W9-BXW-709

Commitment and Sacrifice

Commitment and Sacrifice

Personal Diaries from the Great War

Marilyn Shevin-Coetzee
and
Frans Coetzee

OXFORD
UNIVERSITY PRESS

OXFORD
UNIVERSITY PRESS

Oxford University Press is a department of the University of Oxford. It furthers the University's objective of excellence in research, scholarship, and education by publishing worldwide.

Oxford New York
Auckland Cape Town Dar es Salaam Hong Kong Karachi
Kuala Lumpur Madrid Melbourne Mexico City Nairobi
New Delhi Shanghai Taipei Toronto

With offices in
Argentina Austria Brazil Chile Czech Republic France Greece
Guatemala Hungary Italy Japan Poland Portugal Singapore
South Korea Switzerland Thailand Turkey Ukraine Vietnam

Published in the United States of America by
Oxford University Press
198 Madison Avenue, New York, NY 10016

Library of Congress Cataloging-in-Publication Data
Commitment and sacrifice : personal diaries from the Great War / Marilyn Shevin-Coetzee & Frans Coetzee.
pages cm
Includes bibliographical references and index.
ISBN 978–0–19–933607–4 (hardback : alk. paper) 1. World War, 1914–1918—Personal narratives. 2. World War, 1914–1918—Sources. 3. War diaries. I. Coetzee, Marilyn Shevin, 1955– II. Coetzee, Frans, 1955-
D640.A2C65 2015
940.4′81—dc23
2014041488

1 3 5 7 9 8 6 4 2
Printed in the United States of America
on acid-free paper

This book is dedicated to our daughter, Michelle.

CONTENTS

TEXT SOURCES

Philip T. Cate diary (RG1/007) courtesy of the Archives of the American Field Service and AFS Intercultural Programs.

Henri Desagneaux, *A French Soldier's War Diary, 1914-1918*. Edited by Jean Desagneaux, translated by Godfrey J. Adams. Morley, Yorkshire: Elmfield Press, 1975.

Sapper John T. French Diary. Redruth Old Cornwall Society Museum, Redruth, UK.

Sir James D. Hutchison Diaries, MS-Papers-4172. Alexander Turnbull Library, Wellington, New Zealand.

Felix Kaufmann Diary. ME 233. M44. Leo Baeck Institute, New York, New York.

Willie Wolff diary, 1914–1919, Willie Wolff Papers, Louisiana Research Collection Tulane University. Translated from the German by Marilyn Shevin-Coetzee.

Introduction

This book brings to light the previously unpublished diaries of five participants in the First World War and restores to publication much of the diary of a sixth that has long been out of print. The six diarists are a diverse group with varied experiences. John French was a Cornish tin miner who served as a sapper in the British Army, tunneling underground toward German lines in Belgium and northern France to place explosives from January 1916 onward. Philip T. Cate was an idealistic American volunteer who went abroad not to fight but to heal, driving ambulances in the mountainous Vosges sector of eastern France in 1915–16. Willy Wolff, a German-born cotton broker in the Manchester office of a Rhenish textile firm, was arrested in October 1914 by the British and interned as an enemy alien until his release in 1919. New Zealand artilleryman James Douglas Hutchison, having volunteered in the first week of the war only to be rejected as too young, reapplied and formed part of the famous ANZAC contingent dispatched to Gallipoli in 1915. Invalided home, he returned to active service in 1918 on the western front. Henri Desagneaux, whose diary appeared briefly in print after his death in 1969, was a French infantry officer frequently in the thick of the bloodiest fighting whose experiences spanned the rush to the colors of August 1914 to eventual demobilization in 1919. Felix Kaufmann, who served as a machine-gunner in a German infantry unit, was captured in 1917 and endured confinement as a French prisoner of war until 1920.

The diaries that these six men found the opportunity, the will, and the necessary materials to write illuminate what might be called the "intimate history" of the war. Initially, it was the great collections of diplomatic documents, reports of stirring speeches, and the partisan memoirs of the leading participants that shaped analysis of the conflict.[1] As early as 1916, however, the noted British art writer and collector Cecil Reginald Grundy urged local authorities to waste no time in locating and preserving the varied artifacts that could best express to future generations the experience of the war,

[1] Jay Winter and Antoine Prost, *The Great War in History* (Cambridge: Cambridge University Press, 2005), 7–15.

and to recognize that "little things often throw a more intimate light on the period than the great ones." Indeed, he suggested, "illiterate letters from privates at the front giving insight into their experiences in fifty years time may be rated as more interesting than official dispatches."[2] Grundy's prediction was apt, even if it has taken somewhat longer than he anticipated for the social and cultural history of the conflict to displace scholars' initial focus upon the war's diplomatic and strategic outlines. Yet now, a century later, shedding a "more intimate light" on 1914–18 by emphasizing the experiences of ordinary individuals is at the forefront of historians' approaches to the Great War.

Intimate histories of the war have taken several forms. First, there are the broad overviews. Svetlana Palmer's and Sarah Willis's *Intimate Voices from the First World War*, a 2003 by-product of a British television series on the war, blends commentary and brief extracts from twenty-eight published and unpublished diaries to provide personal views of the events.[3] In his justly acclaimed *The Beauty and the Sorrow: An Intimate History of the First World War*, Peter Englund adopts the same approach, mining twenty published accounts in an effort to recapture what the war "was like" rather than simply "what it was."[4] To an extent, these moving and meticulously edited diary extracts may be viewed as complementing the equally carefully edited volumes of letters by fallen soldiers, for whom the collections of their correspondence serve as epistolary headstones.[5] The authors' desire to achieve comprehensive coverage, however, necessitates a reliance on brief quotations and frequent, rapid shifts from one source to another. In achieving breadth, they almost inevitably sacrifice depth.

A second approach is to focus on single combatants, reproducing either their diaries or their correspondence from the front. These sorts of publications are staggering in quantity, though highly variable in quality. Perhaps the most remarkable recent addition to this individual-soldier genre is Martha Hanna's sensitive exploration of the voluminous correspondence (perhaps 2,000 letters over four years) between a French soldier, Paul Pireaud, and his wife, Marie, who sought to cope with the demands of an infant son and the family farm in the Dordogne. She illustrates, as few historians have, the importance of regular correspondence in sustaining personal relationships under the severe wartime strain of enforced separation and omnipresent danger. The written word, Hanna reminds us, underwrote the French war effort, as the nation's perhaps first fully literate generation produced some 4 million letters per day and several billion over the course of the conflict.[6] If,

[2] C. R. Grundy, *Local War Museums: A Suggestion* (London: W. Claude Johnson, 1917), 5–8.

[3] Svetlana Palmer and Sarah Willis, eds., *Intimate Voices from the First World War* (New York: HarperCollins, 2003).

[4] Peter Englund, *The Beauty and the Sorrow: An Intimate History of the First World War* (New York: Knopf, 2011), xi.

[5] The two classic titles are Philipp Witkop, ed., *German Students' War Letters* (London: Methuen, 1929), and Laurence Housman, ed., *War Letters of Fallen Englishmen* (New York: E.P. Dutton, 1930).

[6] Martha Hanna, *Your Death Would Be Mine: Paul and Marie Pireaud in the Great War* (Cambridge, MA: Harvard University Press, 2006), 19. See also two works by Martyn Lyons: "French Soldiers and Their Correspondence: Towards a History of Writing Practices in the First World War," *French History* 17 (2003): 79–95, and *The Writing Culture of Ordinary People in Europe, c.1860-1920* (Cambridge: Cambridge University Press, 2013),

as the Duke of Wellington is alleged to have intimated, the Battle of Waterloo had been won on the aristocratic playing fields of Eton, then a case might be made that Verdun and the Marne (twice) had been won (or those campaigns sustained) in the republican classrooms of French primary schools.

Nonetheless, collections of wartime letters, however revealing, raise issues as historical sources. In many cases it may be difficult to ascertain how complete a run of correspondence might be. Not only are individual letters easily weeded from a collection, but the sheer difficulty involved in delivering so much mail, from soldiers often on the move or in precarious circumstances, suggests that what correspondence survives is often fragmentary. More significantly, the military authorities—and not just in France—imposed censorship on military correspondence. Postal censors were employed to comb selected samples to ensure that soldiers did not unwittingly divulge military secrets (such as their location, operational plans, or casualties) or openly prejudice the war effort (by relating criticisms of officers, instances of defeatism, poor morale, or sympathy with the enemy). Soldiers knew that their letters home might be intercepted and read, so it is not unlikely that on occasion correspondents exercised self-censorship, avoiding either the specific details or controversial opinions that might run afoul of the censors.[7]

Diaries, on the other hand, present their own potential rewards and pitfalls. Officially, soldiers were discouraged from keeping diaries, or even prohibited from doing so, on the assumption that if they were killed or captured, their diaries might yield information of value to the enemy.[8] This supposition immediately distinguishes diaries from letters. It assumes that a personal diary would be a rich source. The diary would remain intimate and private, its secrets (barring capture or death) the sole preserve of the keeper who confided them to its pages. Censorship, beyond official discouragement or prohibition of the practice, was thus impractical or impossible. Moreover, the fact that diary-keeping had been extolled as an aid to both personal self-evaluation and improvement, as well as a means of recording remarkable experiences and circumstances, meant that it was a difficult habit for the military authorities to eradicate. Officers frequently turned a blind eye to the practice, and sometimes engaged in it themselves.

Jean Norton Cru, a pioneer in the analysis of wartime testimony, argued that the habit of making daily entries imposed a certain structural rigor upon diarists and ensured that "diaries [exhibited] an average honesty which surpasses that of the

71–90. Jay Winter suggests a figure of 2 billion letters in his "Families" in Jay Winter, ed., *The Cambridge History of the First World War*, 3 vols. (Cambridge: Cambridge University Press, 2014), vol. 3: *Civil Society*, 52.

[7] There are insightful discussions of this issue in David Omissi, ed., *Indian Voices of the Great War* (Houndmills: Macmillan, 1999), and Bernd Ulrich, *Die Augenzeugen: deutsche Feldpostbriefe in Kriegs- und Nachkriegszeit 1914-1933* (Essen: Klartext, 1997).

[8] An example of what could happen was the case of Joseph Bédier, a famous French philologist, whose use of captured soldiers' diaries lent credence to his influential 1915 pamphlets condemning German atrocities in Belgium and France. John Horne and Alan Kramer, "German 'Atrocities' and Franco-German Opinion, 1914: The Evidence of German Soldiers' Diaries," *Journal of Modern History* 66 (1994): 1–33. See also their magisterial summation, *German Atrocities, 1914: A History of Denial* (New Haven: Yale University Press, 2001).

reminiscences and novels."[9] Cru's purpose was "to give a picture of the war according to those who have seen it at close range," which meant, in his view, excluding the views of anyone who had not served extensively in the trenches.[10] Witnesses of the war could only be trusted if their testimony was based on what veteran and literature professor Samuel Hynes has called "the authority of direct experience."[11] Yet did such "direct experience" guarantee accuracy? Norton Cru abhorred the exaggerations that produced such literary conventions as mountains of corpses and rivers of blood. Cyril Falls, who reviewed many wartime memoirs for the *Times Literary Supplement*, lamented this tendency in which "every sector becomes a bad one, every working-party is shot to pieces; if a man is killed or wounded his brains or his entrails always protrude from his body. ..."[12] It was not so easy, however, to write a good war book. Soldiers struggled to find the language appropriate to express their growing disillusion with a horrific situation in which death was so pervasive, random, and anonymous, and their own contribution, their ability to make an individual difference, so constrained.[13] Tim O'Brien, a Vietnam veteran and accomplished author, has suggested that writing war stories that are "true" to that experience might involve contradictory truths that could not be believed.[14] Norton Cru, the son of a Protestant minister who was imbued with a devout sense of the sanctity of the written word, held himself to a very different standard. He prized the judicial witness, the only one, in his view, whose personal experience and stenographic veracity would disclose the unimpeachable truths about the war.[15] Today, historians are more charitable. They accept that gifted civilians who have never seen combat are capable of evoking the

[9] Jean Norton Cru, *War Books*, trans. Stanley F. Pincetl Jr. (San Diego: San Diego State University Press, 1988), 37. Norton Cru, himself a veteran and French literature professor at Williams College, undertook a massive project during the later 1920s to read and evaluate some 300 French memoirs, diaries, and letter collections on the war by those who had served. After its publication in 1929 as *Témoins* ("Witnesses"), he prepared something of an abridged version that drew upon the original introduction but added several new chapters and illustrative extracts from works he considered representative. This second book, *Du Témoignage* (Paris: Gallimard, 1930), is the basis for the 1988 English translation by Stanley Pincetl Jr. cited above.

[10] Cru, *War Books*, 7. On this basis, the testimony of any officer above the rank of captain would be excluded for he had not "seen" what those more consistently in the front lines had the opportunity to witness. Also failing to make the grade would be prisoners after capture or internees, whose experiences are central to this book. Norton Cru's professed restrictions should be regarded as an attempt to reassert who was entitled to define a particular view of the conflict at a particular historical moment.

[11] Samuel Hynes, *A War Imagined: The First World War and English Culture* (London: Bodley Head, 1990), 158–59.

[12] Cyril Falls, *War Books: An Annotated Bibliography of the Books about the Great War* (London: Peter Davies, 1930), xvii.

[13] Paul Fussell, *The Great War and Modern Memory* (New York: Oxford University Press, 1975). The "high diction" and emphasis on irony that Fussell documents on the basis of a number of articulate, highly educated British soldiers finds fewer echoes among the diarists represented here.

[14] Tim O'Brien, "How to Tell a True War Story" in his *The Things They Carried* (Boston: Houghton Mifflin, 1990), 64–81.

[15] See Jay Winter's introduction to Henri Barbusse, *Under Fire* (Harmondsworth: Penguin, 2003; originally published in 1916); Leonard V. Smith, "Jean Norton Cru

experience of battle in all its fury and complexity, and they recognize that witnesses who seek to craft a narrative inevitably raise issues of representation that cannot be separated from their very personal role (or struggle) as narrator.[16] Diaries are somewhat more problematic than Norton Cru assumed, so it is best to begin with the circumstances under which they were composed.

If a soldier was in action at the front lines, of course, keeping a diary (or writing letters, for that matter) was extremely difficult. John French, Doug Hutchison, and Henri Desagneaux sometimes had to wait several days until they had an opportunity to record their experiences, occasionally supplementing their memories with notes they had hastily scrawled. As an officer, Desagneaux could exploit the time he set aside for writing reports to compose diary entries as well (this may be one reason why his entries are often especially detailed). But apart from time, all the diarists faced periodic difficulties in finding pencils, paper, or blank journals to continue their work.[17] John French, for example, made do with tiny pocket diaries about the size of a modern credit card that were small enough to be easily carried or concealed. Fortunately, his minuscule handwriting was sufficiently legible to make maximum use of such modest materials.

At their best, diary entries manifest a raw immediacy that memoirs, recalled at a distance, composed after the fact, perhaps edited or amended as prevailing attitudes then dictated, simply cannot match. There is no evidence to suggest that any of the six diaries in this collection were ever written for anyone other than the diarist himself (although their contents might perhaps be shared within the family). Writing regular entries afforded the diarists opportunities for reflection or consolation. Keeping a diary played a significant psychological role, by enabling these men to vent their frustrations, celebrate small triumphs of daily life, fend off boredom, and, ultimately, preserve some sense of remaining a literate human being under circumstances all too inhuman. Certainly there was no indication that when these diaries were written they were ever intended for eventual publication. John French's diaries came to light when the three surviving volumes were discovered among his sister's possessions after her death at age ninety-nine. Not until their later years, and long after they had emigrated to the United States to begin new lives, did Willy Wolff and Felix Kaufmann decide to donate their manuscripts to archives in New Orleans and New York. A surviving sister gave Hutchison's diaries to New Zealand's Turnbull Library after he died. Desagneaux's diary, the sole manuscript to be published, appeared in print only after his death. It is also the only one to show occasional traces of having been amended after initial composition.[18]

and Combatants' Literature of the First World War," *Modern & Contemporary France* 9 (2001): 161–69.

[16] The first issue was confronted directly by John Keegan in his remarkable *The Face of Battle* (New York: Viking, 1976), 13–15; the second is best approached through Leonard V. Smith, *The Embattled Self: French Soldiers' Testimony of the Great War* (Ithaca: Cornell University Press, 2007).

[17] Hutchison, entries of June 29 and August 8, 1915.

[18] See his entries of July 6, 1917, and August 14, 1918. The first could have been revised within two days, but the second definitely was updated well after the events it describes.

By reproducing the vast majority of six diaries, we seek to provide the depth of coverage that allows readers to comprehend how the war's impact registered, not in abstract generalities, but on specific individuals over the course of several years. Those long runs of diary entries enable us to eavesdrop, so to speak, on their intimate reactions to whatever the war threw at them, ranging from acute physical danger and the loss (in cases, obliteration) of trusted comrades to exhaustion, hunger, sickness, and boredom. By reproducing six diaries, we also intend to provide the breadth of coverage that almost inevitably is compromised by the focus on a single author or correspondent. Of course, no collection of six diaries can be declared as representative of the war as a whole, and our selection is no exception.[19] Nevertheless, these men—and their diaries—bore witness to many of the iconic episodes of the First World War: the patriotic surge of mobilization; the battles of Verdun, the Somme, and the Chemin des Dames; the invasion at Gallipoli; the 1917 mutinies in the French army, as well as the last desperate campaigns and the Spanish flu of 1918. They also provide rare glimpses behind the lines, at the "other ordeal" endured by internees and prisoners of war.[20] Together, they add new and distinctive voices to the chorus of testimony regarding life during the Great War.

What do these voices tell us? The first broad theme illuminated in these diaries might be loosely labeled as the education of young men, albeit under very particular circumstances. Education pertains here in a dual sense. First, with the exception of Henri Desagneaux, the diarists were in their early twenties, having concluded all, or at least most, of their formal schooling. They had just begun to embrace—or anticipate—their likely careers. Ordinarily, in peacetime, the next few years would have seen them settle into young adulthood, establishing their livelihoods and family households. Second, because their situation was anything but ordinary, they had to learn how to adapt to, and survive under, wartime conditions (and in five of six cases, under fire). They literally came of age in World War I.

Hutchison, who used blank printed diaries, added longer descriptions of certain sites at the end of his 1914 volume, though it is not clear whether he did so because it was the only point at which he had time to reflect or whether it was the only section with sufficient space. Kaufmann most likely added an introductory section when he had the opportunity, but the remainder of his diary betrays no evidence of obvious gaps in composition or retrospective rewriting.

[19] In a perfect world we would have liked to include a diary dealing with the eastern front, as well as one written by a woman. The first alternative is complicated by issues of access and language, the second by the fact that the comparative rarity of women's diaries has meant that those that have turned up invariably have been published. A good example is Elfriede "Piete" Kuhr's *There We'll Meet Again: A Young German Girl's Diary of the First World War* (Gloucester, UK: private printing, 1998), an almost obligatory reprint that has found its way into both of the "intimate history" collections by Palmer and Willis and by Englund. The war at sea is another candidate for inclusion; for these, see the superb account in Daniel Horn, ed., *War, Mutiny, and Revolution in the German Navy: The World War I Diary of Seaman Richard Stumpf* (New Brunswick, NJ: Rutgers University Press, 1967).

[20] See Georges Connes, *A POW's Memoir of the First World War: The Other Ordeal* (Oxford: Berg, 2004).

For men like Hutchison and Cate who had never been far from home, volunteering for service overseas meant that their war began as a voyage of discovery. Hutchison's diary, for example, reflects his initial status as a sort of military tourist and records in considerable detail his lengthy seaborne voyage to the Suez Canal. Once in Egypt, however, he was forced to confront difference; his more telling diary entries are as much about adjusting to a very different cultural environment as to adjusting to life in uniform. It was not long before he wished for his homeland's "absence of noises and smells."[21] After mingling with Frenchmen from various regions, Desagneaux confirmed his distaste for his compatriots from the south.

The second way in which the diarists portrayed the war as a learning experience involved the acquisition of the requisite skills that would enable them to function and survive in a military setting. Hutchison learned how to transport, load, aim, and fire artillery. French learned how to tunnel quietly, listen for enemy activity, recognize deteriorating air quality, and, in an emergency, to rescue endangered comrades. Anyone serving on the front lines had to learn to recognize incoming shells by their characteristic sounds and to gauge, quickly and correctly, where and when they might explode. The likely fate of students who continued to perform poorly in this particular lesson was all too apparent. Cate's diary, for example, relates the difference between the rookie and the veteran; the American ambulance driver, in the unfamiliar position of visiting a trench at the front, ducked for cover unnecessarily while the experienced soldiers around him coolly ignored an incoming round that they recognized posed no threat.[22] He also had to become familiar with the medical terminology he would require to accurately relay diagnoses and conditions, terms that clearly challenged him upon his arrival in France.

Desagneaux and French mastered the vocabulary essential to identify the various elements of the enemy's arsenal, such as "whizzbangs" or "Jack Johnsons," and to take the appropriate action. French's diary also reveals his growing concern with the weather. His frequent meteorological references, however, do not indicate a desire to chronicle the mundane or anodyne no matter what; rather, the state of the weather was crucial to his new career. Temperature and precipitation affected the soil, and hence his tunneling. Fair skies meant German planes would be overhead, and that meant trouble, for they might either strafe his trenches or (as "artillery spotters") observe the fall of shell for more accurate enemy bombardment. It is tempting to attribute French's constant scanning of the skies to the fascination of someone so anonymously and frequently mired underground with the strikingly individual fliers soaring above, effortlessly enjoying their panoramic views, but there were very practical reasons for his vigilance.

[21] Hutchison, supplementary entry at end of 1914.

[22] Robert Pellissier, an elite French infantryman who served near Cate in the Vosges, highlighted this acquisition of knowledge, linking it to his masculinity. "I have now received the 'baptism of fire,' and feel quite like a man," he wrote. "I know the noise of bullets and shells. I can tell from the report whether the gun is French or German." Joshua Brown, ed., *A Good Idea of Hell: Letters from a Chasseur à Pied* (College Station: Texas A & M Press, 2003), 35.

This learning curve was also reflected in the overall increase in the depth and richness of the diary entries as the war progressed. Especially evident in the cases of French and Hutchison, it appears that as these young recruits matured as men, and as veterans, they also evolved as diarists. It is equally likely that as the war dragged on, its apparent lack of resolution encouraged a degree of personal introspection that seemed unnecessary if victory was but a few months away. Desagneaux noted early on how an officer predicting a war of three years' duration was thought mad, whereas Hutchison anticipated that the battle for Gallipoli would be decided in a matter of days. Indeed, one of the foremost challenges facing these men was how to deal with the unfamiliar and unsettling ways in which they now experienced the passage of time.

It is a commonplace that trench warfare disoriented soldiers and disrupted the rhythms of activity/relaxation and day/night to which they had been accustomed.[23] Flares illuminated the dark, and nocturnal bombardments or working parties kept the troops busy. When an offensive was imminent, the apprehensive soldiers could feel, in Desagneaux's words, "separated from the world."[24] When the inevitable casualties poured in, the medical personnel, as Cate noted, found their schedules overwhelmed. Desagneaux registered not knowing whether he would be alive in an hour, and during one especially intense episode, he likened excavating a hole for shelter to digging his own grave. Death itself could strike capriciously, at any moment, as a grizzled veteran sat down for a snack.[25] Shortly after arriving at the front, French was struck by the conjunction of the evocative peals of Sunday-morning church bells with the thunder of cannon fire. In this instance, the accustomed distinctiveness of the Sabbath was yet another casualty at the front.[26] The landscape was simultaneously tilled by farmers plowing their fields and torn apart by artillery shells, while the soil was contaminated by chemical warfare.

Although internees and prisoners may not have been endangered by shellfire or poison gas, they too faced issues with the passage of time. Felix Kaufmann, though he moved frequently among French prisoner-of-war camps, nonetheless found that the monotony of his daily routine dulled his senses to the point that one day simply resembled the next. He sought refuge, perhaps, in the agricultural labor that permitted him more time outdoors and access to French civilians. Willy Wolff, interned on the rainy and windswept Isle of Man, voiced similar complaints and immersed himself in the daily progress of the war as reported in the few newspapers he was permitted to read. Another German internee, Paul Cohen-Portheim, titled his memoirs *When Time Stood Still*, to express the acute discomfort he felt in confinement. He had relinquished his self-defining sense of autonomy, as personal

[23] Mary Habeck, "Technology in the First World War: The View from Below," in *The Great War and the Twentieth Century*, ed. Jay Winter, Geoffrey Parker, and Mary Habeck (New Haven: Yale University Press, 2000), 99–131.

[24] Desagneaux, entry of May 20, 1918.

[25] Desagneaux, entry of August 11, 1918.

[26] French, entries of February 27 and March 2, 1916. The Army sought to maintain the practices of church parades, outdoor religious services attended by the troops spruced up for the occasion.

privacy or even his daily schedule slipped from his control. Time, to him, grew odious, something "to be killed."[27]

This feeling of being dehumanized, either periodically or progressively, was recorded by many of the diarists. Upon emerging from the inferno of Verdun, Desagneaux noted that he and what remained of his unit were so dirty and unshaven as to be virtually unrecognizable (recalling the common description of French soldiers as *poilus*, the "hairy ones"). At such times he no longer felt part of the civilized world. Prolonged bombardment was disempowering, after which "our faces have nothing human about them."[28] Felix Kaufmann recalled calmly eating in the presence of dead comrades, a matter-of-factness reminiscent of the desire of Paul Bäumer's squad not to let the boots of their dead mate go to waste in Remarque's novel *All Quiet on the Western Front*. Willy Wolff described his internment experience as "inhumane" and his Knockaloe Camp as "a stable for men."[29] Yet the reach of civilization was not beyond recall; the mere availability of soap and the opportunity to wash reminded Kaufmann of what he had forgone in captivity. For Wolff, the trigger was a warm fire and a leather chair. He felt not just his humanity under siege but (as the two were interwoven) his German identity as well. Wolff scorned the dietary changes on camp menus that brought herring and rice. It was not just a matter of hunger or diminished nutrition that he resented, but also the fact that he and the internees were being treated as Russians and Chinese.

These experiences point toward a second broad theme, that of endurance. An English infantryman, C. C. May, cut to the heart of the matter when he confided to his diary in February 1916 that "This war is a war of endurance, of human bodies against machines and against the elements."[30] With that characteristic stoicism so prized by proponents of Victorian masculinity, he emphasized "the stolid, uncomplaining endurance of the men under the utter discomforts they are called upon to put up with, their sober pluck and quiet good-heartedness" that enabled them to make "something grand and inspiring" of their service. The static, constrictive, and physically uncomfortable nature of trench warfare, the persistence of attrition and stalemate, and the seemingly purposeless nature of military operations all challenged the participants' resilience, their ability to preserve their physical and mental health and somehow make it through the war.[31]

[27] Paul Cohen-Portheim, *Time Stood Still: My Internment in England, 1914-1918* (London: Duckworth, 1931). Tammy Proctor, *Civilians in a World at War, 1914-1918* (New York: New York University Press, 2010), 205, aptly describes the impact on men of military age as the "purgatory of internment."

[28] Desagneaux, entry of June 30, 1916. After heavy combat in the Vosges, Robert Pellissier confessed to "leading a perfectly animal life." Brown, *Good Idea of Hell*, 59.

[29] Wolff, entries of October 26, 1916, and October 26, 1917.

[30] Jessica Meyer, *Men of War: Masculinity and the First World War in Britain* (Houndmills: Palgrave Macmillan, 2009), 62.

[31] There is an excellent discussion of these issues in Alexander Watson, *Enduring the Great War* (Cambridge: Cambridge University Press, 2008). See also J. G. Fuller, *Troop Morale and Popular Culture in the British and Dominion Armies, 1914-1918* (Oxford: Oxford University Press, 1990); Alexander Watson, "Morale," in *Cambridge History of First World War*, vol. 2: *The State*, 174–95.

The defense of homes and families, the socialization of military training to promote loyalty to comrades, even the deterrent influence of military discipline—all played a role in motivating men to fight. So, too, did the quality of leadership at the junior level and the ability of the soldiers themselves to assess risk.[32] The diarists all confronted the challenge of endurance, one which they successfully surmounted and which they addressed in their diaries.

The first prerequisite for enduring the conflict, indeed just surviving it, was luck. Each diarist who served under fire recorded "near misses" where he might easily have been hit or where a nearby comrade was not so fortunate. Sapper French had "a narrow squeak myself . . . [when] a big shell dropped a few yards away in a ditch," wounding the man beside him. This incident capped an eventful week, for six days earlier three comrades nearby were killed by shellfire, and French himself "had a rather narrow escape." As he recounted, "a shell splinter struck me full in the left side, ripped through my tunic but was stopped by a thick leather belt I was wearing at the time. I escaped with nothing worse than a bruise."[33] On another occasion an officer next to him was hit by a sniper and died as French cradled his head.[34] Desagneaux's miraculous escape came when a heavy German 150 mm shell landed nearby with a thump. "Everyone thought that this was the end," the French veteran noted, but because the shell failed to explode, "there's still some hope, our turn won't come today."[35] The capriciousness of death at the front was illustrated two months later, when the unit's only other captain with comparable experience, "old man Trillat," was killed by a shell as he sat by the roadside just "having a bite to eat."[36]

Doug Hutchison had been ashore at Gallipoli for only two days when he had the first of "some very narrow escapes."[37] A companion beside him was hit by shrapnel, but Hutchison himself emerged unscathed. Three months later to the day, his overcoat, set aside nearby, was perforated in twelve places by shrapnel, and one month after that (again to the day) a shell penetrated the roof of his dugout shelter but failed to explode.[38] While Hutchison was moving guns into position in October 1918, a shell burst within several yards of him. Having escaped again without a scratch, he briefly remarked on having been "very lucky" and then laconically concluded that he reset his watch to wintertime.[39] Philip Cate, though he drove

[32] Watson argues that a degree of self-deception in evaluating risk (such as exaggerating how soon the war might end or underestimating the tenacity of the enemy) helped the men to endure. There is some evidence for this in Desagneaux's diaries, especially the entry of June 11, 1918.

[33] French, entries of August 16 and 22, 1917. A comrade was struck in the chest but survived with barely a scratch because the bullet's progress was impeded by a pocket Bible and a change purse.

[34] French, entry of April 9, 1917.

[35] Desagneaux, entry of June 11, 1918.

[36] Desagneaux, entry of August 11, 1918.

[37] Hutchison, entry of April 28, 1915.

[38] Hutchison, entries of July 28, 1915, and August 28, 1915. He also witnessed an unexploded shell in the hospital on May 1, 1915.

[39] Hutchison, entry of October 6, 1918. Keeping accurate time was essential for artillery barrages coordinated with infantry assaults.

an ambulance rather than fighting on the lines, and whose service was limited to six months, was not immune, either. Taking shelter from a German bombardment, Cate was "blown off" his seat by a near miss.[40] Felix Kaufmann narrowly avoided shell fragments when bringing soup back to his dugout, being hit instead with clumps of earth displaced by the explosion. A comrade had not been so lucky, killed as he sat quietly reading at the shelter's entrance.[41]

The ability to cope emotionally with the prospect of imminent and anonymous death, and to gain access to the accumulated experience and advice that might improve one's odds of survival, were facilitated by primary group membership. It is now widely accepted that whatever pride soldiers may have taken in their parent unit's military traditions (often on the regimental level), or however they may have identified on an ideological level with justifications for war, what sustained them on a daily basis were the friendship and support of the men within their particular micro-unit (often a squad). In combat, they fought not just to protect their families at home; they fought for each other as well.[42] Within these diaries there are frequent references to the health (or otherwise) of valued comrades and to the disruptive impact of transferring and accommodating to new units.

Primary group loyalty was no less crucial, however, to internees or prisoners than to frontline soldiers. Willy Wolff, whose life in Knockaloe was more static and sedentary than that of men in uniform, depended on the companionship of his fellow hut residents to survive the monotony of internment. The internees nurtured a degree of cohesion as they waged a cat-and-mouse war with the camp administration over conditions and privileges, appealing periodically to Swiss or American authorities (as long as the United States remained neutral) to validate their grievances and seek redress. Felix Kaufmann observed a similar struggle at play in the prison camps. The French, he complained, subjected the prisoners to a series of "pinpricks" to retaliate for German military successes.[43] Moreover, he suspected, the French engaged in a tit-for-tat policy of meting out punishments that corresponded to the mistreatment (mere rumors, Kaufmann thought) suffered by French prisoners at the hands of their German captors.[44] The German prisoners waged their own retaliatory campaigns (such as the strike of May 2, 1918) and sought to enlist Swiss support. After these communal efforts, Kaufmann enjoyed a "firm feeling of comradeship."[45]

Nonetheless, however beneficial the varied primary groups may have been, they were not immune to the stresses of war. One major divide, for internees and prisoners alike, was over the issue of work. Willy Wolff could not understand why anyone

[40] Cate, entry of January 10, 1916.

[41] Kaufmann, initial entry. He attributed his survival to a presentiment of danger, a sensation also observed in others by Sapper French, as in his entry of November 15, 1917.

[42] The classic exposition of this argument, drawn from the experience of German troops during the Second World War, remains Edward Shils and Morris Janowitz, "Cohesion and Disintegration in the Wehrmacht in World War II," *Public Opinion Quarterly* 12 (1948): 280–315. See also the discussion in Hew Strachan, "Training, Morale and Modern War," *Journal of Contemporary History* 41 (2006): 211–27.

[43] Kaufmann, entry of September 12, 1917.

[44] Kaufmann, entry of December 23, 1918.

[45] Kaufmann, entry of September 19, 1918.

would aid the enemy in any way, and excoriated those internees who did civilian labor for the British (usually agricultural work). On the other hand, Felix Kaufmann welcomed the diversion (and pocket change) that unloading cargoes or harvesting crops entailed. Gambling was another issue that threatened group solidarity, so much so that it was prohibited in Knockaloe in 1916. So were attempts to escape, a flurry of which prompted the British authorities to crack down and impose martial law in the camp in October 1916. A year later, the compound's active theater group dissolved due to "disunity."[46] Felix Kaufmann noted how an influx of new arrivals disrupted the cooperative order that had prevailed, with unpleasant consequences, including the recurrence of lice.[47]

A third element that sustained these diarists during the war, obvious enough in retrospect, was recreation. Both French and Hutchison took frequent advantage of opportunities to swim (Hutchison in the Mediterranean when at Gallipoli, and both in local canals when in Belgium or northern France). On rare occasions, Desagneaux did as well. Rugby and soccer matches between units not only released stress but also reaffirmed group loyalties. The most extensive array of leisure activities, not surprisingly, could be found in the internment camps. Wolff's diaries detail a remarkable range of such efforts, from gardening and theater clubs to tennis and soccer tournaments. The theater groups, in particular, provided both a diversion from the monotony of camp life and a way to reinforce and maintain a sense of Germanic culture (and of home) under disorienting circumstances.

The primary means of retaining contact with home was through mail, parcels, and newspapers. Doug Hutchison meticulously noted letters received and continued to follow local sporting events through clippings or enclosures from the New Zealand press. He complained when notes home were censored (in one case his letter was returned because he indicated it was written at the Suez Canal) and plotted how to slip a longer and more detailed account through when censorship eased. Interestingly, he often distinguished between letters to or from his mother or his father. When, for example, he wrote home to explain that he had transferred to the artillery (to a more "masculine" assignment), he directed it to his father.[48] A full epistolary cycle, with a letter sent and a reply received, could take up to four months, requiring considerable patience. The newly embarked John French was impatient, or perhaps he had not yet developed realistic expectations of wartime postal delivery. His first six diary entries each concluded by anxiously noting the absence of mail, only to be supplanted by relief when the post from home finally arrived. Nonetheless, even as a veteran, he continued to remark on disconcerting interruptions in correspondence when they occurred.

Felix Kaufmann had made a habit of surreptitiously recording notebook entries and then shipping the pages home to be read in the event of his death, yet he also

[46] Wolff, entry of October 17, 1917.
[47] Kaufmann, entry of January 15, 1919.
[48] Michael Roper notes these distinctions in his *The Secret Battle: Emotional Survival in the Great War* (Manchester: Manchester University Press, 2009), 58–63. See also Meyer, *Men of War*, 14–46.

valued regular correspondence. After his capture on April 30, 1917, his first challenge was to dispose of his diary while in military custody (he would resume making entries once he settled behind the lines and was no longer discussing anything of operational significance), but he endured a wait until August 3, when his mail finally caught up to him. Given how frequently Kaufmann moved as a prisoner, it is worth reflecting on the fact that the more remarkable aspect of his postal experience was not that it took so long for him to receive mail but that the letters were delivered to him at all. Yet it was not unusual for his mail to arrive so heavily censored, lines excised with scissors, as to be illegible. For Willy Wolff, mail delivery was one of the contentious subjects at issue between internees and camp administrators. He was especially irritated by the inconsistencies in deliveries; after all, unlike Kaufmann or the frontline soldiers, he remained in the same place. Letters or parcels from Germany might arrive as quickly as six weeks or lag for two to three months. Once received, the contents of packages (and of letters) would be shared with hut-mates, thus reinforcing the primary group loyalties and sustaining the links with home.

Finally, one might ask whether these diarists found it easier to persevere by cultivating a hatred of the enemy. The answer might prove surprising, for the frontline soldiers actually had very little face-to-face contact with their opponents.[49] French's unit had several fierce engagements underground with German sappers, but his closest encounter was with disheveled German prisoners stained with mud and blood. On another occasion, marked by "shouting and laughing," men from his unit conversed for some thirty minutes with their counterparts in the German lines about seventy-five yards away. Three days later, his unit was reminded that Germans were to be shot on sight and that Englishmen found talking instead of shooting were to be arrested.[50] Hutchison described a one-day armistice during which each side could bury its dead. Quiet sectors were noted for a "live and let live" system, in which offensive action was carefully regulated (artillery fire at specified times, for example) to minimize casualties.[51]

Desagneaux briefly experienced this respite after Verdun, transferring to a sector that had been manned for eighteen months by the same reservists. Stability on both sides was a prerequisite for any durable tacit mutual commitment to keep the peace, which in this case apparently extended to passing cigarettes and singing songs together. Desagneaux's unit arrived with "orders to stop all this and to harass the Boches."[52] Having suffered so from German artillery fire the past month, the newly arrived French gunners were clearly in the mood to shell the enemy and puncture the relative calm that had prevailed. Yet the only specific instances of Franco-German enmity he cited do not concern the respective armies in the trenches. Instead, he remarked upon the animosity of Rottweiler's inhabitants toward their postwar

[49] This was not unusual. Fussell, *Great War*, 75–77.

[50] French, entries of August 10 and 13, 1916.

[51] Tony Ashworth, *Trench Warfare, 1914-1918: The Live and Let Live System* (New York: Holmes & Meier, 1980).

[52] Desagneaux, entry of July 25, 1916.

French occupiers, which in turn elicited his personal revulsion at the behavior of German occupation forces in northern France since 1914.[53]

The clearest and most frequent references to antagonism can be found in the diaries of the two men who actually did encounter the enemy (though not in combat) on a daily basis, Willy Wolff and Felix Kaufmann. In both cases, the German diarists chose not to express any particular personal animosity toward their captors; they recognized acts of kindness. Wolff generally regarded the English as manipulative and duplicitous rather than evil, though he bitterly criticized the reductions in rations that sapped internees of their energy and spirit. He noted receiving a positive reception upon arrival on the Isle of Man, but also being denounced by local housewives as a "baby-killer" or being provided virtually inedible marmalade that was nonetheless "fine for Huns."[54] Wolff retaliated, so to speak, by poring over his newspapers for evidence of German successes. Victories in Serbia, the fall of ministries in France, advances in Russia, the death of Lord Kitchener—all prompted approving entries from this resolutely patriotic German. For much of his internment the passage of time did not quell his ardor for German victory. At the outbreak of the Battle of the Somme in July 1916, for example, he wished that the "enemies will bleed to death." Only in 1918 did his optimism wane and his diary-keeping deteriorate.

Felix Kaufmann recorded examples of French officials who had been "rabid" or "violent" German-haters and he encountered similar sentiments from some French civilians. Nonetheless, he professed to fully understand such feelings near the front lines and his nuanced account differentiated between harsh and sympathetic treatment from his guards. His experience provided "a lesson how different men behave."[55] Kaufmann was not blind to the same diversity of behavior among his fellow prisoners. "Two of my co-workers couldn't suppress their hate of everything French," he observed when loading a cargo ship," and they "dropped quite a few cases of champagne in the hold."[56] Like Wolff, Kaufmann was an ardent patriot who sought to refute allegations of German atrocities, but he admitted to being unable to justify the violation of Belgian neutrality. Moreover, when he witnessed the devastation in Reims (including the damage to the historic cathedral from German shelling), he lamented that the "work and genius of generations lay in ruins."[57] Quite simply, Kaufmann was not an implacable foe of France sustained by wartime hatred. Indeed, as a German Jew well aware of the persistent anti-Semitism within the German officer corps, Kaufmann in his more reflective moments admitted to feeling ambivalent over his wartime service.[58]

[53] Desagneaux, entry of December 6, 1918. In fact, some of the harshest criticism he reported was reserved for English troops who supposedly lacked the fighting spirit of the Australians, Canadians, and Indians.

[54] Wolff, entry of June 10, 1917.

[55] Kaufmann, initial entry.

[56] Kaufmann, entry of October 21, 1917.

[57] Kaufmann, entry of January 26, 1919.

[58] Recent work has tended to downplay the pervasiveness of overt anti-Semitism among ordinary German soldiers. Thomas Weber, *Hitler's First War* (Oxford: Oxford University Press, 2010); David J. Fine, *Jewish Integration in the German Army in the First World War* (Berlin: Walter de Gruyter, 2012); Gregory Caplan, *Wicked Sons, German Heroes: Jewish*

Evidence of war weariness runs like a persistent thread woven through the diaries. Soldiers yearned for minor wounds, and even the resolute Desagneaux admitted that because it seemed impossible to escape unharmed, the "only wish is to leave as little of yourself behind on the battlefield."[59] After heavy fighting in August 1918 he reported that "the men can't take any more; there have been cases of men breaking down in tears and rolling on the ground crying."[60] Some men surpassed the absolute limit of their endurance and committed suicide, both on the battlefield and in an internment camp. These six diarists, however, all held up under the strain and did not stumble into the postwar world as broken men. With the exception of John French, who was plagued by medical issues related to his prewar employment and wartime service, these men went on to enjoy long and productive lives after the war.

So, apart from good luck, the influence of the cohesive and supportive small groups to which they belonged, the opportunities to release stress through recreational and leisure activities, and the beneficial impact of periodic contacts with home through letters or parcels, what else sustained them through the conflict?

The final significant factor, so pervasive it was left unspoken, was a sense of duty. Three of the diarists—Cate, French, and Hutchison—were volunteers who never wavered in their conviction that they were doing the right thing. Hutchison returned to combat when he could have remained in New Zealand. French and Desagneaux condemned the shirkers who not only failed to pull their own weight but also effectively repudiated the notions of duty and sacrifice that underlay military service.[61] Away from the fighting, Willy Wolff and Felix Kaufmann sought to remain true in their loyalties whatever the hardships. Both retained their confidence in the validity of Germany's cause and the inevitability of its triumph until nearly the end. Kaufmann, still expecting a German victory in 1917 after his extensive service, only began to harbor doubts when he saw increasing numbers of American troops in France. Collectively, these diaries illuminate the sacrifices of war, whether willingly volunteered or stoically endured, and document these sacrifices across six lifetimes.

Soldiers, Veterans and Memories of World War I in Germany (Saarbrucken: VDM Verlag, 2008); Tim Grady, *German-Jewish Soldiers of the First World War* (Liverpool: Liverpool University Press, 2011). On the so-called Jewish Census, however, which some senior officers mistakenly anticipated would expose a pattern of Jewish shirking behind the lines, see Werner Angress, "The German Army's *Judenzählung* of 1916: Genesis, Consequences, Significance," in *Leo Baeck Institute Yearbook* 23 (1978): 117–37; Jacob Rosenthal, *Die Ehre des jűdischen Soldaten: Die Judenzählung im Ersten Weltkrieg und ihre Folgen* (Frankfurt: Campus Verlag, 2007).

[59] Desagneaux, entry of May 5, 1918.

[60] Desagneaux, entry of August 31, 1918.

[61] French, entry of November 24, 1917; Desagneaux, entry of June 5, 1917.

John French in military uniform. *Courtesy of Diana Dowson.*

CHAPTER 1

"It was like ten thousand devils let loose"

John French, British sapper

By the time he sailed from Chatham in December 1915 for service in France, John Thomas French had already earned accolades as a keen sportsman and experienced adventurer in the American West. French was born on February 14, 1892, near the southwestern tip of England in the Cornish town of Redruth. One of eleven children, he helped to support the family by working in the local tin mines, though he also found time to play rugby for the town and win several trophies as a long-distance runner in half-marathons. The Cornish tin industry, however, was contracting, so in 1912 he and one of his brothers, Harold, emigrated to the United States to find work in the Arizona copper mines.[1] *Upon their arrival in the town of Morenci, dominated by the Scottish-owned Arizona Copper Company, they found a resilient community of fellow Cornish expatriates whose institutions and fellowship eased the transition to frontier life.*

However well the French brothers may have accommodated themselves to their new surroundings in Arizona, when war broke in Europe they had no doubts about where their loyalties lay. In 1915, John and Harold left the safety of America to return to England and volunteer for military service. Given their mining experience, it was logical for them to enlist in the Royal Engineers, where their duties normally would include digging trenches and dugouts, as well as repairing roads and bridges. Yet as John French was returning to his native Cornwall, the war took a sudden turn that would shape his future military career. On December 20, 1914, German sappers detonated eight 50-kilogram (110-pound) mines underneath the positions held by troops from an Indian brigade near Givenchy, a French village close to the Belgian border. The shock from the explosions stunned the Indian defenders, temporarily rupturing the British lines, and

[1] N. M. Penzer, *The Tin Resources of the British Empire* (London: W. Rider, 1921), 17.

also prompted British commanders to reconsider the military value of tunneling and mining operations they had assumed were nothing more than outmoded relics from the siege operations of the medieval and early modern eras.

Within two months, Major John Norton-Griffiths, who had overseen military and civil engineering projects after the Boer War, was authorized to seek recruits for tunneling companies. These men would be expected both to dig beneath German lines to lay and detonate underground explosive charges and to thwart German efforts to replicate their success at Givenchy. Because the Royal Engineers had no such existing units, Norton-Griffiths searched everywhere–in the military and among civilians–for men with the requisite experience. Coal or tin miners, sewer workers, subway tunnelers—all were pressed into service. Among them was John French.

From the spring of 1915 until early 1918, one particular sector of the western front, from southern Belgium through northern France, was the scene of an underground war.[2] *It took hold because of a particular set of circumstances. Tunneling beneath enemy lines was a time-consuming process and required static warfare, with no major shifts in the contending armies' positions. It also required suitable soil, and Flanders' wet clay provided, as Norton-Griffiths had suspected it would, a familiar environment for tunnelers already versed in the "clay-kicking" method of excavation common in the British Isles. Finally, the dominance of artillery, of the bombardments that devastated whatever moved above ground, only accentuated the search for concealment and the necessity for countermeasures below ground.*

This underground war was John French's war. He would spend much of the next two years in dark, cold, damp tunnels, facing the persistent threat of being buried by a cave-in or asphyxiated by carbon monoxide. He would plant explosives in an unstable environment, risk discovery and attack by German sappers whose own operations periodically breached British tunnels, and lay still for hours listening for the muffled but telltale sounds of German spades at work underground. French's patience, calm demeanor under pressure, and meticulous powers of observation were reflected in both his military career and the diaries in which he recorded his experiences at the front. He was selected for special training in the perilous task of mine rescue and the use of the cumbersome breathing equipment it required. He rose through the ranks, ending the war as a second lieutenant, and earned decorations for bravery, including the Military Cross.

French participated in two of the most famous mining-related episodes of the war. The first, which he records in his diary, concerned the strenuous efforts to rescue five men trapped underground when the shaft in which they were working collapsed as a result of a German mine explosion on June 22, 1916. A rescue party successfully dug its way to the trapped men two days later, and three were pulled to safety. The fourth was too

[2] See *The Work of the Royal Engineers in the European War, 1914-19: Military Mining* (Chatham: W. & J. Mackay, 1922); W. Grant Grieve and Bernard Newman, *Tunnellers: The Story of the Tunnelling Companies, Royal Engineers, during the World War* (London: Herbert Jenkins, 1936); Alexander Barrie, *Underground War* (London: Muller, 1962); Peter Barton, Peter Doyle, and Johan Vandewalle, *Beneath Flanders Fields: The Tunnellers' War, 1914-1918* (Montreal: McGill-Queen's Press, 2005).

badly injured to return through the narrow rescue shaft, so the fifth man, Sapper William Hackett, elected to remain with him until the shaft could be widened. Hackett, then age forty-three, had been rejected for service as too old, but constantly reapplied until he was accepted; when greeting his rescuers, he is believed to have said that as a tunneler he was obliged to look after the other men first. Despite desperate efforts to clear the gallery (all while under frequent bombardment), it collapsed completely, permanently burying both men. For his heroism, Hackett was awarded the Victoria Cross, Britain's highest decoration for valor.[3] He was the only tunneler so honored.

The second episode, at a time for which French's diary does not survive, was the remarkable preparation by the Allies of some 8,000 meters (nearly five miles) of underground shafts toward the German lines at Messines Ridge, a prominent defensive position near Ypres. The sappers laid twenty-one heavy mines, to be detonated in the early morning of June 7, 1917, to be followed by an attack by General Herbert Plumer's Second Army. Nineteen of the mines detonated, nearly simultaneously, and the resulting explosions could be heard as far away as London (including by British Prime Minister David Lloyd George in his study at 10 Downing Street). The largest mine, Spanbroekmolen, produced a crater 250 feet in diameter.[4] Thousands of German soldiers were killed outright or buried alive, and Plumer's troops succeeded in capturing the ridge. It remains the most dramatic mining operation of the war.

Yet John French's diary also illuminates the less dramatic daily rhythms of life on the western front. His entries, inscribed in an elegant copperplate hand, detail his service without melodrama or any effort to exaggerate his own role. As such, they reflect his dedication to duty, his unflinching willingness to fulfill his obligations without dissent or the expectation of special recognition. By late 1917, mining operations began to wind down and French's later diary entries, as they record his increasing exposure to bombardment above ground, finally betray intermittent signs of war-weariness.

On November 11, 1918, "after watches were looked at frequently until 11 o'clock came," French registered that he had survived the war. He could not, however, escape its long shadow. After his demobilization in June 1919, his search for work took him not home but back to the United States, to the Detroit Motor Bus Company. He married an American pianist, Eve, but war-related lung problems prompted him to return to Cornwall in the hope that the sea air might improve his condition. After two years in Tehidy Sanitarium, John French died from tuberculosis on December 24, 1929. He was just thirty-seven years old.

[3] Barton, *Beneath Flanders Fields*, 290–93; Grieve and Newman, *Tunnellers*, 166–67.

[4] The mine was named for the nearby windmill that had been erected long before the war to drain the marshy local terrain.

December 31, 1915. Left Chatham Friday morning 7.30; sailed from—by the C— on same night 7.00 p.m. Arrived at Rouen[5] Saturday at 1 p.m. Had several miles to march with full kit—feeling pretty rough—effects of sea-sickness—had a bad dose—got through the march alright.

1916

January 2. Feeling pretty fit today—inoculated—second dose—does not seem so bad as first one. Rifle drill.

January 3. Girl came round selling "Daily Mail" 1½ d each. Went outside camp. Nothing much to see, could only go half mile each way. Rifle Drill.

January 4. Received orders today to go up the line tomorrow—attached to 250th Coy[6]—Feeling alright. No letters yet. Saw pole marking spot where first French airman fell. Rifle Drill.

January 5. Was notified today that I wasn't going up the line with this draft, nearly all my chums are going—Been working today—pretty soft—no letters yet.

January 6. Went to the Rouen docks to work today. Easy work but wet and dirty. Lots of ships coming and going. Saw several German prisoners working at Brick-laying and various other jobs. No letters yet.

January 7. Been working at No. 9 Hospital today, putting sacking around the water pipes; very glad for it has been raining heavy today. Pay-day tomorrow.[7] Very glad. Everybody seems hard up. No letters yet.

January 8. Heavy rain during the night and blowing a gale, thought the tent was coming down. Been to the docks working today, rode down on a motor-bus—looks like one of the London ones. Worked in a timber yard in the morning and making roads in the afternoon. Saw several hundred German prisoners including a good many of the Prussian Guard. Marched back to Camp about four miles, got our pay, I got ten francs and three packets of cigarettes. No letters yet.

January 9. Lovely weather today and no work, it being Sunday. Went to Church in the morning in the Y.M.C.A. . . . Met some old friends. No letters yet.

January 10. Been to the docks to work again to-day, unloading timber from trucks. Rode down and back this time. They are saying tonight that we are going away tomorrow. Can't tell. Got letters tonight, very glad.

[5] City in Normandy, France, on the River Seine that was used as a depot during the war. A number of Allied hospitals were located in the city's outskirts.

[6] company

[7] Janet S. K. Watson, *Fighting Different Wars: Experience, Memory, and the First World War in Britain* (Cambridge: Cambridge University Press, 2004), argues that individuals were disposed to view their contribution to the war effort, frequently but not exclusively, according to their own social class, either in terms of work (especially manual laborers) or of service (members of the middle class). French's references to his paydays are suggestive, but they are hardly surprising given that many of the available opportunities to enjoy the intervals of leisure required money.

John French's family in 1918. John is third from left in the back row. *Courtesy of Diana Dowson.*

January 11. Working at docks again today. Nothing said about going up the line yet, expecting to go every day. Saw a big crowd of German prisoners again today. Several N.C.O.s[8] picked out for a draft but no men yet.

January 12. Been working at the Remount Depot today, thousands of horses there of all descriptions. Several N.C.O.s left the line including some Redruth men. The N.C.O. who slept in our tent is gone with them he . . . is a nice fellow.

January 13. Been tarring houses today, getting to be a regular jack-of-all trades. Saw another Redruth man, Thomas from King St. A draft of Scotch men went off this after-noon with their Kilts on and the Pipers playing in front. Looked alright.

January 14. Had frost last night, first since I've been in France. Get many more nights like that and I shall alter my opinion about the climate being mild. It was colder than the North Pole. Been putting up barbed wire today. What next I wonder.

January 15. Working at docks again today, dirty job, up to eyes in mud. Went to concert in Y.M.C.A. Very good. Paid a shilling lots of times to see worse.

January 16. Notified this morning that we were going up the line. Took us all morning for kit inspection and getting more kit. Left by 5 a.m. Train. Kit felt as if it weighed a ton by the time got to station. Travelling all night.

[8] non-commissioned officers (i.e., junior officers)

January 17. Arrived at firing line 3 a.m. Saw about a dozen aeroplanes from the train and Germans shelling ones. . . . Taken from station to billet on a motor bus. What a billet, one blanket and on bare boards. Still might be worse. Can hear firing very plain, artillery and machine guns.

January 18. Had to dip water out of pond to wash this morning, water nice and green. Been to trenches today on 1 a.m. shift, ducked when I heard first shot. Germans 75 yards away. Plenty of firing and flares going up. Got back 10.30 a.m. dead tired and covered with mud.

January 19. Got some better water to wash with out of stream. Saw several aeroplanes of both sides. Being shelled during night (I was in trenches all night). Bombing parties very active during night and our artillery bombarded enemy pretty heavy. Came out of trenches without being shelled, some-thing unusual. Germans [have] been shelling roads pretty heavy to-day.

January 26. Things rather quiet today, got some letters from home, first since I've been up here. German airman dropped a petrol bomb on town but did not do any damage. Kaiser's birthday to-morrow, expect Germans will try something.

January 27. Up in trenches all day today. Our artillery made a heavy bombardment of enemy's positions during night. Our fellows pushed bundles of straw over the parapet.[9] Germans thought we were going to attack and they stood to their parapet, our guns then opened rapid fire on them with shrapnel. Must have inflicted heavy losses. I watched the Germans shelling one of our support trenches this after-noon.

January 28. Brisk artillery fire both sides otherwise things rather quiet. Rather heavy rifle and machine fire as we were going out of trenches. It is surprising how quickly you duck when you hear a bullet whiz over your head and then you make up our mind that you won't duck for the next one—but when one comes down you go again like your neck is on a wire.

January 29. Lovely morning but cold and frosty. One would not think there was a war on coming into the trenches this morning. From one dug-out comes the smell of bacon frying, in another some-one is playing a tin whistle and a little farther on there are some Pipers playing. One finds it hard to realize that the Germans are only seventy-five yards away until a machine gun or two opens fire.

January 30. Got paid yesterday ten francs for two weeks, will have to go very careful to make it last that time. Nothing of such importance happened today. Weather dry but cold. Went in a Restaurant and had a good dinner of beef-steak and chip potatoes, cost a shilling.

January 31. Been in trenches all-night tonight and coming out in the early hours of the morning decided to make a short cut out to avoid a party coming in. Got out on road when a German flare went up and someone started sniping at us. I think I did the hundred yards in about ten seconds. No more short cuts for me.

[9] A wall made of stone, wood, or dirt on the exterior side of a defensive trench that protects the soldiers.

February 1. Got issued with four packets of cigarettes and a box of matches today. Went down to the town and had a look at the old church almost totally destroyed by the Germans when they occupied the town, also a bridge that was blown up but has since been repaired. Went to the Picture Show and it was fine, good Orchestra, good singing and dancing, good comedians and good pictures. It is not far behind the firing line and you can plainly hear rifle and machine gunfire.

February 2. Things rather quiet in the trenches to-day. Some artillery fire on both sides. Trenches drying up fine with the recent dry weather. Infantry busy building dug-outs and doing repair work. Some of the dug-outs are very dry and cosy, with a table, chairs and stove and there are very often some very appetizing smells coming from them.

February 3. Bitter cold wind blowing today, just like a day in March. Went down to the town, nothing much to see but scores of transport wagons continually passing and of course plenty of troops of various regiments.

February 4. Was on guard last night, my first attempt. There were no complaints so I suppose I got on alright. Some rapid fire going on at the trenches. Weather not so cold and coming in rainy.

February 5. Been in trenches all day. Watched the Germans shell our communications trench. Some of them seemed to be very big shells throwing the earth and stones forty or fifty feet in the air. Seems remarkable that no one was hurt. Great day for aeroplanes. Our party had up more than a dozen and the Germans wasted hundreds of shells trying to bring them down. Their armoured cars shelled a group of five planes until the sky was full of rings of smoke, but they got away alright.

Another of our planes hovered over the German position like a big bird trying to draw the fire of their batteries but they kept very quiet, letting a shell go every now and then. The pilot was very daring, coming down very low. I had a splendid view of it. I also saw a trench mortar in action for the first time. Our men sending over three, the first two fell short but the third fell right in their trench doing considerable damage judging by the amount of debris thrown. During the afternoon our party and the enemy sent up a couple of Observation Balloons[10] each. They were captive balloons and looked like huge sausages, they were up for about a couple of hours. Altogether it has been a very interesting day.

February 6. Nothing much doing today. Weather showery and the roads soon get very muddy with so much traffic. Got a nice parcel today from Aunt M. with some very handy things in it. Went to the Picture Show again. It was very good. You have to go early to get a seat as the place is crowded every night. I think it is run by the Military Authorities.

February 7. Germans were shelling the roads today, knocked down a house or two. Our artillery replied with interest. Things rather quiet in the trenches tonight. Our party gave them a little rapid fire once. Very difficult to find your way along the trenches

[10] Nicknamed "sausages" by the British, owing to their elongated shape with rounded ends, observation balloons carried a wicker basket in which an "observer," equipped with a wireless set, viewed the enemy's position through binoculars. Because they were filled with hydrogen, the balloons were highly flammable and often easy targets for enemy planes.

there being so many turns, twists and holes and it being so dark. It's worse for the man in the lead for when the others see him tumble in a hole they naturally avoid it.

February 8. Weather very showery but hardly so cold. Went to the Y.M.C.A.[11] about 2 miles from here, very nice place. I think I will go there oftener for it is alright to be able to sit down and write. You don't appreciate a Y.M.C.A. so much until you go to a place where there is none.

February 9. Went to the sergeant today and asked him for a new suit, got it first time somewhat contrary to expectations. Watched our party send over a few trench mortars again today. They sent over a dummy first to ascertain the range. I had a look at the country around the lines, a very desolate scene. It seems to be mostly fruit growing land for there are fruit trees everywhere and houses with no doors or windows and in some cases no roofs. Of course no one lives there for it is death to be seen out in the open around this part.

February 10. The Germans dropped some big shells from long distance guns, very close to our billet this morning. I was in bed when the first one burst and it fairly shook the house. They sent over seven in succession which did not burst at all. There was no damage done with all their shelling, even as I am writing now I can hear them dropping some-where pretty close.

February 11. Miserable weather today, rain and sleet, did not feel much like getting up this morning at four o'clock but there is no such thing as having ten minutes longer in bed after you are once told to get out on Active Service. Artillery very active on both sides today, sending over hundreds of shells. It's not so bad when you hear them whistling over your head and you know that they are going to burst about a mile away from you. Saw a lot of aeroplanes coming back this evening, they were flying very low and looked very much like big crows coming back to roost.

February 12. Weather very cold again today and showery, keeps a regular army of men busy keeping the roads in repair. This work is mostly done by Belgians and Frenchmen over or under military age. A good many of them wear the new French shrapnel proof helmet.[12] These helmets may keep off a few bits of shrapnel if they don't come too fast but they are certainly not bullet proof.

February 13. Saw one of our Observation Balloons up again today. Went to the Y.M.C.A. today again and did some writing. German shelling again, could hear them bursting quite near whilst writing. I think our party must have made an air-raid some-where for nine or ten planes passed over this place to-day flying together. Things rather quiet in the trenches.

February 14. Was on sentry duty last night. Got on alright, plenty of rats for company, some of them as big as small cats. My birthday today, twenty-four, coming

[11] During the war, the Young Men's Christian Association sought to provide soldiers with more wholesome, morally irreproachable options for entertainment and leisure than they would otherwise encounter.

[12] In 1914, soldiers went to war wearing only cloth caps, which could not shield them from head wounds. As a result of mounting head injuries, the French introduced the first modern

on a bit. You never know where you'll be from one year to another. Last year I was a good many thousands of miles away. I wonder where I'll be next year by this time.

February 15. Been to the Soldiers Club today. It was opened yesterday and is a splendid place. You can get tea and cake at reasonable prices. There are plenty of books and magazines to read and a band playing part of the time, an A1 place. It makes a lot of difference when you have a place to go and sit down when you have a little time.

February 16. Been in the trenches all night. Packing sand-bags most of the time in torrents of rain and a gale of wind. Got soaking wet through and covered with mud. About ten o'clock we had orders to scatter and get under cover for our artillery were going to bombard the German trenches to be followed by Trench Mortars. Sure enough no sooner was the signal flare in the sky than our artillery started. It was like ten thousand devils let loose, with the scream of the shells just passing over our heads and the crash as they burst in the German trenches only seventy-five yards away. Our party had the range to a nicety and they must have done considerable damage for we could see the German working party repairing the parapet after-wards.

February 17. Been in trenches all day. Weather a little better. There was a Trench Mortar duel between our party and the Germans. You could see the mortar coming over just like a big sausage, providing you see it in time you are alright. The enemy then started to shell our trench. One burst so close that it sent a shower of earth and stones onto the roof of our dug-out. Our artillery trenches replied with interest. You could see the shells bursting right in their trenches. They soon made the Germans quit. About from four to six o'clock this morning there was a terrific bombardment on the left of our line. I think it was our party judging by the flashes of the guns which we could see very plainly. Rather interesting day.

February 18. Things rather quiet today. Had to clean up our billet and make it tidy for the General was coming to inspect us. Got the place tidy alright but the General did not turn up. Weather still very wet and dirty.

February 19. Had two of our men gassed tonight but they got around alright after treatment. Artillery active during the night also trench mortars. Our artillery seem to do more work by night than the enemy. I think the Germans must be afraid of the gun flashes giving away their position. They have a battery just behind their lines that our party have been trying to find for a long time. Walked over to E—s about three miles away, to get a new glass for my watch. Very pretty place with some nice shops. The Germans occupied it at one time but were driven out.

February 20. Splendid weather today. Dozens of aeroplanes of both sides up over the lines followed as usual by heavy artillery bombardment. Saw a farm set on fire by German shells and burnt down.

steel helmets in the summer of 1915. These bowl-shaped steel helmets were worn beneath their caps but did not provide much protection from modern warfare. The British improved upon the French design with a helmet that was crafted from a single piece of steel.

One curious incident of the day was a German plane being shelled by its own guns. It was heavily shelled by our aircraft guns as it passed over our lines and as it got over the German lines they started to shell it. The airman at once threw out a couple of star signals and the shelling ceased.

February 21. Five German aeroplanes passed over our place today, one of them dropped a bomb but did not do any damage beyond making a big hole and breaking some glass. They were heavily shelled and I think one was brought down. I only saw two come back of the five but very likely the others went back another way; anyhow our machines soon broke up their formation.

February 22. Been in trenches all night, very heavy frost and it looks as if we were going to get snow. We always ride to the trenches in a motor lorry. A wild ride this in the dark, all packed in tight and not daring to show a light for fear of drawing the enemy's artillery fire. One minute the wheel is in a shell ditch, but no-one seems to care whether we go in the ditch or not when we are going up, but it is very different when we are coming back. If we get anywhere near it the driver is told in very choice terms what everybody thinks of him.

February 23. Heavy snow today and very hard frost. My leather coat was frozen as stiff as a board while I was wearing it. It is a regular white world; everywhere in the trenches you see fire buckets with a ring of soldiers clad in their skin coats sitting around, every spare bit of wood carefully picked up and used as firewood.

February 24. Snow and hard frost again today. Had to break ice to get water to wash, cold while you are about it, but makes you feel fine afterwards. The Germans sent over two or three hundred shells quite close to our billet trying to locate a battery concealed somewhere around. They did not do much damage. I stood and watched them burst for quite a while.

February 25. Been in trenches all night. About midnight we were told to come out of the pit at once and stand to [be on alert] for the Germans were making an attack on our left. We stood to for about an hour and then word came to stand down as it was alright. It appears the enemy launched a gas attack on our left but the wind turned and the gas came back on them, making it a failure. I've often wondered how I should feel in case of an attack and I was surprised to find that I did not feel the least bit excited and I felt very confident that our party could stop them. It was very dark and bitterly cold. More snow and frost.

February 26. Snow again today and still very cold. Things rather quiet with the exception of some pretty stiff artillery work. One of the sections of our Coy broke into an old German gallery. The fellow at the face was working away when his spade went through at the bottom and then he fell through with it. It was a gallery that had been blown up, but the timber was intact at this place. Got paid today—ten francs, we also got issued with tobacco and cigs.

February 27. Sunday today. Can hear the church bells ringing on one side and the guns going off on the other. I went to the Cemetery and had a look at some of the graves there. There were a good number of Canadians buried there. They all have the same kind of cross with Canada in big letters at the top. You see graves everywhere, behind the trenches, beside the road and in fields with farmers ploughing all around them. Sometimes you see the dead soldier's hat placed on the grave.

February 28. A thaw has set in today and it has started to rain heavy. Plenty of mud again. Had gas helmet inspection this after-noon. We get this about once a week and rifle inspection every other day. Our party are doing some heavy shelling and even as I am writing the batteries are booming all around. Going to the trenches last night a machine gun started spitting bullets across and we had to drop what we were carrying and lie flat on the road in about six inches of mud and we were glad to do it, too. I don't think the enemy saw us, they were just stray bullets. This war game is rather exciting alright for you never know what's coming next.

February 29. Weather much milder today but plenty of mud about. Dozens of aeroplanes flying around. Ours in particular being very daring. One came so low that the Germans started rapid rifle fire at it. Our machine then peppered them with a machine gun. Plenty of trench mortar and rifle grenade fighting to-day. Our party doing a lot of it especially when getting dusk when they are very difficult to see coming.

March 1. Been in the trenches all day. Coming back tonight saw a large number of signal lights being sent up by our party. These lights are red, blue and green as the case may be. They go up like a rocket and remain suspended in the air for two or three minutes just like a star. When we were having tea in the billet a terrific rapid rifle fire started up the line and hundreds of flares went up. Must be an attack on somewhere.

March 2. Big bombardment on down the line some-where. Must be a long way away for though we could see the flashes from the guns we could not hear the reports. All the land around here is being cultivated almost up to the firing line. I've often seen shells pitching in the same field as a man was ploughing. Of course the ploughing finished there and then.

March 3. Sorry to say one of our party got killed last night, shot through the head. Weather very rainy again and coming in colder. Things rather quiet in the trenches today. Was going up the road at stand-to time this morning plenty of stray bullets coming across. You can bet I did not waste much time going down.

March 4. Snowing today and very cold. Went to the Y.M.C.A. at B—r, when I was coming out a chap stopped me and said "excuse me but isn't your name French." It turned out to be an old school chum of mine whom I had not seen for several years. We are going tomorrow to see some more pals of mine about two miles out. I had no idea that they were any-where near this place.

March 5. Been up in the trenches all night. Could hear the Germans working in their sap. They appear to be below us which is rather unusual for we are more often under them. We are starting a rabbit hole right away on the down grade to try to get below them. Instructions to be very careful. Got to pad our feet, speak in whispers and not to drop anything heavy. Went up to see those friends of mine today. They were very surprised to see me, thought I was still in America.

March 6. Snow and very cold again today. Did not hear much of the Germans in the sap today, but we are taking the same precautions. Saw several observation balloons up today, but they soon came down again when it started snowing. Aeroplanes too are flying very low owing to the bad weather conditions. Had some fine views of our planes flying low over-head.

March 7. Still snowing and very frosty. Things very quiet in the trenches with the exception of some trench mortars and rifle grenade work on both sides. The weather favouring this kind of warfare making it very difficult to see them coming. Trenches getting very sloppy with so much snow.

March 8. Came out of the trenches this morning about 4 a.m. in a regular snow-storm. Had to walk about four miles in it. It was pretty heavy going. Our Coy had a very exciting experience in one of the saps to-day. They broke through into a German sap with the Germans working in it. Theirs was below ours and had gone past. One of the Germans flashed a light full on one of our chap's faces. Our party kept them at bay with revolvers while they fetched and exploded a box of gun-cotton,[13] blocking their gallery. Going to blow them up good and proper to-night.

March 9. Cleared the debris where we exploded the gun-cotton and got into the German gallery to-night. Our party drove back the enemy with revolver fire and they replied with revolvers, bombs and grenades. We advanced 150 ft. into their gallery and blew it up with 13 boxes of gun-cotton using some of theirs to do it with, for they were trying to blow us up. Our men had taken their boots off and they had to get away in such a hurry that they had to leave them behind and in some cases their rifles, too. But they accomplished a fine piece of work. Our artillery then got to work and wrecked their pit-head. The enemy replied but could only get one shell through ours, wounding three of the Infantry. I think the German parapet is too high to allow their artillery to hit ours very easy, for they very seldom do. Was informed last night that I was to be transferred to the 254 Coy today. Am rather sorry to go, having made friends and kind of settled down.

March 10. Left the old Company yesterday and am now in B-e. We were fourteen of us and we reached here in a motor lorry, a twenty mile ride. We are staying in a big French barracks. This is a fine big town with lovely streets and shops. I expect we will stay here a few days. We were inspected by our officers and informed that we were now a part of the 254 Coy, the Coy with a record, having done all the mining in Gallipoli and had not let the Turks through once. He said it was probably the finest record of any Mining Coy in the British Army and he hoped we would keep it up. We will. Rifle inspection.

March 11. We are still in B-e. A man wants more than 10 Francs a fortnight to stay in this place long. There are so many things you feel like buying. Saw several chaps from Redruth that I knew. Came across them in the street. Another rifle inspection.

March 12. Saw a fight between a German aeroplane and one of ours. Did not see how it finished owing to a cloud, but could hear their machine guns going. Left B-e for our billet this afternoon. We paraded again and our Major told us we were going to a hot part of the line but one that the Germans had never broken through and that he wanted us to do our best to keep them out. Arrived at our billet alright and are going up to the trenches to-morrow morning, rising at three.

[13] nitrocellulose, often used by artillerymen as a projectile charge

March 13. Been up the trenches all day. Our Major said it was a hot part of the line and I should say it was, what with trench mortars, bombs, grenades, shells and explosive bullets it keeps a man on his toes all the time. I never saw anything like it before since I've been out here. In some parts of the trenches you are up to your knees in water and in some places you have just room to get through. There are also snipers galore.

There is another Redruth chap with our Section and we had a fairly easy job on our first day up the trenches, cleaning out the officers dug-out. We had to keep our eyes open for trench mortars and rifle grenades for they were dropping pretty thick. One rifle grenade dropped on top of the parapet about three yards in front of us but failed to explode, just threw up the dirt. It was a narrow escape. We just left it there, did not go to examine it. Going out we had to step over a poor fellow lying dead in the trench, killed by a sniper.

March 14. Lovely weather today and very hot. Took a walk down to the 251 Coy's billet and saw a number of Redruth chaps that I knew. They gave us a good tea. Seems to be pretty country around here and a big Canal runs through the place.

March 15. Up the trenches again today. Our party got lost and we were wandering around the trenches for two hours, sometimes up to our knees in icy cold water and with both sides shelling like fury and sending over trench mortars. One shell pitched close enough to us to splatter us with mud. Had to get under cover while our party bombarded the enemy's trenches with artillery, bombs and every other sort of contrivance. It lasted two hours. On one part of our line there is a pretty smart German sniper and he has killed a number of our men. Yesterday our men baited him with a dummy. They had no sooner raised it above the parapet when smack went a bullet right through the cap. Our relief were an hour and a half late coming up and we again got lost for a while going out.

March 16. Lovely weather again today. Plenty of aeroplanes flying around. Went for a nice walk. Saw our party fire two rounds from a big gun. The concussion was so great that it killed thousands of fish in the canal.

March 17. In trenches all day today. Found way in and out this time alright. Trenches getting a little drier with the fine weather. St. Patrick's Day today but things are rather quiet. Three of the infantry were knocked out by one bullet from a sniper, another bullet knocked three sand-bags off the top of the parapet; it must have been an explosive one which the Germans are very fond of using. During the night the enemy fixed a white flag with a black cross half way between the two lines. It must be a ruse of some kind for they fixed one there before and they say that the officer and two men who went out to investigate never came back. In one place, the enemy occupy a mine crater and our chaps dug a new trench from a sap and are bombing them from a distance of seventeen yards.

March 18. Still lovely weather. During the night a German machine-gunner came over and gave himself up. He also brought the bolt of his machine-gun with him. He said they had plenty of ammunition but very little food, only two meals a day and one of them consisting of biscuits. Our side are heavily bombarding the enemy this afternoon and evening. Can hear the guns roaring all along the front.

March 19. Been working today in a trench only thirty yards from the Germans with a low parapet and the hot sniper on the other side. He got another victim this morning. He kept hitting the sand-bags in one place trying to work through, must have been using the explosive bullet for lumps of dirt came flying over the parapet on to us. In the afternoon we were ordered out of the saps and told to take cover for our artillery were going to bombard the enemy's trenches and there was a chance of a shell dropping short. Sure enough one did drop short and killed five men (including one of our squad) and wounded two others.

March 20. Some German aeroplanes over our place today. Our machines attacked and drove them off. We buried the chap who was killed yesterday, belonging to our Company. I was one of the firing squad [to fire a salute]. Paid today—ten Francs.

March 21. Been working in the same trench today, thirty yards from the enemy. The hot sniper got two victims again today, two brothers they say. Trenches drying up fine with the recent fine weather. Forgot to say that yesterday during the funeral service shells were dropping very close. I saw two flags today that our fellows had fixed between the lines for the Germans to come and fetch, if they can.

March 22. Things are somewhat quieter in the trenches. I think the Saxons[14] must be in, for they are always quiet when they are in. They seem as if they don't want to fight very bad against the British. Been out for a walk around; looks like fine farming country around here and most of it is under cultivation.

March 23. Been up all night and the corporal came around and said "I suppose you know your instructions." I said "what instructions?" He said, "Any man found sleeping at this post, the penalty is death." Got through alright though.

March 24. Bitter cold weather today. Things rather quiet up in the trenches. I hope it will keep quiet. Have had no letters for quite a while now, must be delayed somewhere.

March 25. Been up in trenches all night. Fritz tried to blow us up this morning about 9 o'clock. I was in the sap[15] at the time with some others. We were working away when suddenly there was a terrible rumble and the gallery shook from side to side, but the timber held. We lost no time in getting out. When we reached outside we found that the explosion had blown down a part of the parapet and buried one of the infantry. We soon dug him out, alive. It also blew the body of a Canadian soldier (that had been lying between the lines for months) over into our trench. So taking it all around, Fritz's mine was a failure.

March 26. Rotten weather today, rain and wind. Trenches in bad shape—up to the knees in mud and water. Been snowing a little too. Got a nice parcel from home, soon made short work of it.

[14] "Red Saxony" was the description applied to the kingdom of Saxony to distinguish its more progressive political sympathies from those of Prussia. See James N. Retallack, ed., *Saxony in German History: Culture, Society and Politics 1830-1933* (Ann Arbor: University of Michigan Press, 2000).

[15] tunnel

March 27. Bad weather again today. Went into trenches last night at mid-night. It was dark as pitch, raining in torrents and blowing a gale. Up to knees in water in some parts of trenches. Pretty rotten for the infantry, but they seem cheerful enough.

March 28. Rain again. Fairly quiet up the line. We kept in our huts all day. Not much pleasure in going out walking.

March 29. Weather a little better. The enemy were rather quiet tonight although they sent over a few trench-mortars. Our party peppered them well with rifle grenades early this morning. I think that crack sniper of the Germans must be killed, for there has been no sniping at that corner for a few days.

March 30. Splendid weather today, a perfect Spring morning, makes a man feel 50% better. Heard the A. & S.H.[16] band playing this evening, pipers and drummers. They were fine. A large number of aeroplanes flying around today. Witnessed a fight between some of the German planes and ours which resulted in the enemy being driven off. Did not see any brought down.

March 31. Lovely weather again. It looks as if we are going to get a spell of it. Was looking at the German lines this morning through a periscope to see if I could see any Germans. Was looking a long time but could only see one as he passed a low place in the parapet. Had a good view of our rifle grenades bursting in their trenches.

April 1. Still lovely weather. Went for a walk in the woods around here. Plenty of flowers around including primroses, but they do not smell like the flowers in England. Heard S.W.B.[17] band playing this morning. It was a treat.

April 2. Been in trenches all night. Our bombing parties very active bombing some of the craters occupied by the enemy. Plenty of noise all along the front. It was very cold all night but it has been very hot all day. Made the sweat fly during the four-mile walk back to our huts.

April 3. Very hot again today. Been sitting in the woods most of the time. If it wasn't for going to the trenches things would be alright. Still things seem to be coming our way. The S.W.B. band playing again tonight—some very enjoyable music. This morning about 6 a.m. Fritz exploded a mine near our part of the line which killed about a dozen of the infantry and buried two of the R.E.s.[18]

April 4. Things rather lively in the trenches last night and this morning. Our party tried a new trench-mortar and the explosion in the enemy's trenches fairly made the earth tremble. The Germans then started to shell our first line but did very little damage. We were paid this evening, twenty francs—most I've received at one time since I've been in France.

April 5. Weather cold and dull. Several enemy aeroplanes flying around today. Our aircraft guns brought down one which dropped about two miles from our huts.

[16] Argyll and Sutherland Highlanders
[17] SouthWales Borderers
[18] Royal Engineers

April 6. Things rather lively in the trenches last night and this morning. Had a narrow escape going up on the canal bank. The Germans had a machine gun playing on it. Early in the morning we were taken out of the saps and told to get under cover for our party was going to start a bombardment. It did not last long but it was pretty hot while it lasted for Fritz started to send them over too. Just before entering the trenches we pass through the deserted town of G-. It is a pretty large place with some fairly large buildings but no one lives there and all the houses bear the marks of shellfire, a good many of them are wrecked altogether. There are shops, restaurants, hotels all deserted. You have to move quickly through this place and in single file for it is directly behind the firing line and stray bullets are always whizzing through the streets.

April 7. Cold and dull weather. Several of our Coy wounded by a trench mortar last night and another one killed by a rifle grenade this morning. It was a Welsh chap.

April 8. Things rather quiet in the trenches last night and this morning with the exception of trench mortars and rifle grenades on both sides. These are murderous things for even if you hear them coming you can hardly tell where they are going to pitch. We buried this afternoon the chap who was killed yesterday.

April 9. Forgot to mention that we exploded a mine yesterday doing considerable damage to the enemy's position. Got a pass and went to Bethune for the afternoon. Met several chaps I knew.

April 10. Up in trenches all night. Had to get under cover early this morning while our party bombarded the enemy's trenches. It did not last very long. Was on a listening post all night. Monotonous sort of job. Our officer caught two fellows sleeping at their posts last night. They are to be court-martialed—this makes four for the same thing. A fellow has a job to keep awake for twelve hours especially when the sap is warm and the air bad.

April 11. Things rather quiet today. Heard the R.W.F.[19] band playing in the afternoon. Some very good music. It makes things seem a little brighter.

April 12. Been lots of grenade fighting tonight on both sides. Our fellows have a man on the watch and when he hears or sees a grenade coming he blows a whistle. Saw some of our airmen flying low over the German trenches. They fired at them with rifles, machine-guns and bombarded them with their aircraft guns. It seemed impossible to miss them and yet they did. We shifted tonight from our huts to a big building about five hundred yards behind the firing line. The roof has been blown off by shell fire and there are several shell holes right through it. It is in the deserted town that I mentioned before and it is shelled every day. We are only allowed to enter the building by one end. They are afraid that the enemy might see us if we use the other end. You have to be very careful when walking out around of the stray bullets, especially at stand-to time. Altogether it is a delightful spot, I don't think. Forgot to say that the Germans blew up a mine last night. Gave our sap a good shaking.

[19] Royal Welsh Fusiliers

April 13. The enemy started shelling our billet this morning just as we were leaving to go on shift. We had to race across a piece of open ground to reach the trench with shells dropping all around. Rather exciting five minutes. A very good start for the first morning.

April 14. Very quiet up the line today. After coming back to the billet we were all ordered to get under cover in the cellars for there was a bombardment coming off. We were under cover for half an hour when word was passed around that it was postponed.

April 15. Rather brisk artillery fire on both sides today and grenade fighting in the trenches. I went to the nearest town today after coming out of the trenches and a three mile walk. It felt like coming out of prison. Went in and had a good square meal and then walked back. The Germans were dropping shells all around our billet the early part of the night. I felt so tired that I did not trouble to get out of bed.

April 16. Sorry to say one of our chaps got killed this morning by a sniper. He was just on the point of being relieved when he forgot himself and put his head above the parapet. Got a bullet clean through the head. I helped to carry him out. Not a very nice job owing to the narrowness of the trenches in some parts and the turns and twists. I notice there are three observation balloons up this afternoon—two German and one of ours, which is generally a sign of more shelling.

April 17. Dropping shells pretty close to the billet again today. One went thro' the next building to the cook-house. Gave the cooks a bad scare. Well they need a little waking up for sometimes you can hardly tell the soup from the tea. Forgot to mention that we have to wash in a big shell-hole for there is no water nearer than the La Bassée Canal which is a quarter of a mile away with bullets continually whizzing past. Was working last night in a sap that's almost under a crater near the German lines. Had to work without making the slightest noise and up to the knees in mud and water.

April 18. Up the trenches again last night having the usual narrow escapes from stray bullets before reaching the communications trench and being shelled coming out. Worked in a sap in darkness all night, the air being too bad for a candle to burn. Had a nice bit of sing-song back in the billet. Everyone seems to be in good spirits. Some of the chaps are fair knock-outs.

April 19. Rather exciting times in the trenches last night. In the first place on going in we found sentries posted everywhere and they would pull you up at the point of a bayonet; in some instances men of the R. E.[20] had to show their identification discs. We found out afterwards that there were two German spies in the trenches. They caught one but could not find the other. At half-past four in the morning we were told to come out of the saps at once and stand-to for the Germans were attacking. On coming out we found the trenches swarming with men with fixed bayonets and some with bombs. It appears that three different sentries reported the enemy

[20] Royal Engineers

advancing under cover. The distance between the trenches is about seventy-five yards. When our party thought they were near enough they started bombing them and must have driven them back for none of them reached our parapet. You could also see Germans marching on a road behind their lines. We were ordered to stand down at half-past five. One of our Coy was severely wounded by shrapnel just by the door of our billet this morning.

April 20. Machine guns sweeping across the road in front of our billet again last night. You should hear the bullets striking the bricks and tin cans all around. One of our squads had to put back for a while. We had to sprint to the mouth of the trench. Another of our Coy severely wounded by a rifle grenade this morning about the head.

April 21. Germans exploded a mine yesterday morning and two early this morning, but did no damage. Getting pretty rotten weather again now. Trenches in a very bad state, almost up to the knees in water in some places. Good Friday today. Got a nice parcel from home. Was in bed at the time but soon roused up when it came. Partner and myself ate a whole chicken before going to sleep again.

April 22. In trenches again last night. Torrents of rain all night. Got soaking wet through. Each side sent over a large number of rifle grenades and trench mortars. Machine guns kept sweeping the parapet all night. Must have been a number of working parties out it being an exceptionally dark night.

April 23. Soaking wet through again last night, working in a wet sap. Germans blew up another mine again this morning at six o'clock. Did no damage. Lots of sickness in our Coy. Forty-nine men sent to hospital in five days due no doubt to the wet weather and bad working conditions. Easter Sunday today. Weather a little better.

April 24. Working in the wet sap again last night. Working up past the knees in water, and water coming down on your back like a shower bath. After working about three hours air got so bad that we had to come out. Candles would not burn. Stiff rifle grenade and trench mortar fighting all night. Several bombing parties out.

April 25. Called out of the saps last night to get under cover during a bombardment. Whilst in the saps the explosions overhead were so severe as to shake the gallery and put the candles out. Was provided with a complete set of oil-skins for working in the water. Saw several notices stuck on the side of the communication trench near the firing line marked, "Heads down—sniper." You may depend we kept our heads down.

April 26. Lot of grenade and trench mortar fighting again last night. Had to avoid a certain piece of the road leading to the communication trench that was being played upon by a sniper. Had to lie down flat in the same piece of road three times in about a hundred yards coming back in the early hours of the morning owing to machine-gun fire. Could hear the bullets whizzing by and striking the wall on the other side.

April 27. Very heavy bombardment on our right this morning lasting about five hours. Saw the Germans send over a number of gas shells which burst about two hundred yards from us. They sent out a thick cloud of yellow smoke which rolled along like a fog bank, the wind driving it away from where we were standing. Went to the doctor to see about a cut on the ankle that I got a couple of weeks ago. He said it was septic poisoning and sent me to the hospital. Rode there in a Red Cross car, distance about five miles.

April 28. Spent in hospital. Plenty of company, wounded coming in all the time. Things very quiet and weather very hot. Had to put our gas helmets on the top of our heads ready to pull down over our faces to-night about ten o'clock, there being a gas attack up the line. It did not reach the hospital however.

April 29. Still in hospital. Weather very hot. Several wounded brought in again today. They are going to send me to the Corps Rest Station tomorrow. They brought down a German aeroplane near here this afternoon—took the pilot and observer prisoners.

April 30. Lovely weather again today. Left the hospital for the Rest Station this afternoon in a Red Cross car—distance about eight miles. On getting there the doctor gave me an injection in the chest. The Rest Station seems a nice place. Forgot to mention that the General of the Division went through the Hospital yesterday. He had a chat with several of the fellows in our ward.

May 1. In the Rest Station. It seems like being in a new world, everything is so clean and quiet. All kinds of books to read, plenty of good wholesome food and nice shady grounds where you can sit around in camp chairs. Lots of men coming and leaving every day. One fellow came in with a bullet wound in the shoulder and he kept on telling how he was wounded just as he was going to drink his rum. He seemed more concerned about losing the rum than he did about getting wounded.

May 2. Still in R.S. and still having lovely weather. Saw several aeroplanes coming back this evening flying very low. I think there is an aeroplane base very near here. Can hear the guns booming in the distance. They seem to be very busy. It is hard to realize lying here that men are being slaughtered wholesale only a very few miles away.

May 3. Lovely weather again today. It makes a man feel that life is worth living. They give us plenty of cigarettes in this place and sometimes sweets and chocolates. We had a very good concert last night with some good singing and music. Everything A1 so far with the exception of the ankle, which is very painful.

May 4. Still splendid weather. This sort of life is going to make me feel lazy. When I go back to the line again it will almost be like starting over again; well I should worry. Always see a number of aeroplanes coming back every evening and going away in the mornings flying very low as a rule.

May 5. Well, I am getting hard up for anything interesting to put in this diary for there is very little to see here. Only allowed out an hour a day. The fine weather still continues, long may it do so.

May 6. Nothing much doing. Ankle getting much better. We get a little music here in the evenings now—one of the chaps brought in a concertina and he plays it alright.

May 7. Still here in the Rest Camp. Doctor says getting on fine but need a few days rest. Plenty of wounded and sick coming in and going back to duty every morning.

May 8. Weather seems to be altering and it has been cold and showery to-day. Still going along in the same old way, getting plenty to eat and drink.

May 9. Been out for a march this afternoon for the first time. Seems to be a very nice place around. Saw a number of Australian troops in town, a fine looking lot of fellows.

May 10. Lovely weather again today. Last night we had a lantern [slide] lecture on New Zealand given by the Roman Catholic priest attached to this Division. It was rather interesting. Went out around the town again this afternoon for an hour. Also went to the Y.M.C.A.

May 11. Still in the Rest Camp. Nothing much doing. Have only had one fatigue [task] since I've been here so far. I had to wash the plates in the dining one day. I did not think there were so many plates in France. Do the half an hour's march every afternoon now. They call it a march but we really go about a quarter of mile then lie about the banks of the canal on the grass until it is time to go back again.

May 12. Rather dirty weather today, very showery. Did not go out on any march. Nothing to do but lie around in the hall reading. Have done more reading since I've been here than all the rest of the time I've been in France.

May 13. Showery again today. Went to the Y.M.C.A. in the afternoon and found out there was a Concert to be given that night by Miss Lena Ashwell's[21] party. Went back and asked permission of the Major to go. Nothing doing. It was strictly against the rules he said, so that finished that.

May 14. Rain again. Church Parade today being Sunday. Got our issue of cigs and matches. Too wet for a march again. Have not seen a paper for several days. The old Frenchman doesn't come here anymore. Got a notion to write home and ask them how the War is getting on.

May 15. Still in Rest Camp, expecting to go out any day now. Weather a little better today. Lots of Anzacs [members of the Australian and New Zealand Army Corps] in town.

May 16. Going out tomorrow, fit for duty. Been on dining room fatigue today, washing up basins, cups and plates.

May 17. Left the R.C. this morning at 9 a.m. Marched to the railway station with full pack. Rode to La Gorgue, waited there three hours and then got on one of our military trains. Rode on bales of hay in a box-car to a place named Locon. Passed very close to a big observation balloon. It looks a huge thing when you are close to it. Passed a large number of transport wagons on the road, also some big guns. One of the leading transport horses swerved and fell into a deep ditch full of water. Had a hard time getting it out again. The country around looks very pretty with all

[21] Lena Ashwell (1872–1957), a British actress, organized large-scale entertainment for British troops at the front.

the orchards in bloom and crops springing up. Could not get farther than Locon by train, with several miles still to go so I started to walk. By the time I had gone a couple of miles the pack seemed as if it weighed half a ton. Here I had a piece of luck—got a lift on a motor lorry going to the very place I wanted to go; very glad I was too, for the weather was hotter than blazes. Got back to the Coy about 5 p.m. Going to the trenches 2 o'clock to-morrow morning.

May 18. Been to the trenches to-day. A lot of Grenade and Trench Mortar fighting. Weather very hot. Infantry going about in the trenches in their shirtsleeves. A German aeroplane flew over Gorre and Béthune in the middle of the night before last and dropped a number of bombs. Our search-lights located it and it was heavily shelled by our aircraft guns but it got away. Since I've been to hospital our Coy has had one man killed and over thirty wounded starting a new shaft exposed to heavy grenade fire. There has also been a gas attack since I've been away. The gas reached Gorre where we billeted but did no damage beyond destroying some growing crops. The fields had to be ploughed up again and the ground sprinkled with lime.

May 19. Been up in the trenches again today. Weather still very hot. Things rather quiet with the exception of the usual grenade and trench-mortar fighting. Going to move up to the line tomorrow for ten days.

May 20. Moved up to the line this morning. We are billeted in one of the hundreds of deserted houses in this town. It has no doors or windows and we are sleeping on the tile floor. We are about half a mile behind the first line of trenches. I went around the place this afternoon looking through some of the houses. They were evidently deserted in a hurry for there are papers scattered on the floors and in some there are curtains still up. Right behind our house there is a grave with twelve men of the K.O.S.B.[22] buried in it, a Major, a Lieutenant, a Sergeant and nine privates, all killed in October 1914. Was up the trenches again during the night. Machine guns sweeping the road coming back. Had to lie flat. Could hear the bullets striking the railings.

May 21. Had a nice swim in the La Bassée Canal this morning. Water was fine. Picked up dozens of shrapnel bullets and a nose cap [of a shell] on the bank of the canal and fished a live shell out of the water. We threw it back again. Weather very hot.

May 22. Had another swim in the canal this morning. Weather still very hot. Was up in the trenches last night, one of the worst nights I've ever experienced. It was a regular nightmare from start to finish. As soon as we reached the firing trench our party started a bombardment with artillery, trench mortars and grenades. They gave the Germans socks.[23] After a while the enemy started to reply and both sides went at it tooth and nail. The air was full of pieces of shell, nose caps and shrapnel screaming in all directions. We had to take cover until it was over. This was about seven o'clock in the evening. Just after stand-to time, which is at dusk, the Germans

[22] King's Own Scottish Borderers; infantry regiment created in 1689 to defend Edinburgh against Jacobite forces of James II.

[23] slang for "dealt them a blow"

started to send over some big trench mortars and rifle grenades. Their fire was very accurate, most of them dropping in trench or very close to it. I was standing in the mouth of our sap having just been relieved from a listening post when a grenade dropped in the trench quite close to me and severely wounded one of the infantry. The stretcher-bearers had him on the stretcher and were just going to carry him out when the Germans exploded a mine about fifty yards to our left. This was exactly midnight. It was like an earthquake. The ground fairly shook and it sounded as if the sky was falling. The poor chap on the stretcher was killed and half buried with the dropping stuff. With the explosion of the mine the Germans opened rapid rifle fire. We thought they were going to attack and stood to at the parapet with the infantry. Our artillery started shelling their trenches and things soon went quieter. We were relieved at 1 a.m. and went back to our billet. Had to step over three dead men in the bottom of the trench on the way out. So ended a rather exciting night.

May 23. Another hot time in the trenches last night with the trench-mortars and grenades. You could see the trench mortars coming through the air like rockets with their time-fuses burning and showing plainly in the darkness. Some of them when they burst fairly shook the ground. There was a terrific bombardment on our right towards Loos. We could see the shells and bombs bursting and flares of every colour going up. They use coloured flares as signals. I think there must have been an attack on. After we came back to our billet at 1.30 a.m. our guns all around started to roar. The Germans replied and some of their shells dropped close enough to our house to scatter stones and dirt on the roof. Our shells were all bursting on our right where the trouble was earlier in the night. This afternoon I saw some one of the heaviest bombardments it has been my lot to witness. I watched it from start to finish on a road running parallel with the trenches about half a mile behind them. The Germans started it and they rained every description of shell on a certain section of our line. There were the "coal boxes"[24] with their dense clouds of black smoke and throwing the dirt and stones to a height of forty or fifty feet, the high shells bursting just over the trenches and even tear shells that hurt the eyes so badly. The whole section of the line was nothing but a cloud of dust and smoke and you could hear pieces of shell screaming through the air. Our artillery then started from just behind us and sent hundreds of shells over. The din was terrific. Both sides kept it up for about an hour and then it died away. Forgot to mention that we got a dose of the enemy's tear gas the night before last. Our eyes were sore for hours afterwards.

May 24. Things rather quieter last night but had the usual trench-mortars and rifle grenades to contend with. These grenades are murderous things. You hear the report of the rifle. It sounds a little different from the ordinary rifle shot, and then the only warning you get is a hissing sound as it drops for there is no time fuse. It explodes on contact. Saw one of our air-men make a daring swoop right over the German lines and rake their trenches with a machine gun. He got clear away.

[24] shell burst, generally from a heavy gun that causes a cloud of black smoke

May 25. Things about the same up the line last night. Another mine went off exactly at midnight; it was a good way to our right, could not tell if it was one of ours or the Germans. Watched another bombardment yesterday afternoon from the road half a mile behind the firing line. It was even worse than the one the day before and in the same place. The Germans started it and then our party took a hand in it. Soon the whole line was a cloud of smoke and dust. There has been a large number of aeroplanes flying around lately, mostly all ours. I think our fellows have the Germans beat in the air for we very seldom see any German machines now and those we do see fly very high.

May 26. Weather rather cold and showery today and things were rather quiet in the trenches last night compared with other nights. There were several working parties out from each side, I think, for there was very little rifle or machine gun fire and it was very dark. They take advantage of such nights to repair the wire between the lines and rebuild the parapets.

May 27. Fine weather again today. We went out in the fields around our billet and found a number of strawberry beds with plenty of fruit but not quite ripe yet. My chum this evening received a telegram from home saying that his brother was dead and asking him to come home if possible. He went at once to the captain and he is going home tonight on a special pass.

May 28. Machine gun sweeping the road when we came out of the trenches in the early hours of this morning. We had to lie flat in the road three times coming from the communication trench to our billet, a distance of about a quarter of a mile. The road was muddy too. We were all lying down in our billet and nearly asleep at half past two this morning when we heard a mine go off. It shook our house like an earthquake. It must have been one of ours for before the rumbling had ceased our artillery had opened fire from all around. They sent over hundreds of shells in a very few minutes with rapid fire which must have got Fritz's wind up considerably.

May 29. Same old thing up the trenches last night. Trench mortar and rifle grenade fighting and plenty of it. Our party were bombarding them pretty heavy when we came in at seven in the evening and soon developed into a regular duel. Went out today looking for German nose-caps, found two, also a dud, which we threw in a stream.

May 30. Been out around the fields at the back of the firing line today. Found plenty of fruit trees including currant, gooseberry, strawberry, apple and pear trees covered in fruit but not ripe yet. Also found some grape vines. Goodness knows where the owners of these orchards are for the houses are all deserted and shell-shattered. Had to put on our gas helmets last night in the trenches. The gas bell was going somewhere on our left. We did not keep them on long however. It was more a precaution than anything else I think.

May 31. Still having splendid weather—was notified today that I was promoted from tunneller's mate to a tunneller with pay increased from two shillings and two pence to six shillings a day commencing to-morrow. Brisk bombardment over on our right this evening. Looks as if there is an attack on. Have not seen a newspaper for two weeks.

June 1. A German bullet came in last night through the doorway of our billet and embedded itself in a sand-bag just over a chap's head. Found a lot of watercress growing in a stream to-day—had some for tea. It went alright with the bread and cheese.

June 2. There was a big do on our right last evening. It looked like an attack. We stood in the road and watched it for quite a while. It was a continual roar and that part of the line looked like a sheet of flame. Hundreds of flares were going up including some red, blue and green ones which were evidently signals. It lasted several hours.

June 3. Severe bombardment on again today. Our part doing most of it. There is a battery concealed not far from where we are sleeping. The Germans have been dropping shells all around it but have not located the right spot yet. This battery does considerable damage to the enemy for it is firing continually night and day. Saw the infantry trimming and decorating the soldiers' graves today and there are hundreds of graves around here. They look after them as well.

June 4. We exploded five mines last night between the hours of nine and mid-night. Our artillery also opened a terrific fire on the enemy's trenches sending over a rain of shells which lasted for hours. It made our house fairly rock. There was no sleeping with it and most of our chaps took refuge in the cellar for Fritz was sending some over too and they were dropping pretty close.

June 5. Forgot to mention that after the mines went off the night before last our men took possession of the craters and before morning had dug a trench connecting them. This trench is only twenty-five or thirty yards from the German trench. Two of our squad are to be recommended for the D.C.M.[25] During one dark night some Germans tried to enter our trench near one of the saps and these chaps bombed them off, the Germans fleeing in all directions. Our bombers made a raid on the German trenches the night before last. The party consisted of about eighty men and they went over just after the mines went up. They cleared the enemy's first line first and roamed about at will doing all the damage they could. They returned without loss and bringing with them one officer and two privates as prisoners. The raid was a great success. Been out digging for nose-caps this morning. We found six fine ones in the shell holes made a couple of nights ago just behind our billet.

June 6. One of Coy killed yesterday, shot through the neck by a sniper. He had only just come back from leave. Another of our chaps had a very narrow escape this morning. He was standing in the doorway of our billet when a bullet struck him full in the right breast. It went through a bible and lodged in a sovereign purse he had in his pocket. The point of the bullet was just breaking the skin. It was a German bullet.

June 7. Had a pretty hot time coming into the trenches last night with rifle grenades coming over. They were dropping all around us and we had to keep a good distance apart. We got in alright though. Seven of our aeroplanes flew over the

[25] Distinguished Conduct Medal

German lines last evening. Looked as if they were going on a raid. They were heavily shelled but got through alright.

June 8. Saw one of our air-men to-day make one of the most daring flights that I've seen since I've been out. Flying very low he flew to and fro over the German lines in spite of terrific rifle and shell fire. At last I think he must have been hit for some smoke came from the machine and he turned and flew back to the Flying Base. They did not bring him down.

June 9. We moved down from our billets near the firing line to our billets at Gorre yesterday. Now we have to walk between three and four miles to the trenches every day. Splendid weather and large number of our aeroplanes are up. They seem to have the sky to themselves around this part and it is wonderful to see them turn and twist apparently signaling to the artillery.

June 10. Weather very wet and cold today making the trench boards very slippery and the trenches wet. The infantry have been very busy the past week putting up shelters in the trenches as a protection against rifle grenades. There is no doubt that they need them for the Germans are continually sending them over. Sometimes there are seven or eight in the air at one time. You can hear them leave the rifle for it is a duller sound than the ordinary rifle report and there is a swish-swish kind of sound when they are in the air.

June 11. The Germans blew up a mine today at noon burying one of our listeners. The rescue party were on the spot at once with their apparatus but could not get at him after working all day and night. Weather still very dirty.

June 12. Weather very dirty and misty today. No aeroplanes or observation balloons up. Things rather quiet in the trenches. The Officer Commanding the 39th Division has conveyed his thanks to the 254 Tunnelling Coy for the valuable help given to the raiding party on the 5th of the month by blowing up the two mines which contributed to the success of the venture.

June 13. Weather dirty again today. Not much doing in the trenches beyond the usual rifle, grenade and trench mortar fighting.

June 14. Better weather today. A number of observation balloons up on both sides. Put all watches and clocks on an hour to-day on account of the daylight saving Bill. Germans blew up a mine again today but did not damage beyond giving some of our men a severe shaking.

June 15. A lot of our aeroplanes flying very low again today. The Germans gave them some heavy rifle and machine fire all along the line but did not damage that I could see. Some pieces of the anti-aircraft shells that the enemy were firing at our planes fell very close to us as we were marching to the trenches.

June 16. Saw one of our aeroplanes returning last night after dusk. It sent out some coloured lights or rather burnt some coloured flares at intervals, evidently as a signal to our anti-aircraft gunners.

June 17. Splendid weather again today. We came out of the trenches in the small hours of the morning. Fritz had an observation balloon up, even that early. We exploded a mine at 1 a.m. this morning and after a hot but brief bombardment a party of our bombers went over and raided the enemy's trenches. The raid was a great success. They killed about 30 Germans and brought back one prisoner. We had six men wounded and they brought them all back.

June 18. The Major of the A. & S.H.[26] was shot dead by machine gun fire on the road last night. This is the road that I have mentioned before as being continually swept by machine gun fire after dark. Been working in a sap today with the Germans working right underneath us. You could even hear them throwing sandbags. We had to work very quietly and in very bad air, but we managed to get it in the required distance by driving a rabbit-hole, which is a sap about two and a half feet high and two feet wide. They are going to charge it on the next shift. The air got so bad before we finished that a candle would not burn.

June 19. We have been charging another mine today. It was a rotten job. The air was so bad that candles would not burn at all. Had to use electric lamps. After working in there about four hours conditions got so bad that we all had to come out to let the place clear and then we split up into two parties and worked twenty minutes each at it. It was a big charge, three and a half tons of powder being used. It's going to shift something when it goes off and we are under the Germans in this case. We exploded that mine we charged yesterday tonight at eight o'clock and the artillery followed it with a bombardment.

June 20. We exploded the big mine this morning at half past three. It was terrific. The earth shook like an earthquake. It made a crater well over a hundred feet wide. It is the biggest crater made on this part of the line yet and that's saying something. Before very long our party had occupied and dug a trench to it. The earth on the sides was thrown up to a height of ten feet.

June 21. Enemy shelled the canal road heavily this afternoon as we were going up. They were trying for some batteries concealed around. Some of the shells ploughed up the road to a depth of several feet. One dropped right in the canal and sent the water to an enormous height besides killing a lot of fish. The mine we blew up yesterday must have done considerable damage to the enemy's galleries for it shook some of ours pretty bad. In one in particular it made a mess, breaking a lot of timber. We had a job to repair this gallery this evening, two of us. We got a bad dose of gas from the fumes of the mine. It gave us a very bad headache and made us sick. We had a mouse in a cage with us in the gallery so that we would be warned in time if the gas got very bad. We got enough gas to make us sick and the mouse was still alive and kicking.

June 22. We left for the trenches at two o'clock this morning. We got as far as the canal and found that the Germans were shelling the road. We took cover for a while

[26] Argyll and Sutherland Highlanders of Canada was an infantry regiment composed of Canadians of Scottish heritage.

until the worst of it was over. They must have sent over two or three hundred big shells in a couple of hours. You could hear them coming in the air like express trains. Most of the French people left their homes and made for the town. When we moved up the road we found it full of big shell holes, some as big as small mine craters. The road was covered with branches of trees, earth and telephone wires. When we got near the trenches we heard that the Germans had bombarded our trenches and then blown up a big mine right under our lines at a quarter past two that morning doing a lot of damage. We met some wounded coming out and fellows without rifles, tunics or hats in a dazed state.

We entered the communication trench and started up. We had not gone far before we found the trench blown to pieces and in some places practically leveled. It was just ducking, dodging and crawling over the top from then on. When we reached the place where the mine had gone off, we could not recognize the place it was altered so. Great gaps in the parapets, where you could see the German lines easily and where the mine had gone off or rather series of mines. There was an enormous crater with dead and wounded, both Germans and British for the Germans had made an attack right after the explosion. They got in our trenches but very few got back again, for after the first shock our men got together splendidly and there was some fierce hand to hand fighting. The enemy carried hand grenades and daggers beside rifle and bayonet. Meantime a party of our chaps got around and cut their retreat off and they say that very few ever got back. There was a German Officer lying dead just over the back of our trench with a grenade still in his hand. There was also one of our officers who had killed three Germans in hand to hand fighting finally being killed himself with a dagger thrust. There were a lot of wounded lying about. Some put in dug-outs until they could be taken away. Two of our squad dug out a sergeant of the M—out of the debris. He had a leg and arm broken and was half buried. He said the mine did it and then he saw the Germans coming so he covered his head with sand-bags and they passed him by. I helped with others to take him to the dressing station. I saw our chaps dressing the wound of a German prisoner in the trenches. It was only a scratch but he was making a lot of fuss about it, a big chap too, over six feet high. They took another prisoner back on a stretcher. It must have been a fierce struggle while it lasted for there were scores of German hand grenades and a lot of German equipment lying around and blood on almost everything. Five of our Coy are buried in one of our mine galleries, through the gallery crushing from the force of the mine explosion. We can speak to them through the air-pipe and they are all alive. We have been working all day trying to get to them, pumping air in to them and pumping water out to keep them from being drowned, for it is a very wet place. There are also two of our Corporals missing. Lots of our Coy had very narrow escapes from being buried and being captured. The entrances to some of the saps were blocked and the Germans missed in their hurry the men inside.

June 23. Those five men are still entombed. We have been working night and day trying to get them out. It is twenty-five feet to go and we are in fifteen, but it is still very slow work owing to so much broken timber and running muck. They are still alive and we can speak to them. No trace yet of the two men who are missing. They are still digging out some dead up in the trenches. I saw one of our fellows and a German officer lying in the trench going in today.

June 24. Got out three of the five men last night. One of the others had some ribs broken and could not crawl through the very small hole that had been driven through. The other fellow [Sapper William Hackett] offered to stop in with him until they could make the hole bigger so they passed in some food to them. They had no sooner done that than there was another fall and they are again entombed. The night before last our men expected the Germans to come over again and they were ready for them. The Scotch lay on the ground in front of the parapet and the Welsh stood on the firing step waiting for them. They took their tunics off and stripped up their shirtsleeves so as to give their arms more freedom. When they found the enemy wasn't coming over they made a bombing raid on their trenches. I heard some of the fellows say that they had come through the war right from Mons but for the time it lasted, the German bombardment on the morning the mine went up was the hottest they had seen. I forgot to mention that our artillery heavily bombarded the enemy's trenches the same morning and must have done considerable damage for we could see Germans repairing their trenches afterwards.

June 25. Those two fellows still entombed. Had to start a new gallery to try and get to them but with the water and running muck it is a heart-breaking job. We cannot get any answer from them now. Men are working hard at it night and day. Fritz keeps on sending over rifle-grenades and trench mortars all the time. We had some of our Coy killed with a rifle-grenade yesterday afternoon. It was one of the fellows who came with me from the other Coy and previous to his going on leave last week we worked together for a while. No news of our two men who are missing yet.

June 26. Still trying to get through to those men, but it is painfully slow. We can't get any answer from them. Saw a thrilling air-fight yesterday between three of our machines and six German machines. It took place right over our lines and down pretty low. We had a splendid view and it lasted for quite a while. One of our machines came down afterwards near where we were standing to take the observer to a dressing-station. He had been shot through the chest and died before they got him there. Another of our machines had to come down and an artillery observer said that he saw two of the German planes come down. The German planes seemed much faster and much faster on the turn.

June 27. Abandoned all hope of getting those two chaps out this morning and stopped all rescue work for the condition of the shaft was so bad as to endanger the lives of the men working down there and they think that they are both dead. That chap Hackett died a hero for he could have come out with the others but would not leave his injured comrade.

Saw the armoured train with a big gun in action today. Our artillery has also been very busy today.

July 28. Another of our Coy killed today, accidentally whilst cleaning a revolver. The enemy tried another raid early this morning following the blowing up of a mine, but were easily beaten off leaving a number of dead behind. Our artillery has been very busy again today cutting the enemy's wire and shelling the support trenches. Saw the armoured train in action again today.

June 29. Things very quiet in the trenches today. Our artillery opened fire on a German working party who were working just in front of us. We could plainly hear them working. The shells whizzed over pretty close to our heads. The Germans started to send some back. One pitched right in the trench and wounded two of the infantry.

June 30. Things rather quiet today with the exception of some bombarding by our artillery. We had new iron rations[27] issued to us today. Weather rather cold and showery. We are on the eve of the great British offensive for it starts to-morrow morning. It's going to be something big this time.

July 1. Things very quiet today in the trenches, except for a little wire-cutting by our artillery. The big offensive has started on our right a good many miles away. On the way to the trenches at four o'clock this morning thirteen of our aeroplanes passed overhead, flying together. Later on in the morning whilst in the trenches we saw eight Germans come from behind their lines and attack some of our machines. Soon it was a regular pitched battle in the air and we saw one German plane break off the fight and fly for home evidently hit. Soon afterwards one of our machines started to fall turning over and over like a bird that had been shot. Whilst still several hundred feet above ground it recovered its balance and flew back over our lines. It was a marvelous piece of flying. He must have looped the loop dozens of times.

July 2. Our Coy was inspected today. Gen. Landon commanding our Division. After the inspection he made a speech in which he paid tribute to our Coy for good work done at Givenchy and said how much he appreciated the gallantry of our men on the morning of the 22nd of June, especially that of Hackett who laid down his life. He also spoke of the great offensive that started and that they were making very satisfactory progress. The Germans blew up a mine yesterday burying two more of our Coy. One more chap gone from the party who came from the 181st Coy with me.

July 3. More wire-cutting by our artillery today. The snipers have been very active on both sides. A German sniper killed the Colonel of one of the Battalions. He was looking over the top to watch the effect of one of our shells. One of our snipers killed or shot three Germans including a Staff Officer. The enemy then tried for him with a machine gun but did not damage although the bullets were skimming the parapet. Our man then located the sniper with a telescope, turned a Lewis machine on him and riddled his place with bullets. We did not hear the German sniper any more after that. The enemy have been very quiet indeed to-day.

July 4. Splendid weather today. Rifle inspection and rifle drill this morning. We seem to be making good progress with our offensive on the right. You can plainly hear the thunder of the guns especially at night.

[27] Emergency rations for use when soldiers did not have access to prepared food, usually consisting of cakes containing powdered bouillon and wheat.

July 5. Been charging a mine today. A rotten job, air so bad that a candle would not burn. Gave all of us a bad headache. There is a big "do" coming off tonight on our part of the line.

July 6. The raid last night was a great success. The artillery bombarded the enemy's first line. We exploded a mine and then the raiding party went over and cleared the Germans' first line. A party of Tunnellers picked from our Coy then went over and blew up three mine shafts of the enemy's. A large number of German miners who kept firing up the shafts and refused to come out were buried. Field Coy R.E. blew up some big dug outs. The party held the German first line nearly two hours. The Tunnellers had one officer and two men wounded and the infantry had three killed and about thirty-five wounded. They brought back forty-five German prisoners and they estimate they bowled over about one hundred and fifty more.

July 7. Things very quiet in the trenches today. Forgot to mention they found the bodies of our two missing Corporals buried in a dug-out. It was crushed in by the big mine explosion and they must have been killed outright. They got near enough to identify them but could not get them out so had to bury them there.

July 8. Saw them burying some of the infantry the night before last who were killed the night of the raid. There were eight of them also two German machine gunners who died of wounds. Our party captured the machine gun and found it to be one of ours.

July 9. The enemy blew up a small mine this morning. It did no damage whatever to us beyond giving a couple of our chaps a bad shaking. It also blew up one of the German snipers evidently through some mistake. One of our snipers who was watching him with a telescope distinctly saw him go up in the air with the explosion.

July 10. The enemy tried an attack on our right last night after a severe bombardment. They found our men waiting for them in front of our parapet where they had gone to escape the worst of the bombardment. They easily drove the enemy back with severe losses.

July 11. We blew up a big mine early this morning making a very big crater. Probably did considerable damage to the enemy's workings for they were above us. The enemy sent over some very heavy shells today. They made the earth tremble when they burst.

July 12. One of our Coy got killed today by a sniper, shot through the head. Saw a German six- inch shell in our trenches this morning that had not exploded—otherwise known as a "dud." Splendid weather and plenty of aeroplanes about.

July 13. Enemy tried another attack on our right last night but failed again to reach our trenches. We have some fine troops in that part of the line and the enemy have their work cut out to do anything there.

July 14. The enemy gave our part of the line a terrific bombardment last night, using guns, I should think, of every description. We had to "stand to" for a while.

Could see figures against the skyline moving about in no-man's land but it turned out to be one of our patrols. Enemy did not come over.

July 15. Weather very hot and things fairly quiet in the trenches. Plenty of aeroplanes about but mostly ours.

July 16. Our party are going to start a big bombardment this evening. All miners withdrawn from the trenches. Had to clean up trenches around billet in case the enemy started to retaliate. I am going for a ten-day's course in Mine Rescue work with the Proto apparatus tonight. Went before the C.O. this morning. Am to get a stripe when I come back.

July 17. At the Proto School. Weather rather showery. This is a splendid piece of country around here and plenty of fresh air. We sleep under canvas, which is alright this time of the year. Not a great deal to do to-day, just a lecture and some fatigue work. Went for a walk in the evening with an N.C.O. from our Coy and we came back too late for the mine school roll call.

July 18. Could hear a terrific bombardment all through the night with a lot of rifle and machine gun fire. Must be an attack on somewhere. Had a lesson in listening to-day, practical mining and Proto practice. Went for a nice walk again this evening.

July 19. Went through the same programme again today. Saw one of our aeroplanes come down in a field evidently through engine trouble. They came for a party of our chaps to dig it out of the mud afterwards.

July 20. Still having splendid weather. Went through same programme again today, with a little extra Proto practice.

July 21. Had a listening test today. Came out good.

July 22. Forgot to say that I saw two Brigades of a famous Scotch Division march past a couple of days ago. The General inspected them as they marched past and each battalion had its pipers playing at its head. It was a splendid night.

July 23. Plenty of Proto practice again today. They are making it pretty hard now. Still lovely weather.

July 24. Have seen several aeroplanes during the week and again last night flying when it was almost dark and throwing out coloured rockets to locate the aerodrome. The aerodrome[28] answered with rockets to show them where to land.

July 25. Working pretty hard at the practices now, for the examination is coming off tomorrow. Hope I don't get the wind up.

July 26. Examination today. Came out good in the listening test. I don't know how I came out in the Proto exam but I answered all questions and did everything satisfactorily—at least I think so.

[28] an air base

July 27. Came back to the Coy last night. Before leaving the Proto school I came across a chap that I knew I had not seen for five years; he is a sergeant now.

July 28. Up in the trenches last night. Things fairly quiet. Weather pretty warm. Counted six enemy observation balloons up this morning.

July 29. Still very hot weather. Went for a swim in the Canal today. Two of our Coy awarded the Military Medal for gallantry in the trenches under heavy shell fire.

July 30. In trenches again last night. Some brisk work by our artillery. Saw our Armoured Train with two big guns in action.

July 31. Promoted to acting L/Cpl this morning. Had another swim in Canal. "Fritz" shelled our huts last night. He sent one each side about twenty yards off, sent a shower of earth and stones on to the roofs of the huts.

August 1. Met one of my old chums this morning. He came up to where I was standing and asked if there was a chap named French in the Coy. Things rather quiet in the trenches last night.

August 2. Still having pretty warm weather. Went for a swim in the canal today. Helps a man to keep cool.

August 3. Things pretty warm up in the trenches last night. After a very heavy bombardment our party made a bombing raid on the enemy's trenches. Some of our Coy went over as well to blow up their mine shafts. The bombardment was a great success but the raid itself was a failure. The men from our Coy took over gun-cotton to blow up their shafts but had to bring it back again owing to the bombing party not being able to hold the line long enough. Some of the bombers were terribly injured. Some with arms and others with legs blown off. Our bombardment must have done severe damage to the enemy for it was terrific. Some of our Aerial Torpedoes weighing about 192 pounds were like mines going off and the air was full of Trench Mortars. You could see the fuses burning as they went through the air in the darkness.

August 4. The enemy started dropping shells very close to our huts again last night. One dropped in the yard just in front of our door but strangely enough did no damage. We are covering the huts with branches of trees now to conceal them somewhat from enemy aeroplanes.

August 5. German big long range guns shelled Bethune yesterday. They dropped some big ones right in the square which must have been crowded with civilians for it was Market day at the time. We could see them bursting from where we were standing and hear the big shells traveling overhead. They must have started a fire for we could see a cloud of black smoke rising.

August 6. Some more shells dropped close to our huts again last night. A lot of stones and mud dropped on the roof. A German aeroplane over today flying around. Did not stay long.

August 7. The shells dropped in Bethune the day before yesterday did considerable damage. Some shells dropped in the square, wrecking shops and killing a lot of civilians. Glass broken in every shop and house around.

August 8. Germans brought down one of our planes behind their lines with their aircraft guns last evening. It caught fire but came down easy. Some brisk work by our artillery last night, but otherwise pretty quiet.

August 9. Been swimming in Canal today. Weather pretty warm. Hundreds in swimming. Fritz sent some shrapnel over pretty close.

August 10. Saw a rather curious thing in the trenches this morning. Heard some shouting and laughing and on going to see what it was saw a lot of Germans leaning over the parapet and shouting across to our men who were also leaning over the parapet. The distance between the lines is about 75 yards. One of our men shouted "Come on over Fritz." "No blooming fear," Fritz shouted back in perfect English. In fact they could nearly all speak good English. This went on for half an hour and then heads went down and the war went on the same as usual. Instant death for the first man who put his head above the parapet.

August 11. Aeroplanes flying in the dark over the trenches last night. The Germans were looking for them with searchlights but could not locate them. Some heavy Trench Mortar work on both sides.

August 12. Went to Bethune yesterday, had a good time. Saw a lot of chaps I knew. Still having some splendid weather.

August 13. Up in Orders today that any German seen looking over the parapet is to be shot at and any man found talking to them is to be placed under arrest. That's the result of that affair a few days ago.

August 14. Promoted from L/Cpl to L/Cpl (paid) from today. Our party did some heavy trench mortar work today. You could see four in the air at one time. They kept it up almost all day. The enemy sent over a good many shells trying to locate the trench mortar batteries.

August 15. Things a little quieter in the trenches today. Had a good look at a German sniper through a periscope. Could see his head above the parapet but he kept it very still. I only saw him move it once and that was when a shell came pretty close. Our fellows are going to get a loop-hole[29] through and have a shot at him this morning.

August 16. Weather rather showery today. Several aeroplanes up this afternoon. Several fights took place above the clouds. Could hear the machine guns going but could not see the aeroplanes.

August 17. Splendid weather again today. A lot of observation balloons up. Counted six German Balloons quite close together in one part of the line.

[29] A gap or slit in the parapet through which defenders could fire at the enemy.

August 18. Weather rather showery, soon makes mud in the trenches. One of our Company accidently killed today whilst cleaning a revolver and another wounded. He was an officer's servant.

August 19. Stiff bombardment by our party last night and a bombing raid which I don't think was very successful. The enemy seemed to have wind of what was going to happen and were waiting for them.

August 20. The enemy were again bombarded by trench mortars and rifle grenades to-day. We must have made a mess of their trenches. The infantry have been "standing to" yesterday and today. Some of them have been asking me if I knew when the German mine was going up, as if I knew. They said they heard there was one going up. It beats me how they know.

August 21. The enemy blew a mine last night at 8.10 p.m. burying two of our men in a gallery. I was standing in the trench at the time and saw it go up. The German artillery opened fire on that part of the line at once and for a few minutes had it all their own way and then our men started and for an hour that part of the line looked like a sheet of fire with the bursting shells. We sent over about three to one and they were the first to finish. They have been working all night trying to get those two chaps out, but they are probably dead.

August 22. Gave up all hope of getting those chaps out alive. The chaplain went down the shaft and read the burial service—a very solemn affair.

August 23. Big bombardment on today. We were withdrawn from the trenches at 9.30 a.m. and went back to billets, a stroke of good luck. Been raining in torrents all day.

August 24. Heard old "Fritz" working in one of the saps today. Could hear him working with a pick, walking and dragging sand-bags. Lots of mud in trenches after the rain yesterday.

August 25. Been in Bethune today and had a good time. A number of shops blown down and all the windows broken in the centre of the town caused by the shells sent over by the enemy a few weeks ago.

August 26. Pretty rough in the trenches today. Our party bombarded the German trenches with trench mortars for a solid hour. Must have given them a severe shaking. Old "Fritz" sent some back though but did not do much damage. They were passing over our heads from where we were working. Some of them when they burst were like mines going off, throwing stones and dirt in the air for hundreds of feet. Would have made a mess of any dug-out if one pitched on it.

August 27. A shell burst in the road near our billets today, killing one and wounding several. He has been dropping three or four over a day for a week or two now, but has not done much damage.

August 29. Rather quiet up the trenches last night with the exception of some bombing. One of our infantry got severely wounded in the side by a bomb chucked in over the parapet in the darkness whilst doing some sand-bagging. I think he must have been wounded in the lungs for I had to hold him up in my arms so that he could breathe. Held him in that position until the stretcher bearers came. Poor chap, he was in great pain. He shook his Corporal by the hand and said "Good-bye, I think they have got me this time, remember me to all the boys. I'll try not to be more trouble than I can help." He could only gasp out the words. I acted as a guide to the party when they took him to the dressing station. He seemed a little easier after we got him there. Our armoured train was very busy in the early hours of the morning with their big guns.

August 30. Splendid weather today. Things rather quiet in the trenches around our part of the line but can hear a terrific bombardment going on on our right; it is a continual roar.

August 31. Went to the 251 Coy today to fetch some trolleys. Saw some fellows I knew from Redruth. Been on fatigues nearly all day, fetching timber and sand-bags with a motor-lorry.

September 1.

Red Poppies in the Corn
I've seen them in the morning light
When white mists drifted by;
I've seen them in the dusk of night
Glow against the starry sky.
The slender, waving blossoms red
Mid yellow fields forlorn
A glory on the scene they shed
Red Poppies in the corn.
I've seen them, too, these blossoms red,
Show against the trench lines' screen
A crimson stream that waved and spread
Thro' all the brown and green.
I've seen them dyed a deeper hue
Than ever Nature gave,
Shell-torn from slopes on which they grew
To cover many a grave.
Bright blossoms fair by nature set
Along the dusty ways,
You cheered us, in the battles fret,
Thro' long and weary days.
You gave us hope: if fate be kind,
When home again we march and find
Red poppies in the corn.

One of our best officers was killed last night by a sniper. A.M.C.[30] man named Bernard. It happened about two in the morning. It was brilliant moonlight at the time and

[30] British Army Medical Corps

we were standing outside the shaft on the top. He was giving me some instructions regarding some work to be done that night and we were looking at the bombardment down at Vimy Ridge when suddenly a shot rang out and Mr. Bernard flung himself down. I shouted "Are you hit, Sir" and he said "My God, yes." Those were the last words he ever spoke for he died a couple of minutes later whilst I was holding his head. The bullet struck him under the right armpit. We had rather a job to get his body away owing to the trenches being smashed so by "Fritzy's" big "Minnies"[31] and to the mud and water. I was not sorry when next shift relieved me at six in the morning.

The shift this morning got a bad smashing up. A big "Minnie" dropped in the trench and killed six of them; they were blown to pieces. Things are getting pretty warm around our part lately. "Fritz" keeps lobbing his big trench mortars over in the hopes of hitting our shaft. He has missed it so far although he has blown in one of the entrances.

A big funeral today. One officer and six men. We buried them in Bethune Cemetery. All the Coy not on duty turned out. It was all rather solemn, especially when the buglers sounded the "Last Post."

1917

April 10. Well we are shifting from Givenchy to-morrow, destination unknown, altho' rumour says we are for Ypres. The 251 Coy are taking over our sector. Their O.C.[32] and ours tossed to decide who should go and our O.C. lost. It will be a change for us, though probably for the worst. We have been fifteen months at Givenchy.

April 11. We are moving today to Ypres. Everything has been handed over the 251 Coy. We have been showing their officers and N.C.O. around the saps for the last two days. They were rather surprised at the quality and the amount of work done. Without a doubt we are leaving behind one of the finest series of mines on the whole Front.

April 12. Arrived at Poperinge, Belgium last evening. We traveled from Bethune in char-à-bancs.[33] A nice ride but very dusty. We are living under canvas in a field just outside of Poperinge. Before leaving Bethune a few of us paid a last visit to the cemetery where so many of our chaps lie buried. The graves are well looked after.

April 16. We are going to have our first experience of the Ypres Salient tonight. We are going to make deep dug-outs in the support lines for Battalion Headquarters Dressing Stations. The work has to be finished by such and such a date, so it will be a rush. We are having delightful weather now.

April 21. Well, we are back from the trenches again after being in four days. We left camp on the night of the sixteenth in motor-lorries and proceeded up the ___ road to a certain point where we had to wait until it was dark before going any further. No traffic is allowed within four miles of Ypres until dark for the roads are under direct observation. There was a long line of traffic waiting to go to the head of the lot. On the way up we passed through the town of Vl___ [Vlamertinge].

[31] mortars
[32] commanding officer
[33] open-top motor vehicle

Nearly every house bore marks of shellfire, while the church and a good many houses were completely wrecked. All civilians were cleared out of this town late in 1915.

By the time we reached the city of Ypres it was quite dark and we could not see much of it. Getting past Ypres we had to walk the rest of the way, up the main road to Hell-fire Corner,[34] rather a suggestive name I thought and then up the trench to the front lines.

August 9. Saw a large number of German prisoners brought in this morning, probably about three hundred and what a sight they were, covered with mud and blood, unshaven with clothes in tatters. Several were wounded and had to be supported by the others. Several of our wounded came along at the same time, with different expressions on their faces, however, for they had been over the top early in the morning and advanced on a two-mile front.

August 10. Dull and showery today and bad for observation. Several knocked out on the road last night and blood, shells, equipment and dead horses lying all over the place. Wounded continually being brought in and taken to the White Chateau.[35] But what a place for a dressing station. Fritz shells it all the time and it's a regular deathtrap anywhere near it. As soon as he stops shelling we have to fill in the shell holes in the road. Our casualties today were one killed and five wounded including two officers. This makes sixty-eight men and seven officers killed and wounded this week from our Coy alone.

August 11. Weather dull with bright intervals. Whenever possible both sides promptly put their balloons up. Fritz seemed to be uncomfortably close and ... [why] he did not fire at some of the splendid targets he had on the road today is a mystery to me. Sometimes during the day the road was full of lorries and G.S. wagons[36] carrying road and material and other stuff. At one time about fifty horses and mules went up loaded with shells in ammunition column that was on the road just behind [the] old front line. I counted a dozen dead horses and mules there this morning. An awful mess.

August 12. Weather was a little clearer this morning and Fritz soon had his balloons up. Two of them seemed to be looking straight down the road we were working on. He seemed to content himself with shelling the batteries however, but just to let us know that he knew we were there he every now and then dropped a few on the roads. Salvage parties were busy to-day collecting equipment, rifles, and saddles from dead horses and mules. They also had a number of sets of German

[34] Nickname for the intersection of the Ypres-Rouler railway and the Ypres-Menin Road on which German gunners effectively had zeroed in, reputedly making it the most dangerous spot on the western front. The Ypres-Menin Road was the principal route by which the British reinforced and re-supplied the Ypres Salient, leaving British troops no alternative but to endure deadly shellfire on their way to and from the front.

[35] Located on a ridge in the Ypres Salient, the "White House" was used as a triage center.

[36] General Service wagon

body armour. They seemed rather cumbersome and probably weighing about thirty pounds. Swarms of aeroplanes in the sky again and numerous fights.

August 13. Weather better today. Fritz shelling the roads as usual. There were five horses lying dead at the Menin Gate and two at the White Chateau. Shells scattered all over the road as usual. Our heavies opened up a heavy bombardment first thing this morning and kept it up for half an hour. I heard afterwards that they caught Fritz moving back some guns. They moved all right—some up in the air. Several dead brought in today and buried in the cemetery. They seem to be giving the battlefield a general clean-up. On finishing our shift we could not get down the road owing to it being heavily shelled. Some ammunition caught fire and we had to go around by the fields. It was a good job we did for when about a hundred yards away the dump blew up and for a few seconds it fairly rained shells.

August 14. It has been a little quieter today, enabling us to get up a good deal of road material. It's surprising the amount of stone it takes to keep the roads in repair. On our sector alone we sometimes have as much as eighty lorries a day, but traffic is enormous.

August 15. Our boys went over the top this morning. They captured their objectives in most places but could not hold them. They were held up on the left by some big concrete forts. A few prisoners came in. Our guns have been roaring away all day.

August 16. We had some heavy shelling today on the roads. One shell killed three R.G.A.[37] men close to us, another big shell cut a big tree clean in two. Our Coy had five men wounded. I had a rather narrow escape. A shell splinter struck me full in the left side, ripped through my tunic but was stopped by a thick leather belt I was wearing at the time. I escaped with nothing worse than a bruise. Our officer had his face grazed with another splinter which just made a slight cut.

August 17. The same old thing again today. Wounded a sergeant of ours at the White Chateau. Several direct hits on the road. At the end of the day and coming down at the rear of the men we found two new shell holes in the centre of the road, so the officer, a corporal and myself started to fill them in. We had just nicely got finished when we heard another shell coming. It sounded as if it was going to drop on top of us. We flung ourselves down flat in the road just as it burst twenty yards away on the pave. We got up and did a hundred yards in about ten seconds; it shook our nerves a bit. He put several more over after we left and burnt up two Red Cross cars.

August 18. Torrents of rain today. Everybody soaked to the skin. No balloons up and very few aeroplanes. Shells being taken up to the guns by the thousand all day long. Dragged six horses off the road that had been killed and buried them; not a very pleasant job.

August 19. Our boys went over the top again yesterday. The Irish are in front of us. I saw them going in the line the night before the attack; they were all in fighting

[37] Royal Garrison Artillery

order. They captured most of their objectives but met with a good deal of opposition and Fritz has delivered several heavy counter-attacks since, but our boys are hanging on. All the caterpillars were up ready to move the big guns up, but they decided not to move them.

August 20. The Gothas[38] came over bombing yesterday afternoon. Dropped a good many on the road and wounded three of our Coy. A Police Corporal directing traffic on the Potijze road [just east of Ypres] had both legs blown off. He was quite conscious and tried to reach his revolver to shoot himself, but was prevented by one of our chaps. He then begged this chap to shoot him to put him out of pain. A few minutes afterwards he died.

August 21. Very fierce fighting the last two days. Our chaps have been driven back from some of the positions they captured a few days ago. The gunfire has been terrific.

August 22. Had a sergeant of ours wounded on the road by a bomb yesterday. Had a rather narrow squeak myself at the St. Jean crossroads. A big shell dropped a few yards away in a ditch; the chap beside me had a piece clean through the shoulder.

August 23. Heavy shelling on the road again today. A party of sixteen men came down the road from the line; all that was left of their Coy. They had just reached the White Chateau when a shell dropped in the middle and wounded twelve.

August 28. Several Gothas came over bombing last evening. Dropped a bomb amongst some infantry making an awful mess of them, burning some of them to a cinder. Our planes were continually going over the German lines, bombing, in large numbers.

September 16. A big attack on today. The gunfire was terrible. We had to shout to one another when speaking. The Irish went over in front of us and captured their objectives but suffered rather heavily from machine-gun fire from pill-boxes [concrete emplacements] all night. Heavy rain all day and the mud is awful. We had a sergeant and one man was killed on the road today.

October 3. Weather much better today but the ground is very soft. There's something big coming off pretty soon by the look of things.

October 4. We attacked on a wide front at dawn this morning. Prisoners coming in in hundreds, coming in by themselves without escort. All prisoners able to do so carry stretchers down to the Dressing Stations. There were a lot of wounded Germans and a good many officers among the prisoners. They say our Artillery caught the Germans massing for a counter-attack when we opened out our barrage and the slaughter was awful. The prisoners were from a good many different regiments and some had the word Gibraltar on their sleeves. I never heard such a bombardment before as we put over this morning. The roar of the guns around made one's head swim. We have made a fine advance and captured all objectives. New Zealand and Australian troops went over in front of us. A big percentage of our wounded were walking cases.

[38] a German heavy bomber

October 24. Had a nasty day of it today. We were marching in single file to our work this morning, when in the middle of the road on top of the first ridge past the old front lines, we came across the bodies of an Australian and his horse; the man still astride his horse. They had not been killed long for the horse was still steaming. I being in the lead, quickened the pace to get by. I had only gone about thirty yards when we heard another shell coming. We dropped flat on the road and the shell burst in the same place as the other, right among the men. The scene that followed was awful. Five were killed outright and seven wounded; two dying of their wounds later in the day. Some of the wounded were shouting and screaming for help and there were so many that you hardly knew which to go to first. Some had arms and legs blown off. Anyhow we got them all to the dressing station. Fritz shelled the road and dressing station all day and we had another two men killed. Altogether it has been a nightmare of a day and a bad one for our Coy. One of the chaps was wounded for a sixth time.

October 27. Been putting in a facine[39] [*sic*] road today for heavy guns to go in over the soft ground. We had the job to do and finish. We did not waste much time about it, although we had to knock off an hour owing to shell fire. One man sitting on pile of facines eating his lunch was killed by a shell splinter which went clean through him. Found a lot of aerial torpedoes in one of the pill-boxes left by Fritz. They were all packed neatly in boxes.

October 28. Saw a very gallant deed performed today. Fritz dropped a shell on the road killing two horses and seriously wounding the rider in the legs. All the rest of the men bolted with the exception of one who managed to get the wounded on his shoulders and started to carry him away. He had not gone ten yards when another shell hit the same place knocking over a third horse. We fully expected to find both dead but when the smoke cleared away we saw the chap staggering down the road with the other still on his shoulders. When shelling ceased, we went to repair the damage and drag the horses off the road. One horse was still alive but could not get up, so I took a rifle and shot it. Was not sorry when we finished today.

October 29. The enemy did a bit of bombing around our camp last night with several planes. We lost one of our best officers today. Captain Bayley M.C. He went up the road with a party of men to look for some men who were missing when he was struck in the head with a splinter and died at the dressing station. A Corporal with him was also wounded. The casualties in our Coy today have been one officer and two men killed and seven men wounded. There won't be many of us left soon at this rate.

October 30. Fritz was over our camp bombing last night again. Killed fifteen of our Coy horses and completely wrecked some buildings near Poperinge main street killing several citizens. Seemed to be fairly large bombs, some of them fairly made the

[39] Fascine; cylindrical bundles of sticks bound together to provide better traction.

ground rock. Road heavily shelled again today, had to take cover in some pill boxes for a couple of hours. No casualties.

October 31. We have a day off today. Spent it building sandbags around our tents to keep out bomb splinters. Fritz came over bombing last night, dropped some pretty close—the dirt came down on our tent.

November 1. Left for the line again this morning at 4.50 a.m. Found the road in a bad state with a lot of fresh shell holes made during the night. Fritz caught afire two lorries loaded with shells and both blew up making a huge hole in the road blocking all traffic. Some howitzers were put out of action and one field gun was blown straight out of the gunpit on to the road, all smashed and twisted. Several bodies were lying about and a lot of horses and mules—some horses and men had been blown to pieces. Fritz shelled heavily all day but luckily few hit the road. We had no casualties but there were three killed and ten wounded out of another party. One chap who was sheltering behind a derelict tank had his arm cut off by a shell splinter. Saw one of our aeroplanes wrecked on the V___ road, engine trouble. One squad of ours had been boring today to see if the ground is suitable for dugout making.

November 2. Our guns were bombarding heavy in the early hours of this morning. I asked an artilleryman whether Fritz had tried to come over or not. "No," he said, "It's only a little morning hate." It has been very misty today but he seems to have the road registered alright for he keeps plonking them in the middle.[40] The 171 Coy who are working next to us lost two officers and three men killed and four wounded. We were very lucky.

November 3. Our guns bombarding very heavy again this morning, but it doesn't seem as if the stacks of shells at the guns get any smaller no matter how heavy the bombardment. One of our N.C.O.s placed thirteen bodies in a lorry and sent them to Ypres to get a decent burial. He picked them up by the roadside. Sometimes bodies are lying around for a week or more. As for dead horses and mules there are hundreds of them.

November 4. Been working today on Abraham Heights; it was very misty and I could not get a good view of the land in front. There has been heavy fighting around this part and there are still several bodies lying about. All the pill boxes were smashed with the exception of the very large ones. Five of our Coy pretty severely wounded on the road today with one shell. The country all around is covered with guns with no attempt at concealment and shells by the hundred thousand. There is a standard gauge railway running up about a mile behind the old front lines and light railways running up fairly close to the new lines. I took a walk around the village of Gra___. It is absolutely level with the ground and you have to look closely to see any traces of it.

November 5. Things rather quieter up the line today. Weather very misty all morning; lot of air fighting after weather cleared. Took a stroll around the foot of

[40] Calculated the range and artillery settings, such as elevation and charges, to hit the same target repeatedly.

Abraham Heights today. Scores of our chaps lying dead around some of the Block houses; looks as if they were mown down by machine-gun fire. Also several tanks and one of our aeroplanes lying about. Two of our Coy wounded to-day. Also found the chap [that] has been missing since yesterday. He had been into a shell-hole and was quite dead.

November 6. Another "push" on today. It seemed to be on a big front. The barrage started at about six in the morning and it was like a great fire-works display, with thousands of shells bursting. Verey lights [flares] and red, green and golden rockets going up in the air. Our chaps had taken all objectives by 7:40 and were a thousand yards the other side of Pas___.[41] There was a steady flow of prisoners coming in all morning. "Fritz" did a lot of shelling but he seemed to be doing it blindly. He managed to get a few direct hits on the road and killed several pack-horses taking up shells. Also put up a dump or two. Our artillery gave him a good pounding. All around you could see hundreds of gun flashes and the noise was deafening. You could not hear "Fritz's" shells coming. He made a counter-attack in the morning but our guns soon smashed it up. The weather was fine for the attack but came on rain later on in the day.

November 7. We are still holding all we won yesterday in spite of several counter-attacks. In one of these our barrage cut them off from returning and our men fairly mowed them down with rifle and machine-gun fire, captured a few prisoners including five officers. The enemy did a lot of bombing last night—killed several men and horses on the duck-board track [wooden planks laid for traction in the mud]. Weather very cold and showery.

November 8. We are working quite close to the now famous Somme and Gallipoli Farms. These are massive concrete block-houses and it was here that the Irish received such a cutting up on the 16th of September. These block-houses held them up and they changed hands several times. I took a stroll around this part of the battlefield today and there are scores of our men lying dead, especially near the barbed wire. (The enemy had a belt of wire right around each block-house) You can see arms and legs sticking up everywhere. We dug up three bodies when making a ditch. Our airmen brought down three German planes close to our sector and "Fritz" brought down one of our balloons in flames. Fritz shelled the road heavily at times and killed twelve of another party.

November 9. Another warm time again today. Two German planes came over our lines early in the morning flying very low. The road at the time was crowded with motor lorries, pack horses and G.S. wagons. They had not gone back long before Fritz started "Strafing" the road right along the whole length. Most of the shells missed the road and fell in the soft ground on each side, but one dropped in the middle of a group of horses and men. It looked as if it had dropped on a pile of bricks—everything in the air was red. It was limbs and flesh flying in the air. Some

[41] He is referring to Passchendaele. The third Battle of Ypres or Passchendaele occurred between June and November 1917 for control of the strategic ridges near the Belgian city of Ypres.

horses were wounded and it was a pitiful sight to see them trying to get up as each shell pitched near them. He shelled the road several times like this and on the other road (Zonnebeke). He caught two motor-lorries afire. Our Coy had one man wounded. Later on in the morning twelve enemy planes dropped a shower of bombs behind the lines. About six this morning our guns opened out for half an hour on a wide front. It was just to put the wind up him, that's all.

November 10. Another of our officers severely wounded today. Lt. Turner M.C. News came through that the corporal who was wounded with Cpt. Bayley had died of his wounds. The same old thing on the roads, some shelling and then a run for cover. Everybody's nerves are all to pieces, some worse than others and no wonder. Congratulations came through in orders last night from the 1st Lieutenant on the good work done by the Coy on the roads in the forward area.

November 11. They say that the officer wounded yesterday is dying. He is quite conscious and knows that he is dying. Been up to Abraham Heights today. Boring. Hostile aeroplanes very daring early morning. One came over and fired his machine-gun at a party working close to us. He was close enough to see the fire spitting from his machine gun. We just stood where we were with our hearts in our mouths, not daring to move or look up. Some bullets came very close but no one in our party was hit.

November 12. Lt. Turner died last night. We had a corporal severely wounded today by a shell, one leg blown clean off. Passed the remains of two motor lorries that had been caught afire by shells on the way up this morning. The body of the driver was in the seat of each still, fairly burnt to cinders; must have been killed by the shells and then burnt by the fire.

November 13. The corporal who was wounded yesterday died last night. One of our sergeants has been awarded the Military Medal for gallantry; he deserved it. "Fritz" brought down one of our balloons in flames today. Both observers escaped by parachute.

November 14. "Fritz" put a heavy barrage on the Zonnebeke road today, much heavier than anything he has put on before; fortunately our party had just moved off and there was not a great deal of traffic on the road at the time. Our next party coming on found over a hundred direct hits on the road. All traffic was held up until the road was repaired.

November 15. Saw rather a curious thing today. A quartermaster and six men were going up the road carrying some wooden crosses for graves, when two of the men "fell out" and dropped behind. One of our men asked them why they did not keep up with their party and they said they would let them go ahead a bit first. The words were hardly out of their mouths when a shell landed on the Q.M.[42] and men killing four and wounding the other. If the other two men had kept up with their party they would have been caught by the same shell.

[42] Quartermaster or supply officer

November 16. Came through in orders today that five others and myself had been awarded the Military Medal. "Fritz" put up a dump of ours last night containing ten thousand shells. It made a crater in the ground about sixty yards long, twenty yards wide and fifteen feet deep. The wonderful thing about it is there was only one casualty—a sergeant shell-shocked. There were several wounded though in a radius of half a mile by dropping fragments.

November 17. Had a day off today. Had a good game of football and got licked 1–2. Weather a little better.

November 18. Much quieter up the line today. Weather very misty which probably accounts for it.

November 19. A heavy bombardment by our fellows this morning, lasted for about two hours. One of our planes came down with a crash, with a wing off. It must have got in the way of one of our own shells.

November 20. Two of our men wounded to-day, standing in the entrance of a 'pill-box'. These 'pill-boxes' seem to be good things to keep away from.

November 21. Fairly quiet again today. A shell killed the traffic man at Spree Farm though. His chum broke down and cried when he saw him. Another of our planes came down with engine trouble; made a good landing.

November 22. Another balloon came down on fire today. I don't know how it caught fire for there were no planes about. It has not been so bad on the road today.

November 23. A major general congratulated us on our good work today. He was walking on the road when he stopped near where some of our men were working and said he had heard a lot about the 254 Coy and the good work they had done etc. It bucked the chaps up a bit.

November 24. Been fairly quiet again today with the exception of about half an hour. As soon as the shelling started (the road being in good order) all the men were taken off. It's laughable to see some of the chaps. In the morning they complain of a sore heel or something and they can hardly walk. As soon as a shell drops anywhere near them they do a hundred yards in about eleven seconds.

November 25. Several men knocked out on the road today. A shell dropped on the timber road and cut off some motor lorries and horse teams. A shell or two then dropped amongst them, killing a good many horses and men.

November 26. Our guns put up a big dump of "Fritz's" this morning; it raised a tremendous cloud of smoke. He doesn't have it all his own way. It must be perfect hell on the other side; our guns are pounding him all the time and they seem to fling 9.2 [inch] shells over like rifle grenades.

November 27. Our guns very active on this front again today; been at it all morning and the shells never seem to grow less. A brig. General killed on the road today by a shell. Had two rows of medal ribbons.

November 28. Rather quiet today, nothing much doing beyond the usual bombardment by our guns.

November 29. We moved our camp forward today, worse luck. We are now at V__, a most unhealthy spot. To be shelled or bombed is a daily occurrence. Already he has been dropping shells around and we have had shell splinters through a couple of tents. On the road in front of our camp a shell killed the driver of a G.S. wagon and one of the horses.

November 30. Had a very warm time last night in our new camp. We were shelled all night making it very difficult to get any sleep at all. We were fortunate in having only one casualty—the shoemaker got a shell splinter the size of a walnut clean through his leg just above the knee. We had a stroke of bad luck this morning though, up the line. A shell dropped where we were working and killed a L/Cpl and two men, also wounding one of my chums (Sgt. Swan) and another sapper. All these chaps had been with us a long time and were some of our best sappers.

December 1. Weather turning very cold, with a bitter wind blowing. Plenty of fatigue work now, getting our new camp in order. It's a bit rough yet and we have to get our water to wash out of shell holes. We are still living in tents. Not so much shelling today.

December 2. Still very cold and getting frosty. Doesn't make a man very anxious to leave his blankets at four in the morning. Our guns very active today.

December 3. Our chaps went over the top this morning, about two, to get a few strong points. They went over in bright moonlight. We saw about fifty prisoners come down. They were rather a mixed lot.

December 4. We had two men of Labour Coy attached to us killed by a shell this morning. The shell dropped right in the entrance of a dug-out we were making and blew both chaps down the steps. They were killed outright. We dug another chap out who had been completely buried. He was still alive but unconscious and bleeding from the ears, probably from concussion. This shell dropped only forty feet from where the other chaps were killed.

December 5. Had a day off today. Working all day on fatigues in Camp.

December 6. Our guns very busy today—at it all the time. Saw one of our aeroplanes catch on fire after being struck by shrapnel. It was all ablaze and then seemed as if they put the fire out and then tried to plane down. Suddenly it burst into flames again and the machine crashed. They made a great fight for life though.

December 7. Still quiet again today. More bombing last night.

December 8. Our guns very active last night and all day today; very little shelling from Fritz. A thaw has set in and it is getting muddy again. During the night a big shell dropped very close to our dug-out up the line—the near edge of the hole was only four feet from the dug-out. The shell hole was fifteen feet across and six feet deep.

December 9. A few prisoners came down today; they were in full marching order—probably gave themselves up. Our guns shelling away all day.

December 10. Things were a bit lively up the line today. Fritz shelled the road heavily with big shells. He got three direct hits on a dressing station, one of his big pill-boxes and flying the Red Cross Flag. He must have done some damage for they brought away several stretcher cases. He also smashed three ambulance cars. This afternoon seven Gothas came over bombing very close to where we were working. A bomb splinter wounded one of our corporals in the ankle. Later in the afternoon four more Gothas came right over our camps and dropped bombs. Anti-aircraft guns fired hundreds of rounds at them but could not hit them. Ten enemy balloons up today.

December 11. Some heavy shelling by the enemy today. He put a terrific barrage across the road and around a group of batteries, blowing the road up and knocking out a good many guns. One shell dropped by the dressing station and blew a hut right on top of a pill-box. For about an hour it was nothing but smoke and dust.

December 12. Our aircraft guns put in some good shooting today; brought down a German plane in flames and another just managed to reach the German lines before coming down. The plane that came down crashed about half a mile from where we were working.

December 13. Rather quiet up the line today. No aeroplanes up today owing to a thick mist. They say that the Germans are concentrating troops on this front. He will probably have a try at getting back the ridges.

CHAPTER 2

Commitment and Sacrifice

Phillip Cate in uniform. He served in both the American Field Service (AFS) and the U.S. Navy. *Courtesy of Lisa Stiegel.*

CHAPTER 2

"Young men . . . helping this nation to save its soul"

Philip T. Cate, American ambulance driver

For Americans who wanted to support France and the Allied cause in the early years of the war, American neutrality left them with two options: either enlist in the French Foreign Legion or Lafayette Escadrille (a largely American unit within the French air service) or volunteer with an ambulance group to assist wounded soldiers and civilians in a non-combatant role.[1] *Those who chose the latter route often signed on with the American Field Service (AFS), an organization that began as the ambulance division of the American Hospital built by the American expatriate community in the Parisian suburb of Neuilly-sur-Seine.*[2] *Organized by former U.S. Secretary of the Treasury and professor of economics at Harvard A. Piatt Andrew,*[3] *the AFS drew its recruits largely from the northeastern Ivy League schools of Harvard, Yale, and Princeton.*

[1] According to Douglas Porch, many of the initial American Foreign Legion volunteers were of French heritage and enlisted out of a sense of "patriotism, love for France and ideology." Douglas Porch, *The French Foreign Legion: A Complete History of the Legendary Fighting Force* (New York: HarperCollins, 1991), xiv. See also Edwin W. Morse, *America in the War. The Vanguard of American Volunteers in the Fighting Lines and in Humanitarian Service, August 1914–April 1917* (New York: Scribners, 1919).

[2] Built in 1910, the hospital was too small to handle the number of wounded anticipated from battle. The French government provided the expatriate community with a nearby unfinished school to expand its wartime facilities; when completed, it contained about six hundred beds to accommodate the injured and sick. The hospital's board consisted of wives of American diplomats, politicians and businessmen who also helped finance the hospital itself. K. B. Johnson, "'It's Only the Ones Who Might Live Who Count': Allied Personnel in World War I," in *Personal Perspectives: World War I*, ed. Timothy C. Dowling (Santa Barbara, CA: ABC-CLIO, 2006), 161–203.

[3] Educated at Princeton and Harvard, Andrew (1873–1936) had an impressive career as an assistant professor of economics at Harvard (1900–09), director of the U.S. Mint

Initially, ten ambulances, produced by the Ford Motor Company, were donated by wealthy Americans, among them Anne Harriman Vanderbilt, the wife of railroad magnate Cornelius Vanderbilt. By April 1915, the AFS numbered three sections, each with twenty ambulances, a staff car, and a supply car. The first section was stationed at Dunkirk, the second at Lorraine, and the third in the Vosges.[4] *Phillip Cate was a member of the third section. Assigned to the French army, the ambulance drivers (or* conducteurs*) received their orders from French medical officers and were fed by and received housing from the French army, while the French government supplied the necessary gasoline and tires for the ambulances.*

*The Vosges, in which Cate's third ambulance section operated, was a sector unlike the rolling farmland and waterlogged plains of the Franco-Belgian border. Located in Alsace, toward the Swiss border, the Vosges region was mountainous, with rocky terrain, pine forests, deep valleys, and capricious weather, affording defenders plenty of natural cover and impeding offensive operations. Formerly French, Alsace (like the province of Lorraine) had been annexed by Germany in 1871 after the Franco-Prussian War, so its recapture was a French priority in 1914. When war broke out in August 1914, the French immediately launched a series of offensives to liberate the "lost territories" and tie down German troops, preventing them from moving northward to join in the Battle of the Marne. Stymied by a stout German defense and the rugged terrain, French forces were thrown back by German counterattacks. By December 1914 a stalemate had set in as both sides struggled to make incremental gains. Much of the fighting revolved around possession of one key local topographical feature, the 3,000-foot-high mountain Hartmannswillerkopf (*Vieil Armand *in French). Located some fifteen miles northwest of the city of Mulhouse, it dominated the Rhine valley and offered superb vistas for observation and artillery spotting. During particularly intense combat in March/April 1915, possession of the summit fluctuated between the French and Germans, though by the summer of that year the mountaintop had been so pulverized as to offer little advantage to either side.*

Amid the fighting in Alsace was twenty-four-year-old university student Philip T. Cate, the son of a Harvard alumnus, Martin Luther Cate, and Martha Curtis Cate. Educated in two all-male college preparatory schools, the Ridgefield School for Boys in Connecticut and the Noble and Greenough School near Boston (the latter a preparatory school for Harvard University), he was enrolled in Harvard when the war broke out. When the United States declared its neutrality, Cate volunteered for the AFS and departed Boston for Paris in early 1915, whereupon he was assigned to section three, the Vosges Mountain division. There he served for seven months as an ambulance driver, retrieving both military and civilian casualties in the mountainous region of Alsace that straddled France, Germany, and Switzerland. His section consisted of twenty ambulances and forty

(1909–10), member of the U.S. Monetary Commission (1908–11), and Republican member of the U.S. Congress (1921–36). After an unsuccessful bid for U.S. Congress in the autumn of 1914, Andrew left for France, where he volunteered as a driver for the American Hospital in Paris. It was there that he founded and directed the American Field Service.

[4] *Friends of France: The Field Service of the American Ambulance Described by Its Members* (Boston: Houghton Mifflin, 1916). For the role of field ambulances, see Emily Mayhew, *Wounded: A New History of the Western Front in World War I* (New York: Oxford University Press, 2013), 41–46.

other volunteers, about half of whom hailed from Harvard and the remainder from other Ivy League schools. For his service, albeit brief, Cate received the Croix de guerre. Upon his return to the United States in 1916, Cate re-entered Harvard and graduated with an A.B. in 1917. When the United States entered the war in April 1917, Cate enlisted in the navy, along with a group of twelve friends, serving on a sub-chaser and attaining the rank of lieutenant. After the war he went into the investment business in Boston and later served for more than two decades as an administrator and admissions counselor on the faculty of Deerfield Academy. He died at age eighty in August 1971.

Cate's diary, at times humorous but more often sobering, offers a glimpse into a sector, the Vosges, that has received far less attention from historians than those in Belgium and northern France. The treacherous, winding mountain roads, clogged with slow-moving convoys pulled by stubborn and frightened mules, were often as dangerous as enemy shells to the volunteer ambulance drivers and the wounded or sick patients their vehicles carried. Ambulance drivers were expected to maintain their vehicles in running order and be available for service at a moment's notice. Amid the dangers, however, were moments of relative calm, allowing for snatches of leisure in which Cate and fellow young drivers could engage in sports and simply act their age. Although the diary itself captures only a relatively brief snapshot of life on the Alsatian front, it stands as testimony to a generation of young idealists who chose to volunteer as non-combatants in a war zone rather than continue their studies in the safety of a neutral America. Theodore Roosevelt, distressed at the failure of the U.S. government to prepare for a war against German aggression, lauded the AFS volunteers in September 1916 as "young men . . . helping this nation to save its soul."[5]

October 5th. The first sight of Bordeaux was quite warlike and soldierly. Many uniforms were to be seen; much barbed wire and other military supplies. Of course, the first auto we saw as we tied up to the dock was a Ford. The Military authorities examined our papers and then we disembarked. We passed through Customs with no trouble at all and having several hours to wait for the train to Paris, two of us took a carriage and drove around the town, the driver showing us the various points of interest. Several of the large Hospitals and Public Buildings have been turned over to the Hospitals, and we learned this was the case throughout all the larger Cities in France. At noon we left for Paris and dined on board the train. All along the way we passed guards at every Bridge, Tunnel and culvert. At one place, we passed a squad of German prisoners at work in the fields. There were women porters on the train. We passed through the Chateau section [Loire valley region] just before dark, seeing Chaumont, Amboise and Blois, arriving in Paris where there were more Military authorities to pass before we were free. Paris was quite dark and we went straight to the Hotel. Had supper in our rooms and went to bed.

October 6th. At 8:30 I left for Neuilly and the Hospital of the American Ambulance. This is a large building of four floors, which was built for a school and was near completion when the war broke out. It was turned over to the American Ambulance for a small rental and has served admirably for a Hospital. There are seven hundred

[5] See *Friends of France*, 8.

beds and most of the worst cases that come to Paris are sent here. We have been very fortunate in the low percentage of deaths. The Staff of Doctors is ever changing as they come for a term of three months mostly. The nurses are American, English and French. On the top floor (the attic) the large room is fitted up for a dormitory for the drivers. In the basement there are two dining halls for two services of meals. Breakfast 7:00 to 8:30; luncheon 12:00 to 12:45; dinner 6:00 to 6:45 and midnight supper for those on duty. The Ambulance department is quite separate from the Hospital in organization. There are several offices, a guard room and a garage for repairing. In Paris there are twelve to fifteen Ambulances as well as a service of touring cars to carry the Doctors and Nurses between the bases and Metro station at Port Maillot. There are several French drivers in the Corps; a couple two [*sic*] young to be at the front and others assigned by the authorities. Among the cars are four Fords, the type used at the front, fitted up to carry three stretcher cases, two below and one above, or five sitters, four behind and one with the driver. There are other cars fitted up for four stretchers. There is a bird-cage carrying ten sitters and the jumbo carrying eight sitters and six lyers [*sic*]. On each car there is beside the driver an orderly.

October 7th. Took first step towards getting the necessary papers to stay in Paris and France. There are five papers one must have with him always. Passport, *permit* [*sic*] *de sejour*,[6] matriculation papers, drivers license and identification card written in three languages,—English, French and German. I had my first Ford lesson in Bois Boulogne. . . .

October 8th. Drove out to Versailles during my lesson today. There is a large Hospital there in one of the big Hotels,—in fact all over France many of the big Hotels are turned into Hospitals. In Paris alone there are over two hundred and fifty Hospitals. At 10:00 P.M. a call came to go to La Chapelle, the station where all the wounded arrive in Paris. As they were short of orderlies I borrowed a coat and hat, my uniform not having arrived as yet and went along. There were three trains expected during the night,—at 10:00, 12:00, and 5:00. They all came in, but at 1:00, 3:00 and 8:00, each three hours late. We got to the station at about 10:30 and waited for the first train. The station is an old freight shed fitted up for the present need.

At last the train came in; all the *broncardiers*[7] jumped up and lined up along the track, stretchers were placed along the walls and blankets too. As the train stopped, two *broncardiers* helped with the two men on each car, one a trainman and the other an officer. As they were a little short of *broncardiers*, two of us helped in one of the cars. There are eighteen berths in each car, upper and lower, five sets on one side and four on the other, the door side. In some cases the berths were arranged so as to swing in case the train should come to a sudden stop and thus reduce the chance of hurting the wounded. We held the stretcher close to the berths, so the man could get out of it easily by himself, or with help. He was then covered with one blanket and carried on to the platform where two *broncardiers* would be stopped, lift him up

[6] *Permis de séjour*, or residence permit
[7] stretcher bearers

and carry him off. Thus we helped unload one car. It was time to get our loads now. As I walked down the platform towards the office, I noticed the Stars and Stripes on a couple of the cars. Upon closer examination I found they had been given by some American. There were others given by French people and other private individuals. I met my driver just coming out of the office with a list in his hand. The chief officer had allotted the wounded to the different cars and each man got a sheet. We now went in search of our men, found in cabin "D" and two in "E." With some *broncardiers* to carry the stretchers we got them all out and into the ambulance and off we went. Our destination was written on the list and we headed for 125 Champs Elysees Hospital #167. We were fortunate to have all the men destined for one Hospital, and that Hospital near our headquarters at Neuilly. We drove through the dark streets of Paris where the Ambulances are the only machines allowed to use head lights and with the aid of a couple of Gendarmes,[8] which we picked up near the place, found our destination. We woke up the door-keeper, who very sleepily drew on a pair of trousers and summoned the nurses, of whom five came down to "look us over." Finally, two men appeared and they carried up the wounded with which the Nurses and driver, who was French, conversed. The last man was so badly wounded that the Hospital man, the driver and I carried him up three flights of winding stairs into the ward, where there were already ten or twelve others. Our stretchers and blankets were carried down and on the way the head nurse very kindly offered us a hot drink. We finally departed from the Hospital, arriving at three A.M. for two hours sleep and a light supper.

October 9th. The next call came at 5:00 A.M. to meet the third train. We were excused from the second and we went thru the same process. While waiting, six of us went off to get a bite of breakfast. It seems that each day, each Hospital reports to La Chapelle what number of empty beds they have, so that the officials know where they can send the wounded.

As the wounded are carried out, you are impressed with the calmness of most of them, smoking cigarettes and looking around. They come in there in every sort of condition, either direct from *poste de Secoms*[9] [*sic*] near the front or are evacuated from some Hospital back from the front. Once in awhile a man will die en route, but seldom. As the men are put into the cabins awaiting removal in the ambulance, Red Cross women distribute hot coffee, bread, oranges and cigarettes to them.

After our two trips we returned to the Hospital and I went to bed and slept from noon to breakfast.

October 10th. Four of us started off for a walk down the Ave. Bois du Boulogne, the Champs Elysees to the Invalides across the Seine. Here we encountered a huge crowd and waited in line for thirty minutes before getting to the place. There was a collection of German guns and aeroplanes in the square, taken only recently in Champagne. These caused much interest. . . .

[8] French term for police
[9] first-aid post or dressing station

October 12th. After driving from one side of Paris to the other, we arrived at the house of the officer in charge of driving licenses. The three of us took our tests, and all passed. In the evening I dined with Mrs. Hill[10] and two Doctors from the Hospital at Hotel de Crillon. The work at the Hospital was talked of a lot. The new seirum [*sic*] for grangreen [*sic*] etc. Mrs. Hill talked of work she was doing in connection with refugee children from Belgium and Northern France. There are three institutions which care for such children, who will be kept there until the end of the war, when they will be sent back to their families if it is possible to find them; otherwise they will be placed in Belgian or French families.

October 13th. At ten thirty, four of us left the Hospital for the station in one of the Ambulances. We got our passes filled out and after all the red tape had been gone through left Paris at noon for the front. We went at once into the dining car where there were many officers and one General. At one table there was a General and Colonel, and the headwaiter had left the two seats opposite empty. A young officer came in looking for a seat but the headwaiter said there were none. The General then called him in and asked him to sit at his table. He said he was in company with a Private, so the General asked him also. All during the meal the Private sat with his hat on as it is a custom that a Private shall not take his hat off in the presence of a General unless requested to do so. He was probably very much excited at dining in such high company. We passed through very pretty country all the way. Here and there were scattered small wooden crosses showing where the tide of battle had once been, in the early days of the war when some Prussian Cavalry succeeded in cutting the Railroad. They were soon driven out however, with small loss of life, having done practically no damage.

At Vitry le Francois [*sic*] two of the party got off to go to the tent squad section four. At Nancy two American Ambulance men met my other companion. The four of us took supper at a Café near by. They were bound for Pont-a-Mousson while I took an 8:50 train for Epinal. I ran across a couple of French Officers in a corridor who were talking English and when I asked them why, they said, merely for the practice of it. At Epinal I had a two-hour wait from 11:30 to 1:30. I got in a train for Bussang and slept in one of the compartments. At five o'clock, just as day was breaking, got off at St. Maurice.

October 14th. From the station I carried my duffle bag and blanket roll to the Hotel, outside of which I read until the time came to open up. Marie, as I afterwards learned her name to be, was the one to welcome me in the new place. I went in and ordered chocolate and eggs when Madame Lebouef, the good wife of the Inn keeper, appeared with smiling face—then one by one the drivers came in, those I knew and those I didn't. Was given a billet across the street from the Hotel. The room was good size, but of course had no heat and the only light was a candle. . . . Was then assigned to car #55 given by Mrs. H.P. Whitney of New York.[11] It was

[10] Mrs. Caroline Hill was a field worker for the "Franco-American Committee for the Children of the Frontier" to assist refugee French and Belgian children.

[11] Mrs. Harry Payne Whitney, better known as Gertrude Vanderbilt Whitney, was an American sculptor, art patron, benefactor, and member of the Board of Governors of the American Hospital in Paris. She was the eldest daughter of Cornelius Vanderbilt.

one of the many given by her, one of the original Whitney unit. There were other cars in the section given by Wellesley, Dartmouth, Gloucester, St. Paul's School, Pomfret School, L.Y.S. Ambulance, two other Whitney cars and a couple given by W.K. Vanderbilt, etc.

A call came for a contageous [*sic*] car and as I was to be on that service for a couple of weeks, I went with Graham Carey, a "sous-chef" to show me the way. We took the man from Wesserland to Le Thillot. The following is the process by which a man is carried from one Hospital to another:

If it be contageous [*sic*], they telephone to our headquarters for a special car, if not, the car stationed at the Hospital is used. The man is put in with his sack and gun and the driver given a paper telling where the man is to go, what disease or wound he has, and all about him. They carry three "couches" in back and one sitter in front, or four sitters in back. Of course, the contageous [*sic*] car is usually only one, unless there be more than one with the same sickness. They would not consider putting two men with different diseases in the same car, although if one man can stand it, they will put him in front with the driver if they don't think the fresh air will do him any harm, while the other man is put in back. This man went to Bussang, which is the clearing Hospital through which they all have to go. Being contageous [*sic*], he was sent on at once to Le Thillot, ten kilometers further. Here, the man is received, a receipt given and the car disinfected. The Corporal at this Hospital speaks English quite well. If you arrive there in the day time you drive the car around behind the Hospital and a soldier with a bucket of water and sulphonapthol[12] sweeps out the inside of the car and sprinkles and top and sides as well as the stretcher. They keep the blanket for disinfection and give you another. If however, you arrive there at night, the Corporal disinfects the car by means of a small bottle with a spray attached to it, which he sprays in at the back of the car.

We then returned to St. Maurice for luncheon. The food is regular Army food, which we obtain daily at four P.M. from a camion "truck" section #408 to which we are attached. In the afternoon I went to Krüth, another of our posts for another contageous [*sic*] case. I followed directions given me at headquarters and succeeded in arriving without any trouble. As I was turning to leave the Hospital at Bussang I ran into a truck and bent the radius rods. I telephoned for another car to take my load and proceeded home on very low speed. The country and nature are beautiful, the leaves are just turning. The colors are all shades of red and yellow, mixed with shade of Pine, as glorious a sight as a nature can show anywhere. All the mountainsides are dressed in these brilliant colors. The roads wind up the mountains along the valley to the tunnel which used to be the border between Germany and France. It was a very queer feeling the first time I came out of the tunnel on the other side and realized I was in Germany. This is the one part of Germany occupied by the Allied Troops and is a very small corner indeed. Down on the other side, the road winds to the valley leading through Thann to the Rhine River. Across this valley are other ranges of the Vosges mountains before one gets to the plains of the Rhine.

[12] A coal tar disinfectant that became a well-known household product in the late nineteenth century.

October 15th. My car was repaired in short order. Soon a call came for Thomannsplatz[13] where there was an attack at Hartmannsvillerkopf.[14] The Germans took a French trench by burning oil. The French retook the trench later, driving off the Germans and capturing fifty prisoners. I afterwards learned that this hill was once covered with a thick wood, but now it is entirely cleared of trees—all cut short by artillery fire.

All the other cars went on the call. Mine was the only one left. I slept on guard that night; one stretcher in the *atelier*—work-room—with a lantern outside the door to guide any messenger that might ring in telephone messages. The attack and counter attack took place on October 14-15-16.

October 17th. I got a call today to go over to Alsace and carry civil typhoids[15] from Saint-Amarin to Oderen. Both Hospitals are run by German sisters. I made two trips carrying old men and young girls. Each time a sister went along. One old man offered me a franc for carrying them. I wish I had taken it now and kept it for a souvenir. Carrying the sisters back to St. Amarin, I had a [tire] puncture which I succeeded in repairing with the aid of some passing soldiers. They are always willing to help one.

October 18th. There was an evacuation at Bussang this morning. The hospital is a large group of barrack buildings; six or seven in all. We evacuated to a hospital train which carried the men to the interior.

October 22nd. There was a call today which took me almost to Thann; almost the farthest place in the French lines. Just before arriving at Thann one comes to a large factory which is a military headquarters now. It covers about ten acres; only a small part is still used as a factory, troops are quartered there. In fact, in many of the large factories one finds troops or Red Cross stations.

October 24th–26th. I learned all the intricacies and state secrets of the Ford by means of taking it down, cleaning it, tightening up all bearings and putting it together. I say I, but I was only the on-looker a good part of the time, while the French mechanic from the Paris Ford Co. and our section mechanic did the work. When I did work, it was on the dirty jobs, under the car loosening bolts or cleaning pistons and engine covers etc. with gasoline. Now that she's up and aired it is almost impossible to crank her, she's so stiff. The supply car towed her away to get her going and limbered up a bit. I start her now by pushing her down hill. . . .

[13] a dressing station near the mountain

[14] A strategic peak in the Alsatian Vosges mountains, overlooking the Rhine Valley, where fierce fighting occurred between French and German forces during January, March, April, and December 1915. Also known as Vieil Armand (Old Armand) by the French, its summit of over 3,100 feet, with sweeping views of the Alsatian plain, was of strategic importance to both the French and the Germans. Today, a national monument, museum, and cemetery, built by the French, commemorate the campaign.

[15] Typhoid fever was a common affliction during World War I, spread by infected people through the handling of contaminated food or raw sewage. A vaccine, developed in 1889 by an English physician, helped protect British soldiers from the disease.

October 30th. I went to Treh. One stops at Krüth to see if there are any orders etc. before going up the hill. Leaving the valley at Krüth, the road goes directly up the mountain, passing the station (lower) of a new aerial in process of construction from Krüth to Breit—first to carry up ammunition, supplies etc. and save the slower mule traffic. It is similar to the aerial which is to join the railroad extensions from Wesserling and Bussang. All the way one goes on high, it is very steep and the road narrow. The road has been built only since the war began. It is very pretty, however, through pine forests and glades lined with ferns, through which run little brooks.

All along, the road is lined with mule convoys or ox carts or horse teams carrying up ammunition. It is hard passing, but by both squeezing it can be done. All along one edge of the road falls off to a deep ravine, the trees being the only thing to stop one from going clear down the mountain side. As on all French roads there is a bank about a foot high on this side of the road.

At last one comes up beyond the tree line to the post at Treh. There is a group of buildings here made of logs, mud and boards, hastily built. There is a mule station here also. Behind the small office is a dormitory of about ten beds, one of which the driver on duty occupies. The *broncardiers* sleep here too. The wounded arrive here by mule wagons or on foot and are relayed down by us or by other wagons.

I arrived just before luncheon which we had at 10:30. We eat out of tin plates; soup, meat, vegetables and all. By special favor we eat at a table with the cooks instead of standing with the other men. Great caldrons are brought out and the men dip in and help themselves. Your jack-knife is your table knife with which you cut bread and meat or even eat at times. It's all the same; a piece of bread will clean it for the next meal. Red wine is served—very poor stuff usually—and I don't like it anyway. The food is coarse, but eadable [*sic*], either potato or macaroni, always a soup, meat, bread and coffee.

I made two trips down the mountain to Krüth. The last one was after dark and I had to go pretty carefully, being unfamiliar with the road. When going down the mountain one has to travel in low speed most of the way, this serves as a brake, with the engine throttled down and saves the break [brake] bands from wearing, otherwise we would be burning our break [brake] bands continually and having to change them often; no easy job either. . . .

October 31st. I walked about the place. There is a cemetery at Treh. . . . I saw a lot of mules picketed. They all of one accord began to salute me with their braying. They sound exactly like a tug passing through Martha's Vineyard Sound in a fog—one long blow and two or three short ones to tell the number of tows. It struck me at once. . . . After *dejourner* [lunch] I left for Mitlack [*sic*; Mittlach], passing through Breit-feist [*sic*; Breitenbach].

Just before getting to Breit-feist [*sic*], I came across a lot of barbed wire entanglements. The second line of defense runs along the top of the ridge here. Then I came to the upper end of the aerial and further on some trenches being dug and batter positions. All the buildings here and elsewhere near the front have pine boughs on the roof so that scouting aeroplanes cannot see them.

I then descended through forests to the valley of Metzeral. This road is very narrow with sharp turns. There is little traffic here, our service being the most that goes over the road, and occasional convoys. There is another road into the valley. At one of the turns, there is an enlarged place labeled "garage Poincaré," a resting place on the hill. As one descends to the bottom of the valley following along the stream, one passes many army buildings, shacks built for the soldiers etc.

Our place here is covered by a roof, but has no sides or back. The Lieutenant, Gates, is rather disliked by us. We sleep in our cars here rather than with the *broncardiers* over a stable with a stove and all windows closed. We eat in the open with the soldiers.

Metzeral is just below. There is nothing left now but ruins. The Germans were bombarded out of the place. Last April the Germans were in Mitlack [*sic*] and several companies of chasseurs came down the mountains there on skis at night and attacked so suddenly that the Germans ran, leaving everything behind; horses, carts, guns etc. There was little fighting; in fact it was so quiet that in the morning many of the inhabitants didn't know the French were there. . . .

November 1st. Still at Mitlack [*sic*]. The man who came down today brought my mail and the first clippings of the World's Series Games. It seemed good to read baseball gossip again. It rained all day. I made one trip over to Krüth. On the mountains at Breit-feist [*sic*] there was a blizzard; a lot of wind and snow. I scared one mule in a convoy so blowing my Klaxon [horn] that he broke loose from his driver and started on the run ahead of me. Every time he slowed down I'd sound my Klaxon and off he'd start again. I guess I played with him for two or three kilometers, where he came to another convoy and stopped. He was so far away from his driver when I first caught up with him that I thought a little more wouldn't hurt. . . .

November 2nd. At eight they routed me out and gave me one sick man and the Catholic Priest who had been in the trenches for a week. He alternates with a Protestant Minister. It was very muddy and snowy on the top. I picked up another man at Treh and stopped at Krüth and Wesserling. At Bussang they had six men for another Hospital three kilos distant so I made two trips before returning to St. Maurice for luncheon.

November 3rd. I left at 7:30 for Wesserling where they have a Hospital in a large factory. The work here consists in carrying men who come in from Krüth and Moosch mostly, over to Bussang. They have built a dormitory in the cow yard and we sleep there with the *broncardiers* and some invalids. There is a large dining room seating about 100 men with a small one off it in which there are also six beds. We eat here with the maladies. The men in the office are very agreeable and we go in there to read or write, which is our occupation when there is no "rolling" or work on the cars to be done.

November 4th. From Wesserling the men always go on to Moosch, when relieved. At Moosch the Hospital was run by German sisters who are still there. . . . We have a room on the third floor with electricity and heat, sharing it with a young *sous-officier.* We eat at a very good inn near by where the German Inn-keepers give us very good food at very good prices. Two of us had breakfast here this A.M. for four cents: a huge omelet, coffee, milk hot bread and butter; not bad.

During the morning, three German aeroplanes, at different times, tried to cross from France to Germany. Evidently they had come over in the night. The French guns fired many shots at each, over thirty. It would take from ten to twenty seconds after we could hear the report. A French plane was up at the same time that the last *boche* plane was, but it could not hope to catch it. It had too much of a lead and above.

November 5th. I journeyed to St. Maurice, stopping at Bussang to deliver a load. The force there has just been changed and everything is slow. I had to wait for an hour for the doctors to see my men and have them delivered before I could get my *broncardiers* back. Then they gave me an order for six men for the Louice, a large Hotel Hospital two kilometers away. I made two trips and got back late for lunch.

November 7th. I left for Krüth, another one of our posts. The Red Cross is located in a part of a large factory here as at Wesserling. There is a dormitory, operating room, mess hall, shower room and waiting room. Things are fixed up pretty well and we have a garage for our cars. There is a young volunteer, who speaks some English named August located at Krüth. He is practically the valet of the A.A.; gives us food when we come back late etc. We get very good treatment here. . . .

November 8th. When my relief came an hour later I learned that the whole section was to leave St. Maurice for Collan, a little town back of Wesserling. . . . The town is small, with many soldiers quartered here "en repose.". . .

November 10th. Today I left for Thomannsplatz, the sixth of our posts. This is a two-night stand. The road leading up to it is very steep and narrow; the worst road we have to use. The road was filled with mule trains and supply wagons which made the going much more difficult. The pine forests go right up to the top where the war colony is located. It resembles a logging camp more than anything else and might as well be. The men sit around stove fires talking and joking just as if war was 3,000 miles away or so. There are two or three alleys or streets between log houses and plank shanties where the different groups of men eat and sleep. We sleep in the house with a young doctor who spent thirteen months in Germany as a prisoner. He was at Colmar with another doctor in advance and when the Germans came back the sisters ran out into the street and told the *boches* that there were a couple of Frenchmen in the Hospital, so they were taken prisoners instead of being able to escape at night. Among other things he said the bread was so hard that it wouldn't dissolve or loosen up in soup.

It was snowing or raining all the time I was up there so I couldn't see anything. They say the Rhine and Mulhouse are visible on clear days. Just below Thomannsplatz is Bain Douche [*sic*] about six kilos. [kilometers] It is at Bain Douche where we get nearest to Hartmannsvillerkopf, where the big attack was on October 14-15-16. There, at one time, there was nothing between the Germans and the Ambulances. . . .

We take our meals here with a very congenial group of *broncardiers* who do not understand me because I don't drink wine or coffee and don't smoke. It is the one place where they give me water to drink at meals.

The young doctor here is about 23 or 24 years old. He is a jolly fellow and we have a good time while up there. He is like an equal; does not walk around as if everyone were a dog as some of the men with one *galon*[16] do. We sleep in pens with straw for mattresses. The beds are better than at Mollau where we have mattresses stuffed with ferns. I think I got fleas here. I find a couple of suspicious bites on me. . . . I leave here on the 12th.

November 14th. This is my second day off. . . . Last night we had a regular schoolboy roughhouse. It opened with a bombardment by Matter and Jennings of the Alkali Ike; Moore with tobacco packages. Then Ike's trenches were undermined by L. Hall by tying a rope to the foot of his bed unnoticed; then Hall and Cate pulled and down came Ike's bed. The head came down later. Then Ike started out on the warpath and Lewis' bed suffered. Then with the lights out I could watch Ike against the window. He would advance, someone would strike a match and five of us could be seen poised on the edge of our beds ready to ward off an attack. Things quieted at last and all dosed off peacefully. About 5 A.M. Ike tied a rope to Walter's bed but went to sleep before pulling it. . . .

November 16th. My birthday. I celebrated by having a bully breakfast[17] at Moosch. Two of us had a big *confiture* omelet,[18] hot bread, butter, milk and coffee for two francs, forty cents. All the morning I spent oiling and greasing my car. In the afternoon I had a lot of work. On my first trip to Bussang I had a blowout. The shoe I put on was no good and went flat about half way up the Col, but I rode it all the way over, and then fixed it at the Hospital. Just as I finished a hard job, Jennings came in and I decided to go to St. Maurice for dinner with him, against all rules. I left my car behind a building and went along. He had to go to Le Thillot with a contageous [*sic*] so I dropped off and ordered dinner for two. . . .

November 18th. From Krüth I made three trips to Bussang. . . . I carried over a little boy of thirteen who said he was a Belgian whose parents were both dead; father killed in the war. He had been brought here by the 27th [infantry] which had come from Antwerp or thereabouts. They go to the trenches tonight and so he is left alone. He has been selling post cards among the soldiers. . . .

November 19th. The young Belgian was brought back here and will stay for awhile till I can communicate with Mrs. Hill in Paris.

November 20th. Much football talk all day. At 7:00 P.M., 2 P.M in Cambridge, someone called "Are you ready Harvard" and the game was off. We sat around dinner talking over many of the old games, there being several old players among us. A couple of days ago we sent a telegram to Haughton from the Harvard Club of the Vosges.

I made a trip from Thann to Oderen with a typhoid woman. Before entering the town it is necessary to pass a sentry and show papers. There is a barricade across

[16] French word for military braid
[17] "Bully," meaning first rate or very good
[18] a sweet omelet prepared with jam

the street. It is a quaint old town with stone paved streets and old houses, many of which have been bombarded by the Germans. I finally found the street and house. All was dark, but I heard voices in back so I went through and found a couple of young women bringing in wood. . . .

Feeling our way up the dark stairway we reached the second floor where they showed me a room which had been bombarded. The walls were broken down and the ceiling had all fallen in. On the third floor I found the patient and got them to start dressing her while I went in search of Doctor Winter who told me where to take her and asked me a bit about the service. I returned and escorted the woman amid the sobs of her children and put her on a stretcher in the car. At Oderen I turned her over to the civil hospital run by the sisters. The Belgian boy disappeared and did not return for the night. . . .

November 22nd. When the relief man Doyle came, he and I took a walk around towards Markstein. . . . After luncheon we took another walk and came across some secondary line defense, with a couple of observation trenches. We also found some of last year's artillery placements which were being shoveled out by a couple of territorials.[19] There were two guns to this battery in covered dug-outs with connecting tunnels and side tunnels where they kept the ammunition. It was quite interesting. . . .

November 23rd. After a little probing, this comrade [Doyle], an Eli[20] finally told me he was ashamed to tell me the news he had learned at Krüth; thus I knew the score was pretty big. At last he finally got it out of his system, 41-0.[21] How I wished I had been there to see a bit of it!. . .

November 24th. An early start took me to Bussang for an evacuation. A train got across the road and blocked the morning traffic, which is always heavy. For about half an hour everything was held up; camions [light trucks], haywagons, ambulances and all. Then finally they set the brakes and broke the train to let us pass. It was just like a city block; it quite reminded me of city driving. . . .

November 25th. Thanksgiving Day. The morning was spent by two of us shelling chestnuts for tonight's dinner. In the afternoon I went over to Bussang in the Staff car to get some geese, brandy, cakes and the doctor from the Lource, Mr. Pichard. Returning, I helped clean the geese for dinner. Then I aided in setting things on the table and arranged the dinner a bit. We had an excellent meal; as fine a one as we could have desired in the U.S.A. Our guests were Mr. Piquard, the lieutenant of our section and Mr. Biertux. The dinner was as follows: Pinee [*sic*] soup, Sardines, Salmon mayonnaise, sausage, goose and turkey, cranberry sauce and mairon [*sic*] dressing; salade, plumb [*sic*] pudding with hard sauce; cheese-coffee-crackers-pies-cakes-candies.

[19] volunteer reserve force

[20] Reference to Elihu Yale (1649–1721), English philanthropist and namesake of Yale University. Yale students are often referred to as "Elis."

[21] Reference to the Harvard–Yale football game played November 20, 1915, at Harvard in which Harvard crushed Yale by the score of 40–0.

November 26th. Left for Thomannsplatz. Passed the whole 13th between St. Amarin and Moosch coming back from the trenches. Many new men are going up as well as more guns, 75's and 150's.[22] I took a narrow short cut on the way up and in consequence, had to follow behind a convoy of mules till we got to the main road again. At one place the road is so steep that I couldn't make it and a bunch of passing soldiers had to give me a hand. . . .

In the afternoon I ascended and was stopped three times. Once I slipped my side wheels about six or eight inches off the road, where the snow looked solid, to give a passing team plenty of room. As a result one of the horses was unhitched from behind and put onto the Ford and with five or six men pushing we finally pulled the machine back onto the road.

Next I ran into a convoy of mules and as passing one he took most of the road and I landed in the ditch opposite leaning against the bank. I waited to let my engines cool down before going on. At the sharp steep curve I encountered a wagon coming down sideways across the whole road and had to stop. In consequence I had to back down and get a start for the grade and made it without further trouble.

November 27th. In the morning Jennings and I walked to Bain Douche [*sic*] and beyond, passing through Herrenflue. The road is not good, very steep in parts, and narrow. A great deal of the way there are small pine trees tied along the road so that the Germans may not be able to locate it or see what passes over it. No lights are allowed at night. At one place, a great deal of wood has been cut down by the *boches* so that the Germans could see if the French cross the section, but these transferred pine trees cut off view of the road from the Germans and besides they have lost the positions from which they were able to watch this place.

Herrenflue is merely a collection of huts . . . where the *broncardiers* . . . live. Two kilos beyond is Bain Douche [*sic*]. Along this road and just below it is a trench, built to guard the road in case of an unforeseen retreat by the French. Pine trees line the road and hide it from view of the Germans. This section is open to the view from the famous Hartmannsvillerkopf, where there has been so much fighting. It was not possible to see this battle scarred hill.

During the attack of October 14-18 when the Germans captured the French trenches for about one hundred meters and drove the French away, there was nothing between our cars running to Bain Douche [*sic*] and the Germans. If they had had sufficient reinforcements they would have been able to capture a great deal of territory. As it was, however, the French reinforcement came up and drove off the Germans taking a small part of their trenches.

We walked on beyond Bain Douche [*sic*] and came to a boyau,[23] which is a connecting trench leading to the front. Just beyond there is a sign "*defense de passes*" because the *boches* can see the place beyond. We stopped in a cabin dug in the hillside where a sergeant holds forth.

[22] The 75mm was the superb light field artillery used by the French; the 150mm was a howitzer that was especially useful against troops entrenched or concealed in forests or hilly terrain, as in Alsace.

[23] communication trench

Nearby is a cemetery among the shell and shrapnel torn trees. Here, one gets the first real glimpse of the waste of war, other than human. It was a striking sight. . . .

We returned for *dejourner*[24] [*sic*]. Hill came up with the new lieutenant to show him our posts. I got a call to go to Bain Douche for a sick captain and set out in the Ford. Trip back was hard with two besides myself aboard and the engine not doing its best; I failed to make three of the grades. I had the captain out cranking my motor as I stalled it and the other *Malade*[25] pushing with a crowd of territorials. It was convenient to have the captain there to direct the work for he had sense enough, more than can be said of many, and to crank the motor. Then when I'd get started, I would run onto the nearest level space before stopping to take on my passengers again. They certainly worked for their passage this time. . . .

November 28th. Not content with yesterday's walk, Lewis and I decided to go to Bain Douches [*sic*] in his machine and take a walk out to the same place and get a look at Hartmannsvillerkopf. We went as far as allowed on the road; a real old Maine logging road beyond Bain Douche. We met here a group of men inhabiting one of the dug-out huts. I took their picture, which always pleases the Frenchmen. They will come from almost anywhere to have their picture taken.

I happened to ask one if it was forbidden to go into the boyaus and he said no. He conducted us to a telephone station near the road dug in from one boyau. The only light the operator had was two or three candles and a couple of cracks in the wall. They suggested going up farther and the operator telephoned to see if it would be possible. At first the answer came "no." Then, just as we were leaving, the phone rang and they asked if we had our Red Crosses on. We had no ... arm bands but had crosses on our collars, so that was enough. Then we got permission and put on the French metal helmets and gas protectors were tied onto us. Our guide led us through a labyrinth of trenches until we caught up with a *service sanitaire*[26] man who was taking in the *loupe*[27] for his group. This man led us to the doctor in charge, who after inquiries detached a guide to take us to the front line.

All along the trenches there are covered places, bomb proofs, every so often so that men passing back and forth may seek shelter under them if necessary. The trenches are about six or seven feet deep in most places, dug through what was once forest but is now merely a network of trenches and tree stumps. The trenches are wide enough to pass in.

We had not gone fifty when our guide spotted an aeroplane and refused to go farther. He watched it for ten minutes and then seeing that it still hovered above he decided it too dangerous to proceed. The truth was, it was just meal-time and he was hungry. Fortunately, however, another Red Cross man happened along at that time and he offered to take us, so off we set again.

The boyaus are all lettered. We took boyau "H" and followed it to the front. All along are little dug outs in the side, often below the level of the boyau where the

[24] lunch
[25] French word for ill or sick people
[26] sanitary section
[27] a small magnification device

men sleep and sit when off duty. They are hung with a canvas curtain door and are quite warm. It is like an underground city. Then as you get up towards the front there are little raised places where a soldier can stand and a peephole where he keeps watch of the enemies' trenches. They stay on duty at these ports for stretches of two hours. Most of the men took us for English soldiers and were quite surprised when we told them we were of the American Ambulance. A *sous-lieutenant*[28] asked us if we had permission to go up there and when we told that a lieutenant had said yes, he was quick to apologize for stopping us.

The trenches became narrower; we were in the front line. There were hand grenades by the peep holes and the soldiers kept watch in block houses. Above were screens to keep off the grenades of the *boches*. We looked through a peephole and below could see the outside of the German trenches. Between the two was a great mass of barbed wire all tangled up.

A little further on everyone was talking in whispers. There was a look-out with two holes. At night there are two men located in it. Behind the men is a canvas screen to keep off the light. The place is covered over and sand-bagged for walls. Through these walls are the peepholes, small, so as not to be visible to the enemy. They said that the Germans were but two meters away, six feet is not a great distance.[29] Hence the whispering. Some sharp-eared Germans heard us and fired a chance shot. Of course, we soon ducked which must have greatly amused the soldiers because they didn't move a bit, reassuring us with a "*ce n'est rien.*"[30] There was the difference between a man hardened by months of war and a couple of sightseers.

Around the corner from this look-out we were shown a trench blocked with sandbags. This trench continued right through to the Germans. During the attack of October 14–16 when the French recaptured their trenches, they also took a part of the German lines, hence this connecting trench. There we were within a few feet of the Germans. Only one shot was fired the whole time. Men were sitting in their dug-outs chatting or writing letters while others slept or watched. That was war. There are occasional attacks, but between them, everything is quiet.

We then retreated by another boyau. Curious heads popping out to see us pass. This one was more open and we had to crouch down as we walked. It had evidently been somewhat shattered during an attack. As our guide left us at the *sanitaire* headquarters we gave him a couple of francs for wine or tobacco and started down the hill by ourselves to find the telephone station when we would swap our helmets and gas bags for our own hats and coats. We missed the side entrance and without noticing went under the road and on up the hill in back until the trench came to an end. We found we were lost among some deserted camps. After wandering about a bit trying to locate ourselves, we decided to retrace our steps through the trench again, looking into all the side alleys. In this way we discovered the road and soon were at our telephone post.

[28] second lieutenant
[29] If true, which is doubtful, this would be unusually close.
[30] "It's nothing"

We hastened back to Bain Douche [*sic*] and picked up a *Malade* here and another at Herrenflue. I then took my machine and descended to Moosch and on home to Mollau.

I shall never forget this trip, which was entirely against our orders, although the French gave us permission to go. It is a chance few men have and one for which we were grateful to those who made it possible.

November 29th. My day of rest was broken into by two calls for extra service; one from Urlest to Bussang and one from Weiler to Moosch. The latter was absolutely needless because it is but two kilos and the Moosch car could easily have done it, but no, that is not the way the French wish; they believe in doing things the longest way.

One thing I did see however, is worthy of mention. It was a horse-shoeing party. There were six or eight men connected with the work. One had a noose around the horse's nose; another a stick to hit the horse in the head to make him stand still; two were on a rope pulling the horse's leg; another held the foot, while a sixth did the shoeing. The rest looked on. The scene usually takes place in a field where there is plenty of room. Wouldn't those men be astonished to see an American village smithy do the whole thing all by himself? I have seen them take three days to do one shoe. The first two they had to give up because the horse was terrified to such a state that six men couldn't manage him. . . .

November 30th. Lewis and Moore left for home. It is still drizzling disagreeably. I am at Kruth for the day and tomorrow till 5:00 P.M.

I made one Bussang trip and a Moosch trip. There is a lot of talk about an expected attack; lots of guns are coming over the "Col" and going to Thomannsplatz. There are also endless convoys of hay wagons, said to carry concealed ammunition.

Troops are moving along the roads, and ammunition is being stored in the dug-outs along the roads near the posts. The guns are of the "75" "155" and "220"[31] variety, real ones. One man was heard to say that in two weeks or so the French would be in Mulhouse; that remains to be seen.

December 1st. At 7:30 I left to get a rheumatic on the Huss road. There was little to do all day. One Bussang and ending with a St. Cenarin.

Having no head lights I had to use my flash light to see things. I passed a camion which in the dark without headlights had misjudged the road and was on its side in the ditch. On returning to Mollau I learned that we may all be moved. It is rumored that they want to put all the American section together somewhere near Pont-a-Mousson. We hope it won't be until after the attack. We hate to leave this country but there's no going against the Military. . . .

December 2nd. In the evening we had a musical. Rice officiated on the oldest piano in existence and the rest of us sang every song we ever knew. Three Frenchmen came in to be amused.

December 3rd. It still continues to rain, about five days steady now. All along the roads the fields are flooded and the rivers overflowing. I go to Treh today. All up the

[31] The 220mm gun was a trench mortar.

road the water has been drained at places to keep it in the gutters lest it wash out the road. The wind is blowing hard.

I made one trip down to Krüth. About half-way my brake band gave way; my hand brake is no good. I had several narrow escapes, almost running into mules and wagons before they got out of the way. My low speed was somewhat of a brake, but not always enough. My Klaxon is no good and I had to use a whistle to make the men hear. They never seem to be able to hear the ordinary hand horn. . . .

December 4th. The rain began again and today it is at it just as hard with a high wind blowing. I didn't get up until 10:00; thirteen hours in bed sleeping. Read and wrote letters. Made only one trip to Krüth.

December 5th. When the relief car came (Putnam) he told us that we would probably leave this section on Wednesday. This news has been in the air for some time. We expect we shall be transferred near to Pont-a-Mousson, but have had no official notification as yet . . .

The head of the English Section, which expects to replace us, came over from Rupt, where they are now. He took over the town etc.

At 5:30 news came of the Krüth car . . . for Bussang in distress, so I went over to relieve him of his load. . . . From Bussang I went to St. Maurice for dinner. . . .

On the way over and back I passed a large convoy of big 330 mm. guns. There were 115 vehicles in all, including camions which towed the guns and carriages; two large tractors, staff cars, red cross cars and a camion section with supplies etc. The whole thing stretched a long way, either side of Urbes and filled the town. It was guarded by soldiers all along. It certainly looks more and more like an attack. The man who came down from Thomannsplatz reports about 15,000 men thereabouts and much activity.

December 6th. The English came to town again. It seems we are to leave on the eighth. The morning was spent in packing the cars and belongings.

At 2:00 o'clock a bunch of us went down to Husseren to witness the decoration of Hill and the section. It took place in front of the church there, where there were three sides of a square made by *broncardiers* of the posts near-by. They told us; four of us, the other two being photographers, to line up too, so we took our places on the end of the line facing the open side of the square, back to the church. After a little talking, Hill and the French lieutenant lined up beside us, everyone stood at attention as the *Divisionaire*[32] [*sic*] came up the street. A Captain unsheathed his sword and advanced to meet him. After saluting the *Divisionaire* [*sic*] inspected everyone.

Then Hill and the Trauffault went out in front of the tanks with us four behind him. He was decorated and M. Trauffault received the Croix[33] in his name of the section. . . .

December 7th. There was a Bussang evacuation at 7:30 so I unloaded my car and went over. It was a big one, taking several hours. I alone carried forty men and there were seven cars. We evacuated about two hundred fifty men. While waiting to carry back

[32] *Divisionnaire*, or major-general

[33] Reference to *Croix de Guerre*, or Cross of War, a French military decoration created in 1915 and awarded for valor.

the stretchers L. Hall and I went into the station to look over the train. It was quite different from the Red Cross trains which one sees in Paris. There were third class cars with the compartments fixed up to hold two stretchers and five sitters in some cases, or in others, four stretchers. Chains being suspended from the roof to hold the one side of the stretcher while the other rested on a place cut out in the arm of the seat. Some of the men recognized me as the driver who had carried them from one place to another when they had just come in from the front.

The last German from the attack of October 14–16 was aboard. We talked to him a bit in German; he seemed smiling and happy, glad probably that he was alive and out of it for good.

We visited the kitchen car, which was neat and well kept. Sandwiches were being made for the men; not delicate ones, but good husky ones, made, of course, from army bread, good and thick. Half the car was given up to sleeping quarters for the two cooks; quite a palatial place it was too.

Orders came not to move at present, so we unloaded the cars which had been filled up and prepared to resume regular service again. . . .

December 8th. We are all much pleased at not having to move because that means we shall stay through the attack. General Lunt of the Division kept the wires hot to Paris to get the orders held up and then changed.

I went to Wesserling, took my first bath, then made four trips in quick succession. On one of these I had to go to the station to get the bags and sack of one man who insisted on giving me a fifty centime tip; Emile Manfield of the 8th Artillery, 60th Division, 7th Army. I tried to refuse but he forced me and I shall keep it as a souvenir of the war. This is my second tip. . . .

December 10th. I made a trip to Moosch with four men. On the way back I was held up in the road by cars ahead. I got out to see what was going on and found three flat cars loaded with 370 mm[34] shells for a battery near Colbach. There were about sixteen on each car. Besides there were two large traction engines and a staff car. These two engines straddled the track, which was in the middle of the road, their steering wheel between the small rails and caterpillers[35] [*sic*] on each side. The two engines hooked onto one car and off they went, very slowly. That it took those two engines to draw sixteen shells shows the weight of the shells, and also how steep the road must be.

December 11th. After a late rising, Rice and I went out to an old observation post where we could look over the Rhine valley. It certainly did not look in the least bit warlike. The heavy rains had flooded the valley. We could see several small towns, roads running between them and the forts where the Germans are said to have much artillery. Way beyond, topping some clouds, we could see some Alpine peaks. . . .

December 12th. Shortly after luncheon I had a trip down and came by a new road into Bitche Ville [Bitschwiller-lès-Thann], which we shall use for down work during the attack. There is more level running on it than on the other road but the descents

[34] French mortar that was so large it had to be mounted on rail and its ammunition loaded separately.

[35] The Caterpillar was a tractor designed to move artillery.

are steeper; it seems broader too. At many places one can look off towards the Rhine Valley, down the Valley by Thann, and the road is screened here by fir trees. It will be impossible to use the lights here as it is exposed to the view of the Germans. It is somewhat longer than the other way, but will make just one thing less to pass when the attack comes off. . . .

Our mail finally came back from the first army where it had been sent with the expectation that we were going to move. It was sent for about a week and we were mighty glad to lay hold of it again. . . .

December 14th. Today was the first day for two weeks since November 28th that we didn't have some rain. More mail—I have received twenty letters in the last three days. . . .

In the afternoon I went for rations. We get our food from tickets; vegetables, bread and meat all at different places. The bread is all piled in one large storeroom from where it is doled out to the many "camions" and wagons carrying food to the different sections. The meat is obtained in a different town, where the slaughter-house is situated. It is quite interesting seeing how the food is distributed from the centers at Wesserling and Fellering to the army nearby.

The English are on duty nearby in the valley from today on, so we have cars at Treh and Thomannsplatz only. It looks as if something were coming soon. The English cars are bigger than ours and can't do the mountains work as well, but carry more in the valley work. There are two men on each car, gentleman and chauffeur. They have two Fords just acquired, one given the French by the students at Eton.

December 15th. Only one car out now daily, at Thomannsplatz. The petrol throwers[36] passed through the valley today. They have been brought in for the attack. We hear rumors of ninety train loads of Germans recently arrived in the Rhine Valley; also notes thrown across from one trench to another by the Germans, asking when the big attack is coming off.

December 16th. We all went to Husseren to get these new French helmets. We look really military with them. Gas masks are to be added.

From now on, the traffic goes one way, only on the Thomannsplatz roads. The names of places are also changed. Thomannsplatz, Herrenflue and Paslettenplatz are now—Tenenre, Hosch and Pyramids respectively. During the attack we are to have three cars at Frennolstein, seven at Thomannsplatz, two at Herrenflue and one at Pyramids, the other at Moosch. We have room there where our cook will serve us food as we pass to and fro. There has been talk about the attack, but we still are waiting. The latest is, that the English and us are going to move on the 24th. Who knows?

December 18th. I went along on a car to Huss for an extra call to get a man. There used to be a post there until along in September when the wind blew off the roof of the house they used. . . .

[36] The Germans were the first to use the *Flammenwerfer,* or flamethrower, as a weapon in the war, but the Allies soon followed. Designed for portable use, the canister, carried by soldiers on their backs, used pressurized air and carbon dioxide or nitrogen to ignite burning oil when aimed at the enemy. It was most effective when used at close range.

From the post Galatti[37] and I walked up on one of the knolls to get a view. The summit was covered with trenches, second defense lines.

From here we looked down the Unitlach Valley. We could see both Unitlach and Untzeral beyond, then the town just behind the German lines, Munster. On either side, the hills rise to great heights. To the left there is a hotel on the top of a hill, which has all been shot to pieces. Below are three smaller knolls which were taken in the last attack. On the right, hill 955, where the trees are all shot off—this was also captured in the last attack in June. The hill is lined with trenches. Some of the men have visited these shortly after they were captured and tell of finding much plunder; new uniforms, personal letters, much ammunition, etc. Behind this is the Petit Ballon,[38] which is German. The valley beyond was filled with mist, but on the horizon the mountains of the Black Forest were easily seen. We were all the time in sight of the Germans, and so stood behind brush so as not to be seen.

Coming down, we got a fine view of the Krüth Valley all the way along. At Ocleru, we passed the whole seventh regiment of chasseurs on their way towards Thomannsplatz.

December 20th. Our gas masks came. They consist of a pair of goggles with a wire at the bottom, which is pinched to close the nose. Then the chemicals are tied on over the mouth so that the air when you breathe in is purified before getting to the mouth. They certainly make good disguises.

I went to the Military dentist at Wesserling this afternoon. He is a Paris dentist with an office in one of the factory buildings; he does pretty good work. Being military, he is free.

On the way back I passed about twenty men all strung out along the road, making maps. Maybe they were getting practice for when the French advance.

There is some firing going on, but as yet no sign of an attack.

December 21–22nd. The attack[39]: Last night about 9:30 Lieut. Trauffault came to the barrack and told us that all cars would be needed today. At breakfast we were distributed as follows: 1 at Pasletenplatz, 2 at Frenndstein, 3 at Herrenflue, and 7 each at Moosch and Thomannsplatz. At eight all except the Moosch cars left, and at 9:30 the rest of us.

Last night the *boches* shelled Bain Douche getting about eighty men. I was at Moosch and at noon I was sent up in place of some of the men that had come down. I went straight to Herrenflue and got a load at once. I rolled steadily all day Monday and Tuesday. Tuesday night I got four and one half hours sleep in two snatches of two and two and one half hours. Finally, on the 23rd I got a bit of sleep in the evening to makeup for the lost time. Perkins was hit by a piece of stone from a bursting shell on the 21st.

The first night of working, the French had attacked and so we had many wounded, both French and Germans. All our cars and some of the English worked steadily.

[37] Stephen Galatti, Harvard class of 1910, who rose to the rank of major.
[38] A nearly 4,000-foot peak in the Vosges Mountains
[39] The third and final phase of the Battle of Hartmannswillerkopf, December 21–22, 1915.

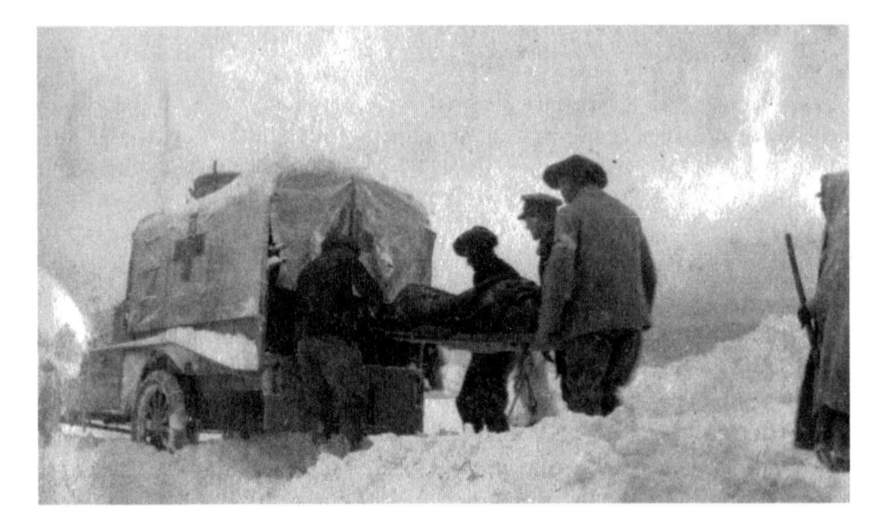

AFS staff loading a wounded soldier onto an ambulance in Alsace, 1915. *Courtesy of the archives of the American Field Service and AFS Intercultural Programs.*

On my second trip, it had begun to snow and the down road was terrible; almost sheer ice. For some reason I started down without chains and had not gone far before I was sliding from side to side. The poor man beside me almost passed out. Finally, when I came to a stop across the road I put on my chains and hugging the inside as much as possible, continued on my way barely moving. . . . I finally succeeded in getting through and when I got below again most of those cars were still waiting to be unloaded.

The work continued all night steadily; as quickly as a car came up it was loaded and sent off again. . . . On one trip the second night I was held up for three hours at the Moosch hospital, so I took the opportunity to look through the hospital. . . .

The "Beneanid Entrees" is in the back of the hospital where there is floor space for about nine stretchers and sitting and standing room for about seventy-five or eighty, and they were there, Germans and French crowded into this room, not able to move out. Some were trying to sleep leaning against the walls; others just looking around. The hall leading from here to the front of the hospital was lined on both sides with stretchers and the larger corridor running across the hospital was filled on one end with about twenty five stretcher cases and on the other with innumerable *assis*[40] sitting around the room or crowding around the door of a doctor's room where they were to be attended to.

In the front hall were cases waiting to be evacuated to Bussang. This process was slower than the arrivals, and so the hospital became terribly congested. I heard one man tell about having both feet wounded and managing to crawl along by himself

[40] French verb meaning "sat down." Here he uses the word as a noun to refer to those injured who were sitting down.

to a *passé de Secoms*[41] [*sic*] where he was loaded on a stretcher and carried back. He seemed very cheerful and was laughing and joking with another cheerful soul who had had the top of his head shot off.

The sisters who run the hospital brought some soup and I helped them distribute it. One man had his face so done up that his mouth was all that showed and so they had to get him a "bud"[42] to drink his soup with. After this I got tea for some of them and cigarettes. They were not grumbling at all or complaining. Those occasional ones who did were at once taken away and seen to.

This second night I got two snatches of well needed sleep, one of two and the other of two and one half hours.

All during the night, German prisoners were going down into the valley in large convoys. In all, I think there were 1,317 taken, not including the wounded. This shows that the French have advanced a good deal to have the prisoners and wounded on their side.

December 23rd. There was a slight let-up in operations today, but still many wounded to be carried out. Today Doyle was wounded by a piece of *éclat*[43] in his right arm and forced to retire from the service. Douglas when going to Bain Douche to get him was held up by a bombardment of the road; one shell coming so near as to knock him over with its concussion.

The Germans made a counter-attack with some success. The French 7th and 23rd held on the sides of Hartmannsvillerkopf, the ground they had taken in their first attack down on the other side. In the middle, however, where the 152nd[44] were, the best French troops in the district, the Germans came up through an underground passage and surrounded the 152nd taking all but about 200. That is, unless they are able to hold out until help comes to them.

There was little doing during the night and I got a good sleep.

December 24th. Today I only made one trip, which shows comparative quietude or German action. The French seem to have stood well, however, except for the 152nd which seems to be lost now.

We had quite a gay little party the night before Xmas with 213 *broncardiers*, singing etc. A lot of Xmas mail came in too.

December 25th. Christmas morning dawned rather sadly for us. We learned that last night about 10:00 P.M. a German *obus*[45] had landed in the back of Dick Hall's car on the way up and killed him instantly with a wound behind the ear, one in the abdomen, and a broken leg. The rear of the car was all blown to pieces but the front assemblage remained intact, even though the whole was thrown about fifteen yards off the road. He was found by two other of our men about four A.M. and his

[41] *Passé de secours*. Reference to a medical aide or assistant.
[42] slang for a buddy or friend
[43] splinter
[44] Reference to France's elite mountain warfare division, the "Blue Devils" (*Chasseurs Alpins*).
[45] shell or bullet

body carried to Moosch, where he will be buried. It must have happened at about 10:00 P.M. last night because Cahey heard rumors of it at midnight in the valley. . . .

The Germans bombard the towns in the valley daily with little effect.

The roads are very muddy, quite a lot of rain having fallen for the last few days. We have had several minor accidents and now only about fifteen cars are in working order all the time. Two men are out sick.

Two French sections are now in the valley as well and they have cleaned out the Moosch hospital. . . .

In the evening the 213th *broncardiers* had a Christmas celebration; there was wine, which they always have in great quantities, buying extra in the valley; a plum pudding which we gave them, and song. They lit little candles and sang their quiet simple little Xmas songs, lead by the Sergeant who is the life of the group.

December 26th. I went out onto a nearby road, where the valley can be plainly seen. The French were bombarding a wood below where German batteries are said to be located. It was a wonderful sight to see these shells break, and the clouds of white smoke and dirt fly up. They kept up the bombardment for quite a time. We also saw one German shell land on a hill up the valley, but no damage was done. Ternay could easily be seen below us and far off the chimneys of the Mulhouse factories could be distinguished plainly.

The French and German shells went whizzing overhead. We could make them out by their whistling. . . .

December 27th. Hall's funeral was today.[46] The *Divisionaire Medicin Chef* at Moosch and Trent, Truffaultall, made very nice remarks at the service. The English section attended and many others who are friends of the section. . . .

The French have attacked again, but found little resistance from the Germans whose morale seems to be pretty low. One story is told how a cook of the 152nd while carrying soup to some of his men lost his way in the trenches and found himself surrounded by about 125 Germans, all of whom surrendered to him. I guess the smell of soup was stronger than the gun.

I carried one German in front with me and tried to talk to him a bit in my broken German. I enquired as to the German feeling towards the United States and found him quite bitter. He couldn't see why we should sell munitions to the Allies and not Germany. He didn't realize that for some time we have been selling to Germany and that we would still, if Germany were able to buy. She can buy, but cannot collect. He couldn't see that it would be unnatural to stop selling to one just because the other couldn't buy. . . .

December 28th. Gen. Serret was wounded and had to have his leg amputated. . . .

Things are about the same; bombarding by both sides.

I asked a Frenchman about the rumors of killing the first few prisoners taken, but he denied it. Also said that he didn't think the Germans did either. He said that probably some soldiers lose their heads and kill right and left, but as a whole they do not, and have no orders to do so.

[46] See *Friends of France*, 305–306.

December 31st. For the past two days things have let up a bit. There has been a slight bombarding but no important action.

Today, however, it was fine and clear and more action. At Herrenflue I was kept in an *abri*[47] with about one hundred others for over a half hour while the Germans bombarded the place. I found several pieces of shell near the machine. I saw the smoke of one little 77 [mm shell] just after it arrived. . . .

After it let up I went to Moosch and there saw four German and one French aeroplane up in the air. The Germans were signaling by little balloons and star bombs to their lines. Three times the French and Germans got near enough to bring their machine guns into action, but no serious damage was done.

At five o'clock, three of us started up to Thomannsplatz and took three hours on the road, because there was a convoy of 150 wagons ahead of us who were held up because the Germans had bombarded and blocked the road with trees. Upon arrival, we learned that two other ambulances had been held up earlier owing to bombardment.

As I tried to mount after an evening trip I failed and turned home to Moosch, spending my first night there. . . .

During the attack so far, Dec. 21-31 I have traveled 654 kilos and carried 97 men. I celebrated the advent of the New Year by sleeping in pajamas and undressing for the first time in ten days; my blanket roll being at Moosch.

January 1st. . . . All along the way, trees were scarred by yesterday's bombardment. I could see how the road had been blocked by fallen trees and one stable stuck, killing a couple of mules. From three to about four the Germans bombarded near Thomannsplatz, probably the road again. They have never struck it before.

The French welcome in the New Year at Thomannsplatz by shooting off seventy 75mm shells at twelve. . . .

January 4th. Had a good day of rest, wrote letters and sat around. The work has become so quiet that we are beginning to have lay-offs.

January 6th. General Serret died today. Could not stand the strain of the amputation. Nothing else doing. Two trips. We had a party in the evening; the English men brought up champagne and we had songs and music. They are very nice chaps.

January 7th. I went to Herrenflue in the morning with Jennings. During the morning the Germans bombarded the place. We were sitting in the bureau alone when two burst right over us, the pieces falling on the roof of the building. Everyone made a quick rush for the *abri*. . . . On the way down the steps to the *abri*, which is below the room we were in, we heard a man yelling and everyone stopped to look back. Shells were liable to drop at any minute. We pushed them ahead, however, and just after I entered the *abri* I turned around and saw the "yelling" man come in. It was just as one might see in an illustration. A crowd of men looking towards the open door, a man with arms outstretched and drawn face burst in through the door

[47] a shelter or dugout

with a terrific yell, more from fear than pain I guess. They bandaged him up and after the bombardment was over, I took him down to the valley. About four men were wounded during the "barding."

The shelling continued for about half or three quarters of an hour while we all sat safely in our shelter.

When it was over I went out to the cars and found that one shell had hit within five feet of them and covered them with loose dirt and stones.

I took my load up and all along the road there were traces of the shelling; trees fallen here and there. . . .

January 8th. General Serret's funeral this morning. I didn't go but they say there were several Generals there, to say nothing of high officers. . . .

A shell lit in Thomannsplatz, right where we park our cars but fortunately the cars weren't any of them there. No serious damage was done, other than breaking windows.

January 10th. I sent off to Thomannsplatz with Pierce. The road all along shows signs of shelling. Trees cut off about three feet from the ground, just as neat as one could wish; great holes by the side of the road where they had landed. A little farther down, there are depressions in the middle of the road where shells have found their mark and the *geine*[48] [*sic*] have filled the holes up with rocks and earth. There is a smell of newly cut pine which is quite agreeable, but the associations, thoughts and broken and scarred trees, are not as pleasant as might be. On the way up we could ear shells whistling and landing below us. . . .

We stopped at the place where Hall had been killed and put a stake up by the side of the road and a few stones. . . .

After luncheon we were sitting in the room of the 213th when a shell came whistling in and lit somewhere near Thomannsplatz. There was a mad rush for the *abri* which is about three feet by twenty. Pierce and I stuck near the outside, and every time we heard a whistle we'd duck for the entrance.

I was sitting just outside when there was a terrific crash, which blew us off the seat. The door on one side blew open, ripping off the wood to which the hinges were fastened; the window on the other side blew down and the stovepipe toppled over. The room filled with smoke and for a minute we thought of the possibility of a gas bomb, but water soon put the fire out and we saw it was only good old wood smoke.

After a few minutes we became bold and re-entered to look out at the front room. Peeking around the corner from the bunk house we saw a great sight. The front of the house was all blown in, the shell having struck three feet from the corner. The poor old horse tied out in front was wounded, and had to be killed. The stove pipe was down and consequently there was much smoke here too. Everything was in a heap on the floor, from graphophone[49] to medical bottles. Pieces of shell were sticking into the bunk sides. A more complete ruin I never saw.

[48] Perhaps he meant *Génie*, or engineers.
[49] an early form of the phonograph

We soon heard the noise of a Ford and running out found Rice plowing through with a load of wounded. Just below the 213th abode is a clearing in one corner of which was a shelter. A shell lit directly on this, killing the two men who were in it and throwing the tin roof pieces across the road. We tried to move these, but decided it quicker to run the machines over them. Wires were all down and tangled up in everything, but we finally got the machines over and shot off so as to get out of range as soon as possible.

The Germans certainly found Thomannsplatz at last and put the fear into everyone. I went to Herrenflue soon after and was glad to be safely away.

On the way up from the valley later, Pierce Carey and I all waited under the shelter of a cliff while the Germans were bombarding the road below. At eight o'clock a few shells whistled over Thomannsplatz and all the *poilus*[50] beat it for the *abris*. However, nothing came of it.

January 11th. At six thirty there were three shells which went overhead and again everyone was scared. There were only two trips the entire day and at evening four cars went down empty. During the day practically everyone left Thomannsplatz. The 213th have gone to France for a rest. There was great activity in *abri* building. When everything is underground, they are going to move back. . . .

Mo Naught and I slept at Thoms while the others preferred their cars and slept cold. The place was practically deserted; the few people left, slept in an *abri* where the rain leaked in and spent an uncomfortable night. We slept in the *Divisionaire* Post and had a good night except that men kept arriving all through the night; some to sleep, others to move on again. . . .

January 12th. After luncheon, Potter and I walked up over the hills in back. German shells were whistling overhead and dropping into the valley. They are looking for batteries there. We ran across an unexploded German shell lying in the dirt; there was not a scratch on it. Potter wanted it but discretion kept him from attempting to unscrew the head and empty the powder out.

In my load was the man who used to cook for the section when they were at Huss; he died on the operating table this evening.

From Bitche Ville to Willer the road was packed with troops going up and camions coming down. The 140th and 75th with all their soup kitchens were on their way to the front somewhere, while the 57th was piling into camions going back. From Willer to Moosch the congestion was worse and it took a long while to pass between the two halted lines of vehicles. . . .

January 13th-16th. A good deal of rain as usual. During these days I relieved my conscience by getting a bath and haircut. Letters were written in an attempt to catch up and quite a bit of bridge played.

The Belgian boy who was with us in November has returned after spending sometime in the Bitche Ville hospital with a bad knee. On the 16th he left with Auley and Galatti for Paris where he will be taken care of in one of Mrs. Hills'

[50] slang for French infantryman, which literally means "hairy one"

depots for frontier children. Auley goes back to New York and Galatti to Paris for six weeks to work at Neuilly. . . .

January 17th. At Herrenflue there was absolutely nothing to do. I took a walk with Brown and ran across a soldier who offered to show me where the French had attacked. Looking over an *abri* we could see the *roche*[51] where there had been such fierce fighting and the little plateau over which the armies have flowed back and forth; the tide having finally carried the French across it, beyond the *roche* and over the crest. The Germans, we were told, are down on the plain in a wood we could see. There is from one half to one kilometer of plain between the trenches.

At the post where we were was located a French 65 mm. gun;[52] the first gun I have seen in position. It was indeed most interesting to see the workings of a battery. It was located in an *abri* with the front, of course, open to the Germans. Just behind it was the shell *abri* and down in front an *abri* for the men themselves. Their sleeping quarters are just below, a sort of semi-*abri* but a shell burst through it during a German bombardment and destroyed practically everything inside. The men were in the *abri* at the time. All around were shell holes, and an exploded shell had a little wire barricade around it. The men were at work on rings of aluminum made from German fuse heads.

We were shown the shells—both shrapnel and percussion, together with the timing machine which was most interesting. The shells are set in a copper base, which contains the explosive powder for shooting them. On the other end is the cap, around which is wound the fuse with time marks on it. The marking apparatus has a wheel marked with kilometers which they set, then they press a lever which shoots out a little pin which in turn dents the fuse on the head of the shell, which has been screwed into its place.

One man works this during an attack, while four men are occupied in shooting the gun, sighting, elevating, etc. It was most interesting seeing how these things worked.

There was no work all day for . . . me. I started *Tom Sawyer* later in the afternoon. It is the first of Mark Twain's books I have ever read. We are very well off at Herrenflue because the man who is in charge of the room in which we sleep, the *blesse*[53] [*sic*] room, is the same as a valet to us. Fetches our food; cleans up the place; tucks our blankets in at night and keeps all intruders quiet. He is a nice old chap . . . and having no wounded to look out for, he takes care of us.

I read *Tom Sawyer* well into the night. . . .

January 20th. After helping Hill[54] change a tire, he asked Jackson, Walker and me to go to Thann with him on a joy ride. We toured the town and I saw a great deal more than I had seen before. We went over across the river and through the older part, which was certainly quaint. . . .

[51] rock
[52] gun favored by French mountain troops
[53] *blessé*, injured or wounded
[54] Levering Hill, Harvard class of 1910, was Cate's AFS section commander. After the U.S. entry in the war in 1917, Hill served as a captain in the artillery.

Across on the other side of the town, is the railroad station and track. Here are many marks of German shelling. One shell landed right in the middle of the station. The houses all along the railroad are absolutely demolished; the Germans in their attempt to shell the railroad have destroyed every house along it. The windows of the church have all been taken out in order to save them. . . .

January 26th–28th. Final arrangements were made for our departure on Saturday; cars were loaded; on the 28th the beds were taken away. The spare time was given up to letters, etc.

January 29th. Cars were running here and there to get blankets and last things for the trip. Coffee and chocolate were snatched on the run from 7:00 to 7:30. Goodbyes said, and by seven forty-five most of the cars had lined up on the road to Urbes waiting for the starting whistle from the chief. At 8:05 the staff car came around the corner, everyone cranked up as it came by and at last we were off; having served from one to nine months most of us were somewhat sorry to leave the old haunts, but *C'est la guerre*[55] and military orders are hard to change. So we winded our way forth for the last time up over the "col"[56] with its convoys of hay wagons, camions, and little steam trains going back and forth just as always. At the top, we ran through the tunnel into France and left Alsace behind us in the care of the Anglo-French section of Fords. . . .

At St. Maurice we waved a farewell to all our old friends and were well on our way to Rupt. We arrived at ten and after parking our cars, looked over the sleeping quarters for the night. The rest of the day was given to strolling about the town and the nearby hills.

In the evening we were invited to a show given by soldiers. It was good in parts, but quite boring in others. Good music, bad songs, card tricks and other stunts made up the program. At ten o'clock we withdrew in favor of our straw beds to sleep for the next days trip. . . .

January 30th. We then were off for Epinal for luncheon, passing through towns where the whole population turned out to look us over. They waved and smiled as *les Américaines*[57] went by. . . .

In the afternoon we pushed on to Nancy where we arrived at 5:00 P.M. On the way, at one of our stops, we had to stop the whole convoy for a tire or other trouble. We stopped in the middle of a vast manoeuver field where for long distances, trenches were outlined as far as one could see, from one to six feet deep.

At Nancy we were unheard of and unexpected. While Hill was arranging for our future, we were the center of attraction for most of the town, which gathered about the cars asking questions and receiving answers from all. At last two whistles were blown; we lit our lights and started our engines. We were off again, back on the road. . . .

February 2nd. We travel to any of the towns within about forty kilometers on errands or to get one *invalide* or so. The 20th Corps is now on repose so we will have

[55] "That's war"
[56] a pass between two mountain peaks
[57] the Americans

little work to do. This Corps is a fighting one, moving around from place to place where there is any amount of action.

In the evening, we had a long talk with our landlady and learned the history of the place. The Germans had been here three weeks a year ago September and had acted quite decently she said, although in a few cases they had pillaged some houses. There was a great battle fought on the rise beyond the town as the Germans were driven off. The Germans had advanced by a pontoon bridge across the river and placed themselves in the woods on the far slope, then the French sneaked around and destroyed the bridge; then they attacked and drove many of the *boches* into the river where they were drowned owing to the knapsacks and other equipment they had on. The French then advanced up the rise on the other side, at the top of which the battle was fought. The Germans were entrenched in the woods while the French had to charge across open fields. Finally, the Germans retired, leaving the town at about two A.M. One French soldier arrived at five but the main body didn't get in until about eight. The townspeople all went out to meet them.

The girls of the town, she said, all went out and buried the dead. It must have been a terrible piece of work. . . .

February 3rd. Went to Maguiers with Pierce[58] to get gasoline. The town has been pretty much shelled in parts. The church is absolutely cleaned out.

In the afternoon Doyle and I took a long walk through the woods of Framboise, where the German retreat had taken place. . . . There were many graves; parts of trenches, shell holes, shirts, socks and cartridge boxes with German names on them. These remnants spoke a great deal. . . .

February 4th. There is talk of our leaving this part of France soon. They wanted a new section in the 20th Corps and we seem to have been sent here by mistake, so it looks as if we would be off again. . . .

February 5th. After washing a car as penalty for being late to breakfast, Dawson and I went with Hill to Gerberviller[59] [*sic*]. . . .

Gerberviller [*sic*] is a martyr town. When the Germans advanced the French put a barricade across the road and left sixty *chasseurs*[60] to fire at the Germans. The latter claimed it was the citizens who had done this so they so they burned the town and after castrating the men, killed many.[61] They saved the hospital because some of their wounded were there and they also spared the brewery, so that the other men who were to follow them to Paris might find drink. The town reminds one of the pictures of Pompeii somewhat. We wandered about a bit and bought a couple of shells for curiosities. . . .

[58] Waldo Pierce, Harvard class of 1907, an artist

[59] Gerbéviller

[60] French term for light infantry

[61] On August 24, 1914, German troops murdered sixty of the town's civilian inhabitants. See John Horne and Alan Kramer, *German Atrocities 1914: A History of Denial* (New Haven: Yale University Press, 2001), 65–66.

*February 6th*. All the towns we passed through showed signs of battle. Burned or bombarded houses and roadside graves told the story. It seems strange that Moyen escaped a like fate. The Germans never got to Rambervillers, being two kilos away. . . .

After luncheon we set off, passing through Gerberville [*sic*] and Bayon. We passed a captive balloon, with all its paraphernalia, wagons, winding apparatus etc.

We arrived at Tautonville about four. . . .

*February 8th*. Along about two o'clock a couple of *broncardiers* were coming up the path with a dead man on a stretcher; a shell struck a tree felling it on one man and killing the other. A little later, a shell struck in the midst of three horses, killing one, apparently only dazing a second, but wounding the third as well as severing his rope. He fled up the road and stampeded a convoy of mules. . . . Things are pretty hot and the wounded were crowding every space. At three a shell struck near four or five men in the doorway and Doyle being on the outside stopped a few pieces of *éclat* with his right arm. Fortunately, he had on five coats and so the force was somewhat abated. He was immediately attended to and found to have one piece lodged in the elbow. He was bandaged up, but they wouldn't let him drive his car.

Shortly before this they had told him to crank up and prepare to leave with a very serious case, but in a couple of minutes an attendant came running out to say that the man had died. Just then a shell burst nearby and struck a soldier but luckily through his knapsack, so by the time it reached his body it was dead and did no damage. It was a piece about an inch square and would have done considerable business anywhere.

At three thirty Douglas arrived in the room and challenged Doyle[62] with an account of how he had stopped a second to look at Doyle's car, when a shell burst nearby and he found himself face down on the ground. He was thinking of his narrow escape when Doyle told him how he had gone him one better. They started about four for Thomannsplatz, dark and hard-going. Twice they got held up by wagons, while the shells whistled overhead. . . .

Douglas has been called the human magnet, because wherever he is, he seems to draw shellfire. . . .

*February 10th*. Today I went to Nancy. . . . There is little to say about the place. It is a city, which is, of course, a sight for us from the country. . . . We went into a bank where they had the floor covered with sand bags, three deep, to protect the safe deposit vaults underneath from the bombs which the Germans have recently taken to throwing into the city, those of the 420 mm. variety. The station is usually the target. . . .

This evening Trauffault read the citations of Putnam, Mellen, Galatti and Walker who were cited for the last attack to the order of something or other which means a bronze star. There are to be six more citations later. Hill asked the *Divisionnaire* for two more, for Pierce and me, but the Div. said he couldn't. It's tough to be the eleventh man on a ten-man list, but *C'est la guerre*.

[62] Luke Doyle, Yale class of 1909, later a major in the U.S. Sanitary Corps

February 11th. Three of us left for Unicourt for two, four and six days respectively. . . .

We traveled about twenty kilometers over bully [good] roads to the town which contains about six thousand inhabitants, a veritable city. . . .

February 13th. Sunday is the file day at Unicourt. They have movies twice a day. We went to the afternoon show at three o'clock. It was quite a homelike feeling to be watching a "movie.". . .

February 15th. The rain of the last few days continues and the wind also with it. The fields are flooded, the roads muddy and the riding in a gale anything but pleasant. It clears up and then comes on to rain in a moment's notice. . . .

In the evening . . . we played cribbage and spent a comfortable evening until nine o'clock. . . . The place was quiet and free from soldiers. It is patronized by the gentry of the town.

February 16th. I had my picture drawn by a boy who was studying in the Beaux Arts at Nancy, but their house having been demolished in the bombardment, the family had moved to Unicourt. . . .

February 17th. At 3:30 Jackson, Clark and I left with some *invalides* for Vittel to help evacuate a sanitary train. We arrived at 4:15 but the train was two hours late, so we cast about for supper, which we had at 5:30. . . . All the hotels of this big watering place are converted into hospitals. About six the train came in, but as the men were being fed, we had to wait. There was an embankment or platform such as is used to easily unload freight at the level of the cars, but instead of backing the train in here, they left it on the third track over, and were to unload the "blesses" and pass them up again to us. We protested but they wouldn't move the train; however, they did consent to our going around on the other side where the men could be loaded right from the ground level. We showed them some quick work in evacuations when we finally got started.

We finished about eight P.M. and then I started out for town. I made Unicourt in twenty-five minutes, got my blankets etc. and came onto Tautonville in about thirty more. The evening was fine and the roads in excellent condition. I was in bed by 9:30. . . .

February 21st. I left for Bayon, a two day stand. . . . The town is a good deal smaller than Unicourt. There is a large civil hospital which now, of course, is given over to the military.

Just before entering town, I passed a good many troops from the 2nd brigade of *Chasseurs*. They soon passed through the town. In fact all day long troops came through with bugles and drums or bands playing. Clark said they had been marching all the day and night before. A good many embarked at Bayon while the others went on to Charmes, 14 kilometers, before entraining. The 143rd was among them.

I spent the morning in a café reading, but after luncheon I discovered a green house in the corner of the garden of the house in which I slept. The sun beat in upon the glass and gave me a very warm place in which to write letters. I was thus occupied when one of the *broncardiers* came and told me to get ready to go out. There is also a French ambulance in the place and as it was going too, I followed. We went down towards the river but turned off towards St. Mard just before we came to it. The recent heavy rains have flooded the whole river and surrounding low fields. The road we traveled was in part submerged with water running over it. . . .

Upon returning late for supper we learned of a trip to Enivaux for a man with a broken leg; so after a hasty meal off we went. More troops passed and they had all manner of remarks for us, such as "Ambuscades" etc. On the way back we were stopped in the road by a group and asked to take a man struck with epilepsy along. . . . A little farther on we were again stopped and asked to take a man along, but a lieutenant came up and refused to have us on the ground. That he was simply drunk and must make it the best he could, which was perfectly right.

When we arrived at Bayon we helped carry up the two men and get them to bed. The epileptic gave them quite a struggle before they finally got him tied down. Just as we were leaving, word came to close all the shutters as a Zeppelin had been seen over Mehoncourt, six kilometers away. Streetlights and all were turned out. We could see searchlights looking for it, but didn't see it ourselves. . . .

February 22nd. I began early my celebration of [George] Washington's birthday. Just after midnight I was called to go to Enivaux station for a sick man. Three of us went because we though they would have no *broncardiers* handy, which was a good supposition. We arrived to find more troops embarking. . . .

February 23rd. There seems to be a big German attack near Verdun,[63] whether all these troops are going there or not, I don't know. One Zeppelin and about six German aeroplanes were brought down yesterday.

It seems our section at Pont à Moussan has moved towards Airas, with eight hours notice only. We almost went, for an hour they say it was nip and tuck. However, as we were out of repair we stayed here. Too bad we weren't ready as we would have liked to have gone.

February 25th. I relieved MacManagle at Neuves Maisons. . . . All the way over there was a terrible wind driving snow across the vast stretches of open fields. In some places it was so bad that I had to drop into low to keep up headway. Off to one side a lot of soldiers passed by, going to some drill ground I guess. There were four groups of them. One group stopped and they pointed their guns at me, just for the sake of giving the boys a bit of practice. I later passed the 17th cavalry coming down from the direction of Neuves Maisons and going, no one knows where. . . .

February 26th. The Germans bombarded Nancy today; fourteen shells in the morning and eight in the afternoon. One landed in the prison but none of them did much harm. Potter was in town at the time and said all the church bells began to ring a warning when the first shells arrived.

From the Fort is a bully view of the whole country. Tautonville lies off to the south. Nancy, however, is over a hill and cannot be seen. There are six hangars for aeroplanes on the plateau near the fort.

[63] The Battle of Verdun, a German offensive launched on February 21, 1916, resulted in more than 700,000 total casualties and a victory of sorts for the French.

This morning we saw eleven aeroplanes in the air at once, coming back from the German lines. Cavalry and artillery passed by all day, going from Nancy. There seems to be an attack at Verdun; many troops passed Neuves Maisons today; artillery mostly. . . .

February 27th. I took doctor to Nancy on a joy ride and we closed up the car so no one would know we had no sick men along. He was much worried that he would be caught so he told me that if anyone said anything to me to tell them I couldn't speak French, but we were not troubled. The *boches* seem to have pushed forward a bit at Verdun, although the French had prepared to evacuate some lines two weeks ago.

February 28th. Took another doctor to Nancy to get more for the hospital we both did errands. The fight at Verdun seems to favor the Germans. . . .

March 1st. Hill told me to prepare for Paris tomorrow, so I packed the things I wouldn't need and wanted to leave in Paris until my departure for home in about five weeks.

March 2nd. At nine thirty we finally got away for Paris. We had to go via Nancy to pick up a *convoyer*. . . . All the way entering Toul we passed defences erected at the time of the first German advance. They may still be seen intact at various strategic places, edges of woods or brows of hills. They were short trenches on either side of the road for about twenty yards; they were dug and banked to about the height of a man and only just wide enough. Along the top was a sort of wicker work of small branches. I suppose this was done to prevent having a straight line, as being easier to destroy.

Then supporting these trench posts would be dug-outs for a battery of four guns and a little place nearer for a *mitraelleuse*[64] machine gun. . . .

At Toul there is an aviation park where we saw several aeroplanes flying about. While at luncheon a Mr. Bartlett-Dadely came in and talked to us. He is in section four and spoke of dissension in the ranks with regard to the leader. He said if things weren't changed the whole crowd would resign.

About the middle of the afternoon we stopped at Bar C Duc for gasoline. The park there was filled with machines of every kind, in for repairs. . . . Bar C Duc was filled with machines, staff cars, cameons etc. all busy in some connection with the battle of Verdun. . . .

In all the little towns through which we passed that afternoon were many troops passing to and fro while on each village had its allotment of several hundred camions, lining the streets. . . .

We passed through interesting country all day and were quite surprised to be called Americans and not English by many mockers. They must have seen many of us before, because we are usually taken for English wherever we go, on account of our Khaki uniform.

[64] From the French word *mitraille*, for "grapeshot." The *mitrailleuse* was a type of machine gun.

March 3rd. We were called at five but it was too dark and we did not get up until six. Changed my tire in a light drizzle and set off about seven for Paris. . . . We were in Paris by three thirty and out at the hospital by four P.M. . . .

After a couple of cocktails, we all went over to Zezis for supper, wherever that may be. After a good meal which was like a five and ten cent store as compared to Tiffany's when compared with our wine bill; extra prices were put on the wine list for the benefit of the Americans, written in ink in front of us. The place closed at ten, as do all cafes in Paris now. . . .

March 5th. I spent the morning diligently writing a history of my car #163, the Lys Ambulance given by Mr. and Mrs. L.G. Spear. None had been written for some time so I took it from the time I arrived in the Vosges . . . through to the present. It was a masterpiece. . . .

March 7th. I took supper with Doyle at the Grand Cafe which is run by Constans, a man who served thirteen months with the Ambulance until his son was called, and he figured on man in the family was enough. He treats all Americans very well indeed. We went to the *Follie Bergus*[65] [*sic*] afterwards. It is quite different from anything we have in the States. There is a large café arrangement before one gets into the theatre itself. Here are tables with a promenade around them where one gets drinks during intermission, and throughout the whole show in fact. Inside a great many people take standing room; conspicuous among these are women who want to be "picked up"; they are continually asking you to buy them a drink, catching your arm as you walk by and keeping at you with great perseverance. . . .

March 8th. In the afternoon I went as an extra to La Chapelle to answer a call. The train was about an hour late. The American cars are now driven into the garage or loading end of the building. When I was there in October they stayed outside. Another change is the lining up of the men, marching them by twos onto the platform because there are usually but ten cars to the train. Only twenty are allowed on the platform. . . . By two's we are told off to the cars and we go in and unload them, depositing the *blesses* outside on the platform where the *broncardiers* take them to the sorting pavilions. It is by order of the Minister of War that the American Ambulance unloads the trains. The Frenchmen were too careless and dropped several men. This also applies to the loading of the Ambulances. The men are brought to the Ambulances and we load them in. It is a real hard job now to go to La Chapelle. We do all the work now, whereas heretofore, it was all done by *broncardiers*. The work lasted late. . . .

March 9th. Four of us dined in town and then saw a terribly poor show at the Nouveau Cirque. It was an American Circus and the worst exhibition I have ever seen pawned off on the public.

During the day I went around to the American Embassy to get my passport renewed. . . . A lot of Harvard Sophomores have come over for six months with the Ambulance, among them twenty new men. . . . There are two men from Bowdoin, one who goes to Cornell next year, Eli's and others. . . .

[65] The Folies Bergère was a cabaret music hall in Paris known for its female dancers.

March 11th. Went out to Versailles . . . but arrived just as the palace closed. . . .

In the evening . . . I supped alone at the Restaurant Larne. I bought a *New York Herald* of February 29th to keep me company. There were several other American and English people there. I took in the Follies afterwards. There was a new show on, quite good in parts. I left early, however, to get a good sleep.

CHAPTER 3

Commitment and Sacrifice

Willy Wolff in 1924. *Courtesy of Seymour Dreyfus and Elton White.*

CHAPTER 3

"Behind barbed wire in . . . a stable for men"

Willy Wolff, German internee in Britain

The internment of twenty-four-year-old German business apprentice Willy Wolff in Knockaloe Aliens Camp on the windswept Isle of Man was the immediate result of the Aliens Restriction Act of August 5, 1914,[1] *enacted by the British government to target the activities and movement of all resident aliens to prevent them from undermining the war effort. The government's decision to limit the freedom of its immigrant population in August 1914 had antecedents in the mid- to late nineteenth century, however, as waves of refugees from religious and political persecution in central and eastern Europe made their way to the island nation.*[2] *The perception of these new immigrants, some of them*

[1] Without possession of a permit, no alien was able either to enter or leave the country, and all Germans who remained in Britain were required to register at a registration office (a local police station) and provide their name, nationality, occupation, and residence. They were not allowed to travel more than five miles from their home without a permit and were prohibited from residing in specific prohibited areas. The same restrictions were applied to all aliens of neutral nationalities. Additional restrictions were added as time went on: alien enemies could not change their names; own firearms, ammunition or explosives; or own any means of communication, photographic equipment, military maps, or vehicles. The suspicion with which aliens, whether naturalized or not, were viewed can be observed in the parliamentary debates in the House of Commons, especially *Hansard*, September 10, 1914. The Defense of the Realm Act (DORA) followed on August 8, giving the government the prerogative to control print media through censorship and imprison anyone, without the right to *habeas corpus*, suspected of interfering with the war effort or assisting the enemy. In March 1915 suspects were allowed to have a trial by jury. The act was continually modified over the course of the war as conditions warranted.

[2] At least half of the German population (including Jews) of England resided in London during the Victorian and Edwardian eras. Those outside the capital lived primarily in

Jews, as both indigent and illiterate, combined with a renewed sense of nationalism in light of escalating military tensions with Germany, prompted the passage of the first modern piece of legislation regulating alien immigration into Britain, the Aliens Act of 1905,[3] *and exacerbated xenophobia and anti-Semitism.*[4]

The war's outbreak only increased anti-alien sentiment, and by the end of August 1914, the government chose to accept the General Staff's recommendation of August 7 that all Germans and Austrians between the ages of seventeen and forty-two be interned. During the first week in September police officials rounded up Germans and Austrians of this age group whose eligibility for military service in their native countries made them suspect for potential espionage.[5] *On September 14, 1914, Willy Wolff, a German Jew from the small village of Böchingen*[6] *in the Rhineland-Palatinate, who had been sent by his German textile firm in 1912 to work at a cotton brokerage in Salford, England, an important textile hub near Manchester,*[7] *was arrested at his office. He was held for three days in the*

the northern cities of Manchester and Liverpool. Germans played a significant role in Manchester's development in the nineteenth century. See Panikos Panayi, *The Enemy in Our Midst: Germans in Britain during the First World War* (Oxford: Berg, 1991), 17–20, and Bill Williams, *The Making of Manchester Jewry, 1740–1875* (New York: Holmes and Meier, 1976).

[3] The Act empowered immigration and medical officers at ports to evaluate the "desirability" of individual immigrants seeking shelter in Britain. The idea of self-selection by port authorities of immigrants was directed against paupers, thieves, and other undesirables. Immigrants (and their dependents) were required to demonstrate self-support as a condition for entrance. Jill Pellew, "The Home Office and the Aliens Act, 1905," *Historical Journal* 32, no. 2 (1989): 369–85; Bernard Gainer, *The Alien Invasion: The Origins of the Aliens Act of 1905* (London: Heinemann, 1972); David Feldman, *Englishmen and Jews: Social Relations and Political Culture 1840–1914* (New Haven: Yale University Press, 1994), 288–90; John A. Garrard, *The English and Immigration: A Comparative Study of the Jewish Influx 1880–1910* (London: Oxford University Press for the Institute of Race Relations, 1971).

[4] Two of Britain's more influential novelists, Erskine Childers and William Le Queux, wrote widely read pulp-fiction thrillers. With its premise of a surprise German invasion of England, Childers's *Riddle of the Sands* (1903) was seemingly so realistic that it influenced the selection of three new naval bases with access to the North Sea. Similarly, Le Queux's *The Invasion of 1910*, serialized in 1906 in the jingoistic newspaper *Daily Mail*, not only stoked the already smoldering fires of the anti-alien movement with his tale of a German invasion of the British isles but also prompted the creation of Britain's modern intelligence service.

[5] Arrests of military-aged Germans occurred on September 3–6 in the Manchester area.

[6] Böchingen is considered to be one of the "lost" German-Jewish villages. Although records indicate that three Jewish families inhabited the small village in the mid-sixteenth century, it was not until the eighteenth century that Jews actually maintained a presence there. During the nineteenth century their numbers increased steadily through mid-century, reaching a zenith of 240 people or 40 families, followed by a decline to approximately 90 individuals in 1910. By 1933 only 42 Jews remained. Its synagogue, school, and ritual bath (*mikvah*) were destroyed during Kristallnacht (Night of the Broken Glass, November 9/10, 1938), and the remaining Jews were rounded up and sent to a concentration camp in France in 1940. See Bernhard Kukatzki, *Juden in Böchingen: Spuren ihrer Geschichte, 1548-1840* (Landau in der Pfalz: Gesellschaft für Christlich-Jüdische Zusammenarbeit, 1996).

[7] By the early nineteenth century, Manchester was recognized as a manufacturing center for wool, silk, and cotton goods, earning the nickname of "Cottonopolis" as the most

town hall. Released only temporarily, Wolff was forcibly removed from his apartment in West Didsbury,[8] *a suburb south of Manchester, on Sunday, October 4. He and three other Germans apprehended that day were transported to a temporary "internment camp," a disused wagon factory*[9] *in Lancaster, until more permanent quarters were constructed. By the end of September, 13,600 people throughout Britain had joined Wolff as internees, roughly three-quarters of whom were civilians and the remainder were prisoners of war.*[10]

The government's rapid round-up of "enemy aliens" and lack of planning for it, however, led to a shortage of accommodations in which to house the internees, forcing the War Office temporarily to suspend arrests on September 20. Internment resumed briefly in mid-October following a wave of anti-German riots,[11] *only to be interrupted yet again by a dearth of suitable housing. With the outbreak of more serious and widespread riots following the sinking of the British ocean liner* Lusitania *by a German submarine*[12] *in May 1915, Prime Minister Herbert Asquith chose to commit to a more comprehensive internment policy implemented later that month.*[13] *The upshot was the*

important center of British cotton industry. Bill Williams examines the early expansion of Manchester's textile industry and the immigration of Jews to the city in his *Making of Manchester Jewry.*

[8] The suburb was often nicknamed "Yidsbury" owing to the preponderance of Jews who in the mid-nineteeth century had emigrated from Eastern Europe to escape pogroms.

[9] Built between 1863 and 1866, and extended sometime in the 1880s, the Lancaster Carriage and Wagon Works on Canton Street closed in 1908. During World War I, the building was used for the internment of enemy aliens. See Robert Graves, *Goodbye to All That* (Providence: Berghahn Books, 1995 reprint), 72–74.

[10] Exempt from internment were women, children, men not of military age, clergy, physicians, and men unfit for military service. Such individuals were given the opportunity to leave, in accordance with reciprocal agreements with other countries.

[11] While the initial riots in October/November 1914 against Germans were limited to a few British cities, they also reflected an anti-Semitic undercurrent. Catriona Pennell, *A Kingdom United: Popular Responses to the Outbreak of the First World War* (Oxford: Oxford University Press, 2012), 108–14. See also Panayi, *Enemy*, 223–58.

[12] The British naval blockade of Germany ultimately led to Germany retaliating by declaring a war zone around the British Isles and pursuing a campaign of unrestricted warfare against American and British merchant vessels in February 1915. The German Embassy had warned passengers on the *Lusitania* prior to its departure on May 1, 1915, from New York for Liverpool, about the inherent risks of traveling through that imposed war zone. On May 7, 1915, at 1:20 P.M. the German submarine *U-20* torpedoed the liner off the Irish coast. A total of 1,195 passengers and crew members died in the sinking, including 128 Americans. Germany claimed that the *Lusitania* was carrying a secret munitions cargo and therefore was justified in sinking it.

[13] Panikos Panayi, *Prisoners of Britain. German Civilians and Combatant Internees During the First World War* (Manchester: Manchester University Press, 2012), 50. Incensed public opinion, including one extreme call in a populist right-wing magazine, *John Bull*, calling for all German-born men in Britain to be "exterminated," led Asquith to decide that internment for enemy aliens would serve to protect both Germans from further acts of violence and the British public from any potential military danger. This new policy of May 13, 1915, mandated the internment of all male enemy aliens of military age between the ages of seventeen and fifty-five. Naturalized aliens were exempt from internment unless their actions warranted otherwise. Women, children, and men no longer considered of military age (i.e., over fifty-five) were to be repatriated. Panayi, *Prisoners of Britain*, 51–52.

rapid expansion of internment camps,[14] *the largest of which was located on the Isle of Man.*[15]

Willy Wolff and his fellow internees were moved from their temporary Lancaster Wagon quarters to Knockaloe Internment Camp on the Isle of Man in September 1915. Located in the middle of the northern Irish Sea, only thirty-two miles long and approximately thirteen miles wide, the Isle of Man seemed an ideal spot for a British internment camp, as escape would have been difficult if not impossible.[16] *Already by late September 1914, a former holiday camp, Cunningham's Camp, near Douglas, had opened as the Isle of Man's first internment camp.*[17] *The largest of the British internment sites, however, and the second to be established on the Isle of Man, was Knockaloe. Built on a former farm known as Knockaloe Moar, and previously used as a camping ground for troops of the Territorial Forces, Knockaloe opened in its new capacity on November 17, 1914. Although it was originally constructed to hold 5,000, its numbers doubled in 1915 and ultimately swelled to well over 20,000 by the end of the war.*

Wolff's diary from September 1915 until his release in March 1919 throws into sharp relief the daily life of "enemy aliens" in Knockaloe, an inhospitable, desolate place with a circumference of about three miles surrounded by 695 miles of barbed wire.[18] *The camp's location, in a valley basin surrounded by hills, meant that it was frequently buffeted by strong winds, heavy rain, and hail. "The Isle of Man was a romantic and historic land, full of beauty, until you came to Knockaloe," one contemporary mused. There were "rows and rows of the black roofs and the brown wooden sides of army huts, miles and miles of sleeper-tracks between them."*[19] *An Austrian writer and frequent visitor to Britain, Paul Cohen-Portheim, who spent a brief summer interned in Knockaloe, wrote that fellow internees "considered [it] the most distasteful of all camps, the one where hardships were worst and conditions most unpleasant."*[20]

[14] British internment camps of varying sizes existed at one time or another throughout the war in Scotland, England, and even one in India.

[15] Men were interned at a rate of 1,000 per week beginning in the summer of 1915. By November 1915 more than 42,000 were interned in locations throughout Britain. Yvonne M. Cresswell, ed., *Living with the Wire. Civilian Internment in the Isle of Man during the Two World Wars* (Douglas, Isle of Man: Manx National Heritage, 2010), 7.

[16] The island's 55,000 inhabitants resided largely in three towns—Douglas, Ramsey, and Peel—and relied primarily on trade, fishing, and tourism for economic survival. Population statistics based on the 1901 census. A. W. Moore, *A History of the Isle of Man* (London: T. Fisher Unwin, 1900).

[17] Douglas internment camp included a privilege camp in which men who paid 10 shillings weekly could share a small hut with two or three internees. For £1 per week, an individual could have his own tent or hut with servants and imbibe two bottles of beer or a bottle of light wine daily. A second option was a Jewish camp, whose members were provided with kosher food and facilities for praying on Jewish holidays. Everyone else lived in the ordinary camp. Of the roughly 2,700 internees, only 400 or 500 could afford "private living." Cresswell, *Living with the Wire*, 12–13.

[18] Cresswell, *Living with the Wire*, 16.

[19] James T. Bailey, "Personal Papers," MS 10417, as quoted in Cresswell, *Living with the Wire*, 17.

[20] Paul Cohen-Portheim, *Time Stood Still: My Internment in England, 1914–1918* (London: Duckworth, 1931). Cohen-Portheim was interned in May 1915 and served in various internment camps—Stratford, East London, Knockaloe, and Wakefield. In February

Knockaloe was divided into four sub-camps, each in turn subdivided into compounds that could hold upward of 1,000 men and operated independently, monitored by subcommanders and deputies.[21] *Throughout the war a seemingly constant influx of new internees arrived at Knockaloe from other internment camps throughout Britain, whereas only a lucky few received permission to return to their prewar homes.*[22] *Strict protocol was maintained: camp inspections were held several times daily at which internees were required to present themselves to an officer; communications with internees of different camps were forbidden unless they obtained special permission; internees were allowed to write only two letters a week, which were censored; incoming letters and packages from relatives and friends were always inspected and often delayed by weeks or, occasionally, months. Insubordination, brawls, and escape attempts resulted in punishment, ranging from the withholding of mail and food to lengthy imprisonment.*

Huts served as accommodations for upward of 200 and contained only the most basic of necessities—tables and chairs for groups of ten men and "beds" made of straw upon wooden planks.[23] *Roofs leaked and proper heating was absent, making the huts cold, damp, and unhealthy for residents.*[24] *Sloping floors in the huts coupled with loamy soil walkways to and from them were perilously slippery when wet—a frequent problem in view of the rainy climate. Washbasins and toilets were located outside the huts. These not only lacked drying areas for clothing but also a sufficient number of washbasins and urinals, given the number of men who used them.*[25] *Internees also received one meager piece of soap for washing every*

1918 he was deported to the Netherlands. While Cohen-Portheim realized the distaste with which his fellow internees viewed Knockaloe, his first impressions were relatively favorable in comparison to his own experience in Stratford Camp. Cohen-Portheim's time in Knockaloe was brief and during the summertime when weather conditions were somewhat more favorable.

[21] In 1916, Knockaloe had twenty-three compounds divided among the four camps. Camp 1 had seven, Camp 2 had five, Camp 3 had six, and Camp 4 had five. Panayi, *Prisoners of Britain*, 99–100.

[22] As smaller camps grew overcrowded as the war dragged on, the government sent some of the "overflow" to Knockaloe. These newcomers, however, just as often did not remain there for the war's duration but were herded off to Douglas Camp or returned to other ones in England. On the one hand, the in-and-out flow of internees may have been a source of instability within the camp. On the other hand, the fact that some internees were granted their release because they, for a variety of circumstances, were no longer considered a threat to security or were in need of greater medical care, gave hope to many Knockaloe inhabitants that someday soon they, too, might return home.

[23] According to a 1916 inspection report by a U.S. Embassy official, each camp covered approximately four acres and was subdivided into compounds that measured roughly 100 by 150 yards. In turn, each compound comprised five or so huts, for a total of about 1,000 internees each. *Foreign Office: Reports of Visits of Inspection by US Embassy Officials, 1916* (London: H.M.S.O, 1916), 20–22.

[24] Because the huts' walls were not tarred, they leaked and sprouted mold, a health hazard to those who occupied them. Willy Wolff's relatives remembered him having had a "persistent hacking cough." Seymour Dreyfus, *The Willy Wolff Story: A Treasured Contributor to Family and Community* (private printing). The huts also had electricity, but it was usually turned off around 10:00 P.M. or 10:30 at the latest.

[25] According to Wolff, from October through December 1915, Knockaloe possessed only two bathtubs for 2,000 men; by December, however, that number increased to four.

two weeks. Each compound of one thousand men had its own kitchen, operated by fellow internees. Food, often in short supply and inferior in quality, remained a consistent source of complaint among Knockaloe's residents, Wolff included. Meals consisted of rationed, small amounts of tinned meats, weak broths with questionable leftover tidbits, some potatoes, a meager serving of vegetables, tea, coffee, butter or margarine, and bread.[26] *As the war dragged on, food became scarcer and its quality, already poor, deteriorated. In extreme cases, some internees slaughtered dogs and cats as food rations dwindled.*[27]

To offset the monotony and hardships of camp life, administrators allowed internees to establish various outlets for stimulating the mind and the body. Internees replicated their prewar fondness for associations by founding numerous theater, literary, singing, and sports clubs. They produced both serious (historical) and light-hearted (comic) plays and operettas for their enjoyment, discussed literary works, sang favorite songs from home, listened to concerts, and even celebrated special events such as the kaiser's birthday with dinners cooked by their kitchen staff. Internees like Wolff also availed themselves of all types of sports activities, including boxing, wrestling, gymnastics, soccer, tennis, bowling, and even cricket, and occasionally held miniature Olympic competitions among the four sub-camps.[28]

There were educational opportunities as well, as interned teachers and academics taught courses on business, languages, handicrafts, and agriculture.[29] *Additionally, each sub-camp possessed a library with approximately four thousand books, which were "in constant circulation."*[30] *A limited number of approved newspapers were made available to internees, enabling them to keep abreast of the war's events, albeit through a "British" lens. Wolff eagerly searched for good news from German forces. From 1915 onward, Knockaloe's residents published their own newspaper, which detailed events around the camp and contained personal reflections and poems about their internment experience.*[31]

[26] Internees could purchase extra food from canteens, but as the war progressed, dwindling supplies and high prices prevented them from doing so. Special gift packages, often containing biscuits, tinned meat, and cigarettes from Germans abroad were sent to internees, usually at Christmas, but also at other times throughout the year. Initially, internees sent their complaints (often unanswered) about lack of food, clothing, and sanitary conditions to American representatives, but once the United States entered the war in April 1917, Swiss officials became their emissaries. Other avenues of assistance were available through the Society of Friends (Quakers) and the Prisoners of War Relief Agency, established by a German-born naturalized Briton, Emil Markel, who provided musical instruments, sporting equipment, and medical supplies, as well as books for the libraries. See especially Panayi, *Prisoners of Britain*, 244–45.

[27] Wolff, entry of May 26, 1917. Even an adjutant's dog became a meal for some internees. Theft of food was also common, but those caught received severe sentences. Requests for more rations (and better-quality ones) to Americans and Swiss representatives often went unanswered.

[28] Cresswell, *Living with the Wire*, 44–47.

[29] Panayi, *Prisoners of Britain*, 178–79. They produced woodworking pieces, ivory goods, and woven baskets in the camp's handicrafts workshops.

[30] Panayi, *Prisoners of Britain*, 179.

[31] No single newspaper served the camp for the duration of the war. The earliest was *Werden* (April/May 1915), followed by *Quousque Tandem* ([How Much Longer], October 1915), *Lager Echo* (Camp 3, intermittently 1916–1918), and *Knockaloe Lager Zeitung* [Knockaloe Camp Newspaper], from September 1916, published monthly with a

For many in the camp, that experience also included manual labor. Although Article 6 of the Hague Convention of 1907 permitted the utilization of POW labor as long as "the tasks shall not be excessive and shall have no connection with the operations of the war," technically no specific provisions existed for civilian internees.[32] *Some internees, however, remained steadfastly opposed to such assignments, equating such work "for the enemy" with treason.*[33] *Others accepted the offer of work as a way to escape boredom and to acquire money for purchasing extra goods (when available) from the canteens. Work generally meant assisting in agriculture in the surrounding countryside or in nearby quarries, unloading coal supplies for a minimal daily wage.*[34]

The monotony of camp life, close quarters, unpleasant conditions, and impatience over the length of their captivity led to escape attempts and even to some criminal activity.[35] *Dr. Adolf Lukas Vischer, a representative of the Swiss delegation who heard internees' complaints, termed such actions as symptoms of "barbed wire disease," resulting from confined living and strict regulations that disrupted normal patterns of behavior and thus provoked aggression among "captives" and toward camp authorities.*[36] *Escape attempts, of which there were a number over the course of the war, all ultimately failed. One of Knockaloe's more daring attempts, as Wolff's diary details, was committed by four young men who cut through barbed wire, hoping to commandeer a boat in Peel Harbor. They were given stiff prison sentences of between six months and a year.*[37] *By October 1916, disillusionment and despair had led to enough "acts of insubordination" that the camp's commander, Lt. Colonel Panzera, issued a proclamation warning that individuals would face "penal servitude for life," or worse, being shot at by a guard.*[38]

circulation of between 1,500 and 1,600). Panayi, *Prisoners of Britain*, 181–82; Cresswell, *Living with the Wire*, 40.

[32] Article 6 also stipulated that prisoners could work for public service or private individuals or "on their own account." Work done for the state was to be paid at the rates "for work of a similar kind done by soldiers of the national army, or, if there are none in force, at a rate according to the work executed. The wages of the prisoners shall go towards improving their position, and the balance shall be paid them on their release, after deducting the cost of their maintenance." *Convention (IV) respecting the Laws and Customs of War on Land and its annex: Regulations concerning the Laws and Customs on Land; Annex to the Convention: Regulations respecting the Laws and Customs of War on Land: Section I: On Belligerents—Chapter II: Prisoners of War—Regulations: Art. 6*, in James Brown Scott, ed., *Texts of the Peace Conferences at the Hague, 1899 and 1907* (Boston and London: Ginn & Co., 1908), 211–12.

[33] Willy Wolff objected to internees working for the British government. See his diary entry of October 11, 1915.

[34] A group of internees who worked in the fields left at 7:30 A.M., traveling eleven miles by train, and returned around 6:00 P.M.; they received a meager six pence or fifty pfennig for their labor. Wolff, entry of June 12, 1917.

[35] Panayi, *Prisoners of Britain*, 154–57.

[36] A. L. Vischer, *Barbed Wire Disease: A Psychological Study of the Prisoner of War* (London: Bale and Danielsson, 1919). The book was originally published in 1918 as *Die Stacheldraht-Krankheit: Beiträge zur Psychologie der Kriegsgefangenen*. The psychosis might be viewed as a counterpart to shell shock on the battlefield.

[37] Wolff, entries of January 12 and 14, 1916; February 2, 1916.

[38] Wolff, Proclamation of October 16, 1916.

"Subversive" action was not directed exclusively at camp administrators but also extended to fellow internees. Crimes by internees against fellow hut-mates, including theft of personal items, increased with the paucity of food and clothing. In one particular case, a group of "thieves" dug a hole in a wooden floor of a hut hoping to steal a box of money placed there by a "wealthier" internee. Physical violence, however, occurred infrequently. Of note, however, was a case in which internees in compound 2 discovered one of their own to have been an informant for the camp administrators. The "snitch" was thoroughly beaten but escaped with his life by running to the guards, who protected him from further injury.[39] Gambling, although strictly prohibited, was a frequent problem and creditors sometimes found themselves fearing for their well-being, even taking extreme measures of hiding in other compounds or underneath floorboards for safety.[40]

Nothing could have prepared Wolff and his fellow internees for such harsh realities behind barbed wire. Held against their will simply because they had been born in countries now fighting against Britain and her allies, enduring intolerable living conditions and facing hunger on a daily basis, most of Knockaloe's internees remained captive until after the war's conclusion. Not until the autumn of 1919 did the pace of repatriation intensify, largely the result of stipulations in the Treaty of Versailles.[41] The vast majority of the "enemy aliens" who had been interned during the war were deported to their original homelands, while only a minority were granted permission to start lives anew in Britain. For some, like Wolff, repatriation meant only a brief reprieve before more ominous threats to his freedom would materialize under Hitler.

Upon his release from internment in 1919, Willy Wolff returned to Germany, hoping to start anew a life interrupted by the tragic events of war. At age twenty-nine, he resumed employment in a cotton brokerage, and he remained there for sixteen years. Willy's hopes for normalcy, however, were shattered with the accession to power of Adolf Hitler and the National Socialist German Workers Party NSDAP in 1933. From April 1933 onward, new laws imposed upon Germany's Jews severely curtailed their livelihoods and educational opportunities. In September 1935, following the implementation of a series of anti-Semitic measures known as the Nuremberg Laws, Germany's Jews became personae non gratae, banned from intermarriage and German citizenship. Not wishing to relive his wartime experiences of xenophobia and deprivation, and now forbidden to work, Wolff left Germany for Luxembourg sometime in 1935 or 1936, and then for Switzerland. In May 1936, while in Switzerland, he requested an immigration visa for the United States. Four years later, in 1940, with the financial and moral support of American relatives, Willy finally arrived in the United States to begin his life yet again at age fifty, this time in New Orleans.

Wolff quickly adjusted to his new home and to the opportunities afforded him by his relatives. He was described in 1940 by a cousin as a person of "short stature" with a "very

[39] Wolff, entry of April 6, 1916. A ruckus ensued and shots were fired by camp guards, wounding a number of internees. The accused "snitch" was transferred immediately to another camp.

[40] Wolff, entry of September 21, 1916. Consumption of alcohol was also prohibited, resulting in punishment for those who somehow managed to sneak it in from their work shifts beyond the camp walls.

[41] Clauses 214 through 221 of the Versailles Treaty. According to Panayi, 84 percent of all interned enemy aliens had been repatriated by October 1919. Panayi, *Prisoners of Britain*, 279.

ruddy facial complexion" and "hacking cough" (thanks to damp, unheated rooms and a fondness for cigars), who spoke "understandable English with a strange twist and dressed like a gentleman in suit and tie." Wolff established himself as a successful purveyor of fabric to clothing manufacturers in New Orleans, working out of a space in a relative's business. Years of suffering as an internee on the Isle of Man and as a pariah in Nazi Germany, however, failed to sour him on humanity. He became an active volunteer in the Jewish community and belonged to a local synagogue. On April 23, 1987, at age ninety-seven, Willy Wolff died, leaving behind a testament both to the injustices of war and his enduring spirit.

1914

At the office: detained on September 14 in Salford Town Hall until the evening of September 17; arrested in my flat in West Didsbury on October 4th (Sunday morning).

October 5. Brought to Lancaster (3 captive Germans; 3 Policemen); Lancaster camp—an old, very dirty wagon factory[42] that already had been shuttered for ten years. The appearance of the thousand internees already there was deplorable. The ovens were terribly primitive—built by the internees themselves. Nearly all of the people slept on straw mattresses on the damp floor. I had a very small straw mattress for three nights until I built myself a bed from 8 boards. . . . The writing of one letter was allowed twice weekly. . . .

The Adjutant is Lt. Deane. The Camp commander is Colonel Ainsley. Then there was an incident with our captain; Weber was dismissed. From October 19 until November 6 the Company was not allowed to write. Additionally, for a few days we were denied receiving packages and letters. Received a lecture from the commander on October 28. The commander was accompanied by a nine-man escort, 2 officers and 2 non-commissioned officers. The company was forced to line up against the wall! What theatrics! "I have spoken"!!!

End of October. Regular exercise in the courtyard (guarded by Gewehr 98 rifles).[43] In mid November [the use of the rifle to guard internees] was banned.

Mid November. Huge uproar with Lt. Deane because of wood theft. A man was dismissed by Lt. Deane for having stabbed someone in the leg with a bayonet. 14 days no letters and the canteen closed. As a result, a deputation was dispatched to the commander. The aforementioned decision was annulled; however, 28 internees (men) were sent to detention for fourteen days.

From November 27 until December 10 absolutely no mail was delivered[44] (without explanation). The colonel blamed it on the officials in London (Home Office and War Office). Internees who wished to immigrate to America had to deposit £15.

November 14. Young man not allowed to attend funeral of his father in Manchester.

November 29. Everyone received one shirt, one brief, one pair of socks, one coat and one handkerchief.

[42] Lancaster Carriage and Wagon Works

[43] Manually operated rifles first used by German army in the Boxer Rebellion (1898–1901).

[44] The Defence of the Realm Act was amended on November 27, 1914, to give the government the power to prevent individuals from communicating with the enemy.

December 2. Alsatians freed. Huge brawl. Soldiers . . . with bayonets in camp!! From October through December only 2 bathtubs for 2000 men in camp. Beginning of December we received 2 additional tubs.

December 8. Inspection by a General.

December 9. Today everyone received a wooden plank bed that consisted of 4 small planks and 2 [other] planks.

December 10. Twenty Austrians. . . freed.

December 14. A man, who should have been released, was detained for four weeks because he tried to get a letter out of the camp. On September 22, prisoners received a second blanket, middle November, a third, and middle December, a fourth.

December 16. Twenty so-called representatives of the Douglas Camp denied [permission] to go to Lancaster.

December 17. 18 boys and 5 missionaries discharged to Germany.

December 18. Twice shots fired in camp without apparent reason; thankfully, no one wounded.

December 28. A camp school is opened. The halls remain open until 12:30 A.M.

1915

January 2. Everyone receives a pair of boots.

January 3. Complaints about conduct by Camp Major Nanschütz. Dissent against W., yet not acknowledged by commander; rather viewed as riot. Three ringleaders incarcerated.

January 5. Butter ration reduced from 2 to 1 ounce.

January 8. Six men prohibited from writing for fourteen days because they wrote to Germany about their incarceration (with handcuffs and the like). The art of bone cutting[45] has begun: ashtrays, lamps, etc. are produced.

January 12. The infirmary . . . 200 feet long, 160 feet wide, 25 feet high (800,000 cubic feet) that can accommodate 600 men but only 4 gas lamps. . . .

January 14. Today the first person (Vogel) was released to America.

January 20. Instead of bread received biscuits; instead of beef received canned meat. Three men will be released to America. Beds are being installed in infirmary!!

January 21. Drying room set up. For the first time Deane wears his sabre today!!

January 23. Finally newspapers are supposed to come.

January 25. Today we received the first newspapers (official!!).

[45] Internees used cattle bones for this kind of art.

January 27. Parade in honor of the Kaiser's birthday.

January 28. Today [feel] a cold coming on for the first time.

Meal Rations:

½ ounce of meat including bones
½ ounce of potatoes
1½ ounces of bread
½ ounces of tea
1 ounce of coffee
1 ounce of butter
Salt, pepper
2 tins of milk
2 ounces of vegetables (beans, peas, lentils, rice) or ½ ounce kohlrabi

Since Jan 15 (1915) [allowed] an additional half tin of milk; 4 ounces of bread to be substituted for 3 ounces of flour—something that will be frequently used (allowed since December 1, 1914).

Every fourteen days we receive a piece of soap. Since December 14, letters may be written only on official government-issued paper. Dimensions of the court for strolling: until mid October: 7 x 117 m. and 44 x 68m. = 3811m.; middle of October an additional 14m. x 50m. (700 m.) = 4511 m.

February 1. Youth company formed. . .

February 11. For the benefit of those interned, a concert of Blücher, Scharnhorst, Gneisenau etc.[46]

Result: £12.10.0. . . .

June 16. Finally a proper bathing room is erected. Until now there were only 4 bathing rooms but now an additional 16 urinals (trenches?). [*Only the entry of June 16 was recorded in the span between February 11 and September 3*]

September 3. Failed escape attempt by some internees. As punishment, from now on we are counted 3 times per day instead of twice.

September 4. Departure for the Isle of Man.

September 12. Early this morning at 9:30 (precise departure time 10:30) approximately 625 men, representing a third of prisoners in the Lancaster camp, [departed] as the first transport from Lancaster. Certainly, we had no idea where our journey, paid for by the English government, would take us; however, our guess that they would be bringing us to the Isle of Man in the Irish Sea proved correct. The journey itself was a rather pleasant one and so different given, that for 12 months and many others for 13 ½ months, we were held behind barbed wire. We were loaded into two "extra" trains with open carriages [and] about eight [internees] per carriage guarded by an English soldier. We were given a daily portion of tinned meat and bread for the journey.

[46] odd reference to three prominent Prussian generals from the Napoleonic Wars

The journey brought us via Preston to Fleetwood, where we arrived at 12:30 in the afternoon. Directly from the train, that brought us to a ship, we immediately boarded *The Duke of Connaught*, that in peacetime had been a steamer that carried passengers between Fleetwood and Belfast but now was converted into a troop transport. It remained approximately an hour in port during which our luggage (about 10 baggage cars full), belonging to 100 of our internees, were loaded . . . by the Fleetwood port officials.

Around 1:30 we left the port and arrived at 4:30 in the afternoon in Douglas on the Isle of Man. The journey over was splendid, because the weather was so beautiful and clear; the sun shone so magnificently and the sea was totally calm. When we arrived in Douglas there was a small incident in which the English officer ordered us to carry our own luggage onto the wharf. At first we weren't eager to undertake such an endeavor but finally [we realized] we had no choice, and, so to speak, we got to work and within an hour's time all the luggage was on the wharf.

Next we all had to assemble again on board and were counted with precision, and then we were ceremoniously accepted by the officers and ranks of the Knockaloe Aliens Camp near Peel. After that we had to walk in pairs holding hands in formation that in typical English manner took up a full hour.

Especially because today was Sunday, a big crowd of onlookers had assembled on the wharf and in the streets of Douglas to gawk at the arrival of this new transport of "Huns." The march from the wharf to the Douglas train station took about twenty minutes and the public's reception [of us] was friendly throughout the entire route. Only now and then one saw a group of women of genuinely questionable character, who spoke their minds and called us "Baby Killers,"[47] as those in England generally refer to us. These can only cheer us up. Overall, we were in really good hands.

Two "extra" trains, which we immediately boarded, were waiting for us in the Douglas train station. Still, about half an hour passed until our little train departed and, we thought, [that] would bring us to Peel. Fortunately, around a quarter of nine in the evening, we departed Douglas; however, we didn't go to Peel but to St. John instead, where we arrived at 8:45. At the very small train station here we disembarked and for the first time our destination became apparent, namely "Knockaloe," which, as the soldiers told us, was about a half an hour from the station. A half an hour passed at the St. John train station before we finally began our march to "Knockaloe." The path was a really poor one and, in addition, it was very dark. Here and there we saw the lights of our new home, then around 10:45 we arrived. After we were divided up into roughly the same companies as in Lancaster, we stumbled dead tired into our quarters. What surprised most of us was the [existence of] electric lights and proper, new chairs, of which we had neither in Lancaster. The tables were already prepared with the same kind of primitive dishes and cutlery etc., naturally. Also palliasses[48] and covers were already there for us. Of course, all of these [items] were arranged by our fellow internees, who had been here longer. Also we were immediately served our

[47] A reference to atrocities against children, women, and men committed by German troops in occupied Belgium in 1914.

[48] mattresses consisting of a thin pad filled with straw

evening meal that consisted of tea, tinned meat, and bread. All of us were extremely tired, ate very little as a result, but [the food] hastened our exhausted limbs to find peace even on rather short and very meagerly stuffed palliasses.

On the march from the Douglas wharf to the Douglas train station, and also on the way from the St. John train station to Knockaloe Camp, the officers had their swords drawn, something that we thought was really theatrical, as until now we had been accustomed to this only from privates and non-commissioned officers. In every instance, the English officials forget that they are dealing with civilians.

September 13

After I had slept quite well the first night . . . I got up shortly after 6 o'clock, like everyone else. Many had slept rather poorly and the frustration was amplified [by the fact that] there was an insufficient amount of water with which to wash themselves. That was really a rude awakening by the English government. We were told that the pipelines were not working at the moment. In short, two to three men had to wash in the same water! A pretty picture for the future!! In the course of the day we were told that the times for running water would be from 5:00 a.m. until 6:00 a.m., 9:00 a.m. until 10:00 a.m., and 2:00 p.m. until 3:00 p.m.

Around 7:30am we have breakfast that consists of tea, margarine and bread (white and black). Both kinds are very good and are nothing like the horrible stuff we received in Lancaster.

Around 9:00am we receive new numbers, so-called "Dog Tags." In addition, we have to provide details about our name, address, occupation, age, etc. Then, finally, a physical examination of our hearts and lungs takes place.

About 11:00 I exchange my tiny palliasse for a longer one in my yet unoccupied, adjacent quarters.

Around 12:30 we receive our large lunch that consists of, believe it or not, a tiny potato, some tinned meat (1/4 lb) and bread. This small lunch naturally caused a considerable uproar in the entire compound. Some individuals complained to the Sergeant and informed him that we need our own kitchen and should have [the opportunity] to elect a kitchen committee as already has been the case in other camps. These [demands] were made over the course of the afternoon.

Around 2:00 in the afternoon we had our first inspection that was conducted by an officer and the Sergeant. We assembled according to respective huts in the courtyard around which stood approximately twenty soldiers with bayonets.

After the inspection the former first and second officers of the Lancaster companies of hut number 5 switched to number 1, because hut number 1 is smaller than the other huts and [has] only 120 men, almost the exact number of our former company, while the other huts have 180 men. We received an additional sixty men who were not part of our group.

Around 4:30 we have supper that consists of tea, margarine and bread. There's more tea around 7:00.

Knockaloe Camp, which is located approximately two miles from Peel and four miles from St. John, received its name from the estate "Knock eloe," upon which it lies. It is about one mile long and one mile wide and lies in a valley basin that is notable because the Isle of Man is rather hilly. To the east, south and west [the camp] is surrounded by higher hills, while it is rather flat to the north and [offers] a beautiful view, especially from our compound, towards the open sea.

The entire camp is divided into four different camps, namely camps 1, 2, 3, and 4, that house 7,000 men.

These four camps are broken down further into seven smaller compounds that are divided by two rows of barbed wire at three-meter intervals that separate each compound from the other. Each compound houses 1000 men. The compound is approximately ___ [left blank by Wolff] long and approximately _______ [left blank by Wolff] wide. Our living spaces are on one side (the wood huts) of which there are six in total. Those are approximately _____ [left blank by Wolff], _____ [left blank by Wolff] long, ______ [left blank by Wolff] high and ______ [left blank by Wolff] wide. The huts are divided lengthwise into A and B and each of these two halves are divided into three rooms for thirty men. In these rooms of _____ [blank] long and _____[blank] wide reside thirty men who live, eat, and sleep with all of their possessions.

On the other side of the compound is the so-called dining hall, separate from the kitchen, and further separate from the lavatory, baths and W.C. Everything is constructed of wood. The remainder of the area, approximately _____ [blank] wide and _____ [blank] long is for strolling.

In addition to the water standpipes and showers in the lavatory there is also an approximately three meter long washing trough with three pipes. On the whole, the lavatory, bathing and drying areas are deficient (they are appropriate for 200-300 men but not for 1,000 men) and much worse than in Lancaster.

As for the kitchen, in Lancaster, every company of fifty men had its own oven, kitchen and committee, with Government provisions cooked and adjusted to one's taste. Anything else such as vegetables and the like could be purchased in the canteen. Here, however, things are different. Meals for 1,000 men are prepared in one and the same kitchen, that is, in the same pot. The kitchen is a rather large room containing 10 kettles, exactly as each company had in Lancaster, and a single hearth. The hearth that is meant for 1,000 men is the same as that in Lancaster for fifty men.

Behind the wood huts is the canteen, which contains very few items one would wish to purchase and only at crazy prices. Additionally, there are postcards and a small room in which money is distributed every Wednesday.

Around 8:00 this evening another transport of internees from Lancaster arrived with another six hundred or so men of which four hundred were placed in our compound and the rest in neighboring compound number five. Through these internees we got today's newspaper that once again contained good news [with regard to the German war effort].

Around 10:30 we turned in for the night.

September 14. Today we got up shortly before 7:00. Unfortunately, yet again, we didn't have enough water for washing up. Following breakfast at shortly after 9:00 there was a big inspection with the Commander himself and his entire staff consisting of six officers and six non-commissioned officers. The commander of our compounds and camps, a lieutenant colonel, put on an air of such seriousness as someone responsible for fifty thousand battlefield prisoners, and instructs us in the

A Knockaloe Camp street with huts and barbed wire. *Courtesy of Manx National Heritage.*

articles of war, that is, regulations, that contain something new for us. In Lancaster, we didn't have to salute soldiers, only the commander himself, by removing the caps from our heads. Here, however, we are ordered to salute all officers according to military regulations. And we are even supposed to salute with and also without our caps. On the whole, it appears to be much more militarized than in Lancaster.

Today lunch is somewhat better. We got soup, soup meat and potatoes.

Today we had to surrender our luggage yet again for examination by the censor, even though it had already been inspected in Lancaster when we handed them over to train officials.

Captain Nanschutz is named yet again as Camp Major.

Whoever desires to have a newspaper for next week must order one today. The following newspapers are approved [for reading by prisoners]: *The Times, The Morning Post, The Telegraph*, and *The Standard*. Furthermore, a few weekly newspapers such as . . . *The Bystander, Sphere, Graphic, London Illustrated News, Economist* . . . and a few trade papers.

We receive no news today because there aren't any compounds nearby able to get the news to us.

September 15. Meals are precisely the same as yesterday. Breakfast around 7:30, lunch around 12:30 and dinner at 4:30 are comprised of tea, margarine and bread. Today we were notified that in future those wishing to make hot water for a cup of tea can do so every Wednesday after dinner. In future, the same will also be the case after 7:00 p.m.

Captain Fritz Raff was appointed today as Postmaster General for our compound as well as for the entire camp No. 4. Today we received our first notepaper. It is basically the same [kind] as in Lancaster. Simultaneously, it was also announced here that just two letters, pertaining to private matters only and absolutely nothing about the war, are allowed per week, and no extra letters can be written. In Lancaster, company captains, police and postal workers, etc., could write additional letters, but here that is not possible. Additional letters can be written only with special permission of the commander.

September 16. Everything's the same as yesterday. Henceforth, every morning around 9:30 an officer will make an inspection of the entire camp for which we must assemble. Afternoons around 2:00 we must reassemble at which time we are counted.

Around 11:00 a.m. the remaining Lancaster comrades [internees] arrived and were housed in a neighboring compound. Our comrades spent the night aboard the *Duke of Connaught* and complained bitterly that they were detained overnight aboard, even though they had arrived at Douglas at 4:30 in the afternoon.

We were taken out for a walk around the so-called meadow around 2:30. The meadow is about 500 meters from our compound. It's located in the southeastern corner of the camp, is rather flat and covers roughly 700 meters long and 1,000 meters wide. Of course, the meadow is surrounded by barbed wire. Countless watch towers dot the exterior and interior of the barbed wire fences. A boxing ring lies in the center of the meadow; in addition, there are six goals for playing soccer and areas for handball. Around 4:30 we returned from the meadow.

Our Lancaster comrades that arrived early today tossed over some newspapers to us.

September 17. Early today we had to drag ourselves to the dining hall and take away our own breakfast. On the whole, this unpleasantness caused great uproar, even more so when we heard that internees in the other compounds also couldn't take their breakfast in the dining hall. In brief, the Compound sergeant told us that, upon the commander's orders and with the compliance of Nanschütz (our camp major), we had to go to the dining hall. Thereupon there was a huge quarrel with Nanschütz. He wanted to give a report to the commander but decided finally to remain calm and keep his fist in his pocket.

Yesterday, we Jews were asked by the censor whether we wished to attend services this evening and tomorrow morning for Yom Kippur[49] to which we replied, "yes." At the same time, we made a request to be transferred to the Jewish camp in Douglas.[50] Tonight we'll go to services in camp #2, compound #2.

[49] Day of Atonement; the most holy day in the Jewish calendar, when Jews fast and pray from sundown to sunset to atone for their sins of the past year.

[50] The Douglas internment camp was the only one to offer special provisions for Jewish internees.

Jewish internees at Knockaloe on Yom Kippur, September 18, 1915. Wolff is second from left in the second row. *Courtesy of Hartley Library, University of Southampton.*

September 18. I went again today to Camp #2 to attend services. I also had *Yahrzeit*[51] for my dear father. About sixty to seventy men attended services yesterday and today. Around 1:00 our group was photographed by two officers.

Yesterday and the day before yesterday I received some letters that were forwarded to me here.

September 19. Today I received a package from Thekla Katz with some very nice things inside.

We heard in the camp that Vilna is in danger,[52] something that is very good news.

The food leaves a lot to be desired, and a new chef is supposed to be sent to the kitchen. Still, we know very well that the government rations provided to us are not very abundant and also that the all around quality with the exception of bread—that is prepared by German bakers—is lacking. Still, at the very least, we can expect to receive decent food from the cooks.

September 20. Thought that we would receive our first newspapers today; unfortunately, here we are at the end of the world on the Isle of Man and, therefore, get our newspapers a day late, meaning that we receive newspapers dated September 20 on September 21 and so on.

[51] Yiddish term (from the German *Jahrzeit*, meaning "time of the year") marking the anniversary of the day of death, according to the Jewish calendar, of a deceased relative. It is observed with the lighting of a candle and reciting of the mourner's prayer called the Kaddish.

[52] German troops forced Russian troops out of Vilna and occupied the city.

Our huts, like some of the others, decided not to eat in the dining hall any more but rather in our huts. We use our chairs in place of our dishes . . . and for chairs we use our straw sacks.

September 21. Today is my sister Erna's birthday

Yesterday's newspapers bring us the good news that Vilna has fallen.

Now water flows the entire day.

The compound sergeant often demonstrates his authority by commandeering the best internees, who cross his path, into various work details. As soon as internees get a whiff of him, they avoid his area. Work isn't difficult; it consists mainly of stuffing straw items for new internees, sweeping wood shavings and paper and the like—nothing that takes too long and isn't really complained about. On the whole, the sergeant doesn't leave a great impression but he isn't a bad fellow. One only has to understand him and consider his former occupation. He was a dockworker in Liverpool and it's known that this class of people aren't very well educated, especially so in England.

Lunch consists once again of a potato and ¼ lb of tinned meat.

September 22. Nothing really happened today in the compound. We got an additional cotton blanket so that we now have two small and one large blanket with which to cover ourselves when sleeping. Also today was the first monetary distribution. At that time we were told that regularly every Wednesday morning we have to change a portion of our money, the highest amount is set at £1. For the money we deposit we receive a receipt, which unfortunately was not the case in Lancaster.

Yesterday's paper reports that the retreating Russian army from Vilna is in great trouble.

September 23. Early today we stood around for an hour as we were told that we would be going to the meadow. After an hour's waiting, the authorities informed us that today's stroll would not happen.

Yesterday the English Finance Minister, McKenna, unveiled his vast budget. It included new taxes that should bring in £100,000,000. In addition, he estimated England's expenditures between April 1915 and April 1916 to be 1,590 Million Pound Sterling.

September 24. Every morning from now on between 11:00 and noon Herr Ulbrecht will offer gymnastics. We are approximately [a group of] seventy gymnasts. Today the brass band accompanied us to the meadow.

Yesterday's newspapers reported that Bulgaria[53] is mobilizing, something that we all are pleased about.

September 25. Yesterday's newspaper revealed that the Russian army in Vilna was safe. . .

[53] Bulgaria signed an alliance with Germany in early September and declared war on Serbia the following month.

September 26. Today's meal was especially miserable; the cooking committee dismissed the [old] cook and named a new one. According to today's newspaper, the Russians once again had a big victory against the Austrians.

September 27. This afternoon a rumor circulated during inspection that twenty thousand of our troops were taken prisoners by the French. The rumor was started by the sergeant. It caused enormous excitement throughout the entire compound. Personally, I don't believe any of it. Throughout the entire afternoon and evening [the rumor] was discussed [among internees].

September 28. Yesterday's newspaper was eagerly awaited. Unfortunately, there was nothing about yesterday's rumor. The entire newspaper is full of news about Allied victories. The French took 12,000 and the English 2,600 [prisoners] and lots of war material.

September 29. Once again the newspaper is full of [news] of French and English victories. They supposedly took 23,000 prisoners. Fortunately, today's *Berliner Bericht* [Berlin Report] brings more soothing news that our troops have taken 6,500 prisoners. . . . On the day that the truth is revealed, [it will turn out that] our troops will have taken more than 6,500 prisoners. This afternoon we were on the meadow again. Meals have improved considerably now.

September 30. Today nothing special happened. The newspaper doesn't have much to say about the victories in the west.

October 1. Nothing special.

October 2. The map in today's newspaper again indicates what huge progress our army has made in the east in the last months. Fortunately, the number of newly captured prisoners from Champagne has increased to over 7,000.

October 3. Only relatively few internees take their meals in the dining hall. Presently, the situation with Bulgaria seems to be favorable. Sir E. [Edward] Grey confirmed it as such in the press.

October 4. Once again today crazy rumors swirl around the camp. Such is the case every Monday because that's the day that we don't receive any newspapers. According to the rumor, no fewer that 350,000 Russians and 120,000 French and English were taken prisoners [by the Germans].

This evening we had a lovely concert by the string quartet Kruse.

Early today a library was opened in our compound. The books were brought from the Lancaster library. Also, a singing club was established today. Some internees are taking English, French and mathematics as school courses.

This evening a new transport from the Handforth Camp[54]of about 120 [prisoners] who brought the welcoming news that Russia presented Bulgaria with an

[54] Located in Handforth, Cheshire, in an old calico printing works, the camp opened early in the war and initially housed interned German civilians; in March 1915, six hundred German soldiers were imprisoned there from northern France.

ultimatum and that now our troops have a total of 13,000 English and French captured in the latest bloody battles in France.

October 5. Many former Lancaster internees as well as boys as young as seventeen and eighteen (who were interned in Lancaster three weeks ago but who are supposed to be sent to Germany) are among the latest arrivals, who we can see through the barbed wire and with whom we can talk.

This evening more internees bringing good news arrived from Handforth. Also, today internees from Alexandra Palace Camp,[55] London, arrived, suggesting that the English Government intends to put all civilian internees in our camp.

October 6. The kitchen committee sold about ten sacks of cheap flour for approximately £20 that will go into their kitty. That [amount] will allow us to purchase vegetables, extra milk, etc. on a regular basis. Additionally, from now on our kitchen will receive government-allotted flour with which to make bread instead of government delivered [already prepared] bread. The internees here complain bitterly about being hungry because the food is not as abundant as it was in Lancaster. Camp Major Nanschütz lives in a separate room.

The newspapers write that the Allied Troops want to land in Greece in order to help Serbia because they are very afraid that we will launch an invasion in Serbia.[56]

Once again about 180 internees arrived in our camp from Handforth (near Manchester). They told us that Greece will join the English side in any case. This afternoon we went to the meadow again.

October 7. Tonight yet again more internees from Handforth arrived who brought us the good news about Venezolos[57] [*sic*]. . . This swine is very much on the side of France and England. . . .

October 8. The new camp newspaper appeared today with the title *Quousque Tandem,* Cicero's famous words "How much longer?" The newspaper is written in a very comical style and is well maintained. It is published by our own here in Camp #1. The print is wonderful. It couldn't have been printed better in any other print shop. A nice post office will be built in our compound.

It's worth noting that more internees from Handforth are expected; [they] bring us today's newspaper; otherwise, we wouldn't receive [it] until tomorrow. This

[55] Originally built in 1873 in north London as a public center for recreation and entertainment, and as a counterpart to the Crystal Palace in south London, the camp housed German and Austrian internees during the war.

[56] In October 1915, upon the behest of the Greek Prime Minister, a Franco-British force landed at Salonika (Thessalonika) to assist Serbian troops in their struggle against Bulgaria.

[57] Wolff meant Greek prime minister Elefthérios Venizélos, who early in the war had hoped to bring Greece in on the side of the Allies, but whose efforts were thwarted by King Constantine I of Greece, brother-in-law of Wilhelm II. Venizélos was dismissed by the king in October 1915, only to return to the political scene in October 1916 to set up a rival government in Salonika. When King Constantine abdicated in June 1917, Venizélos assumed control of the entire country, and Greece joined the Allies on July 2.

evening the good Handforth internees brought us the delightful news of the successful invasion of Serbia. Hopefully, this time this riff-raff will get what they deserve.

October 9. Today it rained nearly the entire day. Because the loam soil produces terrible mud and because our huts are so sloping, one can hardly walk out of them without being in great danger of falling. . . .

We rejected [the idea] that in the future we transform the dining hall into a trade school.

October 10. Yesterday's newspaper reported that the invasion of Serbia is going well. Sir E. Grey's Balkans politics received enormous criticism from various newspapers [about the fact that] the English believed various Balkan states would come in on their side.

This afternoon we were on the meadow and spoke with many internees who came from Handforth.

Today the kitchen is selling Berliner donuts (2 for 1 pence). The '"Cheap Friend," a drinking establishment in Lancaster with its cakes, coffee and the like, has tried several times recently to obtain permission from the Commander to erect a stall but has yet to receive permission. . . .

This evening a nice concert by the brass brand under the direction of the Singing Club took place, at which an altercation occurred between the entertainment committee and the camp major.

October 11. Today the trade school opens in the dining hall.

The entertainment committee and the camp major as well as the sergeant were summoned to the commander because of yesterday's altercation. In the presence of the entertainment committee the sergeant told the commander that he would prefer to leave the compound than work together with Nanschütz any longer. The sergeant, who was a rather decent [person], is leaving and we will get another one.

With regard to yesterday's altercation about the concert Nanschütz unfortunately prevailed. Recently, Nanschütz has been losing supporters. Only the recommendation letter from the Lancaster commander protects him with the authorities here. In any case, he should have resigned his post long ago.

For about two weeks now approximately thirty internees from our compound (from the various camps about six hundred altogether) have been working for the English Government for three shillings per day. The internees work on the streets outside the camp from between 9:00 and 12:00 and 1:00 and 4:00. I strongly condemn this and frankly can't understand how such internees submit to this. In these times, the internees really could use their meager pennies in a better way.

From the beginning gambling was very much frowned upon in Lancaster but later on it was strictly forbidden and the prohibition strongly enforced.

Once again today a representative from the Society of Friends[58] is here. As someone told me, he spent the entire last week in this camp and worked arduously to reopen the trade school [that had existed] in Lancaster. Mr. Clark had already

[58] The Quakers visited Knockaloe early on as advocates for the internees. They also helped establish handicraft classes within the camp.

worked hard on our behalf in Lancaster as had the Society of Friends, in general. Already in peace time [the Society], like the Salvation Army, followed the "love thy neighbor" command and now do a great deal of good for prisoners of war (English, German, Austrian, Turks, etc.) and their families.

October 12. The news from the papers is quite satisfactory. A new entertainment committee is being created. Our hut isn't appointing any candidates because we don't want to have anything to do with any committees or the like. It rained the entire day so that one hardly left the hut. Also the floor was very slippery. In general, though, the weather had been very nice. Until now we didn't need to wear an overcoat. On the contrary, internees would sit [outside] in the afternoons in their free time and read.

We are no longer able to receive the evening newspaper on a regular basis. Tonight we received the happy news about the fall of Belgrade.

October 13. As a result of new taxes, the prices have risen on many items in the canteen, mostly for cigarettes and tobacco. Also fruit has become more expensive again so that the cost of two small pears is 1½ pence. Two small apples already cost ½ pence since we have been here.

In the bathhouse, shelves were finally installed so that we wouldn't have to put our wash on the floor any more. The new sergeant appears to be a calmer fellow.

The rain has stopped, and today we rejoice in beautiful summer weather. So that in future it's safer [for us to walk] when it rains, we made different paths from the court to the train area. We are ordered to have ourselves photographed, and today a photographer from Peel visited our compound. Many internees were photographed in small groups.

October 15. . . The "German Eater" Delcassé[59] has resigned. Once again the zeppelins struck London and its surroundings hard. In the House of Lords a few Lords, Lord Milner[60] and Lord Ribblesdale,[61] proposed that the unfortunate Dardanelles[62] expedition should be abandoned.

Once again the photographer was here in the compound and continued to snap photographs. This fellow earned a pile of money from the camp.

October 16. Nothing of particular interest happened today. More good news comes about Serbia. I talked today with some internees who are so optimistic that they believe we will be going home by Christmas. I am not of the same opinion; however, I believe that we should be home by April or May. The authorities enquire whether there are chemists, experts in the production of soap, iodine, tinned meat, etc. It appears that they want to discharge these internees but, thankfully, no one

[59] Theophile Delcassé, French minister of foreign affairs and an architect of the Anglo-French Entente Cordiale of 1904.

[60] Alfred Lord Milner was a member of the War Cabinet from December 1916 until November 1918.

[61] Thomas Lister, Liberal Party member

[62] Reference to the failed Allied Gallipoli campaign of February 1915–January 1916.

has volunteered. The English do such crazy things. First they lock up people, then they realize that they don't have enough experts and, finally, they want the horrible Germans, whom they locked up and despised, to work for them again.

October 17. Today [the authorities] asked the internees from Camp 10 and the Jewish camp whether they would like to be released [to work for the English].

In the evening we had a big concert.

In the afternoon a fellow from Compound 12 (Camp 4) was buried. An imprisoned German clergyman presided over the burial. Some friends, many acquaintances and an English escort and officer attended the funeral of our deceased countryman. Our band from Compound 2 played the funeral march. The deceased was a young fellow thirty-four years old, who had a managing position in a German-English stove company in Sheffield. When he was imprisoned in Handforth he suffered from severe liver problems and when the internees from Handforth were supposed to be transferred here, the attending doctor [at Handforth] opposed his transfer. Nevertheless, the deathly ill patient was transferred here and was placed in a hut with his friends. The next day he was brought to the infirmary where he died a few days later.

October 18. The evening newspaper brings good news from the front. We also read about the cause of the death of our countryman yesterday by the English authorities. It turns out that the physicians in Handforth and here denied any responsibility [for his death] because the authorities should not have transferred him [to Knockaloe]. . . . Following these proceedings there will be another meeting among the authorities. One of these concerns remuneration, although this is of no use [to the deceased], and therefore, the proceeding is really just a Hun-bashing opportunity (such brutality!!). . . .

October 19. The evening newspaper brings good news of the resignation of Sir Edward Carson,[63] an English minister with a large following and great influence in the Conservative Party. This demonstrates that the English Cabinet is not so unified as the English claim. Also received good news that Ian Hamilton, the commanding general in the Dardanelles, has been recalled to England. A further setback for our cousins!!

October 20. Good news about Serbia.

October 21. More good news and from all war theaters. This evening we had a big concert in support of the soccer club. The soccer club wants to have soccer cleats for all its members. Unfortunately,. . . we are not in the position to buy cleats ourselves. In a previous week a game took place but not with very good results. Therefore, today's concert, which was well attended and in itself very good. Also some internees from other Compounds were present as well as about one dozen English officers. Approximately £1.12.0 was collected—not very much!! . . .

October 22. Nothing noteworthy to report.

[63] Attorney General in 1915 who became First Lord of the Admiralty in 1916 and was a member of the War Cabinet from 1917 to 1918.

October 23. The newspaper reports are quite satisfactory. Unfortunately, I have to stay in bed because I have a cold. Today it rains from morning until evening and is terribly cold.

October 24 Still raining today.

October 25. Today we have splendid weather again. Internees are asked yet again whether anyone from Camp 10 wishes to be transferred to Douglas. The news in the evening newspaper isn't particularly good. Unfortunately, it brings news of the loss of our cruiser the *Prince Adalbert.*[64]

October 26. Improvements like benches and coat hooks are planned for the bathroom. The Austrians are asked whether they would prefer to be transferred to a compound for Austrians only. From the German-Austrian as well as the Bulgarian perspective the Serbian front is going very well.

October 27. Terrible weather and rather cold. Good news from the war.

October 28. For months now the English newspapers have pressed with regard to the Coalition Government, munitions, and again cotton as contraband. Now they're pushing for a smaller Cabinet—fourteen or even seven ministers instead of twenty-two—to lead the war effort. Additionally, the newspapers are clamoring for recruits. Despite the fact that the English Empire extends in all corners of the earth, the press. . .refuses to concede.

Unfortunately, today we did not receive our newspapers. . .

October 29. Today I celebrated my twenty-fifth birthday. As a birthday surprise, I received a post card from cousin Rudolf Teutsch from America from whom I hadn't had any letters until now. The postcard made me very happy. Yesterday's newspaper brought us the good news that our troops are in direct contact with the Bulgarians. What joy this advance party must have felt at that moment and what happiness must have been felt throughout Germany!! The entire English press is scolding their government so terribly over the German [success] in the Balkans.

Nanschütz, our camp major, goes around the camp collecting votes so that he can remain camp major. This is quite a surprise and causes great excitement in our camp as at the moment no one knows the motive behind this. Nanschütz tells the compound that he is being sold out by our hut, that we want an extra kitchen and extra washroom, something that is completely untrue. Nanschütz is pursuing this merely to turn the other internees against us (what was called officer tampering in Lancaster) . . . in order to secure votes for himself. As a result of this political maneuvering, he received seven hundred and fifty votes, but that didn't help him completely. Over the course of the afternoon we heard from the sergeant that he, like his predecessor, also can't work with Nanschütz because of his big talk and attempt to sell him out to the commander by telling him that [the sergeant] supplied us with the evening newspapers, that he sold us wood, etc. I would never have credited him with

[64] German armored cruiser assigned to reconnaissance missions in the Baltic and sunk by a British submarine on October 23, 1915.

such underhandedness. The sergeant's statements circulated throughout the entire compound and inflamed further rumors. Furthermore, the sergeant added that he would refuse to work with Nanschütz any more and that he would do everything possible to convince the commander to remove Nanschütz [from his position]. That [was the situation] in the afternoon. To the enormous surprise of both the pro- and anti-Nanschütz camps, we learned at 6:30 p.m. that the commander had dismissed Nanschütz, ordered him to ready his bags within a half an hour, and transferred him to Camp 3. This happened much more quickly than we had anticipated. Our hut members couldn't believe it. Punctually, at 7:00 p.m., Nanschütz was escorted away. I simply can't imagine how Edwin Nanschütz, [who is] so full of himself, believes the camp cannot manage without his leadership. . . .

October 30. Good news from the papers. Good progress in Serbia, English cruiser stranded, change in French course in Minsk. Election of a new camp major in the compound. It's almost like a parliamentary election. A total of seven candidates are nominated, platforms laid out, [and] the band campaigns for this one and that one from morning until evening. The election results: Landers receives 200 votes, Boch about 130 and the other candidates only a few votes. We from hut #1 don't propose any candidates so that it can't be said that the officer's hut wants to control the compound. Because the candidate with the most votes only received about two hundred [votes] and [because] there are about one thousand internees, the camp commander refused to recognize the results and ordered another election to be held.

October 31. Good news in the papers from Serbia. General Joffre[65] is in London. He will discuss with officials in London how much longer he can hold out. King George, who visited the front in France for the second time in the fourteen month-old war, was thrown by a horse and injured. The newspapers report that a soldier was supposed to have shouted "hurrah" so loudly that King George's horse got skittish twice and the second time threw him. Well, "I thank him."

Talk in compound is still about the election of a camp major. That will take place this afternoon. Boch withdrew his candidacy. Four candidates remain. Landers is elected with four hundred votes. Landers is a young fellow of twenty-three who was only in England a few months. I pity him, just as I would pity anyone else, with what awaits him in the position of major. . . . The position is even more difficult because the largest part of our compound consists of ungrateful beggars.

On Friday until Sunday a guard stood duty the entire time within the compound because of the commotion following Nanschütz's removal.

On October 27 the Government delivered pants and wooden shoes to a number of internees.

About four weeks ago in neighboring compound 5 a few internees assaulted their Head Captain and were brought before a military court. Yesterday, as the special

[65] French general Joseph Joffre steadied the retreating French armies in the face of the rapid German advance on Paris and stabilized the western front with victory at the Battle of the Marne in September 1914.

appeals court's judgment of three, two or one month [in prison] was read in the former compound, a considerable number of internees who hadn't participated [in the assault] yelled "disgrace." The commander wanted to know the names of the internees who had shouted "disgrace" but failed to receive any. At [the commander's] instruction, the former compound was not to receive any further mail, no packages and no newspapers.

November 1. Our new camp major, Landers, took office today. This afternoon a pleasant rumor was spread that Nish[66] had fallen and an Italian cruiser was sunk.

November 2. Unfortunately, yesterday's rumor didn't appear in the newspaper. Still, our troops are making good progress overall. They captured 1,200 French in the Champagne again.

The sergeant inquired who urgently needed clothing. Internees whose money is with the commander don't have to make a claim.

This afternoon a rumor circulated that the entire English cabinet resigned, that King George returned urgently from France[67] and that the largest Serbian arsenal Kragnievatz[68] fell.

Around 6:30 p.m. a surprise roll call occurred and it turned out that the number [of internees] in the camp did not jive.

About 9:30 p.m. we had another [roll call]. This is an unusual occurrence. It was said that these crazy English authorities held a special roll call in another camp around 1:30. Until further notice, sleeping until 7:30 in the morning is allowed. The day before yesterday twenty internees and indeed the oldest in the compound received plank beds for the foundations for their straw mattresses. I wonder how long it will be until the majority receive these plank beds. They were absolutely essential because the ground is really damp.

As the press already had been trumpeting for a week, today Mr. Asquith[69] (Prime Minister) gave his big speech covering the general war situation.

November 3. The other evening's rumors are only partially that. In any case, the newspaper brought us the gratifying news that the largest Serbian arsenal Kragnievatz has fallen. Yesterday, the wounded King George returned with his doctors from France, but this doesn't have anything to do with any kind of cabinet crises.

Our new compound major and sergeant make the rounds in all the huts and announce that in future internees who wish to receive clothing from the government must give in their old clothing. [The reason for this is] that it's been discovered that internees have [been given] the same clothing twice and then they gamble [it].

Furthermore, another decree has been made that the flooring should not be scrubbed until all internees have plank beds.

[66] Wartime Serbian capital captured by Bulgarians (Central Powers) in November 1915.
[67] While inspecting troops in France, King George V fell off his horse and broke his pelvis.
[68] Serbian stronghold about sixty miles southeast of Belgrade.
[69] Herbert Henry Asquith, British prime minister from 1908 to 1916.

From now on we won't have roll call around 1:30 any more; instead a so-called Tally number system will be implemented. Aside from a number that each internee received on the first day of his arrival, each will receive another tally number. The system is constructed in an English manner in which the authorities have precisely so little control over our presence in the compound as it was before. The tally numbers will be given out around 4:30 evenings and collected again in the mornings around 9:00. . . .

November 4. Today we read in the newspapers about Asquith's big speech[70] on the general war situation. The speech is the longest that Asquith has delivered; he spoke no less than an hour and fifty minutes. As far as the content is concerned, it was really very meager. He said what the English have known for a long time. Also he gave official notice that the Dardanelles expedition was a failure from the beginning to the end and that it is the biggest disappointment of his life. The debate that followed was the most lively in the House of Commons since the outbreak of the war. . . .

Today once again for the second time since our arrival in this camp the order came that internees under the age of seventeen and above fifty-five who are totally blind, possess only one limb, extremely ill, crippled or have severe defects should report to the doctor in order to [determine whether] they might be released to return to Germany or Austria. These kinds of internees have already been examined dozens of times but that has not resulted in their freedom.

The Turks from all of the compounds of the camp got their wish to be transferred altogether to a hut in compound 6.

It was rather cold and very windy all of last week. In each hut there is a very small oven that only heats a third, not the entire, hut. The worst is that we don't get any coal to put in it so we have to steal it, so to speak.

November 5. Good progress in Serbia. For the second time since his resignation at the outbreak of the war, Lord Morley,[71] who opposed the war, appeared in the English House of Lords and criticized the government rather harshly because of the censor [that] always prevents the bad news [from the front] from being known.

On November 2 it was also divulged in the House of Commons that in addition to the 100,000 men lost in the Dardanelles since October 9, the English lost an additional 72,000 men through illness.

November 6. Yesterday's newspaper reported of a new cabinet crisis in Greece in which the new Premier, Mr. Zaimis,[72] demanded [a vote of] confidence by the Greek Chamber [but] the majority votes were against him. It appears, however, that Zaimis is working towards new parliamentary elections in which he hopes

[70] Reference to Asquith's speech to the House of Commons on November 2, 1915, addressing Serbia, Lord Derby's recruitment plan, the failure of the Dardanelles campaign, and British war finances.

[71] John Morley, 1st Viscount Morley of Blackburn, British Liberal statesman.

[72] Alexandros Zaimis, Greek prime minister, appointed under King Constantine to succeed Elefthérios Venizélos in October 1915 but forced to resign in November 1915. He became prime minister again in 1917, but once again was forced to resign in June 1917.

that his party (the Neutrality Party) will receive a majority and that Venezelos [*sic*], who is on the Allied side, will be defeated once and for all. It's going faultlessly in Serbia for us.

November 7. Yesterday's newspaper reported that many frightening rumors were circulating in London that Lord Kitchener[73] (the English War Minister) has resigned. The government, however, quashed them. Later on it was announced officially that Kitchener had traveled to the Near East (Balkans) and that Asquith acquired his post at the moment.

Today, after close to seven weeks, the loss of a large English transport with three hundred soldiers on board in the Aegean Sea on September 19 was announced.

A chess tournament will be arranged in which representatives from all seven compounds of camp no. 4 will participate.

In future letters to the American representative and the government in London should no longer be sealed but rather must be left open in order to pass through the censor.

November 8. Today, on a Monday, as usual there are many wild rumors about, one now that claims the King of Serbia and his entire army have been captured.

The wind is blowing very strongly and winter is making its presence known. We can see the high waves of the sea very clearly. An improvement will be made in the toilets. One will not be in use and will be replaced instead with a very primitive type of water flushing apparatus.

Also, finally, there will be an addition to the washhouse that is much too small. The prices for most items in the canteen were increased yet again. This is the third time since our arrival.

November 9. Yesterday's newspaper brought good news about Nish (Serbia's second main city). More important reports with regard to the rumors that circulated in London and in conjunction with Kitchener's mission, and further official news that he has gone to the Balkans. *The Globe*, a well-known London evening paper, was seized around 6:00 p.m. because it maintained that Kitchener had resigned even though the press bureau stated twice officially that it wasn't true. . . .

Once again the Russians have made some successful advances.

Yesterday's newspaper also printed the text of the note that America sent to England in which America protested strongly against the detaining of American ships.

A few hundred young Irishmen, who wanted to emigrate from Liverpool to New York on Sunday, in view of the forthcoming universal military service, [and] although they had already received and paid for their tickets, were not allowed to travel because the crew would not transport military-aged men. The affair is, in any case, nothing more than the power of the government hidden behind the ship's authority. . . .

[73] Lord Horatio Herbert Kitchener, secretary of state for war, 1914–1915, was forced to resign his post following the Gallipoli campaign failure. On a mission to Russia, he died while aboard the cruiser *Hampshire,* which was sunk when it hit a German mine.

November 10. The military prisoners of war sent an official letter to all compounds in which there were civilian internees, who were sent to Handforth a few weeks ago, and thanked the latter for leaving behind £58 for them [to use] in the canteen.

News of the war is good again today with the exception of the sinking of the small German cruiser *Undine*.[74]

In the House of Lords and House of Commons there were very lively debates regarding the general course of the war. The most notable speech was made by Lord Courtney,[75] who said that it was high time to think about peace. Also a very lively debate on the suppression of the *Globe* newspaper followed.

The Greek crisis has been solved in so far as Skouloudis[76] has taken over as Prime Minister and established a new cabinet. It's been reported from Romania that a large number of ships with munitions were headed from Austria down the Donau through Bulgaria to Turkey.

November 11. Lord Mayor's Day was held on November 9 in London. As usual the ministers and all high-ranking personalities attended a banquet with the mayor. The speeches by the ministers and representatives were really laughable. These men ... [think] that they alone and no one else can dictate the peace conditions. ... In general, the speeches were well received.

This evening and yesterday evening we had a wonderful concert by the thirty-two man strong Handforth string orchestra ...

November 12. The news arrives that the large Italian liner *Ancona*[77] sank. About two hundred passengers of the approximately 430 lost their lives. The English are furious over it and say that it had to have been [sunk] by a German submarine and not an Austrian because such an act would be unworthy of an Austrian sailor! Aside from the *Ancona*, a large number of transport ships, auxiliary cruiser and torpedo boats were sunk.

In the House of Commons Asquith demanded a further credit of £400.000.000 that was accepted without issue. A very serious debate regarding the Dardanelles expedition ensued.

November 13. The English are terribly afraid that we [Germany] also are in direct contact via Nish with Sofia [Bulgaria] and Constantinople [Ottoman Empire]. Lord Derby[78] is trying everything to get more recruits. He made it officially known that

[74] SMS *Undine* was a German ship deployed in the Baltic Sea that was sunk on November 7, 1915, by a British submarine.

[75] Leonard Henry Courtney, 1st Baron Courtney of Penwith, British politician.

[76] Stephanos Skouloudis, diplomat and politician, was asked in November 1915 by Greece's King Constantine to form a national unity government. The newly formed government focused on the question of Greece's entry into World War I.

[77] The SS *Ancona* was an Italian passenger ship that was torpedoed and sunk without warning on November 8, 1915. About 200 passengers out of the approximately 430 lost their lives.

[78] Edward George Villiers Stanley, better known as Lord Derby, was appointed director general of recruitment in 1915. Because conscription remained too controversial to implement, Derby introduced a scheme by which men who had not yet volunteered for

individuals who do not report willingly [for military service] by November 30 will be forced to do so. This summons caused extreme agitation throughout the country.

In the House of Commons a lively debate on airships and zeppelins took place. Furthermore Asquith let it be known that Lord Kitchener in view of very, very serious, sudden and unexpected news departed for the East. He also stated that he commissioned a new committee regarding the implementation of the war.

We've had an enormous storm today. It rains, snows and hails. The nearby hills are covered with snow. It's been reported that the Liverpool ship that as a rule docks in Douglas to bring the mail to the Isle of Man could not dock today because of the high waves; instead it had to find a more favorable place in the Peel Harbor.

November 14. It's really cold and the storm continues. We are allowed only one coal for each oven per day.

In Greece the parliament was desolved and new elections are slated for December 19. Venezélos [*sic*] does not want to participate with his party in the new elections. Perhaps he is afraid to lose supporters. Mr. Winston Churchill,[79] who is well known for wanting to remove German war ships out of the Kiel Canal, . . . left his new ministerial post and went to France as an officer with his old regiment. As the reason [for his departure] he explained that he had nothing more to do once he was not included in the new War Committee.

The Russians had a small success in the area of Riga. They immediately created the fairy tale that Hindenburg had threatened to resign should the Kaiser continue to insist that Riga and Dunaberg be taken right away.[80]

A large number of ship accidents as a result of strong storms were reported along all the coasts of England.

The calm, sure progress of our invasion of Serbia is downright wonderful. We've heard very little recently about the Western Front.

November 15. Lots of rumors are swirling again. In the washhouse there has been better water in the last fourteen days from early morning until late evening. From now on there will also be some from 10:00–noon and 2:00–4:30 and 6:00–7:00 in the afternoons.

The cold is still very harsh. The entire courtyard is completely frozen solid. The snow-decked heights create a wonderful view.

November 16. Over the next few days a sixty-four year old internee is supposed to be released to Germany once he pays his £2 for the journey. Otherwise he will

service would attest their willingness to serve if needed, with the understanding that the government would claim single men first before enlisting married men.

[79] Winston Churchill was First Lord of the Admiralty until the disastrous Gallipoli campaign forced him to resign and accept a commission as a lieutenant colonel on the western front until March 1916. He then returned to England, and in July 1917 was appointed minister of munitions.

[80] The rift between General von Hindenburg and Kaiser Wilhelm over military decisions in Riga was related by German prisoners and reported in the press.

have to wait six weeks for his release. If he doesn't have the money [to pay] then a collection will be taken up with him. A large English submarine has been sunk in the Dardanelles.

The English and French absolutely can't align with Bulgaria even though they had promised Serbia to protect it from its enemies. . . . Until now the Italians haven't yet established an active front in Serbia and the English and French have done everything in their power to convince them to take an active role.[81]

November 17. The sub-commander[82] promises that each section of a hut should receive its own oven as long as they will arrive. But when will that be the case?

It turns out that the old internee who is supposed to leave for Germany tomorrow now doesn't have to pay [for his release] and everyone who gave a small contribution [to enable his departure] can get their money back. Most of the internees, however, let the old internee have the few [leftover] Marks.

In Serbia everything's going swimmingly.

In Persia there are uprisings against the English and Russians.

Mr. Winston Churchill delivered an important speech in the House of Commons in which he described his service as First Lord of the Admiralty, defended himself against his accusers and provided the reasons behind his resignation. *The Times*, which not long ago described him as an amateur, now describes him as a hero. . . .

This evening suddenly a rumor circulated that Greece[83] had declared war on England and France.

November 18. Unfortunately, the news about Greece is not true although it's still encouraging to see how we [Germans] and the Bulgarians make daily strides.

In England at the moment there is much doubt about the recruitment system, that the so-called married volunteers remain uncertain whether they will still be called to the colors first if all the single men are drafted.

In the House of Lords there was a vigorous attack on the General Staff.

November 19. The newspapers report that the Ministers Asquith, Lloyd George, Balfour and Grey have gone to a war conference in Paris.[84] A French Minister has arrived in Greece to clarify the situation [there].

[81] Hoping to coax Italy into the war on the Allied side, Britain and France offered it territory in the Adriatic region, and Italy signed the secret Treaty of London. On May 23, 1915, Italy finally declared war on Austria-Hungary.

[82] The officer, usually a major, who exercised authority over one of the four camps into which Knockaloe was divided.

[83] Although officially neutral, Greece split on whether to support the Allies or Central Powers. On the one side was King Constantine I, whose brother-in-law was Wilhelm II, and on the other side was Greek Prime Minister Venizélos, who supported the Allies. When Constantine abdicated in June 1917, Greece joined the Allies against the Central Powers.

[84] Reference to Anglo-French Conference in Paris of November 17, 1915, to discuss aid to Serbia and the Dardanelles.

A large English hospital ship[85] hit a mine in the Channel and about two hundred wounded soldiers and many nurses were killed. Additionally, a lot of ships in the Canal and Mediterranean have been sunk.

The French have received a blow from the Bulgarians.

November 20. More than three quarters of Serbia is already in German-Austrian-Bulgarian hands. What will the Serbs think of their English and French friends?

Lord Lansdowne[86] (a Minister) announced to the House of Lords that General Monro,[87] who was sent to the Dardanelles after General Hamilton's withdrawal order to examine the situation more closely, reported that the troops should be pulled out of Gallipoli. The government was not sufficiently in agreement with his report and, for that reason, sent Kitchener to [Gallipoli] to examine the situation more carefully. ...

November 21. Yesterday's newspaper didn't bring much new, only that Serbia is rapidly disappearing from the map. The situation between the Greeks and English is becoming very critical. The English are no longer allowing any Greek ships to load.

German reports say that in India there's considerable unrest, [something that] the English will deny.[88]

November 22. Today rumors are circulating once again. Greece supposedly declared war on England and France. Likewise, Romania supposedly declares war on Russia, Monastir has reportedly fallen [with] 12,000 Serbian prisoners, and furthermore 40,000 French [prisoners] in the West.

November 23. We were further disillusioned today. Still some [of the rumors] that we heard yesterday are true. Novi Bazar has fallen and over 7000 Serbs have been captured; Prilep has fallen as well and a few other Serbian cities.[89] As far as Greece is concerned, reportedly the Entente has blockaded the Greek coast. . . . Lord Kitchener was in Salonika and Athens last Saturday and tried to persuade King Constantine to demobilize [his troops], because the English and French fear that their troops, in the case of withdrawal from Serbia (something that is very likely), might be interned by Greece. In France and Russia there is nothing new [to report].

Yesterday, as is usual always on Mondays, we had tinned meat. In compound 4 many internees, as they had last Monday, complained about the quality of the tinned meat.

[85] Wolff must be referring to the HMHS *Anglia*, a hospital ship torpedoed on November 17, 1915, by a German U-boat off the coast of Dover in the English Channel.

[86] Henry Charles Keith Petty-Fitzmaurice, the 5th Marquess of Lansdowne, co-leader of the Conservative Party (1911–1916) and minister without portfolio (1915–1916).

[87] When in October 1915 General Ian Hamilton was dismissed from his post as commander-in-chief of the Mediterranean Expeditionary Force because of the Gallipoli fiasco, General Charles Monro replaced him and ordered the evacuation of British troops from Gallipoli.

[88] Allied newspapers reported that unrest in India was a further example of German disinformation.

[89] In the face of a Bulgarian invasion in October 1915, coupled with German and Austro-Hungarian attacks, Serbian forces were driven back and forced to retreat through the Alps. The Serbian army only refitted as an effective fighting force in the spring of 1916 at the Island of Corfu, by which time much of Serbia had been lost.

In reality, a few internees got sick. Naturally, the doctors maintained that their illness was a result of something else. Compound 4 refused to accept the tinned meat. Our compound accepted it initially, although when the tinned meat was opened, it was determined that more of it was rotten. The kitchen committee immediately complained about it, informed the doctor, who ordered that the meat be returned, and we received the previous quality [of meat] once again, about which there were few complaints.

November 24. Yesterday's newspaper did not bring much of interest. The only thing noteworthy is a lead article in *The Times*, in which it explained that people should not give up the crazy opinion that we in Germany have already called up the last of the reserves, as one ½ penny newspaper so eagerly claimed, but that we in Germany have enlisted and classified our human resources in such a wonderful fashion that the Allies could take ours as a model. . . .

November 25. The Foreign Office announced that considerable unrest has occurred in Persia.[90] The Foreign Office also said that no Greek ships will be seized in British ports. That's a true "Edward Grey-style" announcement again. So that the world will be deceived E. Grey says very clearly that no ships will be seized in Great Britain but that he doesn't mention that they will be in the Mediterranean. British Headquarters reported that "Major Churchill" has accepted a new post in the field. I wonder if he will give such big speeches there as in the English Parliament!!

November 26. Today the following statement appeared in *The Times*: "There is no news either of the whereabouts or the present strength of the gallant, still undefeated Serbian Army." Compare these two contradictions. On the one hand, *The Times* knows nothing about the whereabouts of the Serbian Army at present but despite that the newspaper maintains firmly that the Serbian Army remains intact and undefeated.

Prishtina and Metroviza[91] have fallen and the Serbian Government once again has to find a new home. ...

The English had success against the Turks near Baghdad.[92] If one examines the details of the victory more closely, one finds that the English victory was more of a defeat, because even though they allegedly defeated the Turks and took eight hundred prisoners, they themselves lost 2,000 men and had to retreat a few miles owing to a lack of water!!

The Entente has sent a new note to Greece.

November 27. The commander strictly forbids anyone to damage the new plank beds in any way. Internees who recently purchased wood from the sergeant in order to

[90] A weak, neutral Persian government encouraged machinations by both the Allied and Central Powers during the war. While Britain and Russia coveted Persia's (present-day Iran) oil deposits, Germany and the Ottoman Empire hoped to use its strategic position to undermine the British Empire in India.

[91] Once a part of the Ottoman Empire but liberated by Albanian forces in 1912, Prishtina and Metroviza, both in Albania, were fought over by other Balkan forces. Bulgarian troops occupied Prishtina while Austro-Hungarians captured Metroviza in November 1915.

[92] Part of the Mesopotamia (Iraq) Campaign pitting the British against the Ottoman armies.

build their own beds have to stop and [instead] they will receive a very impractical government-designed plank bed. The majority of the internees, however, have not received any as of yet.

We've received the good news that with the fall of Metroviza and Prishtina 17,000 Serbs and twenty-five guns were captured. Supposedly Greece has received favorably the last English note and should have answered satisfactorily. Lord Derby, England's recruitment director, who called Lord Ribbelsdale[93] [*sic*] a traitor to his country in public in the stock exchange because he had openly said in Parliament that General Monro reported that the troops should withdraw from the Dardanelles and, in so doing, passed along a secret to the enemies, . . . today excused himself in the press for his sharp language. This is true English manner—today you affront someone merely for the publicity and then the next day you excuse yourself!!!

November 28. There's not much new in yesterday's news. The only newsworthy item is an article from *The Times'* military expert who admitted that a portion of the Serbian army still exists but that in theory it no longer counts as a military power. Another noteworthy article is namely the news that Russia is concentrating an army of 250,000 on the Romanian border that will advance against us and the Bulgarians in Serbia.

A new decree is out that in future packages that are sent to us by Englishmen and those that are sent by us to Englishmen must be prepaid/stamped.

November 29. Today, as is usual on Mondays or when we don't receive newspapers, a lot of rumors are circulating. Finally, the toilets will be properly fixed.

November 30. Yesterday's newspapers brings us the good news from German Headquarters that the Serbian war machine has already fulfilled its primary goal, that over 100,000 Serbs have been imprisoned and that the rest of the Serbs who are being pursued by us and the Bulgarians are retreating from mountainous Albanian Montenegro.

Apparently a big political conflict broke out between *The Times* and the English Minister of the Interior [Home Secretary], Sir John Simon.

December 1. Today a few internees received plank beds, among them myself.

Yesterday's newspaper admitted that the English were defeated in Baghdad, although the day before yesterday they spoke of the great victory in Baghdad.

Monastir should fall soon.

An English airman supposedly sunk a German U-boat by bombing it off the Belgian coast.

The Russians hope to take an entire German divisional staff prisoner near Pinsk.

December 2. It's been raining evenings until mornings and the other way around. Today there was a big scene on the meadow at a soccer match. The referee couldn't agree on a specific goal with the players and the match was suspended after a few minutes.

[93] Thomas Lister, 4th Baron Ribblesdale, Liberal, trustee of the National Gallery.

According to yesterday's newspaper there was a lively debate in the House of Commons regarding *The Times* and *The Daily Mail*, two leading newspapers. Sir John Simon launched the primary attack in which he pointed out that these newspapers write important articles that many enemies (us) read. *The Times*, he charged, describes the general English news too pessimistically and *The Daily Mail* [erred] because of its map "The Road to India." The map was copied in such a wonderful fashion by us [the Germans].

Once again the situation in Greece is described as rather serious. Pritzrend[94] [*sic*] is conquered by the Bulgarians.

December 3. Next week some of our comrades who are not eligible for military service will be released. Some of the internees from our hut have hope [that they will be released].

The Bulgarians captured 17,000 in Prizren [*sic*]. The train line Monastir-Salonika has been cut by us.

Asquith, McKenna[95] and Renserman[96] [*sic*], three ministers, had a meeting with the largest workers' associations in which they urged workers to save in the interest of the state and to give those savings to war bonds. The speeches of the Ministers had little impact on the representatives.

Furthermore, it was reported that three Ministers resigned from the Austrian Cabinet and were replaced by three others.

December 4. Two internees from our compound (who, by chance, are friends of mine) received definitive news today that they will be released to Germany on Monday. Many internees, who believed that they would be released this time, unfortunately were deceived in their hope.

Once again the Italian Parliament met. The Government explained that it signed an agreement with England, France, Russia and Japan not to conclude a separate peace.

The English Government announced that the total number of casualties through November 9 amounted to 310,000 men.

The conflict between the Government and *The Times* continues. It should please us [Germans] that the English have so much time to spend on such trivialities in their Parliament.

December 5. Monastir has fallen. What a joyous occasion for us. Hopefully, the French and English who currently are in Macedonia will get a good beating.

In general, today's newspaper didn't bring squat. One piece of news [that] is rather interesting and truly English is that English women train young officers in riding and the handling of horses.

[94] Prizren, Albania
[95] Reginald McKenna, Liberal Party member; First Lord of the Admiralty, 1908-1911; Home Secretary 1911-1915, and Chancellor of the Exchequer, 1915–1916.
[96] Walter Runciman, 1st Viscount Runciman of Doxford, Liberal, president of the Board of Trade from 1914 until December 1916.

The sloping lime floors of our compound are terribly slick as a result of this damn rain. Yesterday an internee broke his leg as a result and had to be brought to the hospital and another [internee] today.

December 6. Our two comrades were released this morning at 6:00 a.m., for Germany. What joy for them!

The English consider us innocent lambs to be unusually dangerous because they have erected barbed wire between the two inner rows. In total, we are surrounded by three rows of barbed wire—with a further 1½ meters of thick bundled wire.

December 7. For the [purpose of] dispatching important business, the head commander very kindly allowed me to go, accompanied by a guard, to the private villa of a lawyer who lived nearby, and I spent nearly an hour in his house because the gentleman wasn't at home yet. Together with the guard, I sat in a small, beautifully furnished room close to the fire in a truly comfortable large leather chair. For the first time in fourteen months I felt like a civilized man for a few minutes. Oh, how joyous it would be to be able to live such a life again!! After I settled my business with this gentleman, I left this beautiful house with a heavy heart and returned to [living] behind barbed wire in the camp that . . . should only be described as a stable for men.

Yesterday's news was rather good again. The English admitted that they suffered a beating at Chertiphon[97] [*sic*] in Tigris and that they had to retreat about 140 kilometers (80 miles). Naturally, they didn't call it a defeat but, in their superlative language, a successful, brilliant strategic pullback. Balfour, Asquith and Kitchener were in France again to take part in a war council. The English press brings news of some kind of plan[98] that will be worked out in Berlin and Vienna regarding a clash over what they call the Central Europe movement. The press hopes to learn more about the Plan and is racking its brains about it. *The Morning Post* contains an article from *Vorwärts*[99] in which it says that a poem that appeared in the *Berliner Tageblatt* by a former prisoner of war in England painted the conditions in [English] prisoner of war camps in a much too stark way and that one should assume that the author of the poem was never imprisoned in England. I don't wish the editor of *Vorwärts* ill but only that he be forced to spend the rest of my imprisonment here in Knockaloe. Until December 7 we've had only a tiny oven in one room where one hundred twenty internees live. It's awfully cold in the hut, the rain drips through in many areas, the wooden walls are always wet and everything that one has is damp and moldy. In addition, the food is meager. The English concern themselves with every trifle

[97] Battle of Ctesiphon, late November 1915, between Ottoman and Anglo-Indian forces that halted the British advance to Baghdad.

[98] Reference to the Mitteleuropa Plan, which originally took shape as the September Program (September 9, 1914), in which Germany sought to secure its eastern borders from Russian encroachment. In 1915 it was expanded upon by Friedrich Naumann, a Progressive Party leader, who called for a kind of economic and political union between Germany, Austria-Hungary, and other Central European nations. The plan underwent several revisions during the course of the war, although always maintaining some form of German economic and political hegemony as its basis.

[99] Newspaper of Germany's socialist political organization, the Social Democratic Party (SPD).

that occurs in the German prison camp and articles about this appear continuously in newspapers. In the German newspapers that we have had until now I have never seen an article in which our German newspapers quarrel about the scandalous treatment that we receive here [in England]. We've been here already for three months but unfortunately until now neither the American representative nor any of his bureaucrats have looked out for us.

December 8. The war news is good. Our troops [German] invade Albania.[100] The Bulgarians maintain a stranglehold on the rest of Serbia. The well-known, wealthy American industrialist set out on his peace mission to Europe. The English press considers Ford's undertaking—his entirely private undertaking—as laughable.[101] Unfortunately, the English have sunk a Turkish torpedo boat destroyer. It appears that a revolution has broken out in Shanghai (China) because the rebels have already seized a Chinese cruiser.[102]

December 9. Today we received the excellent news that an Austrian U-boat captured an English officer who was on a passenger ship that went from England to Greece and [then] Greece to England. The Austrians knew exactly the number of his cabin. It also turns out that this fellow is a member of the House of Commons and a big "Germanophobe." Yes, this Mr. Wilson, M.P., must be shaking his head [in disbelief]. Along with him the Austrians snapped up an English colonel who had been the former military attaché in Sofia [Bulgaria]. . . . The official Montenegrin telegram reports that the Montenegrins are withdrawing according to plan, yet . . . the Montenegrins, like their allies, are not necessarily bound to the truth. . . . It's been reported from America that the American Government requested that the Germans recall Captain Boy-Ed and Major Papen.[103] . . . President Wilson gave his inaugural speech in the American Congress. [Judging] from the excerpts that have appeared in the press, the speech is rather biting and unfriendly towards us [Germans].

This afternoon a terrible snowstorm raged. . . . This evening we had a nice concert. . . .

December 10. As mentioned already yesterday, the French have retreated further. Today's German newspapers report that the English have suffered a substantial beating in Macedonia. . . . In the House of Commons Asquith answered the query of

[100] Albania's inhabitants stood divided along religious and political lines between Allied and Central Powers. In December 1915, Albania was invaded and occupied by the Bulgarian army.

[101] American automobile magnate Henry Ford departed on December 4, 1915, with a large group of anti-war supporters aboard a steamship bound for Sweden, hoping to achieve a peaceful settlement to the conflict. The project was a failure.

[102] Japan's intent to become the predominant power in East Asia led to a further assault on Chinese political and territorial sovereignty (especially the Twenty-One Demands) during the war. Its attempt to undermine Chinese President Yuan Shikai's regime and provoke a civil war failed.

[103] Both Karl Boy-Ed, who served as naval attaché in Washington, D.C., and Franz von Papen, member of the Catholic Center Party, who became Germany's chancellor in June 1932, served under the German ambassador to the United States until December 1915, when they were expelled for having allegedly engaged in acts of espionage and sabotage.

a representative about our [German] peace proposal and the restoration of Belgium. [He said] that he would discuss serious peace proposals with all the Allies and also with the House of Commons. His response, that really didn't say much, sounds very different from the speech that he gave upon the outbreak of the war and also a few weeks earlier in which he proclaimed that peace must be dictated in Berlin!!!

December 11. In the Reichstag Mr. Bethmann-Hollweg[104] gave a fine speech in which he thrashed our enemies.

The English and French are forced to retreat even further in Macedonia. Hopefully, they will be stopped short by all of our troops and Bulgaria's.

December 12. Bethmann-Hollweg delivered another speech in the Reichstag with regard to the Social Democrats' interruption about whether he will make his peace terms known. He declined to do so and, in a masterful way, stated that those must come from our defeated enemies. In addition, he mentioned the case in which the English ship *Baralong* boarded a German U-Boat and murdered [crewmembers], [which] would always be a black stain on the English navy.[105] . . . The Serbs, English, French and Montenegrins received yet another beating. It also seems that the English are surrounded. Likewise, in the last few days, [the English] apparently have received another blow in the Dardanelles.

It's hailing and snowing something terribly.

At the beginning of last week the English Government gifted each compound £20, which should be to earmarked for the kitchens for Christmas.

On the 11th of this month we were informed that Baron Schröder made a donation of £575 to the Camp (German internees as well as English guards) for Christmas, roughly 5 ¾ shillings per head. The individual tables determine what they want to use it for. Most choose marmalade, compote, others a Christmas tree, etc. Tobacco was not chosen because of a new tax. Also there's a list of a certain Dr. Lowry (a very benevolent Englishman, who also did a lot for the internees last year), who for Christmas provided those very needy internees with certain smaller items such as socks, wristlets, slippers, toothbrushes, clothes brushes, suspenders, etc.

December 13. Today we were informed that a representative of the American Embassy in London would inspect the camp at the end of the week. As a result, the (camp) authorities are hustling to get things ready. The individuals, who are constructing the new bathrooms, are working overtime to complete them for the end of the week. Also, more stoves are being brought into our compound. My section still doesn't have any. The commander requests that our various hut captains submit to him the complaints that they intend to present to the representative (a direct order!?). In accordance with [the commander's] wishes, the [hut captains] provide him with all the questions. That same evening the huts were made aware of the primary complaints that the captains will bring before the American. In total, there are about twenty-eight points, evidence of just how bad the situation in the camp is.

[104] Theobald von Bethmann-Hollweg, German chancellor, 1909–1917.
[105] Refers to an incident in August 1915, in which a German U-boat's crew was killed in retaliation for the recent sinking of the passenger liners *Lusitania* and *Arabic*.

The main complaints are: terrible condition of the huts (not waterproof; as a result, clothing, wash, boots and packages are always wet); too few covers (only two small and one large one); bad food (too few vegetables); bad pathways in the compound (dirt and water); miserable condition of the wash house; no real drying room; lack of clothing (we want boots and articles of clothing for rich and poor), lack of stoves; absence of a roof in the canteen and post office; poor selection of goods in the canteen, and many more.

A rumor has circulated that Greece declared war on the Allies.

December 14. The Allies admit that they fought hard in Macedonia but maintained that their retreat is an orderly one. The Bulgarians already are on the Greek border. . . .

Lord Derby announced that the rush of recruits of the last days was so strong that he would have to delay the end of his system again in two days. America sent a very impudent note to Austria in view of the sinking of the *Ancona*.

December 15. In accordance with his doctor's orders (!!), King George, who declared himself as a model of abstinence to his subjects for the duration of the war, has to break his promise and regularly drink some alcohol so long as he continues to suffer from his fall in France.

The English Finance Minister suggests a law in which he is ready to request that Englishmen who possess American securities either sell or loan them. This is another means by which England can manipulate the American exchange rate to England's benefit.

December 16. The English and French maintain that they retreated in an orderly fashion from Greece. The Government put forward a bill [that stated that] the next parliamentary elections should take place at the end of January in peacetime, in about twelve months.

December 17. General French resigned and in his place General Douglas Haig[106] was named Commander-in-Chief of the English Army in France. French will be in charge of the troops in England. The Bulgarian and our [German] troops have completely routed the English and French out of Serbia. The latter are erecting more new fortifications in Salonika. Dr. Helfferich[107] was granted a further credit of ten billion Marks from the Reichstag. The English Government put forward a law that would ban Englishmen of any kind from doing business with certain German firms and neutral countries on a "Black List."

December 18. The Government was criticized in the House of Lords because of its trade agreement with two Danish businessmen associations that were allowed to export certain items to Sweden and also to Germany that they had imported before from England.

[106] When, in December 1915, General John French lost the confidence of Kitchener and the Cabinet, Douglas Haig was named his replacement as commander-in-chief of the British Expeditionary Forces.

[107] Karl Helfferich, German finance minister, 1916–1917.

Today the American representative visited us. [His visit] was too short in order to deliver all of our grievances. Nevertheless, this Mr. Littleton [*sic*],[108] who hopes to visit us again on Monday, wants to receive a deputation [of internees] who will present the grievances at that time.

On December 15 an unusually big event occurred in which we finally received a stove but without a cover and the necessary ducts. We got to work quickly to assemble it and the missing pieces so that, fortunately, we could have a fire the same evening. Moreover, this indicates to the world how these noble English gentlemen treat us so well every day!!. . .

December 20. The American Littleton [*sic*] did not visit us again today but allowed our deputation to visit him (three internees). The complaints were delivered and he will pursue. Additionally, he promised that he will come again in four weeks in order to see if any of the improvements have been implemented. He realized that the conditions in the entire camp leave much to be desired.

It's been said within the compound that our troops [Germans] have undertaken a big offensive in France and that Ypres[109] has fallen.

December 21. Following the inspection of huts 1b and 1a, the sub commander allowed us to go to the dining hall and gave us a big sermon about our plank beds not having been made according to instructions and that the general condition of both of our huts was a lot to be desired—something that was not the case in the other huts. In an impertinent manner he also didn't forget to make us aware of the fact that we must stand in front of the door (a real necessity!!!) and because of that he would punish us. If he only knew how touched we were with his moral sermon!!!

Unfortunately, yesterday evening's good news is not confirmed in today's newspaper. We are not a bit disappointed. The newspaper reported only of heavy artillery near Ypres.

The first group, the Lord Derby group, have now received orders to report to military officials on January 20, 1916.

Unfortunately, the small German cruiser *Bremen* was sunk in the Baltic Sea.

December 22. The entertainment committee has finally received permission of the sub-commander to remove the partition in the dining hall and build a larger stage.

In the afternoon of December 20th Mr. Asquith informed the House of Commons that English troops of Anzac and Suvla [Bay] were withdrawn from Gallipoli with good results.[110] He added that it appears that the Turks first noticed the withdrawal as it became light and the troops were on their ships.

[108] Leland Littlefield served as Special Attaché to the U.S. Ambassador in London.

[109] Possible reference to the gas attack launched by German troops on December 19, 1915, against Allied troops along the Ypres Salient. The Germans hoped the gas would cause enough panic among opposing forces to permit a breakthrough. This, however, did not occur.

[110] After visiting Gallipoli in mid-November 1915, Field Marshal Kitchener determined that without a significant increase in troops and artillery, little progress could be made against Turkish forces and, therefore, ANZAC forces were evacuated from the region.

The results of Lord Derby's recruitment system must leave a lot to be desired because Asquith already concluded his report on it. The reports from Greece and Bulgaria are the biggest fabrications and the situation remains unclear.

December 23. Today an enormous number of packages and mail arrived from Germany. These look as if they had been inspected in London.

Another big change has occurred in the English high command and it appears some of this took place behind closed doors. Additionally, Asquith reports in the House [of Commons] that as a result of the withdrawal of Anzac and Suvla troops only six canons and very little war material was left behind and that there were only three [troops] lost in total. . . .

Some Social Democrats in the Reichstag were supposed to have expressed dissatisfaction with Bethmann-Hollweg's speech.

December 24. The newspapers have nothing noteworthy to report. The weather is miserable. Still no letters from Germany. Christmas Eve is really very sad. The kitchen committee gave us Stollen.[111] The five shillings that Baron Schröder gifted each of us for Christmas will be paid out in cash. . . . Thanks to the generosity of donors from abroad each hut received some social games. In addition, each hut with its sixty to ninety inhabitants received smaller presents, namely four cigarettes, some four Christmas cards, two moneybags and three playing cards.

December 25. Nothing special to write about Christmas. There was only Christmas mass. The kitchen prepared a fine Christmas meal this afternoon.

The newspapers have nothing new to say. The Russians registered success in . . . Persia. . . . According to the House of Commons, the total English casualties in the Dardanelles were 113,000 dead and wounded, 96,000 ill, as of December 11. The House of Commons is adjourned until January 4, 1916. There are reports from Serbian refugees that are absolutely not good news for the Allies. They complain that the Allies haven't helped them enough and that as a result our [German troops] have had successful campaigns.

This evening we had a very nice concert in the expanded dining hall. The stage looks very good. The sub-commander attended with his entire staff.

December 26. The whole day was boring.

December 27. Ditto. This evening we had a dance. Lots of rumors circulate again.

December 28. Finally, today we got a newspaper again. . . . On the first day of Christmas in Glasgow before the workers' associations, Lloyd George delivered a speech in which he pleaded and begged the workers to do their utmost to help him.[112] The speech was interrupted frequently by hecklers and it would appear that the workers are not completely in agreement with Lloyd George's suggestions. On

[111] cake

[112] Lloyd George addressed labor union members in Glasgow to allay their fears that the dilution program (using unskilled labor in skilled positions, owing to the severe shortage of skilled laborers who were serving in the army) would undermine their positions and to request an increase in war material production.

the second day of Christmas the Cabinet held a meeting discussing the universal service question because the current voluntary system under Lord Derby isn't sufficient. The Cabinet is divided on the issue.

December 29. Early today one of our chaps (about thirty years old) had a crazy accident. A man knocked a hole in his head.

The English received a further setback in Mesopotamia. They are surrounded in Kut-El-Amara[113] and awaiting reinforcements. The Indian troops, which had been in France earlier, were removed from France and sent elsewhere—a very noteworthy event! As of December 9, English casualties had risen to 528,000. The Cabinet appears to be in a crisis over the issue of conscription. The Finance, Trade and Interior Ministers want to resign [over the issue].

December 30. Unrest is taking place in Russia,[114] the Russian Censor has withheld all telegrams from December 5 until December 20 as a result.

It's been reported that the Arabs have encroached upon the western borders of Egypt but were repelled by the English. The Cabinet has finally decided in favor of universal military service, although it appears that the crisis still has not been overcome. Still no clear reports from Greece.

December 31. The newspaper doesn't bring anything noteworthy. Tonight was quite the colorful evening and was rather splendid. In honor of New Year's Eve, the lights that usually are turned off around 10:30 weren't [turned off] until 11:30. In general, quiet rules and the internees have become more reticent than they were six or even twelve months ago. Today we received a lot of mail from Germany. Throughout the entire month the weather was awful. Not even once did we have a review outside. Last week we were "greeted" three times with tinned meat instead of the prescribed once. . . .

1916

Hopefully, the new year will bring us the final defeat of our enemies and the return to our homes.

January 1. New Year's Day was quite quiet and nothing happened in the camp. Today an amateur chess player from a neighboring compound came to our entertainment room and simultaneously played thirty-six games of chess. Of those he won twenty-four, lost four and drew eight.

January 2. Today fifty-six internees received clothing that they urgently needed, i.e., one received a pair of pants, another a shirt, and a third a pair of wooden shoes, etc. Yesterday and today an exceptionally large amount of mail arrived from Germany. The letters dated from November 12 until December 18.

[113] Reference to Siege of Kut (December 7, 1915–April 26, 1916), in which the Ottoman army led by German General Baron von der Goltz pinned down British and Indian troops under Major-General Charles Townsend, ultimately forcing their surrender.

[114] Possible reference to subsistence riots throughout 1915 that were led by women, protesting both the shortages and the high prices of food.

Aerial view of Knockaloe Camp, about 1916. *Courtesy of Manx National Heritage.*

January 3. Finally today we had nice weather and an inspection outside once again.

January 5. Today another exceedingly large amount of mail arrived.

January 6. Finally today we could go to the meadow again.

January 7. We've been sleeping on the same straw mattresses since we arrived. Today everyone was permitted to exchange their old straw mattress for a new one. Also again today new clothing and wash was distributed.

January 8. Those internees who had paid ten shillings to be transferred to Douglas received the news today that the Douglas Camp was over capacity.

January 9. This evening we had a very nice performance of [a] comedy . . . by the theater group from Compound #2. Two internees from our compound were informed that they would be released the day after tomorrow [to return to] Germany. Both are over fifty-five years old (around sixty years old).

January 10. A school, similar to the one we had in Lancaster, although somewhat smaller, was officially opened today. Approximately twelve different subjects will be taught in it.

We have been waiting for an optometrist for months now. Today one finally arrived.

This evening we had a history lecture.

January 11. "Old Emil" and another older gentleman as well as thirteen young men under the age of seventeen (from Compound #7) were freed to return to Germany around 6:00 this morning. A lecture on German lyric was presented.

January 12. Reportedly, four sailors from Camp #1, who cut through the barbed wire, tried to escape in a boat through Peel harbor.[115]

January 14. The four internees, who broke out yesterday, were apprehended today, unfortunately. The ship's officers petitioned that they be handled separately and receive a better diet.

January 15. The chess tournament ended today. It ended with a small celebration and a small celebratory meal. . . .

January 16. This evening we had another nice theater production. . . . These entertainment evenings are opportune for cheering up the internees.

January 17. Once again there is a crisis in our kitchen committee. Last week we received a notice from the American envoy in London, who promised to submit our grievances to English officials, who promised improvement.

January 19. The weather this month was substantially better than the last and [as a result] we are able to spend our free time outside walking.

January 21. Today, once again, there was clothing distribution. I, myself, was also there and received . . . one under wear, one pair of wooden shoes, one warm coat and one pair of suspenders.

January 25. A notification by the English Government [is received] in which it complains that the English-born wives of Germans [internees], who receive [financial] support from them, are not doing enough to find work and should be deprived of this support in the case that they cannot find work. . . .

January 26. I spoke by accident to the four youth who broke out [of the camp] and tried to commandeer a ship in Peel. They are young men between twenty and twenty-five years old.

January 27. Today is the Kaiser's birthday. Unfortunately, the celebration wasn't as nice as the one we had last year in Lancaster. This morning the Head Captain publicized a letter from the Central Committee stating that in regard to the Kaiser's birthday the commander has forbidden any speeches and processions to take place in public or in the entertainment, including the singing of "Die Wacht am Rhein and Deutschland, Deutschland über Alles."[116] Nevertheless, we had a small celebration this evening, and we believe that our head captain should not have made the letter

[115] On January 12, 1916, four Knockaloe internees (sailors) escaped, and after two days on the lam made their way to a yacht in Peel Harbor, hoping to commandeer it to freedom. They were, however, spotted by fishermen who then reported them to authorities and they were returned to camp.

[116] "The Watch on the Rhine" and "Germany, Germany Above All" were two patriotic songs with origins in the pre-World War I era.

public and that it should have been written more discreetly. . . . Two one act plays were presented, one entitled *Mein Bursche Jochem Besel* [My Boy Jochem Besel] and the other *Waffenbrüder* [Comrades in Arms], the latter updated for the present day.

January 28. One of our former Lancaster comrades departed [died] suddenly yesterday, and today we will take up a collection for a wreath.

January 30. Wild rumors don't circulate now as they had in the weeks before.

January 31. In future postal orders but will not be exchanged by the bank but rather through the canteen. This evening we were told about the case of the *Appam*,[117] the ship that was raided [by Germans] and sailed by German officers via the Atlantic to America. [The event] seems to us at the moment like a fairy tale from "One Thousand and One Nights." Such a master stroke unlike any in this war until now!!

February 1. The Central Committee informed us that in addition to £500 given by Baron Schröder, cigarettes and types of licorice were also given as Christmas gifts.

February 2. The four internees who escaped earlier appeared before the military court today and one of them was sentenced to one year [and] three others to six months in prison.

Another person who also tried to escape was sentenced to three months in prison and one individual, who was found to have letters from the Society of Friends, was sentenced to eighty days imprisonment.

February 3. A trade school, similar to the one in Lancaster, is supposed to be opened here.

February 4. Today we had a lovely theater performance of *Der ungläubige Thomas* [The Incredible Thomas]. Once again yesterday seven internees from our compound were set free to Germany. . . .

February 8. Since February 1 our mail officials and all those individuals, who have passes allowing them to go to other compounds, have had great difficulties because of apparent irregularities with the passes. [As a result] there will be only day passes distributed, [resulting in] many fewer passes.

February 10. In the last few days we have had lots of rain and wind once again and also some snow and hail.

February 12. Today, as will be the case every future Friday, there will be a delivery of goods. Every Friday fifty internees from each compound will have their turn. . . . The American representative who promised to visit us shortly before Christmas . . . still has not shown up.

February 14. Today we had a nice variety show.

[117] British steamship that was captured on January 15, 1916, by the *Moewe* (The Seagull), perhaps the most successful German armed raider.

February 15. The canteen gave notice that in future it will no longer be allowed to sell sugar [and] that the government insists that we be thrifty with sugar [consumption]. This order is not intended just for us internees but also for the entire English population.

Today two internees were sentenced to seven days imprisonment: one for gambling (in my opinion, still too lenient) and the other to eighty-four days in prison for attempting to escape.

February 17. Today our hut held its early year cleaning. For the first time in months the hut was really scrubbed.

February 18. The old commander of the entire camp, Lt. Col. Carpendale, was replaced with Lt-Col. Panzera.[118] In the camp it's been said that the old commander was replaced because many residents of the island complained about the poor conduct of the officers under Lt. Col Carpendale. The officers had too much time on their hands and [as a result] engaged themselves with the weaker sex [i.e., women]. My friend, Cazzini, who has been in hospital for a few weeks, is in poor condition and was transported today to an isolation hospital.

February 20. Today's theater performance was *Der gutsitzende Frak*[119] [*sic*; Frack] and was very well received.

February 22. Today two internees were sentenced to twenty-eight days imprisonment because of drunkenness. Apparently they procured some whisky or alcohol through the mail. Two others, who were in hospital [and] evidently didn't follow the doctor's orders and disobeyed him, were sentenced to fifty-six days imprisonment.

February 23. The new commander informed internees in a letter that they should not continue to direct their grievances to [sources] outside the camp but rather to the appropriate sub-commander, who will do everything within his power to address the grievances. . . .

February 24. Our Singing Association is very much in flux because our conductor, who comes from another compound, has problems with his pass.

February 25. Unfortunately I heard that the condition of my friend, Cazzini, worsens daily. In future, whoever loses his tally number will have to pay 6 pence for a new one. The community of Trier[120] did not send any gifts to any of the Trier internees here. Finally, we get war news once again. The newspapers report about our victory at Verdun! Hopefully, that's the beginning of the end.

February 27. Unfortunately, early this morning Cazzini died. Today's theater presentation is entitled *Die Logen Brüder* [The Lodge Brothers]. In future, only very important letters with postage (that means, only letters to England) will be stamped.

[118] Carpendale was sacked owing to escape attempts by internees. His replacement, Colonel F. W. Panzera, previously had commanded an internment camp in England.
[119] In English, *The Tailor-Made Man*, which was a comedy in four acts, written in 1908 by Hungarian playwright Gábor Drégely.
[120] The oldest city in Germany, located in the Rhineland-Palatinate.

February 28. A new kitchen committee will be elected. An internee was sentenced to eighty-four days imprisonment because of pass falsification. Our friend Cazinni's coroner's inquest happened today. Two of us were present as representatives of the deceased. There was quite a scene between our representatives and the jury, which accused our representatives of inadequate care of the deceased. These people from Peel accused the doctor and those under him [of negligence] and charged him in a second inquest. Finally, they united and . . . declared the inquest as valid.

March 1. Today we buried our deceased friend. Twenty men each from our compound and compound 5 will go the burial. An English priest conducted the service that was nothing more than formulaic. Our band played the last march. Two acquaintances offered a few words at the gravesite and placed a wreath. Cazzini must be the hundredth [person] to have been laid to rest here. No one from the government was present [at the funeral]. Only a few non-commissioned officers and individuals who observed. It rained and snowed.

March 3. Finally for the first time this year we have weather that makes us feel good. A new regulation states that in future we must wake up around 6:30 a.m. The new commander inspected our compound. The government appears to be rather short on money because now they also wish to establish a ten shillings camp. [121] In this sad region and ask if any [internee] would like to apply for it Naturally, almost no one applied.

March 4. Today the commander's proceedings took place because the doctor complained that our representatives at Cazzini's coroner's inquiry had made inappropriate remarks about the circumstances in the hospital. The doctor wanted our representatives to receive a harsh punishment. . .[and] should have known better than to make false statements [regarding his handling of Cazzini's treatment]. Both sides had their witnesses, and the charges against the doctor were dropped. The whole business left much to be desired. Unfortunately, one can't depend on the officials. . . . The old commander probably sentenced our representatives to six months [imprisonment].

March 5. Today in our compound there was a huge disturbance and the guards had to be called in. Now the kitchen sells coffee at ½ pence per cup in the afternoon. This evening a dance took place in the entertainment hall.

March 7. Today the commandant . . . sentenced the wrongdoers to three days arrest and transferred them to another compound.

March 9. An internee, who worked outside of the camp and brought in two flasks of whisky, was sentenced to fifty-six days imprisonment. Another internee, who threatened one of his friends with a knife, was sentenced to eighty-four days imprisonment.

March 10. In the last several days a friend of mine, who is an expert on sewing machines, has been summoned to the commander, who informed him that the

[121] These were camps geared to wealthier inmates who would pay ten shillings a week for superior amenities.

authorities believe it would be worthwhile to construct one of their own to produce underwear, socks, woolen jackets and the like.

March 12. The weather leaves much to be desired. One day we have wind, hail and rain and the next, beautiful sunshine.

March 13. It is strictly forbidden to write letters with violet-colored ink.

March 15. This evening we enjoyed two concerts with two string orchestras.

March 16. Our singing association was disbanded because our choir director is unable to receive a pass.

March 17. Camp 4 trade school's executive committee gave notice that there will be a big trade exhibition March 27-31.

March 19. From today onwards the kitchen will be able to purchase sausage.

March 20. The canteen will be moving to the main street in the camp.

March 22. The exhibitors were requested to appear before the trade school's executive committee.

This evening we had a really good theater presentation of Ibsen's *Ghosts* [*sic*].[122]

March 23. The government seeks internees who are familiar with trees and the transportation of wood and promises them a minimum wage of ten shillings per week but would prefer to offer them wages. Unfortunately, many internees came forward, although it means directly supporting our enemy!! Additionally, the internees know that the English are short on workers, that they put eleven year old school children to work, that wood is crucial for coal mines, that it is necessary for the production of field fortifications and despite this are willing to work for the English state for a few shillings. . . .

March 25. The weather is very changeable once again.

March 27. Today the commander, the various sub-commanders and various other officers opened the highly anticipated trade exhibition. . . . All of the officers supposedly expressed their great admiration. This afternoon the internees from compound 7 visited the exhibition, tomorrow compound 1 will follow and so on and so forth until all of the camp compounds have viewed the exhibition. Finally, the weather is good again and it seems that spring still wants to make its appearance.

March 30. Today it was our compound's turn to visit the exhibition. The entrance fee was two shillings per person. The internees who don't have any money or who don't want to pay for other reasons had to go in the morning when there was no concert. Still, everyone from each compound was given the opportunity to see the exhibition. The exhibition took place in compound 7 (in the dining room) under the direction of various individuals who run the trade school in the different compounds. . . .

[122] Written in 1881 by Norwegian playwright Henrik Ibsen.

The exhibition is really wonderful because every piece of handicraft that is displayed is made by the internees from primitive materials. On the whole, about eight hundred items were displayed and one can only marvel at how it is possible for these internees to create such beautiful things. . . . A portion of the exhibitors are willing to sell their items while the others [do so] for the enjoyment of the crowd. . . .

There are about two hundred thirty different wood working pieces like maps made from wood inserts, fret saws, pictures from various kinds of wood, closets, picture frames and the like; the prices vary from five shilling to about £5.

Furthermore two hundred different kinds of works made from bone in which everything possible is engraved are displayed. Also displayed are flower vases, lights, cigarette holders, ashtrays, brooches, inkpots, napkin holders, trunks, letter openers, condiment holders, etc. . . .

There were also about fifty models, for example, yachts, rowboats, battleships, passenger steamboats, sailboats, camping beds, camping enclosures, car motors, airplanes, etc. Also included were approximately two hundred types of painting—oil, watercolor . . . [and] there were also toys. . . .

For entertainment . . . a string orchestra and a mandolin ensemble played every afternoon. The exhibition also offered a café with coffee and cakes served by female waitresses. . . .

April 1. The exhibition concludes today. This evening we had a nice theater performance.

April 3. This evening there was an inquiry about who would like to participate in one of the following sports during the summer: tennis, handball, cricket or golf. That means that an extra tract of land should be make available to us for sports.

April 6. A really tragic event happened today in compound 2. An informer, who reported everything going on in that compound to the sub-commander, was discovered. As a result, the internees beat him and appealed to the sub-commander to remove him from the compound and place him elsewhere. The sub-commander insisted that this informant remain in the compound. This afternoon he already snitched again and behaved terribly towards his fellow internees. They wanted to beat him again but this little devil bolted towards the guard, who was already rather excited because at that moment a fire alarm had rung throughout the entire camp, called the old [guard] for help and a damn sergeant had nothing more urgent to do but to fire [a shot] from his watch post. This lout got off three shots in which an internee, unfortunately, was badly wounded and two other lightly wounded, although they had absolutely nothing at all to do with the entire affair. The guard was so excited that . . . he managed to shoot through a window of the hut. The aforementioned badly wounded internee was injured with three shots. The shots were heard in almost every nearby compound and caused great excitement throughout the entire camp. A few minutes after the shooting the guard and the head commander, the sub-commander and various adjutants came to compound 2 in order to investigate the incident. The wounded were taken to the hospital immediately and the informer, who was guilty of all this, was transferred to camp 1.

April 7. Today we were led to a different meadow than usual; the new one is located about twenty minutes from our compound and the way to it is much nicer. . . .

April 8. Today four ill internees were released to Germany from our compound; from the entire camp about thirty.

April 9. This evening we had a big variety show put on by the theater association of compound 5. To our great joy it seems that the wounded have improved. On the fifth of this month an inquiry was made as to whether anyone wanted to transfer to the 10-shilling camp in Douglas. I believe that the internees are too sly to fall for this trick now. On the third of this month, notice was given that now, after *The Standard*, a newspaper that we had been allowed [to read] before was discontinued, we are able to order the following four newspapers: *Daily Mail, Manchester Guardian, Daily Mirror,* and *The Daily Chronicle.* Before it was strictly forbidden to have these newspapers. Our officials' orders change from day to day!!

April 10. Today for the first time we received the four aforementioned newspapers. As a result, there's somewhat more time . . . not only to read the conservative but also the liberal papers. The commander has offered compound 8's empty recreation area as a tennis court for our use.

April 12. Finally, we have been given the opportunity once again to stuff our straw mattresses with new [straw]. This is only the second time since we have been here, meaning since September 12, 1915. Those whose straw mattresses are totally torn will receive a new straw mattress.

April 13. Today the tennis site will be divided into seven courts, and each compound receives one court, unfortunately not enough. We have at least sixty players in our compound.

April 14. Today we began to tidy up our tennis courts. The entire area will be raked and trimmed, which will be a lot of work.

April 15. Today our tennis club had its first meeting. First we had hope the government will provide us with nets, balls, tennis rackets, etc. free of charge. Today, however, we were informed that this would not be the case; rather, we all would have to order them for ourselves. For internees, who don't own any rackets, balls or shoes, this is an expensive pastime and, as a result, about thirty internees left the club. Our costs for nets alone will be about two shilling six pence, and this amount will be collected from a club entrance fee.

April 16. The theater society of our own compound put on its premiere with individual one act performances with great success.

April 18/19. Jewish Easter.[123] No prayer service, despite the sub-commander's promise.

[123] Passover

April 20. During this morning's walk to the new meadow an internee from our compound escaped; one hour later he was arrested in Peel.

April 22. A large number of Austrians, Croats, Serbs, Poles and Alsatians were transferred to another camp in England, the Friendly Aliens Camp.

April 23. Easter Sunday. . . . Tonight we have services.

April 24. Easter Monday

April 25. A few older internees were transferred to Camp "Library Hall" in England. Heard about the situation in Ireland,[124] something that brought us great joy.

April 26. Summer finally made its entrance and once again today we were able to go outside.. . . .

April 27. Finally the American representative will visit us again. He hasn't been here since four weeks prior to Christmas. The representatives of our compound have drawn up a sharp letter that should be distributed among the internees and in which the sad conditions of the camp and the families of the internees in England will be detailed.

Now that it's known that the American representative will come tomorrow the authorities finally feel compelled to provide the internees with wood for the stoves in their huts, although we begged for that dozens of times before and had every package removed. In addition, we learned that for months now the censor had removed every package that came for us, even in our presence.

April 28. Despite his promises, the American representative did not come today. We heard that in an adjoining compound an English and an Irish soldier who were guards came to blows over the Irish Revolution.

April 29. Today in compound 2 a springtime gymnastics competition was held in which the gymnasts of compound 2 did not distinguish themselves.

May 1. Today is a fabulously beautiful May day. Finally the American representative confirmed his long promised visit and, in fact, three men from the American embassy were here today.[125] They maintained that they can't do anything for us, that they passed along our complaints to the German Government and that they relayed the instructions they received from Germany with regard to their report, to the English Government. . . . With immense anticipation we look forward to the great things that have been promised us over the course of this month.

May 3. Once again gales, rain and cold greet us for a change.

[124] Reference to the Easter Rising on April 24, 1916, in which Irish nationalists launched an armed rebellion against British rule.

[125] The report by Leland Littlefield, Boylston Boyd, and W. H. Buckler on their visit was printed in *Reports of Visits of Inspection Made by Officials of the United States Embassy to Various Internment Camps in the United Kingdom* (Parliamentary Papers, September 1916, Cd. 8324). The embassy officials noted "no complaints of a serious nature."

May 4. I've been summoned to the doctor with regard to my eventual discharge!! Oh, how happy I would be if I could leave the barbed wire behind one day!

May 7. We had a theater performance today of *Hans Huckebein!*[126]

May 8. We're still stuck in the rainy season. Unfortunately, there's still nothing this month about the war's progression.

May 10. There's an attempt to form a cricket club. . . . A doctor from the Home Office came to our camp today to examine those internees who might be part of the next exchange with Germany.

May 11. A number of internees were transferred today to the so-called Friendly Aliens' Camp in England; these internees were either Alsatians or Schleswig-Holsteiners.[127]

May 12. Tobacco and cigars that were promised to us for Christmas by the Dr. Lowry Committee (a friendly-inclined English committee) were finally distributed today. Most internees received about ten cigarettes or some tobacco.

May 13. In addition, today we received from the Dr. Lowry Committee more items promised us at Christmas such as brushes, sewing kits, suspenders, toothbrushes, etc.

May 16. Internees, who wear women's clothing for theater performances, will not be allowed to be photographed in these in future. Also, no photographs of internees wearing women's clothing will be permitted to be mailed [abroad].[128]

May 17. Finally we have proper summer weather; the heat is overpowering.

May 18. We have been informed that from May 21 until June 4 a soccer world cup between all of the compounds of camp 4 will be held. On the 16th of this month our own compound's theater association put on its second performance with *Der Herr Senator*[129] that received huge applause.

May 21. Today the so-called Summertime Daylight Savings Bill in England and Ireland took effect in our camp as well; as a result, the clock was advanced early this morning from 2:00 a.m. to 3:00 a.m. The good news from the Italian warfront brought us great joy.

[126] a children's story written in 1867 by Wilhelm Busch

[127] Alsace had been French before 1871 and Schleswig generally Danish up to 1864.

[128] Without women in the camp to fill female roles, men obviously were required as substitutes. However, fear of homosexuality spreading within the camps likely prompted the order barring photos of gender role reversal. Panayi, *Prisoners of Britain*, 149–54; Jennifer Kewley Draskau. "Prisoners in Petticoats: Drag Performances in Great War Internment Camps," *Proceedings of the Isle of Man Natural History and Antiquarian Society* 12, no. 2 (2007–2009): 187–204. For comparison, see Alon Rachamimov, "The Disruptive Comforts of Drag: (Trans)Gender Performances among Prisoners of War in Russia, 1914-1920," *American Historical Review* 111 (2006): 362–82.

[129] In English, *Mr. Senator,* a novella written in 1890 by German writer and poet Wilhelm Jensen

May 23. This evening we had a variety show by the theater association of compound 2. We are still hard at work on restoring our tennis courts.

May 24. Summer seems to have ended already because today we endured terrible wind and rain.

May 25. The weather has improved again. Our complaints that many packages haven't arrived recently have been dismissed, as has been the case frequently. This evening Professor Albers gave a lecture on Walter von der Vogelweide.[130]

May 28. Today we had a promenade concert by the Schwarz band.

June 1. Unfortunately, once again, two internees were sentenced to eighty-four days stockade for attempting to escape while working outside the camp.

June 2. Lecture by an engineer about explosives.

June 3. Everyone is very cheerful today because we received the excellent news about the sea victory at Jutland.[131]

June 4. Performance by our theater association; one internee is sentenced to fourteen days stockade for impudence towards the commander.

Late in the evening on May 31 our postmaster, a very upstanding individual, was given an order to pack his bags because he would be transferred the next morning to a camp on the continent. Why the authorities would suddenly dismiss this fellow, who protected our stuff so well, and treat him like a child, no one knows. Apparently, the Central Committee planned it with the commander because the very same evening camp 3's main postal office was transferred to compound 1, where the Central Committee resides.

June 6. This afternoon I had the opportunity to inaugurate our tennis courts. Dr. Markel was so kind to give us four rackets and one net. Everything else we have to provide ourselves. This afternoon we received the good news that Lord Kitchener, the English War Minister, drowned.

June 7. The newspapers confirmed that Kitchener really died. North of Scotland the tides of the sea gobbled him and the cruiser *Hampshire* up as he was traveling to Russia. The English have lost an important person and we, even happier, a keen opponent. We internees are particularly pleased that Kitchener is dead because he was the one most responsible for having civilians incarcerated.

June 8. For the first time today we returned to the meadow. This evening we received radishes from Dr. Nottbey and the garden club for dinner. This evening a big celebration was held in honor of the birthday of our Head Captain, Landers.

June 9. Today about one hundred internees were released to England. It appears that these were required by the government to work in a machine factory.

[130] celebrated twelfth-century German poet
[131] Although the German fleet sank more ships than it lost, the battle was in effect a draw and the Royal Navy retained its command of the sea.

June 10. In Compound 6 a few Germans and Austrians got into a brawl because of the Austrian retreat.[132] One of today's soccer league matches was played so roughly that it caused a huge dispute. . . .

June 11. Today is the first Whitsun holiday.[133] Unfortunately, there's nothing special in the camp to celebrate the holiday, yet our kitchen committee served us an excellent meal. For dinner the canteen gave every internee a small bit of meat free of charge.

June 12. Today it's very stormy once again.

June 13. Two Galicians who are teachers were transferred to the "Friendly Aliens Camp" in England. . . .

June 14. Unfortunately, from now on we receive tinned meat twice per week. Thankfully, we haven't gotten mutton anymore for some months now.

June 15. In order to be released, all Germans who are over fifty-five years old, must provide their names, how, where, and when they were arrested, and where their wives reside and the nationality of [their wives].

June 16. From now on we Jews will have prayer services every Friday night and Saturday.

June 20. Yet again the hut captain was summoned urgently to the sub commander [and reminded] that playing for money is not allowed under any circumstances. . . .

June 23. The commander-in-chief . . . finally came again to inspect our compound.

June 25. The sub-commander circulated a letter in which he requested that in future internees should consult the doctor and not him with their medical issues. If internees don't feel well, they should go directly to the hospital and have themselves examined [instead of] lying around a few days in the huts in their compound. Luckily, it appears that the Russian offensive has been staved off.

July 3. Today we heard that the English and French have launched their long awaited decisive offensive.[134] According to reports, our side gave them quite a reception!! Hopefully, this time our enemies will bleed to death!

It was also reported that in future we will get a hill on another playing field that will belong exclusively to our compound.

July 6. I have the feeling that this time again the English and French won't be coordinated but unfortunately the Russians keep plowing ahead.

[132] Reference to the Brusilov offensive in which Austrian forces were forced to retreat by Russian troops from June 8, 1916, onward.

[133] Name used in the United Kingdom for the festival of Pentecost, the seventh Sunday following Easter.

[134] Reference to the Battle of the Somme that began on July 1, 1916.

This evening one thousand internees arrived here from the Stobs camp[135] in Scotland. All civil internee camps in England are supposed to make room for a few thousand actual prisoners of war.

July 7. The Stobs internees, of which about one hundred are in our compound, left Stobs early yesterday morning (July 6) and arrived here this evening around 10 p.m. Until they went to bed, however, it was about 3 a.m. this morning.

July 8. For three days now we have endured uninterrupted rain and wind!

July 9. Today our head captain had a sharp exchange with the sub-commander and he wanted to resign his post but he conceded to him.

July 11. Herr Raff, who in early June was moved to Stobs as punishment, and who arrived here [the other day] with the Stobs internees, [now] was transferred to Douglas.

July 13. On a placard that's hanging [is written] that a man, who had over £5 of cash in his pocket, was sentenced to four days punitive labor.

July 14. Today more internees were released to Germany and Austria, among them was Herr von Riszha, whose ship was seized before the war's outbreak.

July 17. Today we had a theater performance. Finally, summer has arrived here!!

July 18. I heard that many internees, who agreed to be transferred to the "Friendly Aliens Camp," have returned here; what they had been promised [originally] by the English officials did not transpire!!

July 19. A poster from the "Aliens Aid Society" is hanging [that says] the German Government will allow civil internees to engage in work as long as it is not for war-related purposes and provided that the workers receive full compensation in accordance with the standard of living!!

July 21. Letters no longer arrived already opened but rather remain sealed!. . .

July 23. Today there was a large gymnastics festival in the compound and all of our performances received praise!

July 24. Our head captain Landers resigned today; a new head captain will not be chosen!. . .

July 25. Today a bowling [skittles] alley was opened in our compound. It's an idea the Stobs internees brought with them.

July 26. Various internees [from Stobs] . . . were transferred from here to Wakefield; they had to pay about £1.14.0 for their transfer.

[135] Scottish military camp, located near Hawick in southeastern Scotland, that held both civilian and military internees from November 1914 until July 1916, at which time the former were transferred to Knockaloe.

July 27. Today in the presence of the sub-commander was the official opening of the various tennis courts. At the same time a competition between the various compounds took place in which compound five claimed victory. By and large, the competition wasn't a particular success because it was poorly organized by Herr French.

July 28. From August 1 onwards we will be able to walk about daily on the hill in back of our camp. For a few days already there is no margarine to purchase.

July 29. According to a poster, a small garden exhibition will be held at the end of August.

July 31. Herr Heer, who a few weeks ago went from camp #10 to Douglas, received notice at 10:30 this morning that he was to gather all his belongings to await a transfer. . . .

August 2. Today the field that has been promised to us for some time [and] that lies on the hill behind our camp will be opened for daily walks. We are allowed to go there three times daily and without guards, which is very pleasant. The hut captains are responsible for keeping order. For the first few days only four hundred and fifty internees can go on each walk; later, however, this arrangement will be improved once the [initial] rush has subsided.

August 3. This evening we had very pleasant entertainment that was arranged by the gymnasts for the benefit of our Gymnastics Association. The event was well-attended and the result satisfactory.

Once again the canteen has raised the price of food.

The American representative has been here for a few days. Today he visited our (No. 4) camp, but he didn't visit the individual compounds because the other internees didn't want to see him. Each compound sent representatives to him in the sub-commander's office and those individuals made it clear to him that we are absolutely not satisfied with his representation of our interests. A sharp exchange between him and our representatives followed.

Early this morning our camp was covered in very dense fog that reminded us of last winter's terribly damp days.

August 6. In future a flag at the sub commander's office will be displayed if and when we have outdoor exercise. For us the new path to the hill is a very pleasant change.

August 7. A plot was hatched whereby all those internees, whose wives live in London, would report to the sub-commander, provided that they would be transferred to Alexander [*sic*] Palace Camp[136] in London. The fundamental principle is that their wives are of English or allied origin and that the internees pay thirty shilling for transport costs. Likewise even those who are unable to pay the thirty shillings should be able to report.

This evening we had a very nice theater production entitled *Im Klub-Sessel* [The Lounge Chair].

[136] Alexandra Palace, in north London

August 8. Yesterday Herr Nanschütz, the former Head Captain of our compound who was transferred to camp No. 3 [and then] to the Douglas Camp where he spent the last three months, returned [to Knockaloe]. First he was [sent] for further observation in our camp's [no. 4] hospital. He appears to be completely normal once again. . . .

August 9. Once again today some internees were transferred to the ten-shilling Wakefield camp.[137] Each of the [transferees] must pay £2.10.0 for transportation and guard costs.

August 10. Early this morning in our camp there was a big fight [after] an internee stole money. The actual perpetrator has not been found yet.

All Jews who want to be transferred to the to the Jewish camp in Douglas should report tomorrow to the sub commander.

With regard to the lack of water as a result of the dry weather the washrooms and bathrooms will be closed from 6:00 p.m. onwards. Water then is only available . . . in the courtyard.

August 11. One of my friends from the Stobs camp injured his leg today on the hill and had to be carried from there to the hospital.

Pastor Göring from London, who has visited the camp several times, was here again today and gave us a very nice general lecture. He couldn't say if we would be released. . . .

Today our Gymnastic Association bought another nice apparatus, namely a huge springboard. . . .

August 13. Today we had a really heavy rainfall. This was really necessary because in the last few days it's been very dusty. On the whole, the weather of the last four weeks has been nice.

August 14. As a consequence of the visit of a Rabbi from Liverpool,[138] who was here for a few minutes a few weeks ago (it's worth mentioning that this was the first visit from the Jewish 'side' to us here), created a list on which all Jews requiring assistance can write [their names]. Then the Liverpool community will determine what assistance they can provide these individuals. . . .

The administration, which yesterday searched in vain for a missing internee, believes that he has hidden in the camp somewhere.

August 15. Today we had a festival that consisted of a gymnastics display. The first was held this morning in which nearly ninety internees participated; the last one was this afternoon in which about three hundred fifty internees participated or

[137] Located in Lofthouse Park, near Wakefield, this internment camp held about 500 prisoners, who paid ten shillings per week for their "lodgings."

[138] About 11,000 Jews resided in Liverpool in 1911. Some of the non-naturalized Germans, Austrians, Romanians, and Turks of Jewish descent were shipped to the Isle of Man for internment. The Liverpool Jewish Board of Guardians provided food to Jewish internees and pressured for their release.

about twelve and fifty respectively came from each of the seven compounds of our camp. The festival was held on the hill and went very well.

August 16. It's been said that all of the internees of camp no. 2 who are over forty-five years old were supposed to report to the doctor with regard to their discharge.

The missing internee, who stupidly and for reasons unknown to himself hid, was found today underneath the kitchen on compound 5. That internee really deserves to be beat up because he didn't do anything good for himself and only brought unpleasantness for us.

August 17. The days have shortened noticeably and now it gets dark already by 8:30.

August 18. This evening we celebrated the birthday of Kaiser Franz Josef.

August 20. Soon there will be a tennis tournament with the seven tennis clubs of our camp.

August 22. After having been here nearly an entire year, the sides of the wooden huts finally will be tarred.

Also finally we will be allowed to read the local afternoon newspaper (*Isle of Man Daily Times*) [which] we read yesterday for the first time.

August 24. This evening we had a very nice theater performance, *Die blaue Maus* [The Blue Mouse].

August 25. Yesterday evening shortly after 10:30, after the lights had been turned off, a non-commissioned officer came around to tell us that there would be another head count. A quarter of an hour later the light was turned off again without us having been counted; it turns out that this non-commissioned officer was drunk. . . .

August 29. Our fears yesterday were justified and today we already are reading the serious news that Romania has declared war on Austria. How much longer will this war go on!!

Our camp school, which was closed the last two months for vacation, was opened again today.

On August 26 of this month there was a garden exhibition. Whether our compound will receive a prize is still unknown.

A letter of August 16 by the American representative was posted in which he referred to the grievances we submitted during his last visit and remarked that they were submitted to competent authorities. At the same time, however, the American representative told us that it would be better for us to bring our grievances directly to the commander himself [because] he is really the person who can do the most for us.

An internee was sentenced to ninety-six hour arrest because of gambling. This punishment, however, is much too lenient. . . .

August 30. In the course of the next few months Olympic games will be held within the entire camp.

Unfortunately, the anticipated tennis tournament was not played owing to disunity.

Our compound received three prizes in the garden exhibition. . . .

August 31. This evening we had a variety show.

September 1. The prices in the canteen have risen yet again. Marmalade costs 8 pence, cheese 7 pence. A year ago they were 5 pence and 5 ½ pence.

Dr. Taylor from the American embassy was here a few days ago in camp to check on our provisions. Naturally, he didn't give his opinion, yet at the very least he stated that we don't get enough vegetables ... and that the kitchen should be in better condition. In any case, he is absolutely not satisfied with the conditions here. He also said that of all the military prisons that he has visited in England, this one [Knockaloe] is the worst.

September 2. For every ten men at a table only one gets a napkin. Splendid conditions! In total, within the [last] twelve months the ten men at a table have received three napkins. . . .

September 4. This evening we had a large dinner. The authorities condescended, giving each internee a package of biscuits and one can of meat. In any case, it happened at the behest of Dr. Taylor.

September 6. A poster appeared that said that places were vacant for the ten-shilling camp in Wakefield and that those desiring to pay ten shilling a week should report to be transferred.

September 8. The authorities engage in such clever politics. After Romania entered the war, they wanted to buy off all Austrians and Hungarians in our compound by informing an internee, who represented Austrian interests, that all Austrian and Hungarians would be allowed to transfer to Camp No. 1 and enjoy special preferences. The entire preferences consisted of the [fact that] internees would be allowed to go to the field without guard supervision the entire day in camp 1 (that is surrounded by two rows of barbed wire). The internees did not fall for this bluff and [decided to] remain where they had lived before.

September 10. Today we received extra bread at dinner [as well as] fish and biscuits.

September 11. Our theater association satisfied us this evening with a very good performance from S'dom and Gemorrah. . . .

September 12. Today is a year since we were transported to this sad island. It's been twelve long, difficult months and still there is no end in sight to this terrible war.

September 13. The authorities ask around for internees who make [boatswains'] whistles.[139] Apparently, [the English] are also short of skilled workers.

September 14. Today two internees were punished; the one who tried to escape to six months prison confinement and the other, who hid under the kitchen of compound 5, to nine months imprisonment.

[139] Small high-pitched pipe or whistle used on naval ships to pass commands to the crew and indicate the arrival of officers.

About three hundred internees, whose wives live in London, were transferred today to Alexander [*sic*] Palace Camp in London and three hundred unmarried internees [were transported] here.

September 15. Because of insubordination an internee was sentenced to ten days arrest.

Unfortunately, the Olympic games had to be cancelled owing to lack of participation.

Today two internees were transferred to the Friendly Aliens Camp in England; the one was a Galician, the other from Schleswig-Holstein.

September 17. During a fight in camp No. 2 an internee was killed, unfortunately.

September 20. This evening we had the best entertainment evening we've had in months; the united string orchestra of the entire camp gave us a marvelous concert.

September 21. A young fellow, who was in a lot of debt in our compound and whose creditors were pressing him hard, didn't return to the compound tonight and instead hid himself on the field. The soldiers found him around 9:00 p.m. this evening. The fellow was fearful that he would be beaten up in the compound.

September 22. From now on we are only allowed to be on the field between 10:00 a.m. and noon and 2:00 and 4:00 in the afternoon. . . .

September 23. Our gymnastics association was founded a year ago and this evening we had a small celebration.

September 24. Winter made its entrance today. It's terribly stormy and cold outside.

A London company brought back to London those internees who had worked for it before [the war].

The new soccer field on the hill ... was opened today. Our compound's Education Association offered a lecture this evening on popular astronomy. This association differentiates itself from the Literary Association, which consists of members from the seven compounds of our camp (No. 4) and has its weekly meetings in compound 7, and in which very good lectures are also given. ...

September 26. Last evening five hundred internees arrived from Alexander [*sic*] Palace Camp, London, and early this morning some five hundred married internees, whose wives reside in London and who paid thirty shillings, were transferred to London. Also at the same time a few young internees were released to Germany.

On the 21st of this month a representative of Liverpool's Jewish community was here in order to bring us a few prayer books and clothing. Why this fellow actual came here I don't know, because he had absolutely no time [to spend with us], was very hungry, and only saw one or two internees.

September 28. We had a theater performance today. . . . The weather has improved a little bit. . . .

October 1. Early today as a result of the changeover to Greenwich time we could linger an hour longer in bed. This evening was really too long. ... Unfortunately now the longer nights have returned because at 6:00 p.m. the lights have to be turned on and the light is hardly good enough for reading, playing chess, cards and the like.

Today we had a big singing festival on the meadow in which all of the singing associations of our camp (No. 4) as well as the united orchestras of our camp participated. The number of singers was about three hundred internees. In the morning a sing-off between the individual compounds and in the afternoon a general singing festival took place. Compounds 5 and 3 took first place. There were lots of onlookers from our camps. In the afternoon our sub commander, the head commander with his adjutants and a few civilians also attended the festival in the afternoon. The weather was really cold and windy but despite that everyone had a very pleasant time.

October 2. It turns out that the civilians with the head commander at the festival were from the War Office. Early yesterday we received coal for the first time again. . . . In contrast to last year this year [we are given] wood for fire. It [the wood] consists of old chairs, tables, beds and the like. But they don't provide a small hand tool for cutting them into small pieces.

October 3. It's raining and a terrible wind blows. Every table receives an additional napkin. . . .

October 4. All Croats, Slavs, Czechs, Romanians, Italian, Poles, Alsatians and the like are supposed to provide their names to the commander. . . .

October 5. An internee who attempted to escape was sentenced to 180 days in prison.

The weather, which was much better yesterday, is horrible once again. In future, we will have to deal with "April weather.". . .

October 8. We've all become accustomed to the old time.[140] The difference was really only noticeable on the first day. An acquaintance, who was supposed to have been transferred a few months ago but instead was detained in London because he wasn't sick enough—in reality he was deathly ill—will finally be sent home [to Germany] in a few weeks. There's supposed to be another chess tournament over the course of the next few weeks. . . .

October 10. This evening there was an escape attempt in hut 2a. The internee . . . attempted to dig a hole in the wooden floor of the hut in order to break into the box of an internee who reportedly had quite a bit of money. The noise was heard in the hut, two internees stood up in order to see what was happening. Unfortunately, the thief promptly escaped. Over the course of several days the thief was apprehended. The incident was reported by the sergeant to the sub commander.

October 11. It turns out that more internees were involved in the attempted break out. This band of thieves also wanted to break into the kitchen and, as a result, barbed wire was placed around it. . . .

[140] Reference to Daylight Savings Time, adopted in April 1916, mandating that clocks be moved forward. The idea was to save energy by taking advantage of more sunlight.

October 12. Various internees, who presumably belonged to the theft ring, were transferred to another compound. On October 9 the first issue appeared of the "Knockaloe Camp Newspaper" but it didn't receive a great reception. The newspaper can also be sent to Germany. One article provoked considerable anger because it said that we receive so many vegetables that we can hardly eat them all. The truth is that . . . we get a pitifully small amount of vegetables . . . and that we have to pay a lot for them.

October 14. This evening we had a lecture on Kantian philosophy.

October 16. Four [members] of the theft ring were sentenced yesterday—one to fourteen days and the other three to seven days imprisonment. They say that they got off lightly because a few of them are "friendly aliens," that means Czechs and the like. During the course of the proceedings it was revealed that the internee who [the theft ring] wanted to rob possessed quite a bit of money but presented himself to the authorities as destitute. [As a result] the government presented him with a bill for about £5 for clothing, boots, wash, . . .

During the first few weeks of this month there was lots of excitement in camp no. 3. A few internees, who were about to construct a tunnel, ran away and a few hut captains were seized. New hut captains will be elected, and in regard to this there was a huge quarrel that was viewed by the authorities as a kind of provocation. As a result, the following proclamation was posted on the tenth of this month to all compounds of the four camps:

Proclamation

It has been brought to my notice that it is the intention of some interned aliens to combine together to defy authority and to commit acts of insubordination. They are hereby warned that any combined acts as aforesaid constitute an "offence" of mutiny, which renders those engaged in it liable to be fired on by the troops.

Any person caught persuading or inciting others to commit such acts, or coming to the knowledge of the intention to commit such an act, and failing to report it, will be tried by court martial, and liable to be shot or to suffer penal servitude for life.

Signed: Panzera Lt. Col., Commander

October 22. The weather has been nice the last two to three days. We played tennis for a few hours.

October 23. Today it's stormy again outside. We've heard that the internees, who were released to Germany, always had difficulties with their baggage. [They] asked the Aid Committee of the American Embassy what they should really bring with them. Yesterday the answer was given to us. They gave a few hints.

An internee was transferred to Douglas in the tenth camp, although actually he wanted to go to Wakefield. Late this evening it was noted that now all the internees who for months were supposed to be transferred to Wakefield's Camp 10 would [be transferred] the day after tomorrow. In total, there are forty-eight.

October 25. As a theater performance tonight we had the detective piece, *The Hound of the Baskervilles*.[141]

October 26. Finally it was officially noted (and indeed in the newspaper) that a definitive agreement has been reached in which all internees over the age of forty-five will be sent [to Germany]. What joy this must be for the older internees! Should we have to endure this sad and spiritually draining, inhumane imprisonment much longer?

October 29. Spent my third birthday in captivity.

October 3. Once again today a few invalids were released to Germany. When the over forty-five year olds will be released is still not known. We've had uninterrupted rain and win for the last week.

October 31. A notice appearing stating that because of busy local travel that no packages will be sent from Germany to here between December 10 and 25th.

[There are no surviving diary entries from November 1 until May 7.]

1917

May 7. Recently, many internees, who wish to be supported financially, have directed lots of inquiries to the Swiss Embassy. Now [the Embassy] has replied that Germany will pay ten shillings per month to the indigent, provided that these individuals can prove that they are German. Internees, who have been away from Germany more than ten years and are not in possession of new passports, will not receive support. This statute has aroused bad blood within the camp.

May 8. The representative from the Swiss Embassy, who is here at the moment, was supposed to visit our compound today but he didn't come.

May 10. A few days ago, internees, who had resided for some time in Argentina [before the war], received gift packages from Germans in Argentina [that included] coffee, sugar, cigarettes, cigars and some milk. This brought these internees great happiness because they could really use it. Today's theater was the new comedy, *Der Bursche des Herrn Oberst* [The Colonel's Boy] that was well received.

May 11. The Swiss representative has still not visited our part of the camp. In general, his whereabouts remain a colossal secret.

May 12. Finally, the Swiss representative came to our camp. Our representatives had a long meeting with him and brought him our grievances. The fellow made a very favorable impression on our representatives, even though he warned them not to be overly optimistic.

May 13. Today we had terrible weather again: cold, wind and rain. The second concert cycle began this evening.

[141] First serialized in *The Strand* magazine in 1901–02 and penned by Sir Arthur Conan Doyle.

May 14. Instead of an ounce of margarine, now we receive only ½ ounce of margarine and ¾ ounce of jam per day. Once again this has worsened! In future, any internee who requests new underwear must turn in his old ones.

In order to increase its income, our kitchen bought a skittles alley today. . . . This generates about £2.0.0 of profit.

May 15. The smoking of herring by a few internees has been forbidden from today onwards. All herring must be brought to the kitchen for smoking. Today the Swiss representative visited the individual compounds of the camp. He stayed only a short time so that he could visit all the compounds. He was very decent and listened attentively and seriously to everyone who had something to tell him.

May 16. The administration demands that we use water sparingly.

Today our representatives posted a very thorough report of their detailed discussions with the Swiss representative (Dr. Fischer) [*sic*].[142] The following points received serious consideration: 1) The small and terrible food rations; 2) the lack of supplies in the canteen, the administration of the canteen, the lack of inspection of the books; 3) lack of kitchen implements; 4) lack of blankets and brooms; 5) the reduction in and poor transportation of packages from England; 6) the poor transportation of packages from Germany; 7) the exchange of the sick and over forty-five year olds; 8) reduced news about the condition of those who wish to work in England; 9) our wish to view in the original all of German Government's decrees that concern us; 10) the poor management by the Isle of Man Government; 11) finances; where is the interest on our money in the camp bank? 12) clarification on the official German Government's assistance.

The representative promises to do his best for us; still he doubts that he himself can achieve much. He clearly indicated that really only the German Government could improve our situation in that it could force the English Government [to do so].

May 17. Tonight's theater performance was *The Thief.*

May 20. Today the third concert cycle took place.

May 22. Eighty men from our compound were sent to England today to work. They receive 5 ½ pence per hour. It's believed the internees go to Winchester.

Gradually, we are getting fed up with the daily herring and rice allotment. By and large, we live in part like the Russians who always eat herring and in part like the Chinese, who continually eat rice!! The weather has finally improved a bit.

May 24. This evening's theater performance was *The Handsome Theodore.* At the moment there is an active German officer in camp. He was on a special mission in Spain but unfortunately was captured on his return [trip to Germany]. Understandably, he was in civilian clothing. Now, however, he wears his uniform

[142] Dr. A. L. Vischer, a Swiss physician, visited various internment and prisoner-of-war camps in England and Germany, compiling information on the physical and mental impact of imprisonment for the book he published in 1919, *Barbed-Wire Disease.*

because he will be transferred to an officer's camp. Many internees saw him in his field gray uniform for the first time, along with his iron cross!!

A representative of the Swedish Delegation, who represents the interests of the Austrian internees, was here briefly. He received complaints similar to those that we brought before the Swiss representative. Likewise, he finds the conditions in our camp to be terrible and promises to do the best he can for us.

May 26. Our rations are so small that many internees have slaughtered dogs and cats. An internee went so far as to slaughter the Adjutant's dog. That internee will be called before the courts because of his theft [of the dog]. Recently a number of internees broke into the camp's warehouse and stole food, some tobacco and cigarettes.

May 27. Today is Whitsuntide and Shavuot.[143] By and large, one hardly notices holidays. Only our kitchen tried to prepare enough food for us [to celebrate]. Unfortunately, this is the exception to the rule these days. This evening the fourth and last cycle of concerts took place. It was truly wonderful and is a shame that the cycle is finished.

May 28. Today, to support our kitchen's budget, there was skittles and a theater performance. It was a three-act play that was very well performed.

May 29. Those internees, who have the luxury of owning dogs, now must pay a dog tax! Our margarine ration, that used to be one ounce, has been scandalously reduced to ½ ounce of margarine daily and instead of ½ ounce, ¾ ounce of marmalade or jam, meaning that we don't get any fat [in our diets].

May 30. Since the beginning of March, when our rations were so shamelessly reduced, we've had very little sporting activities. No one thinks about gymnastics anymore because the internees don't feel strong enough [to participate]; the only sport that remains is tennis that about twenty-five internees per compound or 800 internees play; the game has not been played energetically for some time now. In order to increase its revenue, our kitchen purchased the skittles board from its former owner for £2.10.0.

June 1. Once again a change in our daily ration will be proposed and, as a result, our daily ration of five ounces of herring will be dropped and instead two ounces of vegetables are promised; should this not happen, then an additional ounce of rice. We don't get cabbage anymore either.

June 2. At present, our school is up in the air because the teacher could not come to an agreement with the school.

June 4. The head commandant, who inspected our camp (no. 4) this morning, suffered a heart attack suddenly and died on the spot. He was Lieutenant Colonel Panzera. A new committee was formed for our school.

June 5. Once again today fifteen internees were released to work in England. On the other hand, internees, who were released a few months ago, return almost daily

[143] Jewish holiday celebrating the giving of the Torah to the Israelites

to the camp. They say that their treatment was nearly unbearable and that they were treated like slaves. . . .

June 6. Packages from America that many internees had depended on no longer arrive. It appears the censor is prohibiting our letters, in which we complained about the reduction of our rations, from being sent to America. . . .

June 7. Today our theater association from our compound put on *Johannesfeier.* All the actors did a good job and [the play] met with colossal success.

June 8. Our meals consist by and large only of the following:

> Mornings: three ounces of oatmeal cooked like grits; one ounce of marmalade or syrup and one cup of tea or coffee.
> Afternoons: rice soup, six ounces of fresh meat three days a week or three ounces of tinned meat twice weekly or ten ounces of herring and one ration (three ounces) of rice; one cup of tea or coffee.
> Evenings: one ration (about three ounces) of rice.

In addition, each day we received eight ounces (about ½ lb) of bread, always on Sunday afternoons some rice or oatmeal, pudding of some sort of substance that was left over from the week.

It's clear that now we live like the Chinese because our rations consist largely only of rice!!

Finally, summer has arrived. The beets that were planted in compound 8 look very nice because they have sprung up from the earth. Some internees who planted the beets are in the fortuitous situation to [also] have radishes to harvest.

June 9. The administration gave notice today that now it is possible to sell each compound twenty hundredweight [a ton] of corn meal, three hundredweight [336 pounds] of oatmeal, two hundredweight [224 pounds] of cheese and two hundredweight of figs per month. The prices of these have become exorbitant and, therefore, we have to pay for the goods because we are hungry.

Here one can see the deceitfulness of the authorities. Earlier they said that our rations were reduced because they didn't have the necessary quality. Now, suddenly, they have these things and want to sell these items to us at exorbitant prices. But if we agree to this then we are the dummies again . . . our rations won't be increased and also we won't have the opportunity to buy anything!!! Therefore, we must buy everything that is offered to us.

June 10. Today begins the pre-games for our tennis tournament with four camps.

The marmalade that is delivered to us recently is of the worst possible quality. No merchant would dare to bring anything of that kind to market but it's just fine for the Huns!!

June 11. At present, a commission from London is here to examine the camp's administration! Hopefully, some improvements will be forthcoming!

June 12. Today another group of workers went to work in the fields. They leave from here at 7:30 a.m., travel by train about eleven miles, work in the fields, return evenings around 6 p.m. and receive a wage of 6 pence (50 pfennig), two two-ounce rolls (50 grams) and one ounce of cheese!!!

June 13. The first ration of corn meal was delivered to us yesterday. The kitchen baked 400 rolls from it per day. One roll weights 2 ½ ounces and costs one pence. That means a pound costs about 6 ½ pence. This is simply a ridiculous price but we eagerly buy the rolls because we are so hungry.

June 14. No more boots will be soled from the beginning of May. What a scandal! The claim is that a new system for soles is supposed to be introduced. Tonight the play *Triple Entente* was presented. It was a big failure!!

June 15. Finally the administration has come to the view that the marmalade is inedible and from now on we will get one ounce of margarine daily. Perhaps the reason for the change is our energetic complaints to the Swiss representatives last week. Above all, we complained about the terrible marmalade and that for the most part we are fed only rice!

We follow attentively the newspaper coverage of the situation in Russia, because we believe that only from there can peace . . . begin.

At the beginning of this month we received a note from the Swiss representatives concerning the financial support from Germany for the destitute. The conditions are those that were already [established] at the beginning of the previous months. Many internees are quite incensed that the allotment is so one-sided and because for the most part the money will fall into the wrong hands. Either everyone should receive something or no one. A number of internees claim support [and] many of them don't need it!!

June 17. Yesterday the House of Lords met once again to discuss the exchange of wounded prisoners of war, and it came to light that finally someone in our government decided that at the next meeting the release of forty-five year olds would be carried out. . . . This energetic decision was greatly welcomed by all!

June 19. Today the administration delivered turnips but our kitchen administration refused [them]. The impudence of these damn Englishmen!!

June 20. We consider yesterday's turnip delivery a bad omen. Today our theater put on *The Beaver Coat*[144]

June 22. The officers serving under the sub commander are supposed to have gone on strike because they don't want to inspect us any more. The sub commander and his adjutants had to undertake the inspection of all seven compounds themselves!!

June 24. Today we have another theater performance—*Willi's Marriage.*

[144] *Der Biberpelz* [The Beaver Coat] was a satirical play written by Gerhart Hauptmann in 1893.

June 25. The intra-camp tennis tournament (of the four camps within Knockaloe) started today. It was rather well attended. Two singles and two doubles pairs participated from each of the four camps.

June 27. Today we read to our great surprise and joy that at this time German and English delegations are engaged in direct meetings in The Hague [Dutch city] concerning prisoners. Nevertheless, no one is very optimistic as we have been endured too many disappointments. Still it's quite noteworthy that finally German and English politicians are meeting in person and in public.

June 29. Although the boot repair place isn't open yet, today a notice with prices appeared for internees, who have money in the bank, how much they would have to pay in future for boot soles: hand soled 5shilling/9pence and simply built 4 shilling/6pence; 1 shilling/9p.

June 30. Today was the last day for the tennis tournament. Both first prizes went to camp 2, both second prizes from our camp 4 and one from camp 3. A third prize also went to camp 2. No one from camp 1 received a prize. The tennis playing wasn't particularly good as is generally the case in tennis tournaments because [the players] play too cautiously. Nevertheless, the tournament was a welcome change of pace. The weather was downright glorious for the six afternoons. We were really very fortunate in that regard. Daily about one hundred internees from each of the three other camps came and one could meet acquaintances whom one hadn't seen in three years!. . .

July 2. Today's performance of *War and Peace* received enormous applause.

July 5. The Swiss delegation. . .requested a list of needy internees. . . .

July 7. We complained to the Swiss delegation that we still don't have any soles for our boots and that in the two years since we have been here we weren't given any boots with the exception of wooden ones and extremely miserable cloth ones with paper soles.

July 8. Whereas the weather for all of June was very nice, in July until now we have had only strong winds and the sand flies around like that in the Sahara desert!

July 9. Finally we have some sport once again and today a course in Swedish drill[145] will begin. Unfortunately, there's not much participation.

July 11. A poster informs us that from July 23 a new meal ration list will be in place and that finally we will get potatoes again. The [daily] specifics are as follows:

Bread 8 ounces per day
Flour ¾ ounces
Meat 6 or 3 ounces five days a week
Herring 10 ounces two days a week instead of meat
Margarine 1 ounce

[145] a form of physical education developed by Charlotte Mason, a British educator

Tea or 3/8 ounces
Coffee ¾ ounces
Sugar 1 ounce
Milk 1/20 portion of a 1 lb dose per day
Salt ½ ounce per day
Pepper 1/12 ounce
Oatmeal 3 ounces
Syrup or Marmalade 1 ounce
Beans or Peas 2 ounces (if not of reasonable quality, then rice)
Rice 3 ounces per day
Potatoes 4 ounces
Fresh vegetables/fruit 2 ounces (when this is not available then two ounces of potatoes or ½ ounce of rice)

July 12. Regarding our complaint that the water is so bad, we are told that we have the same water as does the civilian population of Peel.

July 13. Compound 1 performed a three-act play today. Once again we are inconvenienced with ½ ounce of margarine instead of a full ounce and ¾ ounce of miserable marmalade [made from] rhubarb!

July 14. The Austrian and Hungarian [internees] have complained to their Swedish representatives that they also want financial support and that [their cause] should be handled like the Germans in The Hague!! The representative reported today that he already has sent [this message] to Vienna. It's sad, however, that until now absolutely nothing definitive has come from the Hague discussions. One thing's for certain—it can't get any worse that it already is. We can only hope for improvement.

July 17. The beets that internees in this compound and especially compound 8 planted have really grown so that they are able to have vegetables.

July 18. The Swiss representative reports that he delivered our complaints about the lack of boots and soles to the British authorities.

July 20. The supposed meetings between the German and English representatives have still not been made public. The English Government has accepted already but Germany has yet to respond!!

July 21. Yesterday and today we received the splendid news from the Galician warfront. Hopefully, this time the Russians will be finished off.

July 24. Today we received the first potatoes we've eaten in four months. Although they were old, they still tasted good. It's scandalous that these Englishmen still give us old potatoes.

July 26. The new Head Commander, Major M. Smith, inspected us today. Fortunately, there aren't many old potatoes because they gave us only four pitiful ounces of them today.

July 27. Today we had a performance of the *Probe Kandidat* [On Probation].[146]

July 28. Once again they are looking for internees to work in England. They receive the usual poor pay.

July 29. Again today some Austrians went away to work. Nearly every week Austrians are released. Finally, the Hague meetings were made public today. Unfortunately until now only some extracts have been publicized yet what is known is that only a small portion of civilians are in favor of [the meetings]. Many were very disillusioned. . . .

July 30. Happily, a new menu has appeared which says that instead of the four ounces of potatoes allowed since the twenty-third of this month, we will receive six ounces from August 8. From then on workers will still receive two ounces of biscuits as well as four ounces of extra bread, in addition to the usual one ounce of cheese.

July 31. On the whole, the weather over the course of this month was beautiful once again. A week earlier the English member of Parliament Mr. Snowden[147] was the first in three years to ask why there have been so many complaints from the internees on the Isle of Man, especially those concerning the lack of food. The Government responded that we [the internees] receive sufficient [food]. Such lies!!!

August 1. Today begins the fourth year of war. Hopefully, it is the last!

A Jewish internee's burial took place today. . . . Although Jewish graves are separate from the Christians and we've asserted that we Jews will not allow ourselves to be buried in mass graves, as we brought the corpse to the cemetery we discovered sadly that, despite all assurances and promises, another deceased Jew had [already] been buried in the grave. What a scene! We . . . brought our complaints [about this] to the authorities immediately. They realized their big mistake, excused themselves and wanted to leave the coffin overnight in the cemetery until a new grave could be dug.[148] Naturally we couldn't allow that and proposed that the grave still be dug today. Unfortunately, there weren't any gravediggers around so a few of us decided to dig the grave. Thereupon most of us returned and in the afternoon the actual burial took place. . . .

August 4. A lot of internees were punished lately because they willfully cut their old clothes they received from the government in order to get new ones.

August 5. Many internees, especially ship crews, have been incarcerated for three full years!! What a long, sad time!

[146] A comedy written in 1899 by Max Dreyer, based on his experiences as a teacher in a German secondary school.

[147] 1st Viscount Phillip Snowden, former Liberal and later Independent Labour Party politician.

[148] Jewish tradition requires that the deceased be buried as soon as possible. Before the burial, a *shomer,* or watchman, remains with the body that is then washed and dressed in a white burial shroud and placed in a simple pine box.

August 6. The distribution of prizes for the Tennis tournament was supposed to be held in conjunction with a festival today. Unfortunately, the authorities wouldn't allow it.

August 7. Today we had heavy rain, the first in many weeks!!

August 8. Today we received an additional two ounces of potatoes so that in the future we will get six ounces daily.

August 9. Today we had a pleasant performance of *The Vicar of Kirchfeld.*[149] Soon a big inspection will take place. Because postal delivery is so abysmal, we complained today to the Swiss embassy. It's not rare for letters from Germany to take two or even three months to reach us. The fastest take six weeks!! Likewise, we've written to the Embassy because the ten-shilling subsidy that we were promised four months ago still hasn't arrived.

August 10. Thankfully, the food is better once again. We also receive quite a bit of fresh vegetables that are in addition to the rations and don't cost us anything. Also, we are able to purchase potatoes in considerable quantities from the available rations. While they cost about 6–7 shillings per ½ pound outside [of the camp], we have to pay 10 shillings.

August 11. For a week now we've had almost uninterrupted heavy rain. Aside from the many schools we have in our camp a hotel school will be opened soon.

August 20. Early this morning there was a big fight in our hut.

August 22. Because of the uproar in the hut, we were summoned to the sub-commander today. A few of us were transferred to compound 2, myself among them, even though I was innocent.

August 23. Everything is foreign here in compound 2. The sub-commander is a hard nut to crack. Yesterday a few of my friends spread a rumor about my return to my old compound.

August 24. The food isn't bad here.

August 26. Today compound 7 was dissolved suddenly in compliance with the Hague agreement that [calls for] youth to reside in a separate compound. About one hundred seventy youth remain in compound7.

August 27. To my joy I discovered that I would be transferred to compound 3.

September 1. After today we will receive eight ounces of potatoes.

September 4. Today I returned to my old place in compound 3. This evening the demise of Russia is reported in the newspaper. That made everyone happy.

September 5. A number of internees from Alexander [*sic*] Palace in London, who reported to a workers' camp in Birmingham, didn't work there, however, because an airplane factory was supposed to have been built. Those internees came here.

[149] Known in German as *Der Pfarrer von Kirchfeld*, this anti-clerical drama was written in 1870 by Austrian writer Ludwig Anzengruber under the pseudonym L. Gruber.

September 10. Today our menu was altered yet again and now we receive the following daily:

Bread 8 ounces
Flour ¾ ounce
Meat 3 ounces for five days
Herring 10 ounces for two days
Margarine 1 ounce
Tea or coffee 3/8 or ¾ ounces
Sugar 1 ounce
Potatoes 1 lb
Milk 1/20 lb
Salt ½ ounce
Pepper 1/72 ounce
Oatmeal 4 ounces
Syrup/marmalade 1 ounce
Fresh vegetables 2 ounces
Beans or peas 3 ounces

September 11. Now we have founded a reading circle in our compound. Aside from our daily ration of one lb of potatoes, we can buy more potatoes in the kitchen almost every day at the price of 2 p per lb.

September 18. A notice was posted by the Swiss Embassy from the German Government which stated that the latter had not yet approved of internees performing work for the British outside. This should really have been banned long ago!!

September 28. Most of the so-called youth in their third year of confinement in compound 7 are now thirty years or older, [and] have complained about their separate internment. Most of them have been transferred to another compound. Now only twenty youth remain in compound 7.

All internees who are ill and believe they are eligible for an exchange must fill out a list once again (perhaps for the twelfth time).

September 30. The following plays were performed in our compound this month: *The Spanish Fly,*[150] *Bakarat, Filmzauber* [Film Magic],[151] *Wohltäte der Menschheit* [Good Deeds of Humanity], *Glück im Winkel* [Happiness in a Quiet Corner],[152] *Pfarrer von Hirschfeld, . . .* and "*Rosenmontag.*" The operetta *Filmzauber* (this is the first operetta performed thus far in our camp) is the hit of the camp. It's been performed about ten times now.

Despite the note from the Swiss Embassy [stating] that no more Germans should be going to England as workers, yesterday a number of them went to England. . . .

[150] In German, *Die Spanische Fliege*, was written in 1913 by German comedians Franz Arnold and Ernst Bach.
[151] a musical drama and parody of silent films written in 1912 by Walter Kollo and Willy Bredschneider
[152] written in 1896 by Hermann Sudermann

October 4. Today it is three years that I've been incarcerated. We have been on this island for two years and today, for the first time, they changed our blankets.

October 9. Our hut captain resigned today and was transferred to compound 6.

October 10. For a few days now there have been no potatoes for purchase. . . .

October 14. From November 1 onwards we will take over the [responsibilities for the] canteen. Now that there is nothing left to sell and nothing more to earn, the government has turned it over to us. . . . The kitchen committee is responsible [now] for the canteen administration. The current Canteen Fund has £6,000 that will be distributed among the various compounds so that each compound will received about £260. . . .

October 15. The internees from Alexander [*sic*] Palace were transferred back there today. In Camp 3 a compound was dissolved today and our compound received about seventy internees [as a result].

October 17. Owing to disunity, our compound's Theater Association broke up.

October 19. Finally, potatoes are available again for purchase. Today our kitchen received an exceptional amount of them. . . .

October 20. The newspaper reports that finally the German and English Governments have decided on which port [to meet for] an exchange of sick internees and those over the age of forty-five. That port will be Boston [Lincolnshire]. All the internees have lost hope for the exchange because the agreement is over a year old and nothing has come of it.

October 21. The workers, who went to England at the beginning of this month, returned today.

End of October. The older youth who were transferred to different compounds at the beginning of this month were returned to the youth compound 7. That is typically English—do something one way today and tomorrow another. A notice from the German Government hopes that all young internees, who have not yet reached the age of twenty-one, will be separated and also transferred to compound 7.

Our Theater Association was put on firm footing again. . . .

In November three hundred internees came here from Douglas Camp of which about one hundred fifty were transferred to our compound, so that our compound is full again! Over the course of November the German Government paid £1 three times to the indigent. Each time about £330 was paid. The actual support amount was ten shillings per month and so the amount above is effective until the month of April. Now the internees have money but there's hardly anything in the canteen to buy.

November 19. The Swiss representative was here today to speak with internees who needed to discuss private issues. . . .

End of November. After having been here for a full two years, we were given a fourth blanket. It was about time because the nights are cold.

At the moment, there is active participation in gymnastics. Additionally, a soccer tournament is taking place among the four camps.

Beginning of December. At the beginning of November the individual kitchens of the compounds have taken over the canteens, something that we have demanded since our arrival here. As long as there were things to buy in the canteen, one didn't consider this. Now, however, when there's nothing to buy, then they hand over the canteen to us. Every few days there are only a few hundred cigarettes available to purchase, some tobacco, a few tins of honey here and there, baking powder, sewing thread, poor writing notebooks and a few other small items, hardly any food with the exception of 1,000 kilos of flour, a few thousand kilos of potatoes that the kitchen uses for itself. The potatoes are sold at a retail value of 1 ½ p per pound. But since the last week of November there are no potatoes to sell! . . . Unfortunately, of the nearly £6,000 received from the canteen fund administered by the English Government, each compound received only about £270. As our kitchen earned £60 pure profit and also saved about £100 in earlier months, our compound now has an income of about £430. The head of our kitchen is an excellent fellow who [works] unselfishly—a rarity in the camp.

December. Finally the release of the forty-five year olds has begun. Today about ten internees of our compound were released to England as a result. The daily ration of government-apportioned margarine (one ounce) is extremely poor of late. One can hardly enjoy it.

Finally a light has been installed in our W.C. (after two years!!).

December 27. Christmas is over once again. It was a very sad holiday. Only our kitchen had prepared something [special to eat]. No compound had such a splendid meal as we did! This was not owing to the English Government but rather our good administration: on the first Christmas eve we had a Christmas party, on the second evening we had a theater [performance]. . . . The Government made an exception and allowed us to leave the lights on until midnight. . . .

In the last three months the weather was rather good; that means it was dry. This year there are rather few Christmas letters and packages. Actually, one can't really expect anything different.

1918

January 1. This evening we celebrated New Year's; "celebrate" isn't really the proper impression. We had a theater performance *Hussar Fever* and made a little noise. The only drink that we got was coffee. The lights were left on until 12:30 a.m.

Right at the New Year a change in our daily rations was made and now we receive six ounces of bread per day and for the rest two ounces of bread and two ounces of biscuits. The rest of the list remains the same as before.

Now we receive a bit more coal—38 per day per section.

January 3. Regarding Christmas . . . Baron Schröder gifted us a can of sardines instead of his usual six pence. Also the Red Cross gave us each a book and fifty cigarettes and twenty cigars each.

During the first week of this month it was very cold here but very mild during the second half. We had a small celebration in honor of his Majesty's [Kaiser Wilhelm] birthday on the 27th. The speech by Rebhahn was very good. Our kitchen provided us with a special Kaiser dinner.

On the 28th of this month the first internees from here were released to Holland. A day later some were released to Germany. Another list of the forty-five year olds was prepared.

Despite the German Government's prohibition, internees continue to go to England to work. On the 31st of this month, however, some returned here at the behest of the Swiss representative, or so it is reported. . . .

February 1. We feared that our rations would be shrunk yet again but fortunately this did not occur. The only change that happened was that instead of the 2,300 pounds of oatmeal that our kitchen gets each month it will only be able to buy 1,800 pounds and there is no cheese available. The tins of honey here and there that can still be purchased now cost 1 shilling/10 pence per piece.

February 28. Over the course of this month more transports of invalids left for Holland. Among these invalids there were, however, many healthy internees, who under one pretext or another were able to leave. Most of these were internees who had money. Rumor has it that shortly the doctor from London will come here in order to examine more internees. Until now the very sick have not been sent away. Also a transport of forty-five year olds have gone to Germany. There's still a number of forty-five year olds here. Most of these are the ones who do not want to go to England and others are naval personnel over forty-five years old. The last is a scandal. There have been a few good theater performances again. . . .

On the 25th of this month our meager rations once again were changed to our disadvantage: instead of six ounces of bread and two ounces of biscuits, we now receive five ounces of bread and three ounces of biscuits. Instead of one ounce of margarine we get only ½ ounce. The tiny ration of milk has also been reduced!! Instead we get one more ounce of oatmeal, so that now we receive five ounces. The weekly soap ration was also reduced. Additional restrictions were replaced on packages from England. All sorts of flour, grain, sugar, butter, milk, margarine, fat and meat can no longer be sent from England. Fortunately, peas, beans, tobacco, cigars and cigarettes are still allowed.

A large number still go to work [in England].

German financial support has not been paid for some time now. A new system is supposed to be introduced.

The canteen, as it were, has absolutely nothing to buy. There's hardly any food except sardines, onions, here and there some crocks of honey for about thirty internees and a very small quantity of cigarettes and tobacco.

March. At the beginning of this month financial support was paid and also for the previous months. According to today's newspaper the German Parliament claimed that things were better here now than in previous months. That is absolutely false, and as a result, we summoned the Swiss representative.

Once again there is a discussion in the House of Lords concerning the general exchange of all civilian internees. Unfortunately, the English Government rejects the exchange of "all for all."[153]

We are all pleased that peace has been made with Russia and Romania.

Finally, the long promised simple pass system has been implemented. Instead of requesting a pass five days ahead of time, now it is enough if one requests it that morning in order to receive it that afternoon.

I received that sad news from the field that L.R. has died.

Most of the military types within the camp do not carry guns now while those outside still carry them. No longer does one have to be accompanied to the authorities' offices by a soldier. . . .

On the eighteenth of this month our rations were unbearably reduced yet again. Instead of the six ounces of frozen meat we now receive only four ounces, two ounces instead of three ounces of tinned meat, ¼ ounce of tea instead of 3/8 ounces or ½ ounce of coffee, and 3/8 ounce instead of ½ ounce of salt. Yet our potato ration increased from 16 ounces to 20 ounces and, additionally, we get 8 ounces more of herring during the week.

Now I also have beets in compound 8 that are about 32 m. in length and 1¼ wide.[154]

On the 20th of this month each German internee received a box of cheese (3/4 lb) from the German Government through the Dutch Red Cross and on the twenty-fourth of this month about ¾ lb of smoked meat and 1/8 lb of sausage. Both items produced great satisfaction yet such rations should be handed out on a weekly basis.

Jewish Easter [Passover] was on the twenty-eighth of this month. Each of us Jews received about 6 lbs of Matzah . . . from a London Jewish community. This ration was supposed to be instead of bread but we also received the latter.

Easter began on the 31st of this month. Our kitchen provided us with exceptionally big and tasty rations!!

From the 30th of this month onwards no more tobacco and cigarettes will be allowed in this camp from England.

On the 21st of this month the big offensive began in France and we are hoping for the best!! Until now the results have been quite good.

The weather was very mild during the entire month.

A smaller transport also left for Holland and Germany again. All reserve officers were sent to Holland. Why not the non-commissioned officers who have been incarcerated for more than eighteen months??

April. On the 1st of this month *Der liebe Augustin*[155] was performed and met with approval; yes, it was so well-received that during the month the play was put on about twenty times!!

[153] Reference to deputation of House of Lords and House of Commons members in March, who urged British Prime Minister Lloyd George to allow for a general exchange of civilian prisoners. Lloyd George rejected the idea, owing to the fact that German prisoners outnumbered British by more than four to one.

[154] Presumably he means a plot to plant beets.

[155] Play was possible reference to Marx Augustin (also known as "Der Liebe Augustin"), a seventeenth-century minstrel and poet who wrote a beloved song, "Oh, You Dear Augustin" during the Great Plague of Vienna in 1679.

On the 10th of this month the Home Office doctor was here in order to examine internees [to be released to] Holland and Germany. Those numbers were extremely large yet, unfortunately, the doctor only examined a few. Also I tried in earnest but it was in vain!

From the 20th-25th of this month two representatives from the Swiss Delegation were here and we complained about everything possible to them. Still we are fearful that again everything will remain as it was before.

Our canteen hardly has anything to sell. With the exception of potatoes and legumes now all food items from England are forbidden!!

The weather through the 20th of this month was very nice but from then on it was rather cold. Many internees already have already planted their beets.

At the end of this month there was another pay out of support [from the German government]. Finally some "players" from the list of receivers were removed!!

The success of the offensive until now is quite good. Already our troops have captured 130,000 English and French. . . . Still the decisive battle is yet to come.

During this month we read much about the Lichnowski Affair[156] and likewise the Czernin-Clemenceau-Kaiser Karl[157] affair! Unfortunately, Czernin must go!

Hardly any mail and packages come from Germany. The first [mail] takes 2-3 months to arrive.

Now also machine guns have been installed around the camp!!. . .

Once again, despite our government's prohibition internees went to work in England. Also a worker camp was erected here on the island.

In recent days the largest amount [of food] that the kitchen could buy is as follows per month:

Rations from July 30, 1918
Bread 5 ounces
Biscuits 3 ounces
Flour ¾ ounces
Meat 4 ounces of fresh/3ounces of frozen for 5 days; 8 ounces herring for 2 days
Herring 12 ounces for two days
Tee ¼ ounce OR
Coffee ½ ounce
Sugar 1 ounce
Salt ½ ounce
Black Pepper 1/72 ounce
Oatmeal 4 ounces
Syrup ½ ounce

[156] Imperial German ambassador to the Court of St. James from 1912 to 1914, Prince Karl Max Lichnowsky wrote *My Mission to London 1912–1914* (published in 1918), in which he blamed the German government for its failure to avert war in 1914.

[157] Reference to the Sixtus Affair involving Emperor Charles I of Austria's failed attempt to conclude a separate peace with the Allies. Count Ottokar von Czernin, Austro-Hungarian foreign minister (1916–1918), who fully supported the initiative, blamed French Prime Minister Georges Clemenceau for being the primary obstacle to peace. The Affair led to Czernin's resignation.

Peas, legumes ½ ounce or rice ½ ounce
Potatoes 20 ounces
Fresh Fruit 4 ounces or ½ ounce rice

1919

March 15. Departed Saturday from Compound 3 of Knockaloe

March 16. Departed Sunday from Compound 7 of Knockaloe

March 17. Monday morning in London at Alexander [*sic*] Palace

March 20. Thursday departed from London

March 21. Friday, departed from Harwich, England

March 22. Saturday, arrived in Rotterdam

March 23–24. In Wesel, Germany

March 24. Monday, departed Wesel

March 25. Tuesday, arrived in Frankfurt am Main

March 26. Wednesday, departed Frankfurt via Friedrichsfeld to Mannheim, Hotel Union

March 26. [presumably March 28] Friday, arrived Greilsheim

May 4. Friday, Bad Kreuznach

CHAPTER 4

Commitment and Sacrifice

James Douglas Hutchison in uniform. *Courtesy of Sheila Douglas Dunbar.*

CHAPTER 4

"A year . . . such as I can never hope to have again"

James D. Hutchison, ANZAC artilleryman

James Douglas "Doug" Hutchison was born on September 29, 1894, the son of a journalist. The eldest of three brothers, he grew up in Dunedin, the principal city of the Otago region of New Zealand's South Island. In 1913 he entered the University of Otago, but was intent on studying the law with a local firm of solicitors. On August 7, 1914, as soon as he had heard of the outbreak of war, Hutchison volunteered for service even though he had not yet turned twenty.[1] *It was the first instance of the exceptionally strong sense of duty that would motivate the young New Zealander throughout the conflict. On this occasion, he was turned away as too young (at this early stage recruiters were not yet desperate for fresh recruits to replenish the ranks that would soon be decimated), but the ever-resourceful Hutchison tried again, and by mid-October 1914 he was in Wellington awaiting the convoy that would transport New Zealand's newly formed expeditionary force to the Middle East and Europe.*

When he arrived in Egypt in December 1914, after an eye-opening voyage (highlighted by narrowly missing the German cruiser Emden *and by sailing the Suez Canal), Hutchison took full advantage of the opportunity to acquaint himself with the local culture and historical sights. Within weeks, however, his appreciation of an ancient civilization was offset by his distaste for the immorality of modern Cairo and a longing for his homeland's "absence of noises and smells." Emblematic of the city's temptations was the so-called Battle of the*

[1] Some 14,000 volunteers came forward during that first week alone, while over the course of the war over 100,000 New Zealanders served abroad (from a country whose population numbered only around one million). Ian McGibbon, "The Shaping of New Zealand's War Effort, August – October 1914," in *New Zealand's Great War*, ed. John Crawford and Ian McGibbon (Auckland: Exisle Publishing, 2007), 65.

Wazzir on April 2, 1915. On that day, Good Friday, Australian and New Zealand soldiers on leave for the holiday and perhaps anxious about the prospect of impending action, rioted in Cairo's Haret Al Wassir red-light district. Accumulated grievances (that local prostitutes cost too much, were inclined to theft, or were infected with venereal disease), exacerbated by the easy availability of alcohol, fueled a rampage of destructive violence. Some 4,000 soldiers ransacked brothels, tossed furniture out windows and onto the street, and set fires. Only with difficulty, and the deployment of mounted military police and other (English) troops, could the British military authorities restore order.

Hutchison was originally detailed to work as a hospital orderly, but soon finagled an appointment to an artillery battery. He regarded his assignment with his new unit to guard the Suez Canal as "proper active service now." It was as an artilleryman that Hutchison would serve out the remainder of the war. As such he would not only represent the lethal military branch whose firepower would dominate the battlefield; he would also participate in the iconic episode of the ANZAC (Australian and New Zealand Army Corps) war experience, the campaign at Gallipoli.[2]

Frustrated by the stalemate on the western front and captivated by the prospect of striking a decisive blow elsewhere, Britain's eloquent First Lord of the Admiralty, Winston Churchill, championed the idea early in 1915 of mounting an attack on the Turkish-controlled Dardanelles, the straits linking the Mediterranean to the Black Sea. Wresting control over this narrow waterway would, in Churchill's estimation, enable supplies to be sent to and from Russia, relieve pressure on beleaguered Serbia, threaten Constantinople, and perhaps knock the Ottoman Empire out of the war altogether. He was also persuaded that the job could be done by naval power alone (and with virtually obsolete battleships at that), an important consideration for British military commanders unwilling to spare manpower from operations in France or Belgium.

Poorly planned and imperfectly executed, the combined Anglo-French naval attack in March 1915 on the Turkish fortifications guarding the straits was a fiasco. In an effort to retrieve the situation, the Allies decided to mount an amphibious assault so that soldiers could disable Turkish artillery and permit safe passage for their ships. The ANZACs stationed in Egypt were close at hand, so it was on April 26, 1915 (the second day of the Gallipoli landings), that Hutchison found himself splashing ashore to man a howitzer battery. For the next six months he would endure heavy fire. Allied troops were often pinned down along the beaches by tenacious Turkish soldiers in superior defensive positions, and their casualties mounted, both from persistent shellfire and the unsanitary conditions. Hutchison himself, like a number of his mates, contracted enteric fever and had to be evacuated in October 1915. With the lack of progress, it was increasingly evident that the remainder of the Allied forces would have to be withdrawn at the end of the year. The evacuation was the most successful aspect of the entire operation, although the Gallipoli campaign is often credited with stimulating a stronger sense of Australian and New Zealand military prowess and cultural identity.[3]

[2] See Robin Prior, *Gallipoli: The End of the Myth* (New Haven: Yale University Press, 2009); Peter Hart, *Gallipoli* (New York: Oxford University Press, 2011).

[3] Christopher Pugsley, *The ANZAC Experience: New Zealand, Australia, and Empire in the First World War* (Auckland: Reed, 2004); Alistair Thomson, *ANZAC Memories: Living with the Legend* (Melbourne: Oxford University Press, 1994).

One might have assumed that the war was now over for Hutchison, as he was sent back to New Zealand to convalesce. Initially too weak to accept civilian employment, he found the next year difficult. Nonetheless, driven by his strong sense of duty, Hutchison insisted on returning to active service. On May 2, 1918, he departed on another epic voyage, traveling through the Panama Canal, evading German U-boats operating in American waters, and finally reaching the French coast at Boulogne. His diary entries point up the importance to Britain of being able to call upon the resources of its empire and, by virtue of its command of the sea, of being able to deploy them wherever it chose, even across thousands of miles.

Up against determined German troops who, even in mid-1918, betrayed no apparent signs of imminent collapse, Hutchison survived snipers, gas attacks, and bombardments. He had recalled 1915 as "a year crammed full of incident such as I can never hope to have again," yet 1918 matched it. When the armistice came, Hutchison welcomed November 11, 1918, as "probably THE day in the world's history." As demobilization approached, he was already pondering his educational opportunities, and once he returned to New Zealand in 1919, he embarked upon what would become a distinguished legal career. James Douglas Hutchison was admitted to the bar in Christchurch later that year and was appointed to New Zealand's Supreme Court in 1948. A knighthood followed in 1959 and retirement in 1965, sixteen years before his death at the age of eighty-six.

August 3, 1914. War declared by Germany on Russia. . . . Germans invaded France

August 4. France declared war on Germany. Germans invaded Belgium and England declared war on Germany. . . .

August 6. Went to National Reserve Meeting in Garrison hall. Immense meeting.

August 7. Volunteered for expeditionary force No. 1. Not quite the min. age (20). . . .

August 12. Drill. Learned I was turned down from artillery of expeditionary force on account of age. . . .

August 19. Got into ambulance corps for exped[itionary] Force, gave age as 20.

August 20. In camp. We leave for Auckland on Friday morning. . . .

Hutchison's entries for the remainder of 1914 are relatively brief. They include his departure from Auckland on September 24 and passage through rough seas, at which point he admitted, with characteristic understatement, to being "a bit sick." After loading horses and stores, his ship sailed for Wellington on October 11, where a convoy and escorts (including a Japanese battleship) began to assemble. Three weeks later, once Australian transports had joined them at Albany, Hutchison and his mates finally sailed into open waters. He had been given no specific idea where the convoy was headed, and speculation ranged from Bombay to Cape Town to Colombo. Colombo it was, followed by Aden and the Suez Canal, and then to Alexandria, where his unit disembarked on December 5. The next six weeks were quiet, with Hutchison noting his receipt and dispatch of mail, a series of marches, and his periodic visits on leave to Cairo.

Indian Ocean

Hutchison appended this and the following more detailed sections on his journey at the end of his printed/bound diary for 1914. Whether he did so because it was the only section of the diary in which there was space for lengthy descriptions, or because he was more inclined to reflection at the end of the year, is not clear. On balance, the former is more likely.

First four days from Albany nothing startling. Nov. 5th[,] two-funneled liner from Freemantle to Colombo[4] overhauled us. She was pounced upon by the *Sydney* which was our rear guard. This was when she was out of sight of convoy. She thought apparently our cruiser was *Emden*[5] and started to run, but was soon hauled up. Glorious sunset like a distant bush fire. On Nov. 7[,] sun appeared to be directly overhead at noon. Saw my first flying fish. It is exactly like a bird when seen from any distance, with whitish wings. This morning the *Minotaur*[6] left at full speed towards southwest, having it is rumoured got news of the whereabouts of the *Emden*. Nov. 8th[,] at midnight we passed the Cocos Islands[7] and early in morning a wireless message was received from there, "Strange warship approaching." About 7 a.m. the S.O.S. signal came through, and *Sydney*[8] left hell-for-leather towards S.W. engaged the *Emden* (for it was she) about 11 a.m. and beached her. News was through by noon. The *Melbourne* and the Jap. Cruiser both went to western (i.e. dangerous) side of convoy. It seems *Minotaur* was recalled for some other duty. When crossing the line [the equator] on Nov. 13[,] it was too wet to hold proper ceremony but a big bath was erected on top deck (it was just our ordinary swimming bath shifted) and nearly everyone on ship, officers (except the one or two heads), men, ship's officers and crew were put through no matter how many times they had already crossed the line. Nov. 14.[,] Wrote note home and Xmas greetings to Daisy, John Lang, Edith H., Podger Pilling. Letters are now censored, and you can only send a note. Arrived Colombo Nov. 15th.

Colombo opens your eyes. It is on a wide bay facing to the south. The harbour itself is formed by a breakwater, and the shipping must get right particular hell in the monsoon season. The shores of the bay are very low and covered with tropical

[4] Because of its strategic importance as a port in the Indian Ocean, Colombo, Ceylon (today Sri Lanka), was occupied first by the Portuguese (early sixteenth century), the Dutch (early seventeenth century), and, ultimately, the British (late eighteenth century until 1948).

[5] the second of the swift Dresden-class light cruisers built for the German Navy

[6] a relatively modern British armored cruiser that had entered service in 1908

[7] Also known as the Keeling Islands after Captain William Keeling of the East India Company, who was the first European to visit them, in 1609.

[8] The *Sydney* was a Royal Australian Navy light cruiser, which, with its sister ship *Melbourne*, was detailed to escort the expeditionary force. It left the convoy on November 9 to investigate an SOS signal from the wireless station in the Cocos Islands, which was under attack from the German light cruiser *Emden*. At the outbreak of the war, the *Emden*, based in China, had detached from the German East Asia Squadron and raided throughout the Indian Ocean, capturing or destroying some two dozen Allied vessels and threatening vital shipping lanes. It was a great relief to Britain's Admiralty, therefore, when the *Sydney* caught the German marauder, crippled it, and forced it to run aground.

vegetation, but behind the town (a good way behind, probably thirty miles) are high tops including one regular sharp peak like Mt. Aspiring.[9] There is all sorts of shipping about. I have never seen so many ships of all sorts together before. Inside the breakwater were five warships, at least thirty more or less sizeable steamships, probably a dozen biggish sailing ships, and innumerable small vessels of all shapes and sizes. Outside the breakwater were at least forty biggish steamers. The ships inside the breakwater were anchored all over the place almost touching each other. The small harbor craft comprise numbers of first class motor launches, native rowboats of all descriptions, catamarans with their outrigggers, and even one with high stem and stern, two masts sloping forward and a huge sail. The natives dress in a sort of running singlet above (or sometimes stripped to the waist) and a gaily coloured skirt below. It is very hard to tell the men from the women. They are a dark brown colour, which looks a sort of dark green when the sun shines on it. The *Sydney* arrived soon after we did, and with her the huge *Empress of Russia*,[10] an armed merchantman (or converted cruiser) with the German prisoners from the *Emden* on board. The *Sydney* showed few signs of conflict. It seems the *Emden* got the first shot into her, and it passed right through the officers' quarters, but after that the *Sydney* registered about one hundred hits and was hardly hit at all herself. Nearly everyone on the ship got ashore for a short time on leave, but I was unfortunate enough to be on duty. Those who went ashore spent nearly all their time in rickshaws and bargaining with the natives. They were delighted with the place. Left twelve noon Nov. 17th.

Colombo to Aden

On 19th or 20th a memorial service was held for Ernest Webb son of Herbert Webb of Dunedin who died at Colombo on the *Arawa* and was, I believe, buried ashore. It seems that during the Neptune celebrations crossing the line two or three days before he dived into the canvas bath, and thinking it was deeper than it was, hit his head on the bottom and broke his neck. On the 20th the fleet parted company for some reason or another. The *Maunganui, Athenic, Ruapehu* and *Star of India*[11] went on ahead. The great body of the ships dropped behind. I suppose it means we will go first into Aden. . . . There is a rumour that we may be disembarked in Ishmailia to protect the Suez canal from the Turks. This was first stated by one of our majors who said to us "We may see service before we expected it. It is quite possible that we will be landed in Ishmailia." There is also a rumour today that two Australian ships collided this morning. This is well supported and is probably true. Nov. 24th[,] sighted Arabia, high land at some distance from coast. Nov. 25th[,] arrived Aden.

Aden is on a bay protected by a great bare rocky promontory and an equally forbidding looking island. There is no vegetation whatever to be seen through glasses except in a few places a sort of thornbush . . . and in one place a few palms. There is very high country and long way to the back. It has been almost invisible through haze all today

[9] New Zealand's tallest peak
[10] At nearly 17,000 tons and 570 feet long, it was a swift passenger liner that had regularly plied the Pacific since her maiden voyage in 1913. When war broke out, it was refitted and armed.
[11] passenger liners converted to serve as troop transports

(25th). The bay offers a good anchorage and the town appears to be practically impregnable against attack. It is protected on the land side by desert and on the sea side by what must be immensely strong fortresses on the rocky promontory and island. There is a garrison of between one and two thousand. It must be the last place on earth to live in. The reflected heat from the bare iron looking rocks must be terrible. It has not really rained here for fifteen years, we were told. Left Aden 6.30 a.m.[,] Nov. 26th.

Red Sea

Passed straits of Bab-el-Mendib[12] (Hell's Gate) into Red Sea, at about 3 p.m. Asia and Africa on either side are both plainly visible and quite near the strait being no more than ten miles wide. There is a small, sunburnt town on the Asia side. It must be quite the last place in the world to live, being much worse than Aden could possibly be. Nov. 28th[,] at night there is very persistent rumour that we are going to land in a day or two. The mounted men have to see to horseshoes, and orders say all men must wear boots to accustom their feet once more. All goods in the holds are being overhauled, and it is now probable we will see fighting against the Turks. The Ambulance will probably be armed. Nov. 29 and 30. It was very cold at night and wind was bitter. Passed numerous islands on 30th. Arrived Suez morning of December 1st.

Suez is situated on the north end of Red Sea. It is not on a harbor, but the sea is so narrowed as to form a very good anchorage. The most noticeable thing at first glance is a series of great concrete tanks for the town's water supply. The white section of the town is formed of nice houses surrounded with verandahs and with lots of palms about, but at best it is very unprotected from heat and winds. The natives are Arabs and are very fine looking chaps.

The Canal is a wonderful work. Before we started we put on an extra rudder, and a searchlight at the bow. On the Arabian side the Canal is well defended. We passed[,] on the afternoon of Dec. 1st[,] detachments of East Lanc regiment, Royal Engineers, Sikhs, Gurkhas and Soudanese all in different entrenched camps not far apart. On the Egypt side there are occasional canal stations with French names and under French control, I suppose. . . .

Tuesday, December 1, 1914. Arrived Suez and dropped anchor 8.30 a.m. Moved off and started through canal about 2.30 p.m. . . .

23 December. Whole division marched to Cairo and back but I was on hospital duty. Got our first N.Z. mail. . . .

December 25 (Christmas Day). Off duty all day. Went to Pyramids, and in evening to Kursaal (rather flash vaudeville show). Ducked into camp 2.30 a.m. . . .

December 31. Had a very pleasant and somewhat noisy evening in Cairo and then in camp. In the afternoon went to old Cairo. . . .

[12] Strategic link between the Indian Ocean and the Mediterranean via the Red Sea and the Suez Canal. Its name is Arabic, meaning "Gate of Grief," perhaps a reference to the dangerous passage between Asia and Africa.

January 25, 1915. In the evening orders came that there is fighting going on at the Suez Canal, and we must leave for there first thing in the morning. Was working packing stores till after midnight. Packed up big kits and handed them in to stay behind. Small kits, blankets and waterproof to go. Slept in the open, tents having been removed to pack for patients.

January 26. Moved off to Zeitoun station about 7.30 a.m. Train left 9.30, reached Kubri 3.30 p.m. Fixed up temporary camp. Got hot tea about 6.30. . . .

January 27. On proper active service now, so there are no bugle calls. We were not called till 6.30, and then were not expected to turn out in a hurry as there was nothing to do. About 4 in the morning a rattle of rifle fire broke out in the canal direction and lasted for about half an hour. It seems the Turks made a sort of reconnaissance in force as soon as moon sank and were easily repulsed. No British casualties, Turkish casualties unknown but thought to be at least half a dozen and one prisoner taken. . . .

Wellington battalion moved off in morning and lined reinforcement trenches on our side of canal. We followed and bivouacked for night behind their trenches, that is the bearer section. Tent section stayed at railway siding 3 miles back.

January 28. Got up when we liked, about 7 a.m. Washed in mess tin full of water.

More sniping last night. I slept through it and so did most of others. It was not quite in front of us, but to both sides. One wounded Indian was brought in by native ambulance.

Erected a good bivouac of sacks and pieces of wood for five of us.

January 29. Was on guard last night 4-6 a.m. There was no firing last night.

7 or 8 Australian transports and 1 N.Z. with reinforcements passed along canal. The other New Zealand one apparently disembarked its men at Suez and they went by train to Cairo. Wrote a note, censored of course, home.

Learned we were to be replaced by A section for a couple of days.

Submarine AE 2 passed through canal.

January 30. We knocked up at 4.30, stood by till daylight. There was considerable movement of troops till daylight but no attack eventuated. Were replaced by A section and marched back to camp at station, arriving back at 11 a.m. Erected bivouac till lunch.

January 31. Church parade. Were paid, drew £1. Had a sort of bath in a big basin of water.

Monday, February 1, 1915. Some chaps who should know reckon they heard big gun shooting last night somewhere Ishmailia way.[13] Went over and joined A section in our original position by the canal. Erected bivouac. Went swim in canal. . . .

February 3. Last night there was brisk rifle firing starting about 12.20 a.m. and lasting till about 2 a.m. There were one or two shots fired by ships guns in canal. Were awakened by first shots, got dressed and lay down again. . . .

[13] city on west bank of the canal

This afternoon there seemed to be considerable movement and bodies of what seemed to be Turks were seen. . . .

Nights very dark, attack expected.

February 4. Had fat boiled bacon for breakfast. Nearly everyone felt a little crook[14] through having too much of it after no butter or other greasy food.

Converted cruiser *Himalaya* fired several rounds at the enemy. We could not see the enemy but saw the burst of the shells.

February 5. On guard last night. 8–10, 2–4. No alarm.

Today a small column went out, Taranaki company. Ghurkas,[15] Haiderabad[16] [*sic*] cavalry, three 15 pr. Guns.[17] Went towards enemy's position. Returned in afternoon. Slight skirmish and one Haiderabad lancer killed, I hear.

Later news of this is that there was no rifle fire but the E. Lancs. Artillery fired 40 rounds at 4000 yards and scattered the enemy. One lancer shot through the head. . . .

February 6. Marched along to next post and examined all our trenches so as to know how to get wounded out if necessary. In afternoon C section played A cricket. . . .

February 11. We had rather a pleasant evening on the canal bank. Ships are coming through tonight after dark. Whether this means the enemy are gone or not I don't know. At any rate several big passenger boats went past all lighted up and we stood on the bank, gave one or two hakas[18] and sang a few songs. Geoff Fisher started to teach some Indian soldiers a Maori haka. They picked it up very well and are very keen on it and very pleased with it. . . .

February 13. 108 Turks including a major were captured by Gurkhas away out in front of Suez, and 60 were killed and wounded. One Gurkha killed and only a few wounded.

February 14. 20 oz. tin of Capstan medium tobacco given out to each man with the inscription "With the compliments of the people of N.Z. collected through the *Dominion* newspaper."

Got a pair of sox from Mother. The note I wrote home on the 11th was returned censored because I had headed it "Suez Canal." Cut this off and posted it again.

February 15. Got paid. Drew £1-12-. . .

February 16. Washing day.

Camel corps went out on a four or five days' reconnaissance assisted by two or three aeroplanes. . . .

February 23. Camel corps returned and reported no Turks within 75 miles. We got orders to pack up ready to move off next morning.

[14] Australian/New Zealand slang for feeling ill

[15] Gurkhas were highly regarded Nepalese military units in the British Army.

[16] mounted troops from the southern Indian princely state of Hyderabad

[17] artillery firing 15-pound shells

[18] traditional war cry or dance

February 24. After a final glorious bathe in canal, we moved off with all baggage to the railway siding, demolishing all signs of the camp.

Bivouacked for the night in the open. . . .

February 26. Cold windy night last night and heavy mist, blankets wet in the morning. Reveille 5 a.m. Loaded train. Left 8.25 a.m. Arrived Zeitoun about 2 p.m. . . . Got about 3 weeks' mail in a lump, a *Bulletin*, two *Times*, about 3 letters from home. . . .

March 8. Busied myself trying to get transfer to howitzer battery. Saw Major Falla who said he would take me. Saw Major O'Neill and wrote application to the Colonel. Saw the Colonel who said he would transfer me if I could get a man to change with me. Quite by chance I came on such a man in a little shop in the camp.

March 9. Was informed over in the artillery that they would try to get me in, but they were not able to let any man go even on an exchange as they were under strength.

On guard again tonight and tomorrow.

Wrote to mother. . . .

March 13. Broke. . . . Chronic lack of funds in the camp and no possibility of borrowing any money. Hence had to stay in through a half holiday.

March 22. Big mobilization scheme of whole N.Z. division including 4 battalions of Australian infantry and Queensland light horse with all transport.

Inspection and march past before Commissioner for Egypt. . . .

March 26. At night Maori Contingent[19] about 500 strong arrived. They expect to stay here as a garrison force till the end of the war, and consequently are dressed in helmets and shorts. They are a fine looking crowd. Late at night advance part of third reinforcements arrived. . . . In the afternoon played for Field Ambulance v. Mounted Ambulance. Lost 3-14. It was played on gravelly sand and under a hot sun, so the football was poor.

March 27. On guard tonight and tomorrow. . . .

More of the reinforcements arrived. . . .

March 28. Hear great stories about the Maoris. An English tommy called one a black bastard and was knocked through a plate glass window. They are a fine crowd, and are making themselves felt.

Now that we have further reinforcements, I again made application for a transfer to the howitzers. . . . Wrote to Mother.

March 29. The Colonel wrote to headquarters to see whether he would transfer me. . . .

Inspection and march past of N.Z. division before Sir Ian Hamilton.[20] Quite a successful afternoon. Hamilton was as cheery as when we saw him at Matarae[21] nearly a year ago.

[19] Indigenous people of New Zealand; the soldiers developed a fearsome reputation.
[20] commander of the Dardanelles expedition
[21] a New Zealand military camp near Otago

March 30. Small field day.

Was told I had got my transfer and was to report to adjutant of artillery brigade tomorrow morning. . . .

March 31. Saw artillery adjutant who sent me to orderly room of howitzer battery, where I got my orders to bring my kit over.

Wrote to Father telling him about it.

Thursday, April 1, 1915. Ordinary routine of howitzer battery:

Reveille 5
Exercise horses & stables 5:30
Breakfast 6:30
Parade 8
Stables 11
Dinner 12
Stables 4
Lights out 10.15

Drew my pay from field amb. . . .

April 2 (Good Friday). Whole holiday. . . .

In the evening there was quite a riot in town. A party of Australian and N.Z.'landers wrecked a brothel for some reason or other and the English military police came on the scene. They used their revolvers and the other chaps, by now quite a big crowd, used pickets, chair legs and a few bayonets. Two men were killed, nearly a dozen wounded, and 50 arrested. Before the police arrived beds, chest of drawers and a piano were thrown from top windows and burnt in the streets. One or two cabs were piled on the fire. The fire brigade's hose was cut in several places, and the firemen used their axes on the soldiers. . . .

April 5. Mobilization parade ready for leaving at any moment. . . .

April 6. Letter from home, 2 *Witnesses*,[22] 2 *Bulletins*, and packet of tobacco.

April 8. Orders were to leave tonight, but they are now postponed till Sunday. . . . Saw five batteries of Australians go.

April 9. No. 1 battery left. Auckland infantry left and some other units.

April 10. Mobilization parade again.

Otago infantry and ambulance among others left. Said au revoir to all the boys.

April 12. Embarked on transport. Moved out into stream in evening. On board are Howitzer battery and amm. [ammunition] column, some ASC,[23] part of 16th Australian infantry, Australian ASC and ambulance, over 1000 men. The ship is a small one about 4000 tons and there is mess accommodation and horse

[22] a paper published weekly in Otago
[23] Army Service Corps for logistical support

accommodation, but none for men to sleep in. The ship had been used to ship troops across channel, but never for a long trip.

Managed to sleep all right on concrete deck.

April 13. Left Alexandria in afternoon.

Wind got up and it was very cold on deck at night.

Busy all day fusing ammunition and filling wagons with it.

There is a very large amount of lyddite[24] among the ammunition, which points to our bombarding ports or something. . . .

April 16. Sea calm. Arrived at island of Lemnos[25] about 7 a.m. Met there about a dozen large warships. English, French and 1 Russian, with a considerable number of torpedo craft, and a considerable number of troopships.

I don't know whether Greece has joined the allies. If she has not this must be a breach of neutrality making a base at one of her islands.

The island is nice and green but without bush, and the anchorage is a good one capable of holding hundreds of ships.

April 17. Great arguments as to who this island belongs to. I have been told that Turkey promised to cede it to Greece after last war, but did not do so and it is still Turkish.

In the morning, we went ashore for an exercise march and a welcome and much needed swim. It was fine. The country is just like the older settled parts of N.Z. except that it is not fenced, and that the houses are old and stone. The people do not live in farmhouses but congregate into townships or villages.

There is a rumour that one of our transports was sunk by a Turkish vessel, which was in turn sunk by a British cruiser. . . .

April 19. All day practicing slinging horses and guns into lighters.[26]

April 20. Went ashore in the afternoon, and went for a march to another village. The country we went through was fine, all young oats and barley crops with red poppies and some blue flowers among them. The village was nice and clean, with a fine big church, full of hand paintings of religious subjects. The people seem very decent and homely and are very friendly to the troops though their prices for figs, biscuits etc. are exorbitant. However this does not trouble us, as most of us have no money.

Met some of the Munster Fusiliers who said there are 20,000 regulars here, Royal Munster Fusiliers, Lancs. Fusiliers, Dublin Fusiliers, K.O. Scottie Borderers, East and West Kents, Surreys. These Munster chaps seem decent fellows, at any rate infinitely preferable to the E. Lancs. Terriers in Egypt.

April 21. There was a heavy wind yesterday, which developed into a gale today. Fortunately, the anchorage here is practically landlocked. Two ships, a transport and a tug went ashore on a sandy spot.

[24] picric acid, an explosive

[25] island in the Aegean Sea on which the Allies marshaled forces in early 1915 for the Gallipoli invasion

[26] smaller boats for transport to the beach

Packet of woodbines[27] given to every man, a gift from an officer unknown.

There seems to be no money at all on the ship and everyone is hoping to be paid something soon.

It seems the true story of the transport and the Turkish torpedo boat is that the Turks fired three torpedoes but all missed. Some of the Tommies[28] on the transport stupidly jumped overboard and a few were drowned. The torpedo boat was settled by one of our own ships. . . .

April 24. Left at 7 a.m. One of the first transports to leave this morning. Hung about outside. Life belts issued to each man owing to possibility of being torpedoed. We ought to be in the real thing in 2 or 3 days. We are taking next to no horses ashore in the first party of the battery, it being understood that we will have to manhandle the guns into position and go into action at once. Truly a pleasant prospect and for, if we can go into action almost on the beach, surely the enemy's artillery can cover the beach, and one of our guns would be a good and very desirable target.

Got on the move again about 7 p.m. No lights tonight. The horse boats are to be lowered at 5 a.m. to-morrow, when I suppose we will be off the hostile shore.

April 25. Arrived off mouth of Dardanelles before daybreak and bombardment started with the light. Fleet, led by *Queen Elizabeth,*[29] bombarded both sides. Half the transports moved in and commenced unloading men about 7 a.m. and rest of transports with portion of fleet went about ten miles along the coast of Gallipoli peninsula. Nearly all Australians, with latter. Some Infantry, N.Z. and Australian, landed. The landing was fairly easy, or seemed to be, but the enemy soon opened from behind a high hill with a battery the ships' guns could not locate. The men on shore clung on and fighting continued till night. Good number of our men killed and wounded. At night fighting lulled, but there was a fierce long range cannonade by our warships and the enemy started to pitch shells among the transports, which were then moved out of range for the night. . . .

April 26. Was not the least scared on going into action, hardly even excited.

Were knocked up at 0.30 a.m. and started to unload. Got ashore by daybreak, leaving most of the horses and drivers on board. Dragged the guns into scrub just off the beach. Concealed them with scrub and built a sand bag wall. Fired about 45 rounds on our gun during the day, whole battery fired 250 rounds but it was mainly the other section.

It seems the landing was far from easy yesterday. The first landing party of Australians were badly shot up, but jumped from the boats and made a great charge up the hill. They went too far, and were badly smacked up, and retreated again with loss. The N.Z. infantry, especially the Canterbury battalion, got hell too, mainly from shrapnel. Tommy Burns of 1st Cant. is dead. The infantry are not so badly off

[27] cigarettes

[28] English soldiers

[29] The most modern battleship in service with the Royal Navy. A nervous Admiralty soon withdrew it to the relative safety of Scottish waters.

now that we have artillery ashore. The only batteries ashore so far are us, one 18 pr. Australian, and one Indian mountain battery. Our fire was very effective keeping their guns quiet and silencing a maxim among other things.

April 27. Got up 4.30, a third day of glorious weather. Hope today will see the end of the battle and the enemy in retreat. We hear that the English troops who landed down the coast have got the Turks in the rear. We did see some rapid firing during the morning and ran out of ammunition. Our infantry were being cut up pretty badly and the enemy's shrapnel was preventing our ammunition from being landed. An Indian mountain battery came into action on our right, and the Wellington and Otago battalions reinforced the Australians who were being driven back. In the afternoon our ammunition arrived and the infantry advanced with the bayonet getting well ahead of yesterday's position. Our firing was very rapid at times and during the day we fired from 2 guns 257 rounds. About tea time the enemy's shrapnel got on to us, but we were not firing at the time so we lay low in our dugouts and got no casualties.

April 28. Got up at 4 a.m. Fine weather.

We're conserving our ammunition and had no particular target, so we did not fire a shot all day. Were twice under rather heavy shrapnel fire from an unlocated 12 pr. battery. There were some very narrow escapes. We lay low in our dugouts. Pussy Thomson was not quick enough in ducking down at one shot, and got a shrapnel bullet on the boot. He was just beside me. The bullet glanced off. Two observation points for the enemy's 12 pr. battery, one a place where a German officer communicated with the battery by carrier pigeons, were destroyed. Also a very big gun brought up by the Turks to control the landing beach was destroyed by the battleships. Strong reinforcements of marines were landed, and relieved those in the first trenches. . . .

April 29. Were knocked up 2 a.m. It was wet last night but I was pretty comfortable. Fine day today.

Everybody was up and every available man was out by about 2.30 a.m. because of signs of a night attack. Two 18 pr. guns came up alongside us, and an infantry company arrived to protect us from a charge of any sort. However, nothing eventuated and the tension was relieved when day broke.

Our men seem to be holding the Turks easily now.

It seems our landing where we did was a mistake but a real stroke of Providence. If we had landed where originally decided men would have been slaughtered as fast as they came ashore, for the Turks apparently had wind of it and had barbed wire and guns mounted etc. As it was the landing was a magnificent piece of work.

April 30. Sixth day of the battle. Fine. Last night we were shelled with shrapnel for a good while but no casualties occurred. I slept right through it and did not know till this morning.

Mail going out this morning so sent a postcard home. Were issued with small packet of cigarettes. Had a swim in the sea.

C section ambulance tent subdivisions came ashore. . . .

Another very quiet day.

Tot of rum issued.

On picquet[30] tonight.

The English force has taken Maidos five miles from here across the peninsula and we should junction with them very shortly. The French are on the Asiatic side, entrenched with the job of carrying the forts there from the land side.

(P.S. Report about taking of Maidos quite false).

Saturday, May 1, 1915. Seventh day. Fine.

Was sent out to the artillery observation post on the left flank from which they observe the warships fire. To do this, had to duck up a watercourse to avoid snipers and then climb a steep clay face. A man was sniped, shot through the head, just as I got there. Back to the battery at nightfall.

Battery fired a few rounds with excellent results. . . .

May 2. Eighth day. Fine.

Things seem pretty quiet this morning.

Did nothing much all day. On picquet tonight.

Our men made a night attack commencing at 7 p.m. when the ships and all the land guns fired. We stood by nearly all night and were firing again at daybreak. The attack does not seem to have been very successful. We progressed slightly on the left and in the centre, but could not do any good on the right. The losses were pretty heavy, the Otago battalion being cut up a bit.

The first howitzer man died today, Sergt. Allan, Specialist Sergeant, being sniped.

May 3. Ninth day. Fine.

Firing at daybreak, but did no more till the afternoon when we fired a few shots about 4 o'clock.

Bill Heaver of the Ambulance was sniped and shot dead today while going out into a dangerous part to get a wounded man.

Last night J.S. Reid, Captain in Otago regt. was killed and Spedding wounded. Jock McQueen was wounded and Snipe Prain missing, Adamson, Otago Uni., killed. Pilling came through all right.[31] He was directly in the line of a Turkish machine gun for an hour and a half but managed to lie hid in a hollow and afterwards escaped back.

May 4. Tenth day, fine.

Fired a few rounds during the morning.

Congratulations from the King to all the troops on effecting a successful landing were read. Information was got from a deserter that the Turks cannot stand our

[30] sentry duty

[31] George Pilling, then a Lieutenant in the 4th Otago Company, figured in one of the more dramatic episodes of the campaign. He led an intrepid small group to seize briefly Chunuk Bair, from the summit of which they could overlook the straits until driven back by a Turkish counterattack. Pilling was killed in the assault on Messines Ridge (for which John French helped lay the mines) in June 1917. Alexander Aitken, *Gallipoli to the Somme: Recollections of a New Zealand Infantryman* (Oxford: Oxford University Press, 1963), 9–10.

shell fire during the day, and that in future their attacks will be made at night, They do not like the bayonet at all.

Picquet tonight, 2-4 a.m.

Had a swim.

Cigarettes issued today.

May 5. Eleventh day. Fine.

Last night there was heavy gun firing over at the Dardanelles. In the evening the whole of the N.Z. infantry were taken aboard, to go as garrison for the time being to Chanak[32] which has fallen, This is to give them a rest. The bearer sections of the ambulance went too. Further reinforcements were landed to replace them.

Very cold wind with some rain at night.

(This story of what the N.Z. infantry were shifted for is a wild rumour and quite incorrect, as afterwards turned out)

May 6. Twelfth day. Fine with cold wind. Again a quiet day. A Turkish officer rode in and surrendered, and said he would surrender 1100 men, if he were sure of good treatment for them.

Very cold again at night.

May 7. Thirteenth day. Fine.

Had a swim.

May 8. Fourteenth day. Fine.

The enemy's intermittent shrapnel fire at the beach and incidentally at us is rather worrying and has resulted in a fair number of casualties among the mules and donkeys tethered on the beach.

Today they used lyddite for the first time to our knowledge. One shot landed about 20 yards to one side of us and knocked one or two holes in the cooking tins, but did no particular harm. Gen. Godley and staff were near us at the time and had to skip to cover.

Issue of rum.

May 9. Fifteenth day. Fine.

Information received that the [Turks] have an aeroplane here now and we were busy all the early part of the morning covering the gun overhead and covering any signs of our presence.

Sent a postcard home.

On picquet tonight.

Our fellows are making an attack on an isolated Turkish gun on the right flank tonight.

Heard that the *Lusitania*[33] has been sunk, not confirmed.

Had a swim.

[32] city on the Asian shore of the Dardanelles

[33] A British ocean liner, touted as the fastest ship in service between America and Europe. It was sunk by a German submarine on May 7, 1915, resulting in the deaths of 1,195 passengers and crew, including 128 Americans.

May 10. Sixteenth day. Light showers at intervals, otherwise fine.

Dose of shrapnel at breakfast time was pretty close.

Fired about twenty rounds from our gun during the morning, results unknown.

Tobacco issued.

Had a swim.

May 11. Seventeenth day. Fine till towards evening, then showery.

A certain amount of ammunition arrived for us, not enough to do much good, but still better than nothing.

While I was down talking to the ambulance chaps, a shell came through the hospital wall, shattered a case and landed in Maj. O'Neill's bed. Fortunately it did not burst.

On picquet tonight.

May 12. Eighteenth day. Pretty heavy rain last night and showery this morning. Managed to sleep fairly dry considering.

First lot of Australian light horse came ashore to act as infantry. Two brigades of them and our mounted rifles are on the transports in the bay.

N.Z. mounted rifles came ashore. The Otago regt. has been left behind to come on as a mounted regt. When the time requires it.[34]

Rum issued.

Had a swim.

May 13. Nineteenth day. Fine.

Had a swim.

Our section quieted one or two guns in the morning, tho' we didn't think we damaged the guns themselves. The left section destroyed one of their guns.

Picquet tonight.

May 14. Twentieth day. Fine.

Learn that H.M.S. *Goliath*[35] was torpedoed or mined yesterday in the Dardanelles and went down with three quarters of her crew.

Had a swim.

May 15. Twenty-first day. Fine.

Fired a few rounds in the afternoon with good results we are told.

Issue of rum.

Had a swim.

Picquet tonight.

Heard the opinion of an Australian sergt-major on the N.Z. and Australian troops. He reckoned that, if anything, the Australians were superior in a bayonet charge, but that once a position was taken the N.Z. men would hang on to it when the Australians possibly could not.

[34] Hutchison means the regiment would be used as cavalry to exploit a breakthrough.

[35] A Royal Navy pre-dreadnought battleship that was sunk on May 13, 1915, off Cape Helles by a Turkish torpedo boat, with the loss of nearly six hundred sailors.

May 16. Twenty-second day. Heavy shower last night, today fine.

The following was read to us –

Please convey to all ranks the following message received from G.O.C. Div[36] by C.R.A. (Commandant Royal Artillery).

"Will you please convey to all your batteries now here my high appreciation of their excellent shooting that they have made while in action here. Commanders of all posts are loud in their praises of the support they have had from the howitzers and No. 2 battery and on behalf of the whole Division I wish to express to them my thanks for the good work which has led to such substantial results."

May 17. Twenty-third day. Fine.

Fired a few rounds today.

Had a swim.

In evening helped to drag a 6 in. garrison howitzer along the beach, fifty men to each drag rope.

Sent a card home.

Cigarettes issued.

May 18. Twenty-fourth day. Fine.

Was busy all morning putting finishing touches to . . . 6 in. howitzer.

Our gun fired a few rounds.

The enemy are supposed to be heavily reinforced today. At any rate the have brought up some big guns. A 4.7 shell (or thereabouts) presumably from a ship's gun brought ashore dropped right beside our two guns.

Picquet tonight. Had a swim.

There are great stories going about concerning Capt. Wallingford of the Auckland infantry. He is still here in charge of some machine guns, tho' his battalion is not. He is champion shot of British army, and shoots one or more snipers every day, is best bag being reckoned to be nearly 30 one day. The Turks have got hold of his name and call out "Come out Wallingford, and let's have a shot at you."

May 19. Twenty-fifth day. Fine

Were knocked up 2.30 a.m. There was an enemy's attack on. We were shelled a good deal. We opened fire at 4 a.m. and fired a few shots now and then throughout the day.

We are told the enemy attacked early in the morning and made some advance. In the afternoon they were driven out of it again. From stories of various chaps, the Turkish losses were enormous, running into thousands.

This is the most exciting day we've had since the first Tuesday we were ashore.

Rum issued.

Got a mail, 3 letters from home. . . .

May 20. Twenty-sixth day. Fine.

What remained of N.Z. infantry came back from Cape Helles. Down there they made a great name for themselves. The N.Z. and Australian infantry down there got

[36] General Officer Commanding Division

the name of the White Gurkhas.[37] They made a considerable advance beyond where the others had got. The men down there have got a big job on. They have to take a tremendously strong hill, and seem to have settled down to sapping it.

Was stopped from having a swim today by snipers who kept up a shower of bullets along the beach.

May 21. Fine. Had 2 swims.

I was busy all afternoon with a part digging holes for ammunition belonging to the 6 in. gun.

Fired a few rounds.

14th Otago mounteds and more Australian light horse arrived.

Saw Pilling who said Bob Duthie was killed at the point. Podger was hit in four places, all scratches that did him no harm. The 4th Coy. of Otago regt. has no officers left, and officered by 3 reinforcement officers, including Sargood. Would be suicide to send them into action under fools like him.

May 22. Wet. Started raining heavily about 7 a.m. Cleared off by noon except for about one shower in the afternoon.

Issue of tobacco, matches and rum.

Had a swim in the afternoon.

Great excitement among the destroyers this afternoon. They are all steaming about here and there, covering the whole bay. There is supposed to be one or more submarines about, Austrians or Germans. . . .

May 24. Soft, steady rain.

Armistice today. 7.30 a.m. to 4.30 p.m. to bury dead.

From accounts of chaps who have been up there the Turkish dead are lying about 3 deep in places. . . .

(Hear that Italy has declared war on Austria).

May 25. Heavy showers at intervals.

We had just finished dinner about 12.45 p.m. when someone shouted a battleship had been torpedoed by a submarine. Sure enough, we saw the whole thing. She heeled slowly over to starboard, and after 10 minutes was keel up. She then soon disappeared in 60 fathoms. They say it is the *Triumph*. Torpedo boats buzzed about rescuing wounded and searching for the enemy submarine. One of the destroyers fired several shots.

May 26. Fine. Swim.

Fired several rounds, gun shooting a bit erratic. Don't know whether it's the gun, the ammunition, or the platform.

Rum issued.

Picquet tonight.

Hear that a Turkish gunboat was sunk off Constantinople by a British submarine.

[37] For a ferocity in combat comparable to that of Gurkha soldiers prized by British recruiters as being among India's "martial races."

May 27. Fine.

Along with others had a touch of gripes in the morning, from eating or drinking something crook, I suppose.

There are rumours about that the *Majestic*[38] is disabled or sunk. . . .

May 29. Fine. Swim.

Were knocked up 3 a.m. The Turks were putting up another attack. Heavy fighting going on from then till about 6 a.m. We fired a few rounds, and more again in the afternoon.

One of our gun team, Ross, sniped, shot through lung and soon died. Another, Olsen, developed appendicitis and was sent away.

Official report read to us that 120,000 Turks have been opposing us here and at Cape Helles. Of these the most conservative estimate of the casualties is 55,000. A submarine has done great work in the Sea of Marmora, sinking two or three gunboats and transports. Commander of it gets V.C. [Victoria Cross] and all the crew D.S.M. [Distinguished Service Medal]. . . .

May 30. An outpost of Wellington mtds. [mounteds, namely cavalry] cut off on the left flank and are reported to be in straits. At night a force went out and safely brought them in. They are reported to have lost 60 out of a squadron (150). . . .

This is the beginning of sixth week.

Tuesday, June 1, 1915. Fine. Swim. Picquet tonight.

The sight on our gun having been tested and rectified we are back on the active list again. Fired a few rounds.

On any afternoon the beach looks just like a holiday resort except that bathing suits are not the fashion. Hundreds of men are bathing every afternoon. Once or twice I have been swimming when the enemy opened shrapnel fire on the beach and we've all had to seize our clothes and get into a communication trench.

Our gun fired a few rounds at a strong body of the enemy preceding north. Don't know whether this is start of a general retirement. The general opinion seems to be that we'll advance very soon.

June 2. Fine. Swim.

Another Austrian submarine reported captured while trying to enter Lemnos. This makes three captured, only one now supposed to be at large in our vicinity. . . .

One of two men sniped while in swimming today. We had to come out hurriedly.

June 3. Fine. Swim. Picquet tonight.

Rumours about that the whole Australasian Army corps is to be relieved here and after a spell is to go to France. I don't think there is anything in it. Certain details are being sent away such as Ammunition Column, for which there is no particular work. . . .

June 4. Fine. Swim.

[38] HMS *Majestic* was a pre-dreadnought Royal Navy battleship that supported Allied troops in the Dardanelles campaign. It was sunk by a German submarine at Cape Hellas on May 27, 1915.

They sent us our sea kits containing our spare uniform and boots, having gone through our big kits to get these. I don't suppose we'll see our big kits again, now. . . .

We are all wearing shorts again now, having cut down old pairs of pants.

Went up into our front trenches and had a good look round with aid of a periscope. On the left the trenches are 300 yards apart, narrowing down till at Quinn's post they are barely 10 or 15 yards apart.

June 5. Fine. Swim. Telephone picquet.

Heavy fighting last night and this morning at Quinn's post in the centre of our position. Our men, Canterbury and Auckland infantry, took the enemy's trenches but owing to lack of support and shortage of ammunition were driven out again by hand grenades. Our casualties, about 200 killed, wounded and missing. Turks heavier, including a good number captured.

Some of the prisoners say that they have been shipped across from Asia, not allowed to land in Constantinople, and shoved straight into the trenches. They did not know who they were fighting, and thought [we] were Bulgarians, who take no prisoners. Otherwise more would surrender.

Persistent rumours that the big hill (Atchibaba[39]) is taken. . . .

June 10. Fine. Swim.

Bread issued today instead of biscuits; a welcome change.

Fired a good few rounds including a rapid series of 10 rounds at a direct target. An 18 pr. battery was also firing at some and we made the dust fly between us for a few minutes. Later a destroyer joined in too. . . .

June 11. Fine, but strong wind. Swim. Picquet.

Things are getting very monotonous. We get up in the mornings have three meals and go to bed at night. Every second night we do two hours' or so picquet, and nearly every day we fire a few rounds, sometimes not even that.

Fired a few rounds today.

Jimmy Bennett and Tod Sloan were talking together on the beach when a shell burst right on to them. Bennett got a bullet through the throat and died almost at once. Sloan was hit in the back the bullet lodging against his spine. The X rays alone will tell if he will live, and if he does live whether he'll be a cripple. . . .

June 14. Fine. Swim.

Morning started with artillery duel, starting about 5 a.m. We were firing for a while.

The remainder of our third and all our fourth reinforcements arrived, apparently sent here by some mistake because we don't want them.

Our B gun tonight fired a series at what is said to be a French 75 mm. gun captured by the Turks at Cape Helles, and are reported to have smashed it. . . .

[39] Achi Baba was a high point overlooking the Gallipoli peninsula and the primary position of the Turkish defense during the Gallipoli campaign. Allied forces under Sir Ian Hamilton failed three times to take the heights in late April, early May, and June 1915 during the battles of Krithia.

June 15. For dinner today there was the following menu—mashed boiled potatoes (dried) and green peas (tinned) with tinned fish mixed in it forming a delightful hash, with Worcester sauce. This was followed by maizena[40] and tinned fruit, and finished by tea with milk in it. This stupendous meal was made of stuff brought for us from Lemnos, and paid for out of the battery fund. (At last we have found a use for a battery fund). . . .

June 18. Centenary of Waterloo.[41]

Rum issue.

Spent the evening along at the ambulance lines. . . .

June 19. Letters from home and a *Bulletin*. More mail must be somewhere. Date of last of these is May 5th and it should run to a week later.[42]

June 22. Poached eggs on toast for breakfast. . . .

Hear the enemy have a Zeppelin here, and no lights are to be allowed after dark.

Fired a few shots for the first time for some days.

Was given tin of Havelock tobacco as my share of tobacco sent by drivers from Alexandria. . . .

June 24. Hear that there is every chance of 4th and 5th year medical students being sent home to complete [their studies]. . . . It'll be rotten if all these chaps go.

June 25. I burst into poetry on the subject of these chaps going home. . . .

Effusion by me 6/25/15

They grew in beauty side by side
They filled one tent with skits
Their voices mingled as they yapped
O'er bottles of wine at night.
The talk was of the Colonel's guts
Of Tewsley's Roman nose
Of sergeants, syphilis and sand
And Egypt's other woes.
And one would talk of lunatics
And one of rocks and ores
And then an argument would start
On Cairo and its whores.
And some would talk of clavicles
And some of quail and deer
And some of good old football

[40] cookies prepared from corn flour

[41] Battle of June 18, 1815, when British forces led by the Duke of Wellington along with Prussian troops under Gerhard von Blücher defeated Napoleon Bonaparte's army in Belgium. The defeat would bring to a close Napoleon's rule as emperor of France.

[42] This remark is a clear indication of the degree to which Hutchison anticipated and relied upon the regular delivery of mail from home.

And some of Strachan's beer.
These were indeed a happy band
With talk and laughter free
But now they're scattered far and wide
By ocean, land and sea.
Alexandria holds McCreary
A man of blighted hope
He daily grooms his horses
Nightly fills himself with dope.
Dick King is still at Cairo
Two stars he now can boast
He's pulling teeth, but longing yet
For Turkey's shell swept coast.
Pat Parker's joined the Maori boys
On Malta's beer he thrives
While Hutchy's now a battery man
He's with the four-point-fives.
And now the greatest rift of all
Hail the few lucky few!
Tom Denniston, long Geoff and Chris
And Fitz are homeward due.
Now there is left a sainted band
Some half-a-dozen or so
To tread the weary road until
The Germans go below.
But there will be a glorious spree
When this damned war is o'er
And we have met in peace again
Upon New Zealand's shore.
We'll meet in Sweeting's upstairs room
And fairly shake the wall
With singing "Here we are again"
And shouting "On the ball."
And then the talk will be once more
Of Egypt, Anzac, shells,
Of snipers, shrapnel, trenches,
Of dead men—and their smells.
Of bully beef and biscuits hard,
Of Kaiser Bill, and Cain.
And then once more we'll raise the yell
Of "Fill 'em up again."

June 28. Fired a good few rounds. Heavy cannonade down Cape Helles way.

Good day for our forces. The men down Cape Helles advanced, two more divisions were landed between them and us, and our right flank (Australian Light Horse) advanced 500 yards.

We always have our swim after dark now as, owing to the persistent attentions of the Koja Tepe gun from one end and the Salt Lake gun from the other end, the beach is not safe in the day. . . .

June 29. The advance made by the force from Cape Helles yesterday was about 1100 yards. The advance made on the right flank by our men was to cut off reinforcements going to the Cape. This they succeeded in doing but did not maintain their advanced position.

My pencil is just about finished and I'll have to raise another bit by hook or crook or give up writing this diary. . . .

June 30. Last night the Turks made a charge against our extreme left held by 8th L.M. They were easily repulsed. Casualties, Turks 250 dead on the field, us 7 killed, 30 or 40 wounded.

At tea time, gun from Salt Lake direction got right on to us with melinite[43] or lyddite and dropped 20 rounds all within about 30 yards of our gun without doing any harm.

New dug out finished, and slept in tonight. . . .

July 3. Not feeling too good yet, headache off and on.

Wagon picquet noon-6 p.m.

The Maoris arrived last night. . . .

July 5. Everything is very monotonous now, and we have no way of spending the day. We are just waiting here till it is necessary for us to make a further advance. . . .

July 10. Inoculation against cholera.[44]. . .

July 12. Mohammedan festival month. Ramadan[45] starts today and fierce attacks are expected.

Stood to arms till 11 p.m. . . .

July 14. Intermittent cannonading down the point.

Got paid £1 in paper. . . .

July 19. Second injection against cholera (double dose this time) which was given us yesterday has me knocked all of a heap to-day, shivering fit, off my food etc. . . .

July 20. Heard that there were two parcels for me at the Ambulance so went along and found they were the ones brought by Mrs. Barnett from N.Z. and posted by her in England. They were a fine cake from home and pair of sox, half a doz. handkerchiefs and a lot of toffee from the aunties.

Feeling better today, but not able to eat much yet. . . .

[43] another high explosive containing picric acid

[44] a highly infectious disease of the small intestine caused by the ingestion of water or food contaminated by feces

[45] Observed by Muslims around the world, the holy month of Ramadan, the ninth in the Islamic lunar-based calendar, requires the faithful to fast from sunrise until sunset for an entire month. If, as the faithful believed, the gates of paradise were open during this month, martyrdom might be easier to achieve and thus more frequent and determined attacks might be anticipated.

July 22. Big attack expected tonight or tomorrow night. We are standing to arms to-night 11.45–12.15 (as the moon sets) and again 3–3.30 (just before dawn). . . .

July 26. About tea time 75 mm gun got on to us, demolished the latrines and altered the landscape considerably, but did no damage.

This gun is a French 75, said to have been captured by the Turks from the Greeks during the Balkan war. She gives no warning, the shell arriving as soon as the sound. . . .

July 27. 75 on to us with a few more shells. Owing to her attentions, and to the fact that we have any amount of other artillery, our guns are not going to fire unless absolutely necessary for the next few days.

Spent the afternoon along at the ambulance. . . .

July 28. Fine. Swim.

Took a trip round the right flank in the afternoon. My overcoat, which was laid in the sun on a bank, got 12 holes through it from shrapnel from 75. I was in the open when this shell arrived and had a lucky escape. . . .

July 29. Taube aeroplane[46] dropped a bomb at us in the evening. Bomb landed about 50 yards from our gun in the sea. Couple of lucky chaps got one or two small fish for breakfast tomorrow as a result of the bomb's effect. . . .

August 2. Spent nearly all day digging more caches for ammunition and bringing up the ammunition to the guns.

The big day when we are to make the grand advance is very close now. All indications show that. We have an extraordinary amount of artillery here, guns of all calibers, and any amount of ammunition.

Rum issued.

August 3. Rum issue every night now till the big attack comes off.

August 4. Fine.

The N.Z. artillery has now been made into two brigades. . . . First brigade is 1st and 3rd batteries and the other howitzer battery which should be in Egypt by now. Second brigade is 2nd battery, us and 4th 18 pr. battery also now in Egypt. . . .

August 5. Visited the Otago infantry in the morning. . . .

Division of Tommies came ashore last night, Worcesters, Gloucesters, Warwicks, Chesters, Essex, South Wales Borderers and Birmingham men. . . .

August 6. Fine.

Battalion each of Sikhs and Pathans and brigade of Ghurkas came ashore last night.

Busy all morning bringing up ammunition till we had 400 rounds per gun stowed handy, and all afternoon fuzing this lot.

[46] The Taube (German for "dove") was a German pre-WWI monoplane, well suited for observation, but that soon proved obsolete in combat. It had the distinction of being the first aircraft from which an aerial bomb was dropped (by an Italian pilot over Libya in November 1911).

The big work started at 4.30 p.m. No. 1 gun fired steadily 4.30 p.m. till 9.30 p.m. when we (No. 2) joined in and both fired almost as rapidly as possible till 11 p.m. Then no. 1 knocked off and we continued right till 4 a.m. firing only 1 round every 10 mins. I turned in at 1.30 and was up again before 4. At 4 a.m. both guns commenced firing rapidly again till 5. . . .

August 7. One or other of guns firing all morning. In afternoon bringing up more ammunition and fuzing it. When morning broke we saw they had been landing troops at Cape Suvla.[47] Several cruisers and many transports are there. On the left flank very big advance made last night by Ghurkas, Sikhs, Australians, N.Z. mounted rifles and infantry and Maoris. Hear Colonel [Arthur] Bauchop is dead or seriously wounded. In centre at Quinn's Post,[48] our attack (by Aus. Light Horse) was repulsed with heavy casualties, but the right is said to have advanced a lot. Several guns have been taken on the left and hundreds of prisoners been brought in. The troops landed at Suvla seem to be advancing well. . . .

August 8. I cannot put down the details of our firing and other work for this Sunday, Monday and Tuesday, but we were firing off and on the whole time, and bringing up ammunition and fuzing it, and doing other necessary jobs. We got perhaps 3 to 4 hours sleep a night on an average from Friday 6th till Tuesday 10th. Owing to the advance of the infantry over the country from which we used to be shelled we are quite free from fire of any sort except a few stray bullets and the result is that up to date (Wednesday 11th) we have had no casualties in this battle.

The fighting has been very severe on the infantry. . . .

August 9. The casualties by now must run into tens of thousands, perhaps 30,000, including seven or eight thousand dead. Our force engaged on the left flank alone must be at least 80,000 and fresh troops arrive every night to be sent straight up. The N.Z. 5th reinforcements arrived Sunday and went into action the following day.

All the N.Z. infantry battalions and mounted regiments and the Maoris also have lost heavily. . . .

August 10. There has been a big advance but the real objective, hill 971,[49] is not yet in our possession. The Turks still hold the summit with our chaps entrenched just below it.

August 11. Fine.

[47] Located on the Aegean coast of the Gallipoli peninsula, Suvla Bay was the site of a British effort to break the deadlock in the Gallipoli campaign. The landing of troops on the night of August 6, 1915, however, was disrupted by enemy sniper fire and the grounding of several ships on shoals and reefs.

[48] A strategic point for ANZAC forces, Quinn's Post was named after Major Hugh Quinn, who perished there on May 29, 1915. Today Quinn's Post is a Commonwealth cemetery for those killed in action during the Gallipoli campaign.

[49] Also known as Koja Chemen Tepe, the highest point of the Sari Bair ridge, Gallipoli. During the night of August 6, 1915, ANZAC troops launched an attack with the objective of capturing Hill 971 and ultimately securing Turkish forts guarding the straits. Owing to rugged terrain, poor maps, and constant enemy attacks, the plan failed.

Everything very quiet today. Got time for a morning swim and a shave. . . .

Got orders to be ready to shift out to left flank at night, but orders were countermanded and our other section is going. Was on party who dragged gun out after dark. . . .

August 13. Everything is quiet again, the lull before a continuation of the storm. Both sides are consolidating as fast as possible. A great deal of artillery is being shifted out to our left flank.

We are spending our time getting further ammunition up and fuzed, and in fatigues necessary in connection with the shift of the other section. . . .

August 19. Twelve months today since I enlisted, I think. . . .

August 23. I have got a touch of dysentery just now. . . .

August 25. Four calendar months today since landing was made. . . .

August 28. This morning while Allan (my dug out mate) was inside the dug out and I was standing in the doorway, a shell came through the roof but fortunately did not burst. The roof was strong timber with a sheet of copper on it and about a foot or 15 inches of earth. It wrecked the place properly but did no damage otherwise. . . .

The entries for the next three weeks are not very informative, reflecting a lull in the action. Hutchison continued to note the state of the weather, the receipt or dispatch of mail, visits from friends, and any unusual meals.

September 19. A few scraps of mail came round. I got another parcel of sox and tobacco from home, and tin of sweets ordered by Father from Selfridges,[50] London. They were first class sweets, quality having evidently been considered, not quantity. . . .

September 27. Big bombardment up the coast in direction of Bulair this evening.

Also considerable bombardment down in Achi-baba direction. . . .

September 28. Owing to reduction of our non coms,[51] by sickness etc., I am appointed bombardier today and transferred to B gun. Would rather have remained with A.

September 29. Fine. Swim.

I am 21 years of age today (my second birthday in the army). . . .

September 30. Allan and I have started on winter residence. We are putting it on the side of a hillock along with others and it is not to be a dug out but a hut of timber, empty ammunition boxes, sacks and waterproof sheets. . . .

October 4. For lunch today had cold lamb and chutney, good bread and butter, digestive biscuits[52] and butter, good cup of tea.

[50] well-regarded, high-end department store, founded in 1909, on Oxford Street in London's West End

[51] junior or non-commissioned officers

[52] semi-sweet biscuit often consumed with tea

This is easily the pleasantest meal I have had since coming on to the peninsula and is quite like lunch at home. Everything, except the tea of course, came off the *Maheno,*[53] and the *Maheno* stores are about cut out now.

Our gun (B) fired about 10 rounds at 5 p.m. . . .

October 5. Cold beef and tomato sauce for lunch. We are living very well just now, fresh beef being issued practically every day and much better bread than usual. . . . Big mail arrived.

October 8. Had 2 or 3 giddy fits,[54] last a bad one.

Greig, Allan and Newsham took me to Aus. hospital on a stretcher and I was sent off to hospital ship.

October 9–11. Lying in [sick] bay.

October 16. My trouble diagnosed as slight enteric, and am shifted to Mtarfa Hospital[55]. . . .

October 17. In bed at Mtarfa. So for some weeks I suppose. Wrote to father, Greig, and orderly room sergt. Telling him where to readdress letters.

October 19. Getting only fluids for food. . . .

During night drink of milk 2 or 3 times if you want it.

You get only about 1/3 pint at the most at a time, and you get pretty hungry on such a diet. . . .

October 29. A Mr. Tobin, N.Z. chaplain, attached Auckland Mounted Rifles but now looking after all New Zealanders in Malta, came up to see me and gave me *Auckland Weekly* Sept. 2 and *Canterbury Times* Sept. 8.

By latter I see school beat Ch'ch [Christchurch] H.S. 17-10 but lost final of tournament to Timaru 9-11, both games being described as very good football.

Monday, November 1, 1915. My temp. being satisfactory, I was today on sort of half milk diet. I got just my ordinary cup of tea for breakfast, got a little bread in my beef tea at noon, and got about 1 ½ or 2 inches square of bread with my tea at 4 p.m. It was just enough to tantalize me, but I suppose one must start very gently. . . .

November 11. On full diet.

> Breakfast Porridge, egg, bread and butter
> Dinner Meat (roast and stew alternatively) and potatoes, bread and pudding
> Tea Egg, bread, butter and jam
> Supper Bread, butter and jam, cocoa

November 12. Got my first letters readdressed from peninsula, one from Connie Beaumont[56] Sept. 21 and one from Mother, same date. A month's letters between

[53] New Zealand ocean liner that served as a hospital ship during the war
[54] dizziness or light-headedness
[55] a naval hospital on Malta
[56] future fiancée of his close friend Gid Fitzgerald

these two and last ones I had, still to come to hand. Wrote to Father, a very short letter because I had nothing to put in it.

Over the next month Hutchison made slow but steady progress in his convalescence, noting when, for example, he could sit up again or walk.

December 10. While down getting paid, we noticed that the number of Australians is increasing rapidly. They will soon have to send us away or the hospital will be full of us. . . .

He was indeed sent away, on December 15, to Alexandria. From there he was transferred to Suez for return passage to New Zealand, eventually leaving for home on December 26.

December 22. News came through that they have evacuated Suvla and Anzac. A bit of a shock to our pride! God knows how they did it successfully. It must be one of the greatest feats in British history, but this thought is not much consolation for the death of the thousands of men who were killed. . . .

December 31. So ends a year crammed full of incident such as I can never hope to have again, unless this coming year is equally eventful.

More than three years after he had sailed halfway around the world to serve in the war, Hutchison once again embarked on an epic journey on May 2, 1918. Now a second lieutenant in the 36th New Zealand Field Artillery, he enjoyed a first-class berth on the 13,000-ton passenger liner Balmoral Castle as it slowly steamed from Wellington, making some 330 nautical miles on its best days (a laborious 14 knots per hour). Because his unit was headed to France this time, not Egypt, the route was eastward, through the Panama Canal, and via Jamaica to Newport News, Virginia. Fresh from the cool late-fall weather of New Zealand, Hutchison found the summertime heat of Virginia stifling, which even his customary swims did little to assuage. Leaving Newport News on June 5, he realized he was "entering on probably the most ticklish part of our journey, as we are unescorted here and U-boats, probably several, are actively employed in these coastal waters, and have sunk numerous vessels in the last three or four days."[57] Hutchison's voyage proved uneventful, and he reached Halifax safely. There the Balmoral Castle waited for the assembly of a convoy of 14 troopships, mostly loaded with American soldiers, and three escorts. On June 21, 1918, he finally disembarked at the port of Tilbury on the river Thames, just east of London. He returned to France on July 8, and to the front lines a week later. His two long voyages had been a testament to the seaborne lifelines that sustained imperial Britain's war effort.

July 14, 1918. Went up to the guns, had a look round positions etc. Fritz exceedingly quiet. Back to wagon lines for night. . . .

July 15. Up to guns again, this time for permanent residence. Stayed at rear sections all day and night. . . .

[57] The U-151 sank three American ships off the Virginia coast on May 25 and another six vessels off the New Jersey coast on June 2. Paul Halpern, *A Naval History of World War I* (Annapolis: Naval Institute Press, 1994), 430–31.

July 20. We started slight advance in afternoon. My communication down and I got mixed up with the infantry in waiting for a bomb attack which was however easily repulsed by bombs and a Stokes [mortar].

July 21. Heavily shelled in afternoon for about four hours. Advanced position consolidated.

July 2. Quiet today. . . . Letters from home (13 May 1918). . . .

August 10. Nice day again, but on this job the trouble is you don't see much of it, as you spend the biggest part of the day in a deep dugout. However, it's great experience to have charge of an isolated section like this, and teaches you things very quickly. . . .

August 14. Huns commenced to evacuate their positions this morning and our fellows are pushing on to keep in touch with them. Our guns are going up this afternoon. Glorious day. We liaison tonight with first Otagos. . . .

August 15. Went on this morning, finally to most extreme point of our advance on Serre ridge to south of Puisieux.[58] Had no communication, however, out there, and after having a look round, came back to Battn [battalion] H.Q. now advanced to C trench beyond Kaiser's Lane. Advance so far has been made with very few casualties, Hun getting out tout suite. Very hot tiring day. . . . Good deal of shelling on all newly occupied area. . . .

August 22. We had just finished work at 5.30 a.m. when Hun countered and put a considerable strafe on us. S.O.S. up, and no firing. Very lucky though, and only 2 wounded. Counter attack repulsed. Other batteries all got the strafe too. . . . Another counter attack in aft. Also repulsed. Our line advanced again at night.

August 23. Doing a lot of firing at night and today, but enemy fire on us very little. Advanced guns again in evening to open position E. of Puisieux and left that 9 a.m.

August 24. Moved as said above 9 a.m. to position ESE of Achiet-le-Petit where we can fire on Bapaume, which is next objective, I suppose. Out of the region of eternal shell holes now. Open position here. The whole N.Z. div. has come here, where there is a mass of troops. Sleep has been very short since Monday, and I am filthy dirty. One wounded. Things pretty rough for the diggers[59] in front here today. . . . Hun planes very active in bombing and machine-gunning our communications, which are crowded with guns and men.

August 25. Further advance at daybreak today. In forenoon I took centre section forward again, got onto position with the gun teams, and had to cut and run for it owing to heavy shelling. Came at it again later and got into position (W. of Grévillers). In evening got orders to come in against [enemy] battery, as Jerry had

[58] town in northern France not far from the Somme; scene of much heavy fighting in 1916
[59] ANZAC troops

been making it pretty hot all afternoon. Heavy thunderstorms at night made it very unpleasant for us in open scrapes in the ground.

August 26. Was awakened up 3.45 a.m. by 4.2 shelling our posy [position]. Blankets and everything soaking wet, but nevertheless had slept pretty well. Just as well I had my blankets as the last night we hadn't them. Beat it out of my scrape into the best shell cover I could find. Moved again 6.30 a.m. to position N.E. of Biefvillers-les-Bapaume and W. of Behagnies—Bapaume Rd.[60] Considerable shelling round about us there all day. Only 4 guns now, as one was put out of action by the shelling this morning, and one was left behind at Brickfield on 23rd so shaken as to be useless. Another gun out of action this evening with shell damage to buffer. Two men wounded today. . . .

August 27. Gun with damaged buffer repaired, and one arrived from W.L. making 5 in action today. Rum ration last night and a quiet night, and everyone slept like a log for ten to twelve hours. Quiet day today. Able to get a mugful of water for shaving, washing etc. and now feel ready to carry on stunt for another week or so. No casualties today. We seem to be temporarily held up now until Bapaume falls. We (the battery) are within 1500 yds of Bapaume. . . .

August 28. Quiet night again and good 11 hours' sleep. Day quiet too. . . . Hun shelling forward area especially Favreuil very severely all day. . . . No casualties today.

August 29. Night again quiet. Home letters complete to 23 June and acknowledged. Wrote home. . . . Our chaps going forward again in the evening. Bapaume evacuated by last of the Huns. Péronne said to have been taken. We are now divisional reserve to be used to follow up a success. Gun limbers and wagons standing by at gun positions.

August 30. Fired a barrage 5-6 a.m. Moved off 8.30 a.m. into position W. of Beunatre, where we came into action. . . . I had a rotten day dodging from one shell hole to another; no trenches; the 4 telephonists could not keep the wire going; enemy shelling forward area heavily. Position in front obscure. On getting in to battery at night, find they have settled down for a stay, however short, at the position, and have sent the firing battery wagons back as usual. Two men wounded at battery today; one man . . . yesterday, also several horses killed and wounded. Hun planes flying low over us bombing and machine gunning to-day; saw one brought down by a Lewis gun. Really good living possy here, some German Bde H.Q. or something. . . .

August 31. S.O.S. 4.30 a.m. to 6 a.m., Hun counter attacking in force with tanks but was repulsed. New position selected forward between Fremicourt and Bancourt.[61] Fairly quiet day. No casualties. Got in good amount of sleep last night, this afternoon and tonight to carry me on for two or three days. . . .

[60] Hutchison's specificity here reflected his need as an artilleryman to be precise about his position relative to the enemy's.
[61] villages just east of Bapaume

Sunday, September 1, 1918. Fired barrage in early morning. Weather continues to be very good. . . . Moved to position between Fremicourt and Bancourt in afternoon. . . .

September 3. Moved forward midday, me taking left X to report to infantry comdr, but this order was countermanded when I was well along road with them, and whole battery came in together W. of Bertincourt. O.P.[62] with Major till evening. We went to our front posts, and there stood up on top of bank with glasses, without provoking any machine gun or sniper. Hun must have gone further still, though we could see movement of him.

September 4. Our chaps advancing again, and I followed up as F.O.O.[63] Had a fairly rotten time with shell fire. Advance did not go as far as desired owing to 42nd. Div. on right not going on and our flank having to bend back to avoid being outflanked. Got a bit of gas last night, also tonight, nothing very bad. One man wounded today. . . .

September 5. Moved 5 a.m. to position W. of Ruyaulcourt. . . . Running a bit short of sleep again the last couple of days. . . . Hot day, very quiet. Managed to get the best wash I've had since, I think, about Aug. 9 when I had a wash down bath. Fired barrage 5.30 to 6.15 p.m. . . . Quiet night too, though some gas came over in early part of it. Got a good sleep. No casualties today.

September 6. Hot day again. Very heavy thunderstorm washed nearly everyone out last night; not me, I kept quite dry, but this morning everyone dried out again. . . . Moved to position between 7ths and Neuville-Bournjonval, but we find that our advance today is such that we are practically out of range again already. The advance today is not being resisted and is practically bloodless. Fritz has evacuated Havrincourt Wood, where difficulty was expected.

September 7. Moved to position between Havrincourt Wood and Metz-en-Couture. Considerable shelling there all day. Our battery was lucky enough to avoid casualties —our luck has been great all through, but 6th and 9th both had a good few among men and horses. I was sent on liaison to battn. H.Q. in Metz. The weather continues to be as good as ever. Advance held up today. We are practically now where our retreat started on March 21st of this year, and almost on to Hindenburg Line.[64]

September 8. At battalion. Heavy shelling all day. Hun obviously has stack of guns here. One man wounded at battery, I hear. The Hun has a very good position on a ridge commanding us, and looks as if he intends to hang on to it.

September 9. Advance made to take ridge starting 4 a.m. Not too successful at first and considerable number of casualties. Advance stopped short of objective. Another

[62] observation post
[63] Forward Observation Officer
[64] The Hindenburg Line referred to the defensive positions prepared during the winter of 1916–17 to which the German army could fall back if necessary.

wounded at battery. Hun gassing considerably today, mainly blue cross (sneezing) stuff.[65] Got a good mouthful today.

Relieved at battalion in evening and glad to get away from it, what with the crowded discomfort, shelling, gas, etc.

September 10. Not feeling too good today, touch of 'flu' I think. Stayed in bed all day as it was very quiet day at battery. . . .

September 11. Still in bed today, as things are quiet and there is no reason why I should get up. Feeling considerably better. . . .

September 12. Barrage 5:25 to 7.

Up today again, feeling fine but a little bit weak. . . .

September 14. Heavily shelled with mustard H.E.[66] shells 4 a.m. to 6.30 a.m. All batteries got it. Five men of ours evacuated gassed. I got down to the W.C. and managed a hot bath. . . .

September 16. At Ytres[67] till 5 p.m. when whole battery moved off S. and established . . . between Equancourt and Nurlu. . . . Heavy thunderstorms at night; we all got thoroughly soaked. . . .

September 17. Battery moved up at dark into position E. of Hendicourt within 700 or 800 yds. of our front line ready for a stunt in the morning. Got in without accident. . . .

September 18. Stunt 5.10 a.m. onwards. Very successful. We had 4 wounded including Sergt. Lane and Austin. Tommies lost some of the taken ground again, but on the whole stunt was quite successful. Day quiet. Small barrage 7 p.m. and S.O.S. immediately following. Night quiet. One more man evacuated as result of gassing last Sat.

September 19. Small barrage 5.30 a.m.

Shot away a lot of ammn. on various targets. . . . No hostile shelling.

September 20. At W.L.[68] awaiting orders. Good day. Several of our men arrived last day or two as reinfs [reinforcements]. Say that 39ths and 40ths should be in Ewshot[69] by now, and that they have had a bad time, several deaths, on the voyage. . . .

September 21. At W. L. getting ready to move. Orders to move in evening to Quéant, a trek of 15 miles or so northward. . . . Moved off 6.30 p.m. Cold trek. Made new position W. of Quéant 1.30 a.m. . . .

September 25. Obviously summer going now; nights and early mornings very cold. Guns went up to position in evenings. Great concentration of infantry here, also

[65] German gas shells so named for the blue crosses marked on them
[66] high explosive
[67] not to be confused with Ypres
[68] wagon line, with logistical support for the batteries
[69] Ewshot, a Hampshire village southwest of London, was the site of a New Zealand army camp housing some 5,000 soldiers.

great mass of guns. All good infantry, 51st and 52nd (Scotch) divisions, naval div., Guards on right, Canadians on left. I am at wagon lines . . . , quite a change for me.

September 26. Cold night and morning again, glorious day. Infantry pouring in tonight. Biggest battle of the war (some say) starts probably tomorrow.

September 27. I left W.L. 5 a.m. with 2nd lot of gun limbers, rt. sec. of limbers having gone on an hour before, guns having to shift forward part at a time so as to keep fire going. At 9.30 a.m. I went forward to reconnoiter possible crossing of canal [du Nord]. Hun holding well and could not get to canal till about 11 a.m. Found good crossing. 2 p.m. went forward as mounted patrol, and further on foot. Attack in aft. on our front going fairly well in afternoon, though held up for some time in morning at canal. Guards on right, Canadians on left, have gone ahead well. Two men wounded today in bty. I went back to W.L. at night. Got Hun dial sight off a whiz-bang.[70]

September 28. Left W. L. 5 a.m. Crossed Canal 6.30. Rendezvoused two or three times, finally got to pos. S. of Fontaine-Notre-Dame. . . . We are in readiness to go forward at any moment, but infantry held up on Canal de L'Escaut for time being. . . .

September 29. 24 years old today. . . . Had a quiet day there. Did some shooting, and saw infantry advance to Cambrai main south road. However, advance met considerable resistance, and, though useful advance, was not a great one, and guns remain in same pos. for to-night, which is alright as we have a good possy.

September 30. Had a really good restful night last night, which is all to the good. . . . Moved soon after midday to position W. of La Folie Wood (still W. of Canal de L'Escaut). . . . Position not changing much in front. Quiet night, but very heavy rain, and we got soaked in our hastily built scrape bivvies.[71]

Tuesday, October 1, 1918. Nice day, but cold wind. . . . The infantry at present in front do not seem to be pushing with any great energy, and we are hung up for the present. One man wounded by apparently stray shell at wagon lines. . . .

October 4. Pretty quiet day again, but Hun shelled up pretty heavily at times. One man wounded. . . .

October 9. Hun got out and we got possession of Cambrai. Guns after firing barrage in the morning limbered up and bridge rendezvoused. W.L. brought across canal. I went forward as mounted patrol with mounted orderlies to send back situation. Had quite a good day.

October 10. Bde. is now in support attached to 19th Div. Advance going on well. I reconnoitred outskirts of Cambrai for water. Town is not damaged much, though outskirts are. Town is, however, mined in places. . . . This is a land of peace and

[70] German 77mm. or similar shell that traveled at high velocity and whose distinctive high-pitched noise could be heard just before impact
[71] bivouacs or tents

plenty, stacks of vegetables everywhere, a pleasant change especially as rations all around have been pretty fine recently.

October 11. Hun, we are informed, is conducting retreat on a big scale. . . .

Had another look at outskirts of Cambrai, and into town. Town out of bounds at present. Centre of town has been destroyed, not by shell fire, but wantonly with fire and mines. . . .

October 13. A miserable sort of day again, though no rain to speak of. Got orders early in afternoon, and shifted battery complete to position S. of Rieux, still in "position of readiness.". . .

October 15. Two parcels arrived today . . . both dated about the beginning of Aug. I think. Wrote home. Saw a paper of Oct. 13, the only recent paper we have seen for days. Peace seems to be in sight, but we must slip into the Hun toute suite and making something in the way of a Modder River on a huge scale, annihilate or capture one of his armies.[72] Then let him talk peace. No move for us today or for a couple of days, so played football.

October 18. Down to Avesnes, next village,[73] with a party to the baths (Hun ones). Had my best bath since Etaples. Guns went up into position, but only a guard there for tonight. Weather pretty cold nowadays also been a bit wet recently, but we are pretty comfortable in our place with quite a good stove. Big show [attack] coming. . . .

October 21. Moved off 8.30 a.m. Got to Northern outskirts of Viesly 11 a.m. and established W. L. Took guns and full echelon onto position S. of Solesmes in afternoon. Hun strafing vigorously all round, and frightful mud on roads and tracks, but had no casualties getting in. . . .

October 23. Guns firing barrage from 3 a.m. I took gun limbers up, whole echelon to be on position 6 a.m. Moved on about 7 a.m. through main street of Solesmes and rendezvoused E. of Solesmes. Eventually came into action N.E. of Solesmes and fired a barrage from midday on. . . . Very heavy shelling on and about position as we came in but we got in without casualty. . . . Show is going well. . . .

October 27. Frosty last night. Enemy put a lot of harassing fire all about in vicinity. . . . Bursts of fire being put down by enemy all over the place. . . . During night enemy harassing fire continued. We had one gun knocked out, but no casualties. . . . 3 horses killed, 5 men wounded. . . .

November 4. Barrage 5.30 to 6.30, then 7.51 to 10.50. Advance went well. Hun put good heavy strafe back, but we had no casualties. . . . Brought bty to position in

[72] Reference to the fierce November 1899 battle during the Boer War when British forces sustained more than five times the casualties of their opponents. Hutchison may have been right to wish for a climactic victory, for the fact that German troops were defeated in Belgium and France, rather than on German soil, was used by ultranationalist agitators (including Hitler) to suggest that the real reason Germany lost the war was that it had been "stabbed in the back" by traitorous Jews and socialists.

[73] Avesnes-les-Aubert, several miles due east of Cambrai

afternoon, 6000 yds. as crow flies from this morning possy. And by nightfall 5000 from front which represents advance for day of almost 10,000 yds. Two men wounded at new possy. Le Quesnoy entirely surrounded but some stout Hun machine gunners and a minnewerfer[74] still hold the place. Early start again tomorrow. Us living in a cellar tonight. . . .

November 5. Enemy shelled us with whizz bangs from close range on left, which is not at all secure as we are well forward in a salient. Most unpleasant as we could not dig down at all, as whole place was water immed. under surface. 3 men wounded, 1 gassed. Raining heavily all day. Beastly rotten day. Transport hampered by heavy going and shortage of horses.

November 6. Had control last night between 2 logs and slept fairly dry considering. Fortunately battery that was shelling us captured soon after dark, and night was quiet. . . . Finally came into action 7 p.m. in pitch dark . . . still in sodden ground, everybody wet and cold only half the amm. waggons up, no rations, but still going strong. . . .

November 10. Another glorious day, the first white frost of the season on the ground in the morning. The war seems to have rolled on and left us here in a backwash. Guns sounding very distantly on the front. It's pretty decent. Football the go today. . . . Marching orders for tomorrow back towards Le Quesnoy to Div.

November 11. Probably THE day in the world's history. Hostilities cease 11 a.m. Only remains now to see what our terms to them are. We moved off 11 a.m. to go back to division, now at Beauvois-en-Cambrésis.[75] Raw day. Halted for night at RAMPONEAU just E. of Le Quesnoy. Got good billets. The news of peace seems to be received most quietly. After all this time, nobody seems to realize what it means.

November 12. Sunny day but very cold wind. Moved off 9.30 a.m. . . . All sorts of rumours, of course, but nothing definite yet as to our terms to Germany, or as to the great question of our future movements.

It's alright to move back in perfect peace past the places you got strafed going up.

November 13. Weather fine during these few days, very hard frost every night, and days sunny and clear, but always a great nip in the air. All divisional officers spoken to by Gen. Russell at Beauvois in aft. He says we go to occupy the Rhineland,[76] that demobilization will go on from there, leave to be as usual. . . .

November 28. Moved off 7.25 a.m. on first stage of our journey to the Rhine. Whole N.Z. division on the move together. . . .

[74] mine thrower

[75] farther to the west

[76] Given the strategic importance of the Rhineland, the German territory lying between the Rhine River to the east and the French frontier to the west, and the French insistence on security guarantees in this region to prevent a future German invasion, Allied forces occupied the Rhineland immediately after the armistice. It was anticipated they would remain for fifteen years, sufficiently long to witness the dissipation of German militarism.

December 4. Pulled out 10 a.m. and trekked to Fontaine-Valmont, crossing Franco-Belgian frontier at 2.20 p.m. and pulling in to one new lines 4.30 p.m. . . . Great diff. between France and Belgium. In France shops etc. are just struggling to begin again, while Belgium seems in comparison all business and prosperity. Belgians are not so friendly to us as French. . . .

Hutchison ends his diary with the following:

She has been a grand year again, 1915 and this year two of the greatest years a fellow could ever wish for. The next thing, of course, is to get back to N.Z., and then it's a case of settle down and work.

CHAPTER 5

Commitment and Sacrifice

Sir James D. Hutchison in judicial robes as member of New Zealand's Supreme Court. *Courtesy of Sheila Douglas Dunbar.*

CHAPTER 5

"Life has been spent among the dead"

Henri Desagneaux, French infantry officer

Henri Desagneaux served in the French army from the war's very beginning, and by its end he could count himself fortunate enough to have survived without serious injury. No doubt the fact that he spent all of 1915 behind the front lines contributed to his relative good fortune, but for the remainder of the conflict Desagneaux endured postings in locations that have since become synonymous with horrific combat, including Verdun, the Somme, and the Chemin des Dames. That he held up under the strain and served with distinction as an officer, earning the respect of his troops, was a testament to his maturity and strength of character.

The war's outbreak found Desagneaux just shy of his thirty-sixth birthday. He had been born east of Paris, in Nogent-sur-Marne, on September 24, 1878. Trained in the law, he worked in the legal department of the Eastern Railway Company until he was mobilized on August 2, 1914, as a reserve lieutenant in the Railway Transport Service. He was ordered to the town of Gray in eastern France to assist in the complex and sometimes chaotic process of getting French recruits to their correct units and positions at the front lines. As such he was well placed to observe the vital importance of rail transport in the war's opening days (without which neither side could have conducted major offensive operations so quickly) and gauge the initial mood of the French populace.

In contrast to what historians too readily assumed was the people's universally enthusiastic and bellicose stance, Desagneaux noted how any excitement had evaporated.[1] *He characterized his own experience as a "sad journey" and remarked on the depressing effect*

[1] Recent work has presented a more nuanced portrait. See Jean-Jacques Becker, *The Great War and the French People* (Oxford/Providence: Berg, 1985); Leonard V. Smith, Stéphane Audoin-Rouzeau, and Annette Becker, *France and the Great War, 1914–1918* (Cambridge: Cambridge University Press, 2003), 25–30.

French infantry preparing to leave for the front. *Library of Congress, LC-DIG-ggbain-16707.*

as wounded soldiers and civilian refugees flowed back from the lines. In the absence of hard information, fantastic rumors flourished, an unsettling climate that made it harder still to grasp the challenges that lay ahead. Even though Desagneaux remained in Gray for a year, safely insulated from the fighting, he was separated from his family and felt "very alone and also quite sad." He was frustrated at being confined to an office that afforded no opportunity for the initiative he yearned to exercise.

That opportunity came in 1916. If Desagneaux's maturity and judgment had not already fitted him for command at the front, the loss of so many officers intensified the search for their replacements. After a month's training course, he was appointed in February 1916 to command a company in the 129th Infantry Division. From that point onward his experiences were dominated by the need to simultaneously repulse German infantry attacks, survive their artillery bombardments, maintain his own unit in fighting condition, and minimize the detrimental impact of superior but frequently incompetent or ill-informed French officers.

Desagneaux's diary illustrates how over the next three years he sought to meet each of these challenges. Periods of intense, numbing combat, where just to survive was to claim a kind of victory, alternated with deployments to quieter sectors and reflected General Pétain's conscious effort to preserve the integrity of units by rotating them just as the revolving wheel of a mill only intermittently came into contact with water (called the noria system). The war as he endured it, however, was not a cycle of mindless repetition. When in combat, Desagneaux had to stay alert to innovatory tactical developments. He documented, for example, the introduction of rolling artillery barrages that in theory were timed to coincide with (and cover) the advance of infantry. He noted how often in practice these efforts went awry. He also described, in July 1917, how small groups of German shock troops penetrated French defenses, a harbinger of tactics in the desperate German offensives the following spring. Nonetheless, it is striking how rarely Desagneaux actually encountered identifiable Germans; in periodic attacks men were cut down by machine-gunners they could not see, but on a daily basis it was the anonymous artillery bombardments that really taxed his nerves and claimed so many of his comrades.

Remarkably, despite his frequent exposure to imminent death, as in the inferno of Verdun, Desagneaux remained unbroken, ready yet again to marshal his men in preparation for the next round of combat. His diary, then, can be read as an extended meditation on the question of leadership. Unfortunately, in Desagneaux's view, all too many of the higher-ranking officers he encountered were deficient on that score. Some were obsessed with "spit and polish," such as General de Villaret, commander of the 7th Army, who turned a potentially instructive inspection into a "grotesque parade" by focusing on his men's bootlaces and buttons. Some spent their time drinking and gambling, like the "real boozer" in the Lorraine whose post Desagneaux assumed in March 1916. This was a relatively quiet sector, and though he had been at the front for no more than a month, he already recognized that the generals would "make the most of [the quiet] to plague us with their visits." Two years later, during a lull near the Franco-Belgian border, he was scathing: "like snails after a storm, the gold braid is appearing from everywhere. . . . [With] no shells [falling], they are happy to make themselves noticed."

Even worse were the officers too cowardly to appear at all. For months during 1918, Desagneaux was plagued with a colonel who hid underground, abdicating real responsibility for the welfare of his men. "He won't come out to see what's happening," lamented Desagneaux, who nonetheless was bombarded with orders to ensure the colonel's safety in his cellar, whether with barbed wire, earthworks, machine gun positions, or even an escape trench. It was a farce, but ultimately "he is in command and I have to obey."

Although Desagneaux's inflexible sense of duty prevented him from directly challenging the army's command structure, others in the ranks, goaded by the mistakes of their superiors and the seemingly interminable stalemate, were willing to defy their superiors. In the late spring and early summer of 1917, the French army was wracked by mutinies after a major offensive along the Chemin des Dames, touted by General Robert Nivelle as a surefire breakthrough that would win the war, deteriorated into yet another bloody round of attrition.[2] *With dissent in the air after the February/March Russian Revolution, increasing numbers of French soldiers refused to participate in new fruitless attacks. The foremost recent study of these incidents, by Leonard V. Smith, emphasizes that they sprang from the men's self-awareness of their status as republican citizen-soldiers.*[3] *By participating in the war as soldiers they affirmed their responsibilities to protect the nation, but as republican citizens their service was framed by their implied consent in return for the promise that their lives would not be squandered. Territorial gains would be proportional to casualties.*

[2] Robert Doughty, *Pyrrhic Victory: French Strategy and Operations in the Great War* (Cambridge, MA: Harvard University Press, 2005), 326–54.

[3] Leonard V. Smith, *Between Mutiny and Obedience: The Case of the French Fifth Infantry Division during World War I* (Princeton: Princeton University Press, 1994).

But the failed offensives of April/May 1917 only confirmed what the bloodletting of the previous years had already made clear—the French army was being squandered to no proportional benefit and that French soldiers, in Smith's argument, felt justified in withdrawing their consent until the proper proportional relationship between gains and losses was reestablished. It is worth noting that these acts of "collective indiscipline" never went so far as to jeopardize French defensive measures, for the poilus remained determined to repulse any German attack. But without renegotiating the basis of their consent, French soldiers would hesitate to take the offensives that were necessary to break the stalemate and win the war.

Desagneaux never minimized the blunders by French commanders that produced disproportionate losses, but he made no excuses for ordinary soldiers who shirked their duty. He blamed the mutinies on seditious troublemakers within the ranks (the "bad hats") and attributed their seductive appeal to a lack of discipline at the front and the wealth of pacifist propaganda soldiers imbibed on leave. A veteran of the French railways, he linked the lack of discipline to the lamentable state of the trains (though the attentive reader will note that he made similar complaints of the railway carriages during the enthusiasm of August 1914). His utter contempt is evident for men who had forcefully urged mutiny only to cringe before a subsequent court-martial. In any event, the soldiers went "back to work," so to speak, after improvements in leave, food, and a tacit understanding not to squander lives needlessly. France would, as Pétain quipped, wait for the tanks and the Americans, although it did not abandon offensive action.

Indeed, Desagneaux was involved in some of his heaviest fighting in Belgium during the summer of 1918. At that point the German army did not appear beaten and dispirited, and he continued to experience close calls from German shellfire. By October, however, victory was obviously within reach, especially given the mounting numbers of artillery pieces and American troops that would sustain a final attack. When peace finally came, Desagneaux's homecoming was delayed for two months by his deployment in the forces occupying Germany. Nonetheless, when he finally returned to Nogent-sur-Marne, it was as a respected veteran and decorated Chevalier of the Legion of Honor. He was active in politics during the interwar period, serving as a municipal councilor and then deputy-mayor until 1942. One can only imagine what he must have thought of the return of German invaders in 1940. He died on November 30, 1969.

Only after his death did his son, Jean Desagneaux, submit the diary for publication. It appeared in print in 1971 as Journal de Guerre 14-18 *from Les Editions Denoël of Paris. An English version,* A French Soldier's War Diary, 1914–1918, *translated by Godfrey Adams, was published four years later by the now defunct Elmfield Press. It is that version which is partially reproduced here.*

1914

1 August. From the early hours, Paris is in turmoil, people still have a glimmer of hope, but nothing suggests that matters can now be settled peacefully. The banks are besieged; one has to queue for two or three hours before getting inside. . . .

In front of the "Gare de L'Est," the conscripts throng the yard ready for departure. Emotion is at its peak; relations and friends accompany those being called up individually. The women are crying, the men too. They have to say good-bye without knowing whether they will ever return.

At last at 4:15 in the afternoon, the news spreads like wild-fire, posters are being put up with the order for mobilization on them! It's every man for himself, you scarcely have the time to shake a few hands before having to go home to make preparations for departure.

It's 5 o'clock, my mobilization order states: first day of mobilization—without delay. The first day is 2 August!

2 August, Sunday. Mobilized as a reserve lieutenant in the Railway Transport Service, I am posted to Gray.[4] At 5 in the morning, after some painful good-byes, I go to Nogent-le-Perreux station, The train service is not yet organized. There are no more passenger or goods trains. The mobilization timetable is now operative but nobody at the station has any idea when a train is due.

Sad day, sad journey. At 7 a.m. a train comes, it arrives at its terminus—Troyes—at 2 p.m. I didn't bring anything to eat, the refreshment room has already sold out. The rush of troops is beginning and consuming everything in its path. Already you find yourself cut off from the world, the newspapers don't come here any more. But on the other hand, how much news there is! Everyone has his bit of information to tell. . . .

At last in the afternoon I catch the first train which comes along: a magnificent row of first-class carriages . . . which is going no one knows precisely where, except that it is in the direction of the Front. The compartments and corridors are bursting at the seams with people from all classes of society. The atmosphere is friendly, enthusiastic, but the train is already clearly suffering from the influx from every stratum of society! The blinds are torn down, luggage-racks and mirrors are broken, and the toilets emptied of their fittings; it's (typical) French destruction. . . .

The most fantastic rumors are going around; everyone is seeing spies unbolting railway track or trying to blow up bridges. . . .

3 August, Monday. Morale is excellent, everyone is extraordinarily quiet and calm. Along the track at level-crossings, in the towns, crowds singing "La Marseillaise"[5] gather to greet the troops.

The French women have set to it. They are handing out drinks, writing paper, and cigarettes. The general impression is the following: it's Kaiser Bill who wanted war, it had to happen, we shall never have such a fine opportunity again. . . .

[4] southeast of Paris near Dijon
[5] French national anthem

6 August, Thursday. The traffic is intense, with the same enthusiasm and the same slogans "Death to the Kaiser," "String the Kaiser up," "Death to the *Boches.*"[6] The same caricatures: pigs' heads in pointed helmets. Bouquets, garlands, flags. . . .

11 August, Tuesday. Casualties are starting to arrive and sunstroke is prevalent; people are not so enthusiastic now as in the first days.

The Territorials and Reservists are now arriving. They are not as orderly as the Regulars. Then there are convoys, lines of carriages of every description and limitless baggage. . . . How many non-combatants, what a burden they are! They have requisitioned everything in the surrounding area, and the troops have to camp in the open.

Organization too is not what it should be. . . .

12 August, Wednesday. Decidedly there is not the same spirit as before. Perhaps it's due to the torrid heat, but the enthusiasm isn't there any more. The trains are not decorated with "Death to the Kaiser" and the flowers have disappeared. Now it's slovenliness and orders bawled out as in maneuvers. The leaders forget it is wartime: the men get irritable when they see that the orders of the day prescribe polish, uniform regulations, and the pettiness of barrack life.

Disorder is rapidly replacing the order of the early days. The maimed and the sick arrive from God knows where; only one train a day to evacuate them. The wounded, sometimes feverish, are forced to spend up to twenty hours at the station, in the open air without food or medical attention, left to themselves. Nothing has been planned for them by their companies, they just get rid of them and that's all. . . .

15–18 August. No news of operations, but people are speaking of some successes in the Vosges[7] and in Belgium. Guns are firing away in the distance. . . .

At last, on the 18th at 1 in the morning, I am ordered back to Gray. The mobilization is over.

At Gray, Desagneaux was ordered to take charge of supplying of the 44th Division at Bruyères.

25 August, Tuesday. The guns roar incessantly. There is fighting at Rambervillers.[8] It appears we have had a setback there. . . . The German heavy artillery is causing severe losses.

Otherwise, no news, the influx of troops just doesn't stop. The evacuation of trains, too, arrive one after the other to carry the inhabitants of the towns and countryside towards the rear. The Germans are advancing and people are fleeing in front of the invader. They run but have no idea where they are going.

It's worse than the destruction of a town. Refugees arrive from all directions, a mixture of every class of society: the peasant carrying his little bundle; the worker with a few old clothes; small farmers, shopkeepers with their cases, finally the bourgeois, dragging along a dog or a trunk. Over Rambervillers, the guns thunder the whole day. One can see a sad procession of town and country folk, panic-stricken,

[6] pejorative slang for German soldiers
[7] along the eastern border with Germany
8 reference to the Battle of Mortagne, August 25–September 11, 1914

fleeing in front to the enemy. ... What a sad sight it is to see the old carts drawn by nags that even the requisition officers refused; these poor people, distressed, leaving their homes and their possessions, without knowing whether they will return.

There are families of seven, eight children walking along the road. An old man supported by a neighbor: he was a refugee in 1870 and is one again in 1914. A young mother pushing a pram in which her months-old baby is crying.

It brings tears to your eyes. All these people waiting, drawn towards the station—the railway is their only hope. They stand crowded together in the cattle-wagons, the youngsters don't understand, the others ask where they will be taken. It's an indescribable mess.

The guns thunder away, and convoys of wounded arrive to increase the confusion. Whole trains of them come, others leave empty to bring back 2,000 wounded announced at Rambervillers. Their limbs shot off, their heads a pulpy mess; all these bandages, spattered with blood mingle with the civilian population. The troops can only speak of the heavy artillery which shoots 10 kilometers and against which our 75s[9] are powerless.

To make the pain even more unbearable, pessimistic rumors are circulating: the Germans are advancing, they will be here soon. The people push, shove, in their desire to leave. . . .

2 September, Wednesday. Convoys of wounded arrive in huge numbers; some German prisoners state that they don't know that England, Russia, and Japan are at war with Germany. They don't know either that Belgium is fighting to stop German troops passing through her territory. They say, also that there is revolution in Berlin and they curse the Kaiser.

6 September, Sunday. A large number of soldiers wound themselves so that they can leave the Front. . . .

11–16 September. The weather is dreadful, troops board the train as the rain pours down. All the soldiers who come back from the front speak about the German artillery. In the beginning, its effect was to start a rout and the officers had to force the men back by threatening them with their revolvers. . . .

25–26 September. We are embarking the Colonial Brigade of Infantry (Colonel Marchand's) . . . to resist a German attack made on Saint-Mihiel. . . .

Colonel Marchand informs us that he has a real epidemic of wounded hands; the men who are fed up with the trenches put their hands in the air to get a bullet and be evacuated.

He says too, that in his opinion the war will be long. He speaks of three years! All those who hear him think he is mad. . . .

8 October, Thursday. I take the chance of two hours off to go to [a nearby village] . . . where a large battle took place. Of the village (800–1,000 inhabitants), only ruins remain and scarcely seven or eight houses which are habitable. Round about, there are only half-destroyed trenches and graves. At every step, there is a cross, indicating

[9] light field artillery

a corpse, then shell-holes, followed by more. Huge fields which are the scene of desolation. There are piles of ruins everywhere, walls and roofs collapsed, and what has not been destroyed by cannon-fire, has been burnt. The burnt carcasses of horses are strewn here and there. Their church was even bombarded during a funeral service. . . .

20 December. I am handed a telegram announcing that I shall be relieved on the 23rd and should put myself at the disposal of Railway Control H.Q. What do they want of me?

24 December. I learn that I have been made assistant to the Senior Officer. An honor, perhaps, but what a change of life.

My life in the open air and journeys to adventure are over. Instead of work that demanded initiative I shall be in an office, amid my bosses from morning to evening with even my meals taken on the spot in the station refreshment room.

How lonely I feel! Won't my former friends have a jealous smile on their lips? What a sad end to my year. And tonight is Christmas, and my kiddies at home will put their shoes in front of the fire-place and I won't be there to see the joy on their faces tomorrow morning. I am alone, very alone and also quite sad. . . .

1916

12 January. Here I am at Remiremont.[10] I arrive at the Army H.Q. There, the same old story, they don't know what to do with us. . . . Finally, in the evening we learn we are to follow a training course for company commanders at Remiremont.

16 January. Sunday—Rest—The first time since 2 August 1914 that I see this word on a program. I go climbing in the mountains . . . to get some fresh air.

18, 19, 20 January. Theory work on machine-guns. Tear gas, poisonous gases, etc., and finally maneuvers to close the session.

The sessions are interesting, but how ordinary the officers are. The last offensive in Champagne, after so many others, cost us dearly in officers and all those who are here are former sergeant-majors or N.C.O.s. The companies are being commanded at the moment by sub-lieutenants.

21 January. Second day of maneuvers in the mountains. We have no orders, we don't know anything—we march aimlessly.

25 January. Beginning of the new course. . . .

An inspection of the battalion which is supposed to teach us something. It turns out to be a grotesque parade where this general is only interested in the men's boot-laces, the buttons on their greatcoats, and the hooks on their cartridge-pouches.

29 January. A Zeppelin flies over Paris and throws down bombs. . . .

1 February. Zeppelins over England. 54 killed, 67 wounded.

2 February. Practice with inflammable liquids, throwing bombs, torpedoes, and rockets. . . .

[10] in the Vosges

4 February. Instruction on how to electrify barbed wire[11]! What don't they invent these days to kill each other with!. . .

15 February. End of course, departure from Remiremont. The regiment is actually resting near Bruyères, where I shall go to join it.

Desagneaux was then posted to the Lorraine Sector from February 17 until May 29.

17 February. I take command of my company: three very ordinary sub-lieutenants (two butchers and a draper's assistant)—all Reservists—I feel the ill-will of the combatants against someone from the rear, but I'm the boss, and they don't dare say anything.

The men are aged between 20 and 42 years of age. A mixture which creates two cliques; the young ones team up with those of their own age, and the old 'uns stick together.

The N.C.O.s could be a lot better; they were corporals or even privates two months ago. They have no notion of leadership or responsibility. They are privates with stripes. . . .

6 March, Monday. My command post is in a cellar, under a group of flattened houses (the whole area is like this). The cellar is swarming with rats, and uncomfortable isn't the word.

In the morning, I go out and explore the sector; my company is guarding a front of 2 kilometers before the village. The Seille (a small stream) separates the lines.

The sector is quiet, some gunfire here and there; I make the most of it to visit the surrounding area. Everything is devastated, it's total ruin everywhere. One can see the fury that went into searching through the furniture and in destroying everything. . . .

It's pitiful. In the presbytery,[12] it's worse, if that's possible. They were even more bent on destruction there, seeing that it was the priest's home. The church is in an indescribable state of devastation.

8 March, Wednesday. At 4 a.m., grenades, machine-gunfire, a German patrol is sighted trying to cut our wire entanglements. Soon all goes quiet.

11 March, Saturday. Order to be relieved. We have been here for six days, and are beginning to get well organized in the sector and now have to hand over to others. That's the reason why our sectors are never organized.

Where are we going? We don't know. I am changing company. I have been given command of the 21st. It's the worst of the battalions. Its captain who has been made adjutant-major is a former regular N.C.O. and a real boozer. The sub-lieutenants who are there join in with their captain and spend their time drinking and gambling. Regretfully, I leave my 22nd Company which I was getting to know well. . . .

[11] In spring 1915, German troops occupying Belgium erected a high-voltage electrified fence that ran nearly 125 miles along the Belgium-Netherlands border.

[12] a priest's rectory or residence

We are going to be quartered at Bouxieres-aux-Chenes where we arrive at 2 in the morning.

12 March, Sunday. We settle in at Bouxieres. I take command of the 21st Company. As officers, I have four sub-lieutenants, a former Regular sergeant who is strong but simple; a wine-barrel of a butcher, a commercial traveler from Marseille . . . a steamboat pilot who can't say one word without swearing.

At mealtimes, two sergeants (why are they there?) come to join the group. The mess has a reputation for gambling and drunkenness. It's the only one in the battalion to which no one comes. My comrades pity me, while my superiors are counting on me to raise the morale of the troops. So, I start by sending the two sergeants to the N.C.O.s mess. That will make two drunkards less with us.

13 March, Monday. I am terribly bored in this unsympathetic atmosphere where I have no friends. We are in a state of alert in a rotten little village of about twenty inhabitants. There's no escape. Even so near the front, with the prospect of leaving for it at any moment, it's barrack life. We clean the streets, in our quarters we make weapon-racks, polish everything, and do theory.

20 March, Monday. After hastily fortifying the front line, it is noticed there is no second line of defence in front of Nancy. Yet again, we work frantically. The guns are more active and it is difficult to go out. What to do besides? We are forbidden to ride, to leave the billet area, and to carry a camera. We would prefer to go to the trenches.

29 March, Wednesday. The sector is quiet, so the generals make the most of it to plague us with their visits.

30 March, Thursday. The artillery thunders. Armancourt receives 260 shells. An attack is expected, we are on the alert. If we were to attack, we would have to cover 1,500 meters of open ground, without a trench or anywhere to shelter.

1 April, Saturday. The day is beautiful, but troubled. There is firing all along the line. At 10 in the evening—it's hell, guns roar everywhere; to the right, to the left, in front, behind. Armancourt is ablaze. Its church is on fire, its steeple collapses. A splendid sight and a terrible one. . . .

26 May. Yet again, there is talk of our being relieved and going to Verdun. They have been fighting over there for three months now, all divisions are going there in turn.[13]

[13] Verdun was less a battle than an interminable campaign consuming the first half of 1916. It began with the effort of Erich von Falkenhayn, chief of the German General Staff, to apply pressure to a sector of the line the French would not abandon, whether for strategic or sentimental reasons. He selected the salient (bulge) in the lines around Verdun, but instead of seeking a conventional breakthrough that would squander German lives, he hoped to lure French forces into a series of costly counteroffensives during which they could be crushed by massed German artillery. The result, he anticipated, would be to "bleed France white," and compel it to sue for peace. Nonetheless, in the face of a resolute defense mounted by General Pétain, the campaign acquired a seemingly inexorable logic of its own, drawing additional German troops into the killing zone as well. With a human cost of more than 700,000 killed, wounded, or missing, Verdun thus came to symbolize the stalemate and slaughter of the western front.

10 June, Saturday. At one in the morning, order for departure at 4 a.m. We are to march in the direction of Verdun. . . .

13 June, Tuesday. Reveille at 2 a.m. At 5, we travel by car and are put down at Nixéville, 6 kilometers from Verdun. We bivouac in a wood in a lake of mud. The guns fire angrily, it's pouring down. . . . We spend the night and the day of the 14th waiting, in torrential rain with mud up to our ankles. Our teeth chatter with cold, we are very uncomfortable. Although the troops have been stopping here for the last four months to go to and from Verdun, there is not one single hut or shelter. We camp in individual tents in thick mud. You should hear what the men say about it!

At 5 p.m., order for departure at 6:30. We are going to be quartered in the Citadel of Verdun. Faces are grave. The guns are thundering over there. It's a real furnace. Everyone realizes that perhaps tomorrow death will come. Numerous rumors are circulating; we are going to "Mort-Homme"[14] which has been captured by the *Boches*; or to the Fort at Vaux. . . . What is certain, nothing good lies in store for us.

We arrive at the Citadel[15] at 10 p.m. after a difficult march through the mud.

15 June, Thursday. We spend the day in the Citadel waiting. The guns fire ceaselessly. Huge shells (380s-420s) crash down on Verdun causing serious damage. I walk as far as the town; it's in ruins and deserted. One can't stay outside for long as shells are dropping everywhere.

The Citadel is a real underground town, with narrow-gauge railway, dormitories, and rooms of every type; it's safe here, but very gloomy.

At 9 in the evening, we leave, not knowing our destination. We advance slowly through the night. At every moment huge shells come and explode on Verdun, at the crossroads, and in the direction of our gun-batteries which are stationed on all sides. We march in silence, everyone conscious of the seriousness of the moment.

At 1 a.m. we arrive at the Bras-Ravin Quarries, where we remain in reserve. No shelter, nothing, we are in the open fields at the mercy of the first shell.

16 June, Friday. Superb weather, not far from us, it's a furnace of artillery fire. The *Boches* pump their shells at us, and our guns reply. What a racket! 150s and 210s scour the land on all sides and there is nothing anyone can do but wait. The battalion is massed in the ravine without any shelter; if their shelling was not at random it would be dreadful for us. The German observation balloons scan the horizon. Up in the sky, their planes search for us; we curl up in a hole when a shell bursts near us and it's like this until evening when orders arrive.

At 6 p.m. my company and another (the 24th) receive the order to advance with a view to reinforcing the 5th Battalion which is to attack on the following day. We leave, not knowing exactly where we are going; and no one has a map. We have a vague idea where the command posts are; guides are rare in this area where death stalks at every step. With difficulty, we move along crumbling trenches, cross a ridge to take up our position in the Ravin des Dames. The shells rain down, still no shelter.

[14] a tactically significant hill named "dead man"

[15] This fortress was originally erected between 1624 and 1636 by Vauban, the foremost military architect of the seventeenth century, to protect Verdun.

We haven't eaten for twenty-four hours and don't know if supplies can arrive tonight.

17 June, Saturday. The attack is due at 9 a.m. The 106th is in charge with the 5th Battalion of the 359th as support. We have to recapture a trench at the top of the ravine that the *Boches* took from us the day before. We spend the night in the Bras-Ravin; hurriedly we dig a trench to give our men some shelter. Just beside us there is a cemetery where the dead are being brought at every moment. The guns fire furiously, from 3 o'clock it's hell. One cannot imagine what the simple phrase of an official statement like "We have recaptured a trench" really means! The attack is prepared from 4 to 9 o'clock; all guns firing together. The Germans fire non-stop, ammunition dumps blow up, it's deadly. There are so many explosions around us that the air reeks of powder and earth; we can't see clearly any more. We wait anxiously without knowing whether we shall be alive an hour later. . . .

At 11, after a relative pause, the cannonade starts up again. At 2 p.m. it's worse still, it's enough to drive you mad; the *Boches* are only firing their 210s and 150s, shrapnel explodes above us, we have no idea of what is happening or of the result. We are infested by huge black flies. You don't know where to put yourself.

At 6 p.m. I receive the order to reconnoiter the gun emplacements in the front line, as our battalion is relieving tonight. The shell-bursts are so continuously heavy that we cannot advance before nightfall and it is impossible to cross the ridge.

The wounded from this morning's attack are beginning to arrive, we learn what happened: our artillery fired too short and demolished our front line trench (evacuated for the attack), instead of firing on the *Boches*. When we attacked the Germans let us advance to 15 meters and then caught us in a hail of machine-gunfire. We succeeded in capturing several parts of the trench but couldn't hold them; at the moment our troops are scattered here and there in shell-craters. During the attack, the German planes bombed our men ceaselessly. Our losses are enormous: the 106th already has 350-400 men out of action, two captains killed and a large number of officers wounded. The 5th Battalion of the 359th, which was advancing in support was caught by gunfire and suffered heavily. The 19th Company hasn't got one officer left, in the 18th, three are missing. We have 32 *Boches* as prisoners. The positions are the same as before the attack—with our troops only being able to maintain the front-line position which they had previously evacuated.

At nightfall, the dead arrive on stretchers at the cemetery. In this, the Ravine of Death, they lay there, lined up, waiting to be put into the holes that are being hastily dug for them. . . .

18 June, Sunday. We have had to leave to occupy our new positions before our food arrived. It's the second day without food. We eat what little we've got amid huge black flies. . . .

It's Sunday! Day breaks amid bursts of gunfire. We await orders. One can't think of washing or sleeping. No news; neither papers, nor letters. It's a void, we are no longer in a civilized world. One suffers, and says nothing; the night has been cold; lying on the damp earth one just shivers, not being able to breathe properly because of the smell. . . .

Orders and counter-orders follow each other; no-one has a map, or even a sketch. We don't know where the *Boches* are, but there is some fear that they will attack us on our right.

My company is all in a line in this trench which collapsed yesterday under the bombardment following our attack. A squad of machine-gunners of the 5th Battalion is buried in it; the following day at dawn we will discover all along the trench, corpses, then legs and arms protruding out of the ground. . . .

19 June, Monday. We are expecting an attack at any moment. There is talk of recapturing the trenches with grenades. But what are our leaders doing? Ah, we don't see them here. We are left to ourselves, they won't come and bother us. . . .

No sleep, no water, impossible to move out of one's hole, to even show your head above the trench. We are filthy dirty and have only cold tinned food to eat. We are not receiving supplies any more and have only been here for four days!. . .

20 June, Tuesday. The food supplies only arrive with great difficulty at 2 this morning. Still no water. When one has exhausted one's ration of coffee and wine, you have to go thirsty. By day, the heat is overpowering, we are surrounded by flies and corpses which give off a nauseating smell. . . .

10 p.m. Great commotion, red and white flares, chatter of machine guns, thunder of artillery. 400 meters from us, a new attack is unleashed upon our lines. Every man is at his post waiting, the whole night through. Will the *Boches* rush us from the top of the ridge?

Shells explode only meters from us and all around men fall wounded. We are blinded by the shells and by the earth they throw up, it's an inferno, one could write about such a day minute by minute. . . .

21 June, Wednesday. Impossible to sleep, even an hour, the deluge of shells continues and the whole night frantic orders follow each other; you may be attacked, be ready! We have been ready for three days. . . .

The shells, the shrapnel, the 210s fall like hail for twenty-four hours noon-stop, the shrapnel, the 210s fall like hail for twenty-four hours non-stop, only to start again; everything trembles, one's nerves as well as the ground. We feel at the end of our tether.

And what a responsibility! The chiefs tell us: keep watch, but no-one can give you any indication about the terrain; on our right, there's the ravine of Hill 321, but we don't even know the positions occupied by our troops and by the *Boches*. Our artillery itself is firing without knowing our positions.

8 p.m. We have been bombarded by 210s for exactly twenty-four hours. The Germans have been attacking on our right since 6 p.m. My company at every moment receives the order to stand by to advance. It's a state of perpetual anguish, not a moment's respite.

We crouch there, with our packs on our backs, waiting, scanning the top of the ridge to see what is happening and this lasts until nightfall. We are haggard, dazed, hungry, and feverishly thirsty, but there is no water. In some companies there have been cases of madness. How much longer are we going to stay in this situation?

Night comes and the guns still fire; our trenches have collapsed, it's a tangle of equipment and guns left by the wounded, there's nothing human about it. Why don't they send the deputies, senators, and generals here?

9 p.m. 210s still, our nerves can't take much more. Can't move or sleep. There are no more shelters, one just clings to the wall of the trench. We wait. At 9:15 the bombardment starts again: the front line troops are so fatigued and jumpy that at every moment they believe they are being attacked and ask for artillery support. Red flares follow, our artillery does its best, it's hellish. . . .

22 June. At 9 p.m. an avalanche of fire bursts on the ridge, the relief has to be delayed, it would be impossible to pass. Is it an attack? There is gas as well as shells, we can't breathe and are forced to put on our masks. . . .

My company occupies a broken line. Impossible to move around in daylight. To the left, no communication with the neighbouring company; just a hole 100 meters long; we don't know if the *Boches* are there. In the centre, the same hole—occupied or not? I have a squad which is completely isolated and stay with it.

The captain I am relieving tries to show me the terrain. He doesn't know it himself, dazed by four days spent up front amid dead and wounded.

In a nightmare advance, we stumble forwards falling in shell-craters, walking on corpses, flinging ourselves repeatedly to the ground.

Ground where there lie forever men of the 106th, of the 359th, still others of regiments who preceded us. It's a graveyard, a glimpse of hell.

23 June, Friday. 5 a.m. The bombardment starts up again fiercely. I get a shell splinter in my lip. Nothing serious fortunately, as the wounded have to wait until evening to get their wounds dressed. One cannot leave the shell-hole even by crawling on one's stomach.

7 a.m. Alert. Commotion. The *Boches* attack. They are driven back by our return of fire. . . .

The heat is oppressive. Around us the stench of the corpses is nauseating. We have to live, eat, and wait in it. Do or die! It's six days now since we had a moment's rest or sleep. The attacks follow each other. The *Boches* have succeeded in advancing towards Hill 321 and in occupying a part of the ravine behind us, where our reinforcements are.

The shelling has completely destroyed the trench where we were yesterday; the dead and the wounded are too numerous to count.

24 June, Sunday. Big German offensive on the right bank of the Meuse. This news arrived during the night. There is no question of our being relieved. Everything is silent and behind us, on Fleury ridge, the *Boches* continue infiltrating. We have been turned! There is no longer any doubt, as we can see enemy columns invading the terrain and their machine-guns are attacking us from behind while our artillery has had to move back.

Now something worse: my men, who have been suffering all sorts of hardships for the last seven days, are becoming demoralized. The word "prisoner" is being whispered. For many this would seem salvation. We must fight against this notion, raise morale. But how? We can't move around, and only those near us can hear. They are all good chaps, devoted, who won't leave us and will form a bodyguard. . . .

At 11 a.m. artillery is heard. Our batteries have taken up new positions and are opening fire, the *Boches* reply.

Impossible to eat, our nerves can't stand it. If we have a call of nature to satisfy, we have to do it in a tin or on a shovel and throw it over the top of our shell-hole. It's like this every day.

25 June, Sunday. Terrible day and night.

At 3 a.m., without warning, our own troops attack us from behind in order to recapture the terrain lost the day before on our right. These troops, without precise orders, without maps, without even knowing where our lines are, ventured off. They fell upon us, believing they had found the *Boches*. But the *Boches* were 100 meters in front, lying in wait and bursts of machine-gunfire cut them down in our trench. We thus have another heap of corpses and wounded crying out, but whom we are powerless to help. Trench!—well almost every evening we bury the dead on the spot and it's they who form the parapets!

At 6 a.m., the guns fire furiously and to add to our plight, our 75s fire at us. Terrible panic; six wounded at one go from a shell-burst, everyone wants to run for it. . . . I have to force these poor devils back by drawing our revolvers. . . .

There's blood everywhere; the wounded have sought refuge with us, thinking that we could help them; the blood flows, the heat is atrocious, the corpses stink, the flies buzz—it's enough to drive one mad. Two men of the 24th Company commit suicide. . . .

26 June, Monday. We attack incessantly. It's four days since we have been in the front line and the relieving troops have been annihilated this morning during the attacks.

Rain replaces the sun; filthy mud. We can't sit down any more. We are covered in slime and yet we have to lie flat. I haven't washed for ten days, my beard is growing. I am unrecognizable, frighteningly dirty. . . .

28 June, Wednesday. Hardest day to endure. The *Boches* begin to pound our positions, we take cover; some try to flee, we have to get our revolvers out again and stand in their way. It's hard, our nerves are frayed and it's difficult to make them see reason. . . .

1 p.m., it's an inferno: the *Boches* undoubtedly are preparing to attack us. Shells scream down on every side: a new panic to be checked. At 6 p.m. when we are dazed and numb, the firing range lengthens and suddenly everyone is on his feet, shouting, the *Boches* are coming. They attack in massed formation, in columns of eight!

These troops who, moments ago were in despair, are at their posts in a twinkling; we hold our grenades until the *Boches* are at 15 meters, then let them have it. Guns bark, and a machine-gun which survived the avalanche of shells is wreaking havoc.

The *Boches* are cut down; amid the smoke, we see dozens of dead and wounded, and the rest retreating back to their trenches. Our commanding officer, thinking that we are hard-pressed, sends us welcome reinforcements. They will be useful for supplies and taking the wounded away.

Only around 9 p.m. is it quieter. We help the wounded who are waiting to be taken away. Our shell-holes are lakes of mud. It is raining and we don't know where to put ourselves: our rifles don't work any more and we can only rely upon our grenades which are in short supply.

This evening, still no relief; another twenty-four hours to get through. It gets colder at night, we lie down in the mud and wait. . . .

30 June, Friday Attacks and counter-attacks. Frightful day—the shelling and the fatigue are becoming harder to bear. At 10 a.m., French attack on Thiaumont; the artillery fires 12,000 rounds of 255s, 550 of 220s, and the 75s fire at will.

The din began at 6 this morning; the *Boches* reply furiously. It's hell, we are getting hit more and more often, as our position is the favourite enemy target. The majority of the shells fall on or around us. The shelling will last ten hours! And during this time we expect an attack at any moment. To make it worse, my own company is hard hit. A 210 falls directly on a group of men sheltering in a hole; 3 killed and 2 seriously wounded who drag themselves up to me to plead for help. A minute later, a second shell sends a machine-gun flying, killing 2 more men and wounding a third. It's panic stations—the men run, and under a hail of gunfire, I have to force them back again with a revolver in my hand. Everyone goes back to his post, we set up another machine-gun and keep watch.

At 10 a.m. and 2 p.m. first and second French attacks on Thiaumont. The *Boches* harass us with their fire. . . . The wounded are increasing in numbers around us. . . . There's death everywhere. At our foot, the wounded groan in a pool of blood; two of them, more seriously hit are breathing their last. One, a machine-gunner, has been blinded, with one eye hanging out of its socket and the other torn out; in addition he has lost a leg. The second has no face, an arm blown off, and a horrible wound in the stomach. Moaning and suffering atrociously, one begs me, "Lieutenant, don't let me die, Lieutenant, I'm suffering, help me." The other, perhaps more gravely wounded and nearer to death, implores me to kill him with these words, "Lieutenant, if you don't want to, give me your revolver!" Frightful, terrible moments, while the cannons hurry us and we are splattered with mud and earth by the shells. For hours, these groans and supplications continue until, at 6 p.m., they die before our eyes without anyone being able to help them. . . .

At last, at 8 p.m., an order: we are to be relieved. What a cry of joy from those of us left. . . . Tiredness disappears, and our limbs regain enough strength to escape from these plains where at every step the guns have done heir work; corpses of men, carcasses of horses, overturned vehicles, it's a horrific graveyard all the way to Verdun. . . .

Our time at Verdun has been awful. Our faces have nothing human abut them. For sixteen days we have neither washed nor slept. Life has been spent amongst dead and dying, hardships of every sort and incessant anguish. Our cheeks are hollow, beards long and our clothes thick with mud. And, above all, we have a vision of these horrific days, the memory of a comrade fallen in action; each one of us thinks of those who have not returned. Despite our joy at being alive, our eyes reveal the crazy horror of it all. . . .

1 July, Saturday. After being relieved, we are quartered at Bois-la-Ville, in the same camp where we stopped on the way here. We arrive at 2 p.m., exhausted. We fall into bed and sleep like brutes.

2 July, Sunday. At 8 a.m., we pile into cars, glad to leave this ill-fated region far behind. We get out at Ligny-en-Barrois at 2 p.m. We spent the evening at ablutions.[16]

5 July, Wednesday. Promoted captain. . . .

Desagneaux served in the Bois-le-Prêtre in the Lorraine Sector from July 14 until October 1.

25 July. Trench life begins anew. It's calm for the moment, but things will soon hot up. This sector was guarded for eighteen months by the same troops; Reservists, they had got into bad habits, and not intending to kill themselves, they even went as far as fraternizing with the *Boches*. They passed cigarettes to each other in the trenches. They even sang songs together. Our division has orders to stop all this and to harass the *Boches*. Our gunners don't have to be asked twice and pound the enemy who are not long in replying. Attacks follow and the sector will become harder.

1 August. Two years of war!

The weather is glorious. Life is spent in the trenches, in shelters crawling with rats and lice. . . .

5 August. Heavy mortar fire; for the second time, my shelter (a fragile cellar) collapses. These mortar-shells are causing huge damage, but the rats, bugs and fleas are even more formidable. The Medical Corps don't even bother about them. We live in filthy squalor.

At 1 a.m. we relieve the front line in the "Marseille" sector near Regnéville. The sector is bad. Every day the trenches are devastated by mortar-fire. My command post is 10 meters below ground, with water streaming in from all sides; every morning we have to bale out 10-15 buckets-full of water coming from a near-by cesspit. How damp and dark it is! Our candles are continuously snuffed out by the gusts of air caused by the mortar shells. When outside, one is at the mercy of these or grenades. . . .

2 September. Relief due at 4 a.m. The mortar-fire is still intense: there are many dead in the 22nd and 23rd Companies who are in the lines. At 3 a.m. there's a dreadful din which recalls Verdun. Firing on all sides. My company is alerted, we are ready to march. Relative calm at 4:30 and the relief takes place at 5. We are going to be billeted at Griscourt.

Captain Desagneau spent most October and November on maneuvers and was then posted to the Somme.

22 November. At 4 a.m., we arrive at Beleuse (Somme). The men are exhausted and, after twenty-eight months of war, we still find the same problems. Our billets are not ready and there is no straw. The locals refuse their rooms because they are not

[16] washing, but with the connotation of ritual purification

paid. And what billets! They are mud-walled sheds, which are half-falling down and draughty. The men grumble and rightly so, the buildings are pigsties rather than habitable dwellings. The artillery was here before us and there's horse dung everywhere—it's disgusting.

I am lodged in a miserable alcove without any heating. With a simple iron bedstead and mattress, neither sheets nor blankets! I manage to get myself a sleeping bag, I am freezing cold.

Food is not cheap in the area; eggs are 35 centimes, ham 10 francs a kilo, bread 2 francs. It's a miserable existence and tomorrow perhaps, the men will be asked to go and get themselves killed.

28 November. We go through Herbécourt, Flaucourt, which are completely destroyed. The sector seems organized and compares favourably with Verdun. There are communication trenches and shelters. It is said that we have nine successive lines of artillery and that we are supposed to attack Mount Saint-Quentin with the 20th Corps, then Biaches, La Maisonnette, and Barleux, reserved for the 12th. . . .

Everyday, there are large numbers of men suffering from frostbitten feet.

20 December. There is shelling with gas the whole day. One could be at Verdun.

There are masses of planes in the sky, through a gap in the clouds I count 45 French ones. Two of them fall in flames on our lines.

In the distance, about 20 balloons observe. Is it the preparation for an attack? The shells rain down and the men are overcome by the gas. On the right, the Moroccan Division attacks unsuccessfully.

22 December. Rain and mud. Many men evacuated with frostbite. Hard day. A lot of gas. Heavy bombardment of our Quarry. The shelters are insufficient and several collapse. Munitions dumps explode all around us. It's enough to drive one mad.

The order for the attack is countermanded. Why? It's a secret. Political reasons they say. Questions in the House on our effective strength and munitions. Also affairs in Greece and Romania.

Our situation is the same, heavy shelling, gas, etc. . . . I go to link up with the Moroccan Division on our right. There, the sector is awful. The Arabs like attacking, but work, never. As a result, the communication trenches fill up more and more every day. You can't use them unless you want to sink in mud up to your waist. If you are unlucky enough to fall into a shell-crater, the mud comes up over your head. There are men in the front line who are buried up to their waists. Some officers tell me that during their last relief, they had to pull men out of this morass by means of ropes.

29 December. At 9 p.m. relief, and what a relief it is! The guns thunder. It is raining and the communication trenches are no more than a cesspool, we advance at 2 kilometers an hour and we have 11 to do before reaching camp at Cappy. The night is black as ink and it's difficult to find one's way. Finally we come out of the trench near Flaucourt. It's the most dangerous cross-roads as gun batteries are installed not far away and the whole zone is shelled. The road is like a quagmire. We get tangled in telephone wires, stumble into holes, the mud coming up to our knees, sometimes to the thighs. We mark time in some places rather than advancing, with only the shell bursts to show us the way. It's a nightmare; some men fall in the holes and are sucked down, we are obliged to help them. Artillery shells explode all around us, but we can't take cover as the mud is too thick. The shells follow us as far as Herbécourt, with mud splashing up on all sides, it's mad.

30 December. The men returning from the trenches are hideous; they are covered from head to toe with a thick coat of sticky mud. Their equipment, rifles, and packs form one huge ball of it. One has only to see this to realize what our troops are suffering. The cry is unanimous here: let Poincaré,[17] let Joffre,[18] the deputies, journalists, and senators come and live here a bit with us. The war will end quicker.

1917

Desagneaux transferred to the Vosges Sector near the German border and served there from January through May.

16 January. Already rumours are circulating: we are supposed to be going to the trenches in four days. The cook heard it from the postman who got it from the Colonel's cyclist, who heard it from the cooks or the orderly or the secretary, etc. It's the same old story. But in this sad existence without ever knowing what tomorrow will bring, one hangs on every word.

10 February. Note from the Colonel: "There are too many men in the rear; keep an eye on your fatigue parties; avoid too many men leaving the trenches. The front line must be attractive and not repulsive!!!" Why, therefore, don't we ever see him in the lines?

15 February. How to launch an attack! The General commanding the Army says: In four days, I need at least three prisoners. The Chief of Staff decides; Division X in 3½ days you will capture a prisoner; Division Y ditto, Division Z ditto.

The General commanding these divisions says to his colonels: In three days you will bring me at least one prisoner.

The Colonel decides therefore: Attack in forty-eight hours on such a position. That's it.

The whole plan is elaborated, of course, kilometers in the rear on a map. Is it possible?—they don't think about that. They need prisoners. When they get down to details and it's a question of placing their mortar-fire—like La Chapelotte—they realize it isn't.

But it is too late. The order has been given and there's no going back as the officers don't want any disgrace. That's how our attacks are always unfruitful and only result in losses and sometimes prisoners taken from our side. How much simpler it would be to study first what is possible and where, then give orders after these details have been settled, rather than say: I need that, there, in such a time!

[17] Raymond Poincaré, French president, 1913–1920

[18] Joseph Joffre, chief of the French General Staff, 1911–1916. His Plan XVII focused on the Franco-German frontier and failed to account adequately for a German invasion through Belgium.

4 April. Many men get drunk. Morale is low. They are fed up with the war. Certain corps court-martial some men for desertion, theft, insolence, etc.; after condemnation (with reprieve in the majority of cases) they are transferred to another corps. My company is infested with them. Special strictly disciplined companies are needed, prison sentences are useless.

1 May. Yet again, we leave this sector for the unknown. General Nivelle[19] is relieved of his command. Pétain[20] now becomes General Chief of Staff for the Army.

1 June. The spirit of the troops is turning sour. There is talk of mutiny and of troops refusing to go to the lines. The "bad hats" amongst them are more vociferous.

3 June. All the companies are in a state of turmoil; the men are receiving letters from friends informing them of the present spirit and urging them not to march; the ringleaders are becoming insolent; others are trying to influence their comrades. My company does not escape this plague: a squad, under the sway of its corporal, refuses to fall in, the men claiming that they are ill. Just as we move to take them to the guardroom, they run off in the fields and insult the N.C.O.s. Some only return the following day.

I have five court-martialed, to get rid of the worst. Alas! That's just what many want—a motive to be court-martialed, so as to spend a year in prison; they are counting on some future amnesty and, during their stay in prison, they will be far from the Front. Once again, it will be the good who will go and get themselves killed and the scoundrels who will be protected.

In addition, a law has just increased the men's pay: first payment today. These men who are getting 20–30 francs rush to spend them on drink; drunkenness all along the line. Command becomes difficult.

5 June. I sit in judgment at the court-martial. What a procession of rogues! How stupid they seem in front of their judges. In their company they tried to be smart, insulted their superiors, tried to get their chums to desert; here they are now, sheepish, not daring to look up, full of repentance.

At 7 p.m. General Garbit and General Méric come and ask for me at my quarters, to entrust me with a confidential mission.

The Army is becoming more and more a prey to this ill-feeling; those on leave on their return home from the front are assailed by agitators who, going as far as uncoupling the trains, urge them not to return. I must go to Meaux[21] to re-establish order.

[19] One of the heroes of Verdun, Robert Nivelle became commander-in-chief of the French Army in December 1916. The unfortunate failure of his 1917 spring offensive (known as the Nivelle Offensive or the Chemin des Dames) resulted in his removal as commander-in-chief and reassignment to North Africa.

[20] Another hero of Verdun, Philippe Pétain, was not promoted to the rank of general until 1914 because of his emphasis on the defensive as opposed to the offensive posture favored by his superiors.

[21] just east of Paris

7 June. On my arrival at Meaux at 9:30 I organize my troops at the station and in town. One platoon for the town and hospital (where there's a load of brutes), two platoons at the station, one in reserve, in case of need.

At 3 p.m. the first train of those on leave arrives at the station from the front. As soon as the train enters, you would see a horde of savages, all the doors opening on both sides and the men flooding out on the platforms.

Shouts, insults, threats fly in all directions: death to the shirkers at home, murderers and pigs that they are; long live the Revolution, down with the war, it's peace we want, etc. We empty the station to avoid conflict; the station staff don't dare show themselves. That's why I'm here. At La Ferté-sous-Jouarre a company of machine-gunners is on guard. At Chateau-Thierry, a company of light infantry; each division has its zone.

4 p.m., second train. The troops invade a garden. The owner kindly offers to let them pick flowers provided that they don't do any damage. There is one mad rush and everything is destroyed; they attack the house too, the windows are broken and the blinds torn down. They shout the same cries and insults: Death, long live the Revolution, down with the war.

5 p.m., third train. As soon as it stops, the troops surge out menacingly. There is an empty train in the station: the men seize stones and break every window. During the journey, a man had fallen on the track and had had his foot cut off. The military superintendent of the station—a lieutenant aged 55—rushes up with four men and a stretcher to carry him away. Seeing his white band the troops call him a murderer and beat him black and blue. It all happened so quickly that the attack passed unnoticed and we found this officer lying unconscious on the platform after the departure of the train. Often scenes such as these happen at the last moment, as the train is leaving, so that we can't intervene.

The trains are in a lamentable state; the doors are wrenched off and thrown on the track during the journey; all the windows are broken, and the seats slashed to ribbons.

That's the state of affairs. My men are well-disciplined and will be ready to act at the first signal. I have no fears in this respect. The situation, however, is delicate, for how can I intervene, should the need arise, with 30 or 40 men, against a frenzied horde of a thousand individuals, the majority of them in a state of intoxication?. . .

8 June. At Meaux my guard duty passes normally. My men, well turned-out, parade in the town and are a source of admiration to everyone. This is because at Meaux, there are only fatigue sections: bakers, drivers who have no idea of smart turnout, good discipline.

The day passes with the usual cries of: down with war, death to the slackers, long live the Revolution and that's all, except for a drunk who got out a razor to show how he cut the *Boches*' heads off; we cart him off to prison.

12 June. The postal service informs me that letters seized are full of threats and plans for revolution. No-one hides the fact things are bad and everyone is fed up. . . .

17 June. The "good days" at Meaux are over and as we return to the lines the shirkers . . . continue their gay life. These gentlemen have got their own restaurant there where no outsiders are allowed and every Saturday the ladies of Paris come and join them. Concert, dancing, it's a real orgy. This is what the men have seen and that's why this evening they grumble. . . .

In mid-June Desagneaux returned to the front lines in the sector of the Chemin des Dames, scene of the failed offensives earlier that spring.

18 June. Superb weather. From 4 a.m., the German planes are above us, two of them flying as low as 50 meters to machine-gun the trenches. It's an awful sensation to hear this tac-tac-tac and the whistling of the bullets. We curl up and anxiously wait until the engine gets fainter. We watch the plane fly casually away—ours aren't there and he can do as he wishes.

Everyday there are repeated attacks on our lines: the Germans are gradually recapturing the ground they lost. The Chemin des Dames is virtually theirs. We have relieved here the 3rd Artillery Company because they refused to march any more and the *Boches* took advantage of this ill-feeling to recapture the terrain.

Throughout the region, there is talk of nothing but mutinies, of troops refusing to relieve their comrades. Near Braisne, they have massed Moroccan and Algerian troops whose role will be to force the troops to go to the trenches if the need arises. It often happens that troops in the line spend three or four days longer there because their replacements refuse to march. It's the spirit of the day. ...

20 June. The day is spent at the mercy of an indescribable barrage of fire, we expect an attack at any second, everyone is at his post. There's no thought of eating, we are dreadfully thirsty, but we haven't had a drop of water to drink, we must wait until nightfall when the fatigue parties will bring some water-bottles. . . .

6 July. My battalion has been on duty in this sector for twenty-five days. We are supposed to be relieved by the 10th Battalion which is returning to the lines. . . .

It is light. The German planes fly over us and signal our movements. Then it's a deluge of shells of all calibers. The trenches are destroyed—we have to cross open spaces in full view; we run, bent double pursued by bursts of machine-gunfire. Miraculously, we reach our position without too much harm.

The departure of the 10th Battalion for this relief was a real epic. . . . To the orders given them, the men reply with sneers and insults. The officers of the division try and intervene, but they are manhandled. Time passes; some men pick up their packs and see reason; their comrades disarm them. The officers, fed up with their lack of success, draw their revolvers and threaten. Immediately a loading of rifles is heard on all sides. The officers parley with the men, trying to inspire some to set a good example, and thus encourage others to go. Failure. Some officers equip with their own hands their loyal soldiers and make them leave one by one. This decides others. And that's how, first of all, we saw small groups arriving.

All this took place before the eyes of the division, the regiment's honor is tarnished. It will be utterly lost on 8 July.

8 July. Memorable day for the regiment. In Champagne (1915) it lost 22 officers. At Verdun, 23. This evening there will be at least 32 officers and 2 battalions (the 5th and

10th) with their commander and their adjutants, almost completely lost to the enemy. It was obvious that the *Boches* would venture an attack on our front: the leveling of the trenches pointed to it as well as the fact that the enemy now had a view of our positions after completing its recent daily series of conquests. The violent bombardment of the past forty-eight hours had slowed down; the night seemed to be calm.

At 3 a.m. suddenly a terrible cannonade rips through the air; everything is a mass of fire in the front and the rear of the regiment, it's a deluge of fire. . . .

At 3:10 a.m. the telephone is cut, nothing works any more, only couriers. . . .

At 4:55 a second note ordering me to come immediately with all my men. At the same time a soldier rushes up like a madman shouting that he had escaped from the hands of the *Boches*, that the whole line is taken, that the 5th and 10th Battalions are prisoners.

We will therefore be expected to counter-attack. I assemble my company; nobody jibs [complains], not a murmur. . . .

At 5:50 a.m. we are all on our way. . . . How we advance, how we get through, how we are not blown to smithereens at every step, nobody knows. We stumble on; explosions everywhere, we fall flat, get up again, it's raining, we are swimming in mud, but we go forward in a hurry to escape this furnace, to get there at last only to find perhaps worse still.

It's impossible to get through this zone unharmed. At every step the trenches have caved in, we have to advance in the open, we go onwards nevertheless, streaming with water, covered in sweat and mud, panting, and with a lump in our throats. They are counting on us and we press on and on. Some wounded are lost en route. We arrive at the Colonel's ravine. I put my company at his disposal.

We have no idea of the situation, except that the few who escaped say that the Germans are in possession of our lines, that the two battalions—5th and 10th—don't exist any more, their commanders . . . their adjutants . . . all the officers . . . are prisoners. The front is wide open. . . .

When I arrive, everyone heaves a sigh of relief. A single squad was guarding the ground occupied by two battalions. Immediately three platoons of my company go into action. The shells fall like hail, we are repeatedly knocked to the ground, it's a miracle even to advance. . . .

One of my platoons supplies fresh munitions and rockets. We left without any food; besides, no one is hungry, the situation is too critical. Three German prisoners are brought in. Some of ours who manage to escape begin to arrive and we learn what happened.

The attack was instantaneous and very violent with special troops. It was made easier by the fact that our companies had evacuated the front line to allow our artillery to destroy the enemy trenches. The *Boches* pressed on and arrived at the second and then the third lines where they caught everyone by surprise. . . .

Time passes; the guns roar, it's awful. I receive the order to organize a line joining what is left of our front line on the right with our third line, our last defense. We have to infiltrate, fighting with grenades. The *Boches* are everywhere.

In my command I have my three platoons, two of the 38th Company, one of the 22nd, one of the 23rd and a few escapees who have returned to fight. The important thing is to hold our ground; the men are hard pressed and covered in mud. We hold nevertheless. Orders come thick and fast, and gradually, we drive back the enemy advance parties and retake some of the lost ground.

The hours seem never-ending, the gunfire relentless, everything trembles. The dead and wounded are numerous. . . .

Night falls, heavy barrage of fire on both sides. Behind us, in the Colonel's ravine, it's a deluge of 210s. I am ordered to lead a counter-attack to recapture the Scutari trench[22] occupied by enemy troops. Their machine-guns decimate one of my platoons; artillery fire pins us to the ground. On three occasions we launch an attack; in vain, the men can't take any more.

At last, the relief arrives, they don't know exactly where the lines are or where the enemy is. It's total confusion. By now the Germans have organized their mortars which are firing in batteries of six, pounding our positions. In one single platoon, I have 7 killed in a twinkling. . . .

There's not a square metre without several shell holes: corpses everywhere, ruin, devastation.

We go out of firing range and breathe at last. I am tired out. We have been in a state of alert for days now and no one has eaten for thirty hours. At the first opportunity I sink into a deep sleep. . . .

Right up to the end of the campaign, the 359th will bear the brunt of responsibility for this day. Those in command will resent the fact it allowed itself to lose two battalions. However, those left, who fought, who prevented the enemy from advancing, are they responsible for this? And those who are captured, who wilted under the attack, are they as responsible as all that?. . .

It was, however, a fatal day for the regiment, all citations were refused to those who had done their duty. Is not war made of capture and of losses of men and terrain on both sides?

Yes, but the chiefs had noticed the ill-will the 10th Battallion had shown in going to the line a few days previously. This was only one step away from accusing these same troops of having surrendered—and this step was soon taken.

10 July. At 6 a.m. motorized transport takes us to our new quarters at Puiseaux.[23] What are they going to do with us? The regiment no longer exists; it is necessary to reform it: only the 6th Battalion has 450 men, the others are reduced to nothing. We have no illusions; if we stay in the area, it's to be back in the lines in a fortnight.

11 July. While waiting we sleep and wash; fleas abound. The men need fresh underwear to be really clean; but as if by chance, there is a shortage of it! The men grumble and indeed it's pitiful to see these men who have not washed for a month, obliged to keep on wearing the same smelly rags, due to the fault of some supply officer who doesn't know what the front is like or to some commander lacking in foresight. Oh, how they ought to make all those in the rear come and see what it's like in the trenches!. . .

[22] a strong defensive position not taken until September 1918
[23] due south of Paris

15 July. Assembly of all officers of the division. General Pétain wants to address us. Everyone is there, from the general to the youngest sub-lieutenant.

Painful meeting which does nothing to raise morale. Pétain enters, cold, stern, "How many deserters in the division?" he asks immediately. We look at each other. We were expecting something else. And, after asking the amount of losses, declaring that we should not count on reinforcements to bridge the gaps, he finishes with these words, "You must re-discipline this undisciplined division. Gentlemen, that's all I have to say to you, good-bye." And he leaves[,] slamming the door of his car.

Brute, is that the way to raise morale and to ask people to go and get themselves killed?

A cloud hangs over us, we are sickened. It's definite, then; the battalions surrendered—they were undisciplined—at least in the minds of these gentlemen. And those of us left, who did their duty, who are still ready to do it to the very end, must they expiate the fault of those who had one moment's discouragement or cowardice?

Pétain has not shown himself a great leader, at the very least not human. There were so many ways to make us feel what he wanted—without saying it!

Who was he talking to?—to Reserve officers in the great majority, who all held their ground. At the beginning of the war, they said scathing things about us, we were considered as duffers, and yet, what would they have done, what would they do without us? We who are alone at the front whilst the Regular soldiers—who had chosen war as their profession—are in the rear, in depots or sheltered in H.Q.s or other services.

Pétain has said that after three years of war the men are tired. Yes, and with these ways of treating them they will end up destroying the goodwill of those men—Reserve officers—who left their homes full of courage and who receive no reward for it. All the "Croixes de Guerre"[24] are for the Regulars, nothing for us.

We return dismayed: an hour later, first note to say that it's urgent to take a firm hold on all units, and to put discipline into action. How many fine words?. . .

17 July. During our marches we have the generals, the Colonel on our back. The men are overloaded with equipment, often wearing worn-out shoes that can't be replaced. They plod along. But they are exhorted to step out firmly, rifles erect, to keep in line, with head up. Perspiration rolls off them, but they must button up their overcoats, put their helmets well over the forehead, guides in their places and ranks-closers in the rear, those blankets are not properly rolled, that haversack isn't in its place, that tool is on the right instead of the left . . . it doesn't stop and, on all sides, the men murmur: "You don't say that when we are in the lines; we never see you there. Come and line us up when we are leaving for an attack."

Then after the troops, it's the vehicles' turn. Too heavily loaded—doesn't conform to the regulations—a favourite word in wartime. In spite of all, our fine bunch of lads, aged between 35 and 40, march, march, to the bitter end.

[24] "Cross of War"; the medal was created in April 1915 to recognize individual soldiers for their valor.

18 July. In the column a soldier has no overcoat. Why? Asks the Colonel in his gruff voice. "Colonel," replies the man, "captured on the 8th, I managed to escape from the hands of the *Boches*, but my overcoat stayed with them." "If it was to return in that state of dress, you would have done better to stay there too," replies the Colonel. That's it, raise morale! But is this the way and is it hardly surprising that there are anti-militarists?

We are all sickened. The notes pile up: forbidden to do this and that. Then, "Those who leave their weapons behind in the trenches are cowards, we will take their *Croixes de Guerre* from them."

And of course the captain is held responsible for everything. Sad, sad life! When will we see the end? When? The Russians are retreating again, there's lassitude everywhere! The same words are on every lip, "I am fed up!"

24 July. Every day exercises are brightened up by a visit from the Colonel. Nothing but criticism. Everything is bad. Never any encouragement, all we do is daft. How he makes us hate the army, and yet again, the men murmur, "Just come to the trenches, we never see your bl—dy face there."

Why criticize all the time? Let them teach us if what we do is wrong. . . . We know what trench life is like, but does he? In that case criticism is safer than advice. Raise morale!

3 August. The fourth year of war is beginning. . . . It rains without stopping the whole day. We are going to be billeted at Taincourt.[25] We are in recaptured territory: there is nothing left, all the houses have been burnt, the trees cut down. It's destruction in all its horror. . . .

4 August. Some local inhabitants are returning to their villages—to see what is left; they are full of sadness and of memories of relations shot on the spot in 1914. The government is supposed to be building huts to lodge the inhabitants, but these poor people, who have lost everything, will only be able to live in them if they can afford the rent!

15 August. Yet another fine sector! Pointed, exposed on two sides with a small command post in a trench which communicates with the *Boches*, the sentries of both sides only 15 meters apart. It's a continual grenade battle. Two platoons in the lines, one as support, and the other in reserve. Only the latter has some form of shelter at Moisy farm, which is itself no more than a heap of stones. The other platoons must live in the trench and dig for themselves under the parapet benches or seats where they can rest. It's impossible, of course, to light a fire; at night when the food arrives we have to eat it cold.

The first day ends badly. At 9 p.m. whilst Agnel and I were having barbed wire installed in front of the command post, the *Boches* take fright. Suddenly, a shower of grenades fall upon us, we are surrounded by fire and smoke. Flares soar in all directions, the *Boches* think they are being attacked and unleash a barrage of mortar fire. With great difficulty we get back to the trench, everyone is on the alert. . . . For an

[25] near Soissons, northeast of Paris

hour the hail of shells covers us with earth, and the trenches cave in. All around us, cries and moans from the wounded. In a flash I have 3 killed and 8 wounded, in one platoon alone. Then towards 11 p.m., calm returns. . . .

26–27 September. It is forty-five days now since the regiment has been in the lines. There's no question of departure, rather we must think of the next attack. It's our punishment for 8 July, which they never let us forget. The men, covered with fleas, grumble. . . .

22 October. Gas the whole night—masks on all the time. We are supposed to attack today—but no news. . . .

We know nothing, how long are we going to stay here? The barrage of fire is getting heavier and heavier, our shelters cave in and the lines are a shapeless chaos of slime in which we have to find some cover. . . .

24 October. Today—Victory. After a heavy artillery bombardment at 11 a.m., supported by gas, we receive the order to advance. We capture in succession the Elfes and Cocotier trenches, then the Ravine of Ailleval. The *Boches* flee and we follow hot on their heels. What a terrain! It's frightful, everything is devastated, we stumble into huge craters, German corpses everywhere, blown to pieces, others overcome by gas, dying. It's dreadful, but superb. The guns thunder in the distance, the battle is ours, for the moment.

25 October. Frenzy, the *Boches* are in full flight. It's hard to hold the men back, they want to pursue them. But we have done our job; the 5th Battalion replaces us to continue the advance in the direction of Pinon.

At 6 p.m. we leave for the rear, without any relief. Are we going to get some rest at last?

1 November. I get ten days' leave.

From November 1917 to April 1918 Captain Desagneaux remained on the move, returning to the Somme, to Alsace, and then to the Somme again.

1918

6 April. Quartered at Laversines, near Beauvais.[26]

The *Boches* are attacking *en masse*, we are dispatched in haste to the front. And, as we advance, so the zone gets worse; poor refugees of all ages; tramping the road, with tears in their eyes carrying what they can, a few clothes, some chickens or rabbits; sometimes followed by a few cattle.

It's misery on the march.

Laversines is teeming with cavalry, artillery, convoys, vehicles. It's complete and utter chaos, difficult to move around. The locality is full of people who are fleeing from the front, we can't find any billets and have to sleep in ruins, cellars, or in the open air.

[26] north of Paris

7 April. We start to learn what happened during the attack; the civilians who fled from this zone, claim that the English gave way and that, in several places, for distances of 10 kilometers there was absolutely nothing to stop the enemy. If the Germans didn't pass, it's because they didn't dare take the risk, fearing an ambush.

It was our troops, yet again, who saved the situation. . . .

11 April. The Germans continue their attacks: towards the sea: Arras, Ypres, Armentières. The Portuguese, in turn, are getting a hiding. We are retreating near Coucy. Everywhere the *Boches* are attacking, they are gaining ground. . . .

13 April. Arrival at Raincheval at midday, where we are quartered. The inhabitants are glad to see the French again. They have no confidence in the English any more. During the last *Boche* attack they lost 25 kilometers; on the first day, regiments—at Amiens—threw down their weapons and fled with the civilians. It is said that they have lost 70,000 men, and 1,100 guns. . . .

People have nothing but praise for the Canadians, Australians, and Hindus—it was they who stopped the enemy advance.

14 April. What a night. We wait in anguish. Sleep is impossible, the guns roar, the houses tremble, even the ground quakes, it's frightful. The weather joins in—rain, gale-force winds, thunder, all the elements are unleashed. . . .

Everyone says the same: the English are hopeless, it's the Scots, the Australians, and Canadians who do all the work. . . .

25 April. Our route is scattered with huge English camps, teeming with vehicles, men, and horses. But these men are more interested in polishing and shining their equipment than in thinking about the trenches.

28 April. I have been made captain adjutant-major in the 5th Battalion. . . .

I leave my 6th Battalion with regret, and especially my 21st Company where the men were always ready to sacrifice themselves for me. With them, I felt sure that they would not give in and, whatever happened, would not leave me behind.

Well, one must follow one's destiny.[27]

5 May. We leave Watou at 1:30 a.m.; the artillery fire is enough to drive one mad. We are now in the firing zone and we pass huge English howitzers, one after the other. The gunners are ramming their shells home like a baker thrusting bread into an oven. The shells go off with a deafening roar and this continues for hours upon end, sometimes their departure coincides with enemy arrivals and there is an almighty spray of fire and earth. We take cover and then move off again. What a march in such an avalanche of fire and by night too! The companies advance half a platoon at a time; we repeatedly come across convoys of artillery trapped in the mud and dead horses blocking the road.

Progress is difficult, our hearts are beating at the thought of what is to come.

Eventually we arrive near Reningelst, in front of Mount Kemmel, where we camp. . . .

[27] in Desagneaux's case, to the Kemmel sector in Belgium

The 27th Infantry Division, which was at Kemmel when the *Boches* attacked, has had many of its men taken prisoner; the 154th which was beside it, was wiped out; it's our turn to march now.

At 9 a.m. we leave to reconnoiter our positions; the terrain is unrecognizable, it is merely holes and muddy quagmires, with wrecked vehicles and a jumble of equipment everywhere: devastation, abominable desolation. Up front, none or very few communication trenches. We can't go any further. From the very first battalion we see in reserve, there is nothing but scared soldiers, huddled in shell-holes, not daring to raise their heads. If this is what it's like in reserve, what is it in the front line? There can be no thought of going there in daylight, the artillery fire is continuous and, further on, their machine-guns are sweeping our positions with bullets.

We leave without seeing anything. The afternoon is spent in chatting about the coming relief, everyone wondering how he will get out alive. The sector is the sole topic of conversation: we shall only be relieved after a 60 per cent loss of troops; the men are beginning to wish for, not death, but just to be wounded so that they can get out as soon as possible. This leads to endless suppositions; one man gives up his hand, another his arm, provided it's the left one; yet another goes as far as a leg, declaring that where he comes from men like this manage quite well. But what frightens them most is being wounded in the stomach or some other vital organ. Then the conversation turns to the ambulance, the hospital, plans for convalescence, rest at home, and what to do so as not to return to the front.

In every sort of sector like this, the conversation revolves around the same topic. There is no longer even any mention of the civilians and their cozy life. No, you are stuck there waiting, simply trying to snatch some part of yourself from death, you don't even ask to escape unharmed, it seems too impossible, your only wish is to leave as little as possible of yourself behind on the battlefield. . . .

At 6:30 p.m. we proceed to relieve the left sector of Mount Kemmel. Our advance is difficult as there are no communication trenches, just shell craters for our protection. We move forward with a lump in our throats; the shells rain down in front of us, but there's no going back, we have to get through. Our only desire is to reach our goal as quickly as possible. A moment's pause, then we are off again. There are explosions on the right, left, everywhere. Sometimes a man stops, wounded; we don't even bother about him, it's such a common occurrence. On we go, knowing full well that he will manage to get to the first-aid post. If his wound is only slight he is envied—he's safe. We advance, the bombardment is heavier, our ranks become thinner, night has fallen, we can't see each other any more, but now and again sheaves of fire bring a sinister gleam to this chaotic terrain.

At last, there's the battalion to be relieved. We shelter in a hole and get our breath. We are in reserve. No dug-outs, nothing, except a simple communication trench which will protect us from shell splinters and that's all. . . .

6 May. What a night. It's an orgy of gunfire. The English artillery and ours shoot away. The *Boches* return the fire, the sky is ablaze. Curled up small and huddled together in our shell-holes we are sprayed with earth and blinded by searing flashes of light. Then, towards midnight, just when the food is due to arrive, gas is unleashed upon us. It's enough to drive you mad. While the distribution of the food is being organized, all masks have to be put on, smoke fills the glasses and we can't see anything any more. We spend hours like this suffocating with parched throats, not daring to take the stifling masks off. During the night, the fatigue parties, which are not familiar with the sector, get lost and we have to go and look for them. Shells burst everywhere. When we do, at last, get the food, the air is full of gas, and we can't take our masks off and the food becomes uneatable.

That night, we have 200 men gassed and evacuated in the 120th Corps, about a similar number in the 297th and in the 359th as well. The loss of relief troops is calculated and the chiefs are struck by the high number of evacuees; the men are accused of having taken their masks off in order to be evacuated. As a result, we get threatening notes from them.

It's Sunday, and there is already talk of us attacking to improve our front-line positions. It's raining. The terrain, the soil of which is clay, is awful. We are eating, sleeping, living in filthy slime.

No shelters, no protection whatsoever. We can't wash, change or sleep. . . .

7 May. Night falls and with it a frightful bombardment starts up again. To avoid the disorder experienced the previous evening in the provisioning of the troops, I am chosen to take charge this evening. The mobile kitchens come as far as Reningelst where the fatigue parties meet them. There are few sectors that I have seen where the rear is so heavily shelled. The *Boches* fire away; the gun batteries, the cross-roads, the surrounding countryside are submerged in fire. . . .

Three kitchens from the battalion arrive; the fourth has been left behind on the way with its two horses killed by the same shell blast. The men run forward to collect the food.

The guns roar and it's just like a rugby scrum there. . . . The cooks are in a hurry, they don't like being in the lines, the sergeant-majors accompanying the kitchens are not the most courageous. The shells burst on all sides, and we can only recognize each other by their flashes of light. People push, shove, and shout to make themselves heard amid the clatter of pots and pans. Then, all of a sudden, a loud whistle is heard very close, everyone dives for cover, with pans flying in all directions. It's over now, the blast was deafening. Shouts of the wounded: "Over here quickly, I'm hit." "Help me, stretcher-bearers, take me to the first-aid post." The tussle for food becomes ever more frantic with men shouting and struggling, two men are lying on the ground, one at his last gasp, the other with his leg blown off. Suddenly, yet another terrible explosion directly on a kitchen, the horses killed, the men scatter, some shouting, others groaning, others running for their lives.

Come on, get on with it! The distribution of the food is now carried out in total darkness, with us standing in pools of blood. Blood from the horses, blood from the wounded, they mingle together and the din of the shells is frightful. Then the news goes round: Sergeant-Major Bonnet has been killed. He's from the 17th. It's panic-stations. Command is impossible, the shells burst all around us. Every man has only one idea—to grab what he needs to get away—coffee, the 3rd, wine, the 5th, what about your bread, you silly beggars!. . .

8 May. Gunfire the whole night long. At 4:15 a.m. our attack is unleashed. We don't know what is supposed to happen. We have simply been told to stand by and be ready for anything. The 359th attacks with two companies. . . .

At the same time as we were launching our offensive, the Germans attacked the English division which was helping the 15th. The English give way and a battalion of the 15th is hard-pressed. . . . Towards evening, with gas shells falling all round us, we are forced to put on our masks and are virtually suffocated for hours on end.

At 8 p.m. we learn that on the left our position has been re-established. This means rest for the time being. How long will it last?

9 May. The artillery has been quieter this evening. The sun rises. We learn the news of yesterday's attacks. It's not very good.

Our two companies encountered the *Boches* and took ten prisoners. . . .

At 9 p.m. we depart to relieve the support battalion at La Clytte, in front of Mount Kemmel. . . . We leave and cross the tiny village with no means of protection, led by a guide who doesn't know his way. The artillery has opened up again and shells splatter us with mud at every step. We advance sliding and slithering in thick slimy mud, with only one desire—to get there. But no one knows the way, the gunfire makes us do a detour and we get caught up in old barbed-wire entanglements. With our clothes and flesh torn to ribbons, they bombard us with gas, which, half-blinded and choking, slows our advance. Miraculously no one in our column is wounded; but it's not the same story for the rest of the battalion. . . .

11–13 May. Still in a state of alert, we are awaiting events. The artillery is as active as ever. . . .

14 May. What a sector. We are on a hilltop—the main target of the German guns. At the bottom of the hill, two companies; near the railway line—one company in reserve with us. No trenches—only holes. . . .

The companies are scattered here and there, anywhere they could find some holes to shelter in. There is no communication between them. From time to time, I come across clusters of corpses, remnants of previous attacks which have not been able to be removed. They are stinking, but when I try to escape them, I merely stumble across more. Grim battlefield where in a few days we shall be fighting in our turn. The German artillery shoots incessantly, and gas shells fall at our feet. . . .

15 May. 1 a.m.—gas again, our shelter is full of it. You can hardly breathe, your throat burns; you cough and spit, tears stream down your face. There can be no thought of sleep, the guns are firing madly, we are in a state of alert as we expect to be attacked at dawn. . . .

Our losses increase daily; about 200 per battalion, i.e. 600 for the regiment. Life is getting harder: no sleep, we are wallowing in mud and filth. We can neither wash nor lie down except on the ground itself and there is not a wisp of straw; our joints are stiff and we are itching all over.

18 May. I receive precise details of the attack: I have been designated to command a communication detachment between the 121st Infantry Division on the left and ours. . . . The attack is for the 20th. The men are exhausted, effectives are reduced to 60 or 70 per company, there are no N.C.O.s and they have been in the sector for fifteen days already.

19 May. The attack is for tomorrow morning. I go and inspect the terrain. The starting point has been fixed at the railway embankment in the ravine. My objective, a nameless farm. We shall have to cross the railway line, then the small stream at Kemmelbeck and then climb a slope. If we get there, I am supposed to hold my position, withstand enemy fire with no shelter of any kind and resist any counter-attacks until relief arrives.

It's a day full of anguish. Orders and counter-orders flood in. You don't know what to believe. Being thus responsible to the 121st Infantry Division for the attack, I am sent to Reningelst to see a major who has nothing to do with me, whereas the one who will be in charge of the attack is still at Poperinge and will only arrive at the lines this evening.

It's utter confusion. And it's Sunday. Whit Sunday. Marvellous weather, not a cloud, brilliant sunshine, and tonight we shall have to go to our deaths. We would love to banish all our hopes and fears until afterwards.

What sadness there is in our shelter rocked by shell-fire. What hope is there? You can't always go on without copping it, won't the fatal moment come when our luck will turn? And while we are here waiting to die, others have been relaxing for the past four years in the rear, or in some headquarters, or in a driving seat! All those fine army circulars have not succeeded in ousting them. Even in the camp up front, there are some who have been vegetating there for one or two years; it's always the same ones who are sent and when reinforcements arrive, it's those who were wounded a few days previously who return, whilst so many others who are fit and capable have never seen a trench and don't know what a shell-burst is.

The hours pass, night spreads its dark cloak over the huge field whilst the artillery pounds the lines and the rear.

The latest orders arrive. I transmit mine: two platoons in line, each with a squad of machine-gunners; as a second wave of attack, two platoons each of infantry and machine-guns. Plans for wiping out the enemy trenches, organization of our position.

Dinner? We aren't hungry, our thoughts are dry, our only thoughts are of what is to come. The major stays at his post, a hand-shake before leaving, a "good luck" and I disappear into the night with Pierre—towards the great unknown.

20 May. Whit Monday. Splendid evening; the stars are shining in the sky, and on the ground shells burst in sheets of light.

At midnight, I make my way to the point where I am supposed to meet the company from the 36th Infantry Regiment which has been placed under my command. I have no information concerning the officers and N.C.O.s in it and I shall have to lead an attack with troops that I have never seen before.

At 1 a.m. the troops arrive at their position near the railway line; then we notice that we are totally unprotected and that there isn't enough room for everyone. How dismal it is to watch in the darkness these files of men, bent in two, each man trying to recognize his neighbor—they are soon forced to spread along the railway line towards the right. But they fall upon a mound of corpses, remnants from previous attacks. The stench is vile. Through the darkness, we perceive shapeless forms, legs folded in two, arms outstretched, eyes wide open. The whole place is littered with bodies, weapons, and equipment; the smell forces us back. We can't think of staying there, the men must be moved away so they are spared this vision of death before confronting it themselves.

Therefore, we fall back towards the left; there will be a gap on our right. Each man digs, as best as he can, a hole to prevent himself from being seen. But aren't we digging our own graves in the night?

At last, we are in position, time ticks by, and dawn is about to break. The officers from the 36th come to discuss the attack with me, their orders don't coincide with mine. Their order is to launch the attack at 3 minutes to 6, whilst we are due to attack at 6. What a confabulation! Everyone is trying to save his own skin and to find some means of escape. Tired of talking, I order them to obey my commands. Then, something else, the bright spark who was supposed to put them there has found it easier not to bother. What organization! Everyone is trying to protect himself and acts just as he pleases—the generals are far away aren't they? No cohesion. Poor soldier? Here's your orders and—get on with it!. . .

5:50. Suddenly, as if by magic, the barrage is unleashed. It's unbelievable: 75s, 90s, 110s, 166s, all firing at once. Shells of every sort shower down in their thousands in front of us. It's just one curtain of smoke, we can't see a thing any more. . . . The din is frightful. The *Boches* do not return the fire. It's such a beautiful sight that everyone comes out of his hole to watch. . . .

6 a.m. Forward, forward. Everyone is on his feet, we join up with the others, we're off. . . .

Suddenly, machine-gun bullets whistle past us; the *Boches* are on to us. We take cover, then move off again. . . .

The barrage lengthens again, and falls beyond the ridge to pound the rear of the enemy's lines. Then, panic-stricken, a group of *Boches* comes stumbling down, without weapons or equipment, and with their hands in the air. They seem half-crazed, with their eyes bulging out of their heads, our barrage has stunned them. We are at the ridge. There are German corpses there, chunks of bloody flesh, with terror written on their faces which are almost black already.

On we go, we are over the ridge, the nameless farm is ours. Spades out, and while everyone is digging away, flinging to one side the evil-smelling corpses, I install my machine-guns and organize communications and positions.

We recapture 4 British guns abandoned here during a previous attack. We take in addition 4 machine-guns and 18 *Boches*.

We take cover, Mount Kemmel looks down on us; the reaction of the *Boches* promises to be terrible. In front of us, it's a plain as far as the foot of Mount Kemmel, no protection anywhere.

Our success is total. The sun is resplendent. We can breathe at last. . . .

10 a.m. The *Boches* react. Our reserves are showered with shells. While awaiting our turn, we hurry to get all our organization complete. We dig, dig, and dig. The heat is torrid, the corpses are giving off an awful stench. . . . The *Boches* really do stink too much and their shells are getting closer. . . .

The afternoon passes without mishap—but relief is not forthcoming, everyone is glum again; they have bitter words for those who leave them here. "Are the pigs going to leave us to die here like dogs? Perhaps they imagine that we haven't done enough already! Twenty-four hours here, I'm fed up. And our food? Who is going to bring it? Nobody here will hear of doing 6 or 7 kilometers and as many back again to go and fetch it! Ah the pigs!"

While these insults fly, evening falls and the artillery opens up. Soon we are in an inferno of fire. . . . Munitions dumps explode, it's a real firework display. The whole plain is alight, it's war in all its horror. . . .

21 May. Night draws to its close and day is about to break. We are hoping for some respite. Suddenly, as well as the violent explosions which splatter us with earth, we have to contend with gas shells which give off a noxious white vapor. "Gas, gas"—the cry echoes all along the line. We shall have to live with our masks on, and be prepared for a counter-attack. . . .

God, how filthy we are! Fifteen days' growth of beard, and for the last eighteen days I haven't taken my shoes off or had a change of underwear. We have no water to wash in, just mud all around us. We can't even satisfy the call of nature any more. . . .

Ah, what a pounding the *Boches* are getting—yes, but we are getting one too. It's one barrage of fire everywhere and the *Boche*s are pouring gas upon us. For the fifteenth or twentieth time of the day, we put our masks on.

We await our relief. Can it take place, will the soldiers be able to cross this wall of metal and flames to reach us? The relief is due at midnight. It is 11 p.m. and the guns rage.

All of a sudden, a shout in front of us: "The *Boches*, the *Boches*." It's a counter-attack. At one and the same time, machine-guns open up, rifles fire at point-blank range, grenades explode everywhere and as soon as a red flare is up, our barrage starts up. The *Boches* suffer heavy losses and those who can escape do so in disorder.

22 May. Midnight. The barrage stops, but there is still heavy firing on the rear and on the lines; we are in a cloud of smoke. . . . Not a drop of water to drink, our throats are parched, we wait. Crash! We are covered with earth. . . . In the hole next to us two men are buried. Help me! One of them runs for it, crazed with fear; another has a broken leg. . . . Carry him to safety?—We can't even think of it in such a hail of fire. . . .

We are ready . . . we anxiously look for a gap which would allow us through. Nothing but smoke. . . . We leave, and we haven't gone 100 meters when we meet the first French body, fallen during tonight's relief. Poor devil with his face crushed, arms outstretched, there's nothing we can do for him. On we go, and all the way we come across wounded making for the rear, or piles of corpses, in fours and fives, no longer red, but black, decomposing on the spot—What an awful sight! Naked, limbs twisted, with sometimes a leg lying on its own covered in blood. We have to step over these bodies, across a maze of holes, strewn with the foul-smelling corpses of men and horses; the ground reeks of gunpowder and gas. The smell gets down into your throat, but there can be no stopping now, the firing seems to be dying down. . . .

Finally, we arrive at the trenches at La Clytte. There's hardly anything left of the dugouts and trenches. . . .

The weather is glorious, we can get some fresh air, without having to keep our heads down. Tomorrow, we'll have water and I shall be able to shave and change my clothes. Oh, just to take off my shirt, and to get rid of these ever-increasing fleas, not to scratch any more! And then not to have to eat chocolate or jam or some tasteless tinned food. And sleep! What a prospect!. . .

5 June. Campremy. We are now in the region of Montdidier,[28] in the American sector.

At 8 in the evening, great commotion. German planes drop a shower of bombs on our quarters. Sometimes there are five or six bombs exploding at once; many casualties. . . .

6 June. Soldiers from Martinique and the 1918 new recruits are brought in to complete the companies' ranks. With these youngsters, we shall be expected to launch an attack before very long.

10 June. I'm in command of the 5th Battalion. The situation is none too brilliant. We have no idea what's in front of us, nor to our right. The artillery does just what it pleases, and there is a successive flow of orders and counter-orders. . . .

11 June. At 3 a.m., just when the companies are acquainted with their positions and the machine-gunners in place. . . . I receive an order to return immediately to Maignelay itself and to make my arrangements for an attack. . . .

The men who are half-asleep complain bitterly, they are fed up. . . .

At 7, the Colonel sends for me. He is very excited and seems tired. In front of him a map. With a finger he explains that the whole division is going to form at the railway-line near Tricot and at 9:45 proceed to attack Courcelles[29] and Mortemer-Grand Bois. Twenty-four tanks will accompany us to Courcelles where our lines are; the artillery preparation is to last half an hour. Five divisions are co-operating in the attack under the command of General Mangin.[30]

And that's all, nothing on paper, no other explanation—how the regiment is marching, its formation, the position occupied by my battalion, liaison with the right and left, nothing.

The Colonel seems overwhelmed, incapable of anything. Perhaps it's because there, he won't be in his dug-out and will have to accompany us? Scrap by scrap I obtain from him the information I judge indispensable. . . .

Direction: Courcelles, then Mortemer. Time of attack: 9:45. . . .

We haven't been able to transmit our orders. The troops don't know what is expected of them. . . .

[28] just southeast of Amiens

[29] the small village of Courcelles-Epayelles

[30] General Charles Mangin was nicknamed "the Butcher" owing to his insistence on fighting to the last man. He was also responsible for incorporating colonial African troops into the French army.

Can a soldier think for one moment that an attack without artillery is possible in 1918? NO. Then the attack can only possibly take place tomorrow morning. Until then . . . all hopes are permissible. . . .

It's 9:45, the regiment sets off noisily. . . .

But scarcely have we crossed the railway when the first shells splatter us with mud and, ahead of us, the leading battalions are submerged in smoke. The enemy has seen our movements, and is firing for all he is worth. . . .

We are in the thick of the barrage, clods of earth are flying in all directions, fire and smoke swirl around us, we hasten to cross this wall. Swearwords ring out everywhere, men stop, killed or wounded, but there is no stopping, we go on and on, we have to get through at any cost. . . .

We move off again. We have difficulty in advancing through these huge cornfields, and from now on we do nothing but stumble across the wounded. They are abandoned here, amid the tall blades of corn, helpless. Those who can walk flee towards the rear; those wounded in the leg, the stomach, or even more seriously patch themselves up while waiting for help. Help; when will it come? The regiment has moved on, will they find them in these huge fields, lying among the tall corn? How many are going to end up dying through lack of attention and will rot where they fell!

We advance nevertheless under the burning sun and the fire of the enemy. The firing grows fiercer. We have to cross the trenches of our second and third lines, then barbed-wire entanglements. We climb over them, scratching and tearing our flesh—but on we go, ever faster, the steeple is still some way off, and we must get there. . . .

10:30. We have been advancing for three-quarters of an hour, the leading companies' lines seem to be wavering, the outlines of the battalions are no longer distinguishable.

The losses must be enormous, how will we reach our goal?

The artillery seems to double in fury, the shells fall like hail—soon the barrage is visible. But what is our artillery doing? We can't even hear anything passing over our heads. Are our guns even in place? And what would they fire with? Tiny little 75s, while the *Boches* are sending us 105s and 150s, and 210s are raining down on Courcelles.

This day seems crazier and crazier. Yet we advance, frightened and worn-out as we are, hastening on, with the idea that the quicker we go the sooner we shall reach our goal. Goal? Who knows what it is? We were told: direction Courcelles, then Mortemer. And then? Do the big chiefs alone know what we are supposed to be doing? Certainly not, for to explain away this day of madness, they are to tell us afterwards that the division was sacrificed, that its mission was to create a diversion, to stop the *Boches* at any price. . . .

What a sight! The *Boches* concentrate all their guns upon them [the tanks], it's a deluge of fire. Some are destroyed on the spot, some are set on fire, some stagger along, trying to reach the plain, only to be blown up further on, others succeed in crossing the lines only to be brought to a crushing halt 100 meters later. In a quarter of an hour, it's all over; this day will have cost us 37 out of the 40 tanks which were escorting the division.

As soon as our tanks are no more, our attention turns to the sky; a swarm of German planes are attacking ours, about ten in number. It's a massacre. The guns chatter; our planes are outnumbered ten to one! Five of ours are shot down immediately. We forget everything happening up front. With a lump in our throats, we watch these planes come crashing down in flames to the ground.

Everyone is dismayed, the battle is so unequal that we felt like asking for pardon for our planes, we would like to shout out to them; no, enough is enough, go home, don't try any more. We, the infantry, will stay here, you can't do anything, there are too few of you, go away. ...

Time marches on. Midday. One o'clock. The sun burns like fire. The artillery has concentrated its fire on Courcelles, which is in flames. At 2 the steeple collapses, the village and the surrounding area are devastated.

What are we doing here? What are our orders? The Colonel? Everyone is seeking the Colonel . . . but he is nowhere to be found. We will shortly learn that on seeing the barrages, he took cover behind the railway-line at Tricot; he will only come and join me later at 2 p.m. . . .

Soon we learn some sad news, brought by our communications messengers, it makes me very depressed; all the old 'uns of the regiment are no more. Two hours ago, I was shaking them by the hand, now they are nothing more than hunks of flesh, carcasses which will probably rot in the sun. All this in an hour, it's brutal, terrifying.

The hours pass slowly by; the Colonel, found at last, sheltering in a dug-out that the sappers have hastily built for him, sends us his orders.

We will attack again at 8 p.m. How and where, nobody knows! Nothing is ready, everyone is seeking his orders—it's one awful confusion. The officers are looking for their men, the men for their officers. Everyone has different orders, and no one knows what precisely he has to do. There are no more N.C.O.s, the companies are reduced to 40 men.

Towards evening a new order: the attack is put off until tomorrow. . . .

12 June. We are in very low spirits all night. This region, which a few days ago had not seen any fighting, suddenly found itself as a result of the German advance, in the front line. . . .

Our regiment is sheltering in a trench 80 centimeters[31] deep which can scarcely contain a battalion. Pushing and shoving the men crawl along on all fours so as not to expose themselves to the enemy's machine-guns. Then they try and find their wounded comrades who can't move on their own. How much devotion is shown during this night despite the enemy's furious gunfire. Ah, if they were to discover our position what butchery there would be. . . .

The hours pass, day will soon be dawning, no orders. It's only at 3 a.m. that these two terse lines are handed to each major: "Proceed with your battalion as far as the front line to re-launch the attack." That's all. Departure time, our positions and objectives, nothing. And daylight is with us, we haven't the time to consult one another, to transmit our orders. It's chaos again. Everyone moves forward

[31] roughly 3 feet

haphazardly as best he can. We fall into shallowly dug trenches occupied by other troops in the sector. These immediately take fright, "Take cover, you silly beggars, you'll get us spotted!" After a lot of jostling, we see that there just isn't enough room for everyone. The men go off in groups on their own to find some shelter, they are no longer under their chief's complete control. . . .

The attack is postponed; what could they expect from our division, decimated and without leaders?. . .

I am at the northern edge of the village, the road is littered with bodies. It's unbelievable. There's a blown-up tank which is lying across and blocking the road. Inside are two burnt corpses, black, unrecognizable. Further on, bunches of men, legs twisted and mangled, or with gaping holes in their bodies, their eyeballs dangling out of their sockets, half their jaws missing, with terror written all over them; we can't take them away, they are too numerous, stretchers-bearers are sorely needed and the *Boches* don't give us a minute's peace. All we can do is to cover them with lime and then with a sheet or a blanket. We pick them up in mounds; but there are still more and more of them. Soon, under the burning sun, the flies will have a feast and the whole road will be nothing more than a cemetery of putrefying dead. . . .

13 June. All night an avalanche of shells fall on Courcelles, the houses are still in flames. This morning, we attacked with three divisions on our right near Méry. We don't know the result yet. We fear an attack on our flank at any moment.

The regiment has no more N.C.O.s, our losses are enormous, and eighteen days ago we left Mount Kemmel with a loss of 800 men.

At 7 p.m. the 18th Infantry Regiment attacks on our left to the north-east of Courcelles. It brings back 50 prisoners, but the *Boches* counter-attack and capture one of our lines. . . . This is the situation when night falls, a night of gunfire, of grenades exploding and of the thundering of guns.

I am now installed in a cellar with my liaison officer and my telephonists. The house above us has collapsed; the floor and the rubble are our only protection.

Inside, some old straw, moldy and dirty. We have only been here twenty-four hours and we're already being eaten by the lice. Sleep is impossible with these continual alerts and heavy artillery fire. A single staircase descends into this dark hole; if it's blocked, we shall be choked to death. There's no time to be lost. Everyone takes a shovel or a pick and starts demolishing and digging. We shall only be happy when we have made a second way out.

14 June. We are expecting to be relieved. After an attack like ours one is usually relieved within forty-eight hours. The regiment needs to be reformed, we can't stay here. We await news of our departure, that's our main preoccupation at the moment.

15 June. Our hope of relief fades away. The division is positioned along a front 4 kilometers long from Courcelles to Méry. All the troops who were behind us have gone elsewhere. There is talk of German attacks on Amiens and Mount Kemmel.

We remain where we are, harassed, exhausted and covered in vermin; thinking we would be here only forty-eight hours, we left everything behind. I haven't a thing, my trousers are torn and I have lost my great coat.

We scarcely see any newspapers here, but those we do see are enough. The journalists claim to have seen it all, but write idiotic articles on the wonderful advance of our troops, the last words of a dying soldier . . . let them come and live a short while with us, then we'll see. . . .

16 June. It's panic stations today. Enemy troop movements have been seen in front of us, near Rollot. Their planes are active, an attack is feared; orders come pouring in: an attack is certain, make ready.

Everyone is on edge; the Colonel sends for me yet again to organize the defense of the village—not really its defense but that of a single man—him, the Colonel! He is the only one that counts. I have to leave what I'm doing, the protection of the companies, exterior defenses, and machine-gun emplacements. He is there in his cellar. If there's an attack, he must be protected. Orders to surround him with barbed wire, orders to build a redoubt in front of him with machine-guns in position; orders to have an escape trench built for him with protective fire on both sides of it.

He won't come out to see what's happening, but he repeatedly calls me in to see if everything is all right and that he will be well protected.

The men grumble; do they count? What disgust they feel in working for this man who doesn't care about them, who couldn't care less if they have only shallow holes for shelter with no protection.

It's war. Every man thinks of his own skin according to his means.

Fortunately it's calmer for the moment, the *Boches* are firing less. It has now been confirmed that our offensive caused a huge German attack to fail and stemmed their advance. We are now being smothered with praise to make us forget the madness of this attack.

18 June. The major returns from leave. I hand back the command of the battalion to him. He has missed the whole business. He tells us that the newspapers are full of the Mangin attacks, of these days which saved the situation. Alas! Who can suspect what we did, in what conditions we attacked. . . .

26 June. Accompanied by one of my men, I set out at 9 p.m. to reconnoiter the lines. But we get lost, the night is very dark, and we can't see a thing. . . .

Not a sound, not a flare, nothing but corn all around us. Do we go forward, back, to the left or to the right? We are utterly lost. We don't dare move forwards for fear of meeting the *Boches*. My only weapons are my stick and my revolver; my companion has his rifle, but no cartridges. It's almost midnight. Are we going to spend the night like this and how shall we get back to our post in daylight? If we make any noise, our sentries may fire at us.

Suddenly, 100 meters from us, we hear shouts in German, three flares, some grenades exploding, a few rifle-shots, then silence falls again. Are we going to get it, have they seen us? However, thanks to the light from the flares, we recognize our positions, we are saved. We make for the post which had come under attack; the *Boches* had ambushed them amid the corn and surprised them at work. One dead corporal and another wounded soldier were brought back. . . .

21–22–23 July. We are now invaded by visitors. The sector is calm, the second line is attractive; these gents will be able to write a fine report on their return. Like snails after a storm, the gold braid is appearing from everywhere. They come by day and even at night, two, three every day. No shells, they are so happy to make themselves noticed . . . in the lines!. . .

2 August. Four years of war!!!

An attack is being prepared. The 5th Battalion is to carry it out. Have they gone off their heads? We must be dreaming. The chiefs have decided that the attack will be effected in total silence. How is it possible to make a battalion of men advance in silence without arousing the attention of the enemy?

Our objective is a small rectangular-shaped wood, about 1,200 meters from our lines. Without artillery preparation, the battalion must surround it and . . . bring back the goods. It's so simple—the German barrage, their machine-guns, nothing matters; just listen to the Colonel explaining the movement to us: you advance up to the wood, one company to the left, one to the right, you surround it and bring back everything inside. There you are, nothing simpler. You might think we were playing with toy soldiers on a table. Yet we have been at war for four years!. . .

11 August. 10:45 a.m., sad news: Trillat, "old man Trillat," has been killed. He and I were the only captains still alive after the battle of Mount Kemmel. Will it be my turn next? Poor old Trillat: in every attack he led his men fearlessly onwards, we saw him at the Chemin des Dames not even ducking when the machine-guns opened fire, at the Kemmel, urging his company on. And now, a shell has fallen right on him as he was having a bit to eat by the roadside! One of his officers has had an arm blown off.

All his men are shocked and have tears in their eyes at such a senseless end to a life. There he is, stretched out at our feet, with a gaping hole in his neck and half of his head missing. One can scarcely recognize him; what remains of his face is covered with blood, and blackened by powder. . . .

14 August. I take command of the 10th Battalion, replacing Major Brébion who has been killed.

I have been recommended for the "Légion d'Honneur" for the attack of 10 August. I will learn later on at Divisional H.Q. that you can receive this decoration only if you have lost a limb! That's how they recognize your devotion. If you haven't got an arm or leg missing, nothing doing. . . .

23–25–26 August. Reinforcements arrive! Our losses since May are the following; Kemmel: 12 officers, 800 men. 11 June: 19 officers, 700 men. 10–25 August: 23 officers, 600–700 men. So in less than four months: 54 officers and 2,200 men. The total strength of the regiment.

28 August. Great news: the *Boches* have taken to their heels.

At 6 a.m. we set off. The terrain is utterly devastated. Gas-shells, we advance with difficulty. . . . It's midday, the heat is overwhelming. . . .

30 August. Our attacks on the right and left are maintained, but without success; the Germans are dug-in at the north canal and are holding it steadfastly. What are our attacks worth? Our exhaustion is total and we can only succeed when the enemy gives way under our artillery fire.

At 6 p.m. the enemy unleash an avalanche of fire on the wood, there is gas swirling everywhere: coughing, spitting, and vomiting with our insides seemingly on fire, our fatigue gets the better of us. Our losses are great and many are seriously wounded. Everyone is bitter at seeing his comrades fall one after the other. Will his be the fate of us all?

I have no more N.C.O.s, with my platoons reduced to half a squad, everything is becoming impossible. No-one wants to leave his emplacement any more and it's only by threats that I can make myself obeyed, and it's hard to do this when you share their state of exhaustion. . . .

31 August. The men can't take any more: there have been cases of men breaking down in tears and rolling on the ground sobbing. As a result of seeing their comrades killed and maimed, their nerves have been broken. . . .

5 September. At last at 4 p.m., we receive the order to leave. What joy! We are going to the rear. Everyone's running around, bursting to tell the good news.

It's not the moment to cop it; some shells explode, men and mules fall to the ground.

Let's get out of here. The artillery fire does not stop, what does it matter, we are going to the rear. We find the strength to walk again. Shortly afterwards we are out of the firing zone, we can breathe. What a relief to feel oneself away from it all. Jokes are cracked; we pass our men and artillery, the plain is in front of us. How good it feels, let's get as far away as possible!

Desagneaux would spend the next two months in the quieter Lorraine sector.

14 September. Is this a sector at all? In broad daylight we can walk along the roads under the very noses of the *Boches* without a shot being fired. We are lodged in huts and nobody thinks of using the dug-outs; the kitchens are installed right in the front line. Their chimneys belch smoke, but nobody bothers. Over the way, the *Boches* do the same, it's a rest sector. You would think you are on stage at the theatre! There's not a shell-hole to be seen in the trenches or along the paths. It's just the sort of sector for the President of the Republic or for parliamentary missions.

On 16 September, I get sixteen days leave. . . .

6 October. I rejoin the regiment at Drouville, in the Serres sector. . . .

7–8–9 October. My relationship with the new major who has been appointed to lead us is becoming more and more strained. We are not speaking to each other any more. I have requested to change battalions, and am awaiting an answer. . . .

15 October. I am informed by the Colonel that my request has been granted. I leave the major and his battalion. He tells me too that I have been proposed to take command of my own battalion.

With my name already on the list, I can be chosen any day now. In the meanwhile, the General wants to send me to Divisional H.Q. to reorganize the instruction centre there and to deliver lectures.

Is this the beginning of the end for me? No, for it is clear that I won't even set foot inside Divisional H. Q., as the Colonel declares he doesn't want to lose me and is going to request my transfer to the 14th Tirailleurs, the 1st Battalion of which has been formed.

21 October. Colonel Dineaux summons me to replace Major Rouchon who is leaving the regiment. My function is that of the Colonel's chief assistant officer.

22–23–24 October. Office life. Shut in all day, surrounded by papers, examining maps, compiling dossiers. Now it's my turn to send for reports and notes! My turn to prepare attacks and order reconnaissances.

An attack is planned for November; our future advance has to be worked out. Ludendorff[32] is overrun. Our hopes increase that the end is nigh, but in the meanwhile there is fighting all along the front and its moving towards us.

We are due to attack along the whole Lorraine Front with two armies and the Americans, 600,000 men, with as many again in reserve, so they say.

The artillery is massing, all calibres are arriving. There are gunners, guns, and piles of shells everywhere. Every night lorries pour in with thousands of projectiles. By day our planes keep watch.

The most extraordinary thing about it is that this is happening so peacefully. The *Boches* are letting us carry out all these preparations without firing a shot. . . .

1–2–3 November. The attack is set for the 6th, then postponed until the 8th, then the 10th.

Then suddenly we learn that Germany is sending envoys to discuss an armistice. Foch[33] has given them seventy-two hours to sign. This is the only thing in our minds at present. If the armistice is signed, it's peace; if not, it's an immediate attack, and butchery in all its horror.

10 November. There's been a real firework display going on over in the German lines all night long. They are letting off all their flares and rockets, green, red, yellow, they all mingle in the sky. A few *Boches* try to come and fraternize with our troops, but they are chased off by rifle fire.

Then we learn that Revolution is brewing in Germany, that the Emperor is abdicating. It's over, the *Boches* are withdrawing everywhere.

We are excited, we wait and hope.

11 November. Firework display continued all night over in the enemy camp. At 6 a.m., we hear on the radio that the armistice has been signed. The end of hostilities is fixed for 11 a.m.

At 11 a.m. it's all over, we are no longer at war. What joy—the champagne flows, the attack won't take place. There's a smile on everyone's lips, no more fighting, we'll be able to move without fearing a bullet, a shell, a rocket, or gas—the war is over!

The *Boches* have thirty days to sign the peace treaty. . . .

[32] German general Erich Ludendorff, who with Paul von Hindenburg proved a formidable duo, had hoped that the German spring offensive in 1918 on the western front would result in a crushing blow to the Allied forces. He was mistaken.

[33] Ferdinand Foch became commander-in-chief of the Allied armies in spring 1918.

17 November. We leave Serres at 6 a.m. We cross Arraucourt, then the German lines. We can't believe our eyes when we see the extent of the barbed-wire entanglements and fortifications in this supposedly calm sector; they represent three years' work and we would have had to take them by force! How good it is to saunter through them with your cane in your hand.

As we proceed, a few curious onlookers appear. The Germans have taken everything with them. There's not a single gun or weapon or value remaining. Only the ammunition dumps which they couldn't destroy have been left.

We camp at Mulcey. The inhabitants welcome us with open arms, but they have been robbed of everything. They welcome us with words and they certainly have some stories to tell. Here, butter costs 18 marks a pound and shoes 200 marks a pair. It's very cold. . . .

18 November. We are going to be billeted at Guermange. All the towns are decked out in the French colours, and the inhabitants are on their doorsteps.

At Guermange, the whole village is in festive mood. We are received by the local dignitaries. Each one has got out his coat, top-hat, and his Sunday-best suit. Everyone, young and old, is wearing a rosette. The children, led by the village priest, are carrying little French flags.

Unbeknown to the *Boches*, the young girls of the village had made dresses in the French colours; when they learnt of the armistice they prepared a welcome for the first French troops.

As the major, quite overcome by the occasion, makes his speech, they surround him and each one has her compliment to pay and a bouquet of flowers to offer.

It's charming for a village of 300 inhabitants. What will it be like when we are surrounded by thousands? These folk, however, are simplicity itself and tell us all they have suffered and endured. Each one has his own sad tale to tell. . . .

19–20–21 November. We stay at Guermange. It is said that they don't want us to have any contact with the *Boches*, so we are waiting until they leave.

We resume exercises, not very enthusiastically—it's merely to keep the men occupied. Our men? They are coloured troops from Africa who don't speak much French, who are lazy and light-fingered. . . .

1 December. We enter Bavaria. The *Boches* stare at us with curiousity. You can feel their pride. Here only German is spoken, and the men can't make themselves understood.

2 December. Billeted at Vogelbach. We are guarding the outposts. Not a word of French here. As we pass through the villages, some inhabitants cry, "Long live France," but others turn their heads.

6 December. Our billets are at Rottweiler. Here the people are German at heart and one can feel their animosity.

The main point of discussion is money. The mark is worth 0.70 francs, but they don't want to understand and demand its nominal value, 1.25 francs. There are long arguments. An interpreter is sent for, but they get kid-glove treatment, no one daring to impose his will upon them. No trouble, no trouble. What would they do however, if they were occupying our country? Here, it's the Frenchman who is fleeced.

When you think of the way they have acted, of the suffering they have inflicted on our compatriots, four years of insults, of fines, of ill-treatment of every sort, it makes you sick.

If we react strongly, the Germans complain, then it's a report to the Colonel, an inquest to be held in the Division, and the paperwork piles up on every desk.

And yet the people here don't know what war is; they haven't seen barbed wire or trenches, all the fields are cultivated. We are the victors, they won't even feel it and we yield before their demands.

7–8–9 December. Exercises again, leave is slow in coming through. The authorities declare: Not enough transport. To which the troops reply: When it was a question of sending us to Ba-li-bou you managed to find trains and vehicles then, but when it's our leave, you don't give a damn!

We stay at Ottenberg. Captain Gérard and I are lodged with a factory-owner, who, fawning and contemptible, put everything at our disposal: bathroom, billiard-room. He offers us cigars, venison—the *Boche* in all his beauty. One feels that these sort of people will sign anything you ask of them, but won't do a thing about it. They have a strong sense of discipline, as we pass by, people salute us. If we complain that the village is dirty, a quarter of an hour later all the people are sweeping the streets and washing.

There are kids swarming everywhere, in the houses, on the streets. . . .

1919

13 January. These days are my last, men are being sent home and my turn will come shortly. There are exercises every day, so we don't get out of the habit.

On 20 January I go and lunch with the Colonel, on the 21st with the General. It's over now. I haven't a friend left, my comrades from the 359th have disappeared, either killed or wounded or posted to other corps. I have no regrets about leaving this regiment where I don't know a soul.

23 January. I put myself at the disposal of the major in charge of transport to carry a detachment of troops home.

There are threats flying everywhere; the men going home speak only of Bolshevism, of revolution: "We'll show the bosses! Our comrades won't have died in the trenches in vain."

Hatred and threats are on many lips.

30 January. I am demobbed [demobilized] from the 163rd Infantry Regiment at Nice.

Formalities, paperwork, queues at desks of all sorts to get my final pay and gratuity booklet, to be returned to civilian life.

At last it's finished. I have fulfilled my duty. I am no longer a soldier.

11 February. 13.411 D. "Chevalier de la Légion d'Honneur"; "Croix de Guerre avec Palme," "Outstanding officer, of proven courage. Frequently distinguished himself in the battles of which he was part, notably when in command of a battalion during the attack of 11 June 1918. Particularly distinguished himself at Verdun, on the Aisne, at Mount Kemmel, at Guiscard, at Montdidier. Mentioned five times in dispatches."

CHAPTER 6

Commitment and Sacrifice

Felix Kaufmann

Erlebnisse in der Gefangenschaft April 1917 – January 1920

Es war am 30. April 1917 gegen 5 1/2 Uhr nachmittags, als die Franzosen, Leute vom I.R. 296 (ein Regiment der Bretagne, wie man mir nachher sagte) sich unser bemächtigten. Unser Unterstand war am sogenannten "Puttkammerstützpunkt" zwischen unserem 2. u. 3. Graben, südlich vom Dörfchen Nauroy, ca. 9–10 Klm. südöstlich von Reims. Von den Franzosen wird diese Gegend "an Marquise" genannt. Der Tag war in jedem Sinne ein heisser gewesen. Wie an den vorhergehenden Tagen herrschte eine Treibhaushitze, dazu fehlte es uns an Trinkwasser. Schon der Weg zu unserem Unterstand, wozu wir die ganze vorhergehende Nacht gebrauchten, war fürchterlich. Im Unterstand selbst verpestete die Leiche eines Kameraden, der 30 Stunden vorher gefallen war, die Luft, sodass wir, kaum angekommen, uns daran machten, diesen Kameraden notdürftig zu begraben. Leider war uns dies nicht möglich, da Minen schwersten Kalibers (bis 4 Zentner) jede Betätigung ausserhalb des Stollens unmöglich machten. Beim Niederfallen dieser Minen bebte die ganze Erde; wir glaubten jeden Moment, verschüttet zu werden. All dieses spannte unsere Nerven aufs äusserste an.

Die Belegstärke unseres Unterstandes bestand nach Abzug der Verluste der vorhergehenden Tage aus 4 Mann meiner Kompagnie, der 2. M.G.K. RIR 53 (Rusche aus Soest, Hitten, Göbel aus Hessen-Darmstadt, Dickert aus Duisburg u. meiner Wenigkeit), ferner 3 Mann der 3. M.G.K. befehligt wurden wir von Feldw. Schwarz der 3. Komp. Ausserdem waren noch 3 Signalgasten vom RIR 16 bei uns. Pickert u. einem der 3. Komp. gelang es, noch vorher zu entweichen. Wir anderen waren umzingelt. Sofort wurden uns unsere Taschenmesser abverlangt. Dann ging es unter Führung eines Soldaten im Laufschritt nach hinten über unseren 2. Graben hinweg zu unserem ehemaligen 1. Graben, einige 50 mtr. vom 2. ab. Der 2. Graben zeigte das Charakteristische einer vollständig eingetrommelten Stellung, d.h. er war fast nicht mehr zu erkennen. Unser 1. Graben war stark von französ. Reserven besetzt, die sich notdürftig in einigen Löchern eingebuddelt hatten. Wir waren unser ca. 12 Mann. Man empfing uns mit den Worten: "Vous êtes contents? La guerre est maintenant finie pour vous!" Da sich nach den furchtbaren vorhergegangenen Aufregungen ein wahnsinniges Durstgefühl bei uns eingestellt hatte, so baten wir um etwas Wasser. Man gab uns bereitwilligst einen Schluck "pinard" (Armeewein) u. auch etwas Brot. Dann ging es nach Meldung beim "Grabenoffizier" unter unserem Artilleriefeuer zum

A page from Felix Kaufmann's manuscript diary. *Courtesy of the Leo Baeck Institute.*

CHAPTER 6

"Hunger was stronger than all punishments"

Felix Kaufmann, German POW in France

In April 1917, Felix Kaufmann's Heavy Machine Gun Company No. 2 was deployed near the village of Nauroy, a few miles to the southeast of the French city of Reims. After heavy fighting in the war's initial months, the sector had been comparatively quiet, one reason perhaps that his reserve unit had been assigned there. But the relative calm was about to be shattered. The French commander-in-chief, Robert Nivelle, was determined to secure a decisive breakthrough with a massive assault on German positions on the Chemin des Dames, a ridge named for the road running along its crest that had been used by daughters of Louis XV. Though the ridge itself, and thus the focus of Nivelle's offensive, lay to the northwest of Reims, the French Fourth Army was to mount an attack on Nauroy and the surrounding region in support of the main effort. Amid persistent drizzle and intermittent snow showers, French troops moved forward on April 16, 1917. After hard fighting, the results around Nauroy, as elsewhere, fell far short of what Nivelle had anticipated. The Fourth Army did, however, manage to capture some 6,000 German prisoners. On April 29, 1917, one of those was twenty-six-year-old Felix Kaufmann, a Jew from Elberfeld, who had served since his induction in August 1914.[1]

Captivity in the First World War, it has been argued, represented a new phenomenon.[2] *Mass incarceration, of military prisoners of war and civilian internees, coupled with the introduction of widespread forced labor, so characteristic of the twentieth century,*

[1] Today Elberfeld is part of the city of Wuppertal in North Rhine-Westphalia, near the heavily industrialized region of the Ruhr Valley.

[2] Heather Jones, "A Missing Paradigm? Military Captivity and the Prisoner of War, 1914–18," in *Captivity, Forced Labour and Forced Migration in Europe during the First World War*, ed. Matthew Stibbe (London: Routledge, 2009), 40.

originated, for all intents and purposes, during the Great War.[3] *Perhaps 8.5 million men were taken prisoner, nearly as many as were killed in the conflict. In response to the challenge of holding so many men captive, military authorities adapted defensive techniques from the battlefield (barbed wire, sentries and so forth) to establish a rationalized, militarized camp system.*[4] *It was this system that Felix Kaufmann entered in April 1917.*

His diary entries suggest that the camp system was not yet fully rationalized or standardized. Kaufmann moved frequently from one camp to another throughout France over the course of two years: from Châlons-sur-Marne (just to the southeast of Reims) to Fort d'Arnières/Fort Brulé, to Roche Maurice and then St. Anne (November 1917) to camp Brest/Kéroriou (February 1918) and then to Bordeaux. Conditions in these different prison camps varied as well. On the whole, however, Kaufmann's treatment was poor. French animosity toward their German captives was a persistent theme, mitigated here and there by occasional kindnesses.[5]

Moreover, Kaufmann, like his fellow prisoners, was a pawn within a system of carefully calibrated reprisals whereby both France and Germany adopted a kind of tit-for-tat attitude. Appeals to international law or inspections by neutral observers achieved little in the way of curbing abuses in the treatment of prisoners, so each country found it more effective to subject some of the captives it held to treatment corresponding to that being meted out (or presumed to be applied) to prisoners held by the enemy. This informal system of demonstrable reciprocity could prompt a mutual commitment to redress the particular grievance (prisoners held too close to the front lines or under particularly inhospitable conditions, such as North Africa).[6] *French policies also had historical roots in France's humiliating defeat by Germany in the Franco-Prussian War of 1871 that culminated in the founding of the German empire and the annexation of Alsace-Lorraine from France. Punishments against German prisoners of war entailing beatings, solitary confinement, and food deprivation were especially common in Kaufmann's early incarceration. Not unexpectedly, he and fellow prisoners were greeted with similar contempt from civilians who assaulted them verbally as they marched from camp to camp or to labor details. Kaufmann did note, however, that not everyone received them in such a manner, particularly toward the war's end and in regions distant from the front.*

Survival as a prisoner of war involved adaptability and ingenuity. Hunger was pervasive, and the scarcity and limited variety of rations led to theft, despite the stiff punishments prescribed for those caught. Labor details ("commandos") at ports unloading ships full of food, providing agricultural labor on farms, or harvesting vineyards all afforded opportunistic prisoners the chance to supplement their diets. Parcels from home were another source of additional calories and a tangible expression that the prisoners had not been forgotten.

[3] To be strictly accurate, precedents can be dated to 1896 and 1900: the "concentration camps" instituted in Cuba by Spanish general Valeriano Weyler to quell guerilla activity and in South Africa by British general Herbert Kitchener to contain Boer civilians. Both initiatives paled, however, in comparison to the continent-wide efforts of 1914–18.

[4] Jones, "Missing Paradigm," 24–25

[5] A September 15, 1916, order in the French Second Army, for example, stipulated that "any act of kindness, any show of consideration for a *Boche* prisoner is an act of culpable weakness and will be severely punished by commanders." Jones, "Missing Paradigm," 33.

[6] Jones, "Missing Paradigm," 26–27

Apart from malnutrition, monotony and boredom were constant threats that Kaufmann sought to counteract by focusing on the prisoners, civilians, and soldiers of different nationalities and races he encountered. One may also speculate about the psychological impact of captivity upon his sense of masculinity. Captured, unable to contribute to the desperate spring offensives of 1918, deprived of female companionship, Kaufmann was now isolated from the conventional attributes of a masculine, military life. It is perhaps suggestive, then, that he savored the occasions when he was able to converse in German with young women.

An armistice was enacted in November 1918, but Kaufmann, like Willy Wolff, remained in French hands for more than another year until January 1920. In effect, he remained a hostage to guarantee German compliance with the terms of the armistice and willingness to accept a permanent peace settlement. More challenges, however, awaited him after his return to Germany. Like Wolff, Kaufmann would be forced to flee his homeland in the 1930s to escape Nazi persecution. He sought refuge in the United States, where he remained until his death in 1988 in California at the age of ninety-eight.

Felix Kaufmann's diary remains as he originally composed it while a prisoner. The exception is the introductory section in which he summarized the events of his capture and initial days in captivity (there are no dated entries over the first few pages). Toward the end of his life, when Kaufmann elected to donate his manuscript diary in German to the Leo Baeck Institute in New York City, he translated the work into English. It is that version that is reproduced here, with Kaufmann's sometimes idiosyncratic and Germanic-sounding grammar intact.

April/May 1917

The wooden barracks of our Rest camp, about a two hours march to the rear from the frontline, were located in a small strip of woods to hide them against French fliers. It did not always work. A few days ago during our rest, a shell landed smack in the middle of a barrack, killing all officers, who, as usual, occupied a separate unit.

For the last two days we heard in our camp the booming of French guns of all calibers, opening a barrage on our sector of the front, without let up, day and night, night and day, forerunner of a coming attack (our guns, although by far not so numerous, answered in kind).

It was April 29, 1917, when suddenly the order came to send four men to the front to replace machine gunners who were killed or wounded the day before. We four—Rüsche from Soest-Witten, Goebel from Hessen-Darmstadt, Pickert from Duisburg and I—were selected.

The days, precursor of summer, were already very hot with cool nights, and soon on the march, with our pack on the back, we were sweating profusely and terribly thirsty without any possibility to quench our thirst. With every step we became more gloomy, but as obedient soldiers we had to follow our orders. We had the presentiment to get either killed, maimed or (only a little bit better) captured. Significant was the answer to our question, before starting our march, where we would get our daily food ration, consisting of hot coffee, black bread, sometimes with marmalade or a piece of bacon, and a hot vegetable soup with potatoes and some occasional canned beef crumbs of meat in it . . . in any field kitchen we can reach. As food was already scarce in the army, we knew what the "any" meant, [that] no field kitchen in our reach. As consolation we were promised to get replaced in four days.

The closer we came to the front, the more we smelled the stench and gunpowder in the air. The whole earth was trembling.

We started our march at four in the afternoon. Soon we found the elaborate dugged [*sic*] and crisscrossed trenches almost leveled. When the night came we couldn't find our way any more. In order to dodge the all around exploding shells we took shelter in the few remaining deep bunkers, and we advanced from one to another. At two in the night we came to a bunker, where an officer showed me on the map our location, and finally at five in the morning, when dawn started already, we arrived at our destination.

It was a so-called "strongpoint" between our second and third trench,[7] near the small village Nauroy, now reduced to rubble, and about eight or nine kilometers southeast of Reims. The French called this region "Au Marquise."[8] There wasn't much left of the trenches to give us cover, but a deep bunker was still in tact. In the bunker we found three men from the third machine gun company with Sergeant Schwarz, a professional soldier with ten years service already, as commander. Besides there were three men from the Signal Corps and one dead soldier. This comrade lost his life thirty hours before in a freak accident. To divert his thoughts he carried a newspaper or book for reading whenever the opportunity existed, the same habit as I had. No daylight penetrated the deep bunker, so he went up the steps behind the wooden door, where there was some faint light from the outside. He was sitting and reading a short while, when a heavy shell exploded close by, one fragment piercing the door, hitting him in the heart and killing him instantly. With shells falling in an uninterrupted succession the soldiers didn't dare to leave the shelter to bury the dead.

Around noon we became very hungry—we hadn't eaten anything in twenty-four hours—but the smell of the dead soldier—due partly to the hot weather—became unbearable. Suppressing our fears, we four men decided to take the body out of the bunker. There was no time for burial. We laid the corpse in a shallow foxhole a few steps away. Then we hurried back and ate our bread.

We were watching and waiting with our nerves at the breaking point. Every time the heavy shells exploded nearby the air pressure in our bunker was so strong that we were afraid our eardrums would crack. Should a shell explode on top of our bunker, we knew we would be buried alive, as it happened to other soldiers before.

When a man is often exposed in a war to dangerous situations he develops a kind of sixth sense or a clairvoyance; at least it was the case with me. Two months ago I was in a bunker, back in the third defense line. We were four soldiers and we alternated every noontime to go to the field kitchen to get our ration. I was on my way back from the kitchen on a clear and crispy winter day with four canteens with hot coffee around my waist, a sack with bread and mail over my shoulder and the four cooking pots with the hot soup in my hand. All of a sudden four guns

[7] an example of the German "defense-in-depth," multiple parallel lines of trenches that made a breakthrough so difficult

[8] "Of the marquis," or a nobleman below the rank of duke. He probably refers to the fact that Reims was the traditional site for the coronation of French kings.

way behind the French lines opened up. Immediately I sensed the shells are coming in my direction and instantly I threw myself flat to the ground. I was hit only with some chunks of frozen earth but not by shell fragments. Still trembling when I came back to my comrades, nobody minded that I had spilled half of the soup.

All of a sudden eerie silence. At exactly 5:30 pm all guns stopped firing. We run out of the bunker to man our machine guns, but in a few minutes French soldiers in overwhelming numbers with fixed bayonets were swarming all over the place in front and in back of us. They had already overrun our first and second line. These were soldiers of the Infantry Regiment 296 (as I heard later, a regiment from Brittany).

The first thing they demanded were our pocket knives. Then under leading of a soldier we had to run at double pace to the rear across our second and first lines. The lines, completely leveled, were occupied by strong French Reserves who were busily entrenching themselves in scanty holes. We twelve prisoners were received with the words: . . . *La guerre est maintenant finie pour vous*!"[9]

Terribly thirsty from the heat of the day and excitement we asked them for some drinking water. To our luck these soldiers were decent human beings. They gave us a gulp of "pinard"[10] from their canteens and a piece of bread. After our French soldier had reported to the officer in charge of the men in the conquered trenches we were sent in a hurry under the shelling of our own artillery to the first French line. Here [we] were told to bring two badly wounded soldiers, our Frenchman and one German buddy to the rear. In order to escape our intense artillery fire as fast as possible, most of the prisoners flocked around the German soldier, who had to be supported in contrast to the Frenchman who was laid on a stretcher, which took a longer time.

Since my capture, I was in a state of apathy and complete indifference. Nothing frightened me any more.

In this state I carried with two comrades the wounded man on the stretcher under guidance of a member of a French regimental band, who worked as a medic as it was the custom also in the German army during the war. It turned out to be my luck as I found out later I saved my watch (while all other prisoners were robbed of them) and I had a shelter for the night.

Alternating, two of us carried the man, who was constantly groaning under severe pain, through a maze of trenches to an ambulance station on the street floor of a completely destroyed house, located on the old Roman highway from Reims through the Champagne. Here we could finally quench our thirst with water. On the courtyard were long rows of dead soldiers covered with their mantle. After the shattered leg of our wounded man was put in a splint, we carried on, this time accompanied by an older French corporal, through elaborate trenches, whose walls had extremely skillful plaiting and which were wide enough to enable the French to install lorries![11]

In a cluster of trees on our left, a short distance away, were French cannons massed and uninterruptedly firing. After ten minutes we reached a highway with heavy traffic, which was under constant fire from our heavy guns. When we saw

[9] "The war is now finished for you!"
[10] cheap wine
[11] British term for trucks

that our corporal didn't think it necessary to help us carry our load, we decided, dead tired as we were, to put the stretcher down in the middle of the road, regardless of the falling shells. Only then he made haste and relieved one of us. Dusk came and in a short while we arrived at a blockhouse, where ambulances were waiting. Our stretcher and two other French stretcher cases were placed into the ambulance and the corporal and we three prisoners climbed in also.

It was my habit to write my daily field experiences in a little notebook. Every week I tore out the written notes and sent them in a sealed envelope home to my dear mother and sister. (I had their promise never to open the envelopes till I came home or something else would happen to me.)

When I was captured I had the last written notes with me and was troubled, how to get rid of them before the French detected it. To my great relief I could tear them into small pieces and throw them out during the ambulance ride.

In the first village we stopped, medic soldiers in white hospital coats, darkened lanterns in their hands, came to inquire about the kind of wounds of the soldiers. They gave each of us prisoners a cup of milled red wine, for us something unheard of. Finally we reached a military hospital in a village, named Beaumont, where the journey ended for our wounded men. When we prisoners came out of the ambulance, the head physician and staff couldn't conceal their astonishment. In a big hall, where we had to wait, he and his whole staff asked me a hundred questions, when they found out that I spoke a little French. An American ambulance driver joined the crowd and regretted that I didn't understand English. We were still plagued with a terrible thirst, so they gave us cold tea.

At 9:30, two field gendarmes appeared to take us way. Running in the darkness under the steady shelling of our artillery close by the houses and around the village church with one gendarme in front and one in the back of us, we halted near a hole in the wall of a house, which led to a deep cellar. Voices received us with: "Voilà des Fritz!"[12] About twenty soldiers with some village beauties were sitting around under the weird shine of flaring candles. In a corner one soldier was singing comic songs amid the laughter of the other. In front of us soldiers on a guard bed were embracing girls, who gave us furtive glances. From time to time came the sound of bursting shells from outside. We prisoners were standing against the cold stonewall in a corner and brooding. Here we got a lesson, how different men behave. One soldier used insulting words, the other invited us to sit on the damp floor, what we refused. Finally two soldiers had pity and gave us their blankets to sit on. In this way we spent the night till one o'clock, when the bombardment ended and we all could leave the protecting cellar. With the soldiers we went to a spacious top floor of a neighboring house. Soon they were fast asleep, on straw on the floor, but not before they had maps to the smallest detail of our position on tables and walls. Another interpreter made notes: name, civilian occupation, residence, family affairs etc.

In a clever way he tried to find out about our combat regiments and especially the position of our artillery. When I insisted I didn't know anything, he threatened

[12] "Here's Fritz"—slang for German soldiers

me twice to bring me before a court martial, which gave me a belly laugh. After five minutes he gave up when he saw he couldn't get anywhere with his questioning. Outside I had to stand isolated against a tree, the same way as my fellow prisoners who were interrogated after me. A soldier of Polish descent stayed more than ¼ hour. I was afraid he would talk, but when he came out he assured me, he didn't betray our country.

A short while later we were sent to an empty enclosure with a bunch of new prisoners. Here we lay down on the ground all day without any protection or shade against the hot sun. At noon they brought a pail of water for our thirst, but this didn't suppress our intense feeling of hunger. Finally in the late afternoon we got a loaf of bread for four men and a box of canned meat. In the meantime we exchanged our experiences and events during our capture the previous day. The soldiers were for the most part from the regiments #142, 144 and 87, forming the division which occupied the sector to our left. As usual they were robbed of their watches. Great numbers of the attacking French soldiers were drunk. A non-commissioned officer of the 142nd regiment fought with his group to the last minute. After they surrendered they were disarmed. Then the French soldiers ordered them to kneel down and all nine men were shot to death. A very young soldier of about eighteen or nineteen years limped pitifully around with a bent back. He told us he and his buddies came out of the bunker without any weapon when the French soldiers tried to kill them with the butt of their rifles. He received several blows and only the interference of a few older Frenchmen saved his life. One other prisoner held his hands on his head for protection and got all his fingers broken. Others told us that when they ran from the second to the third French trench after capture they were shot at, and one of them got hit in one eye and lost it. Six weeks later I met a comrade in Dijon, who was just discharged from the hospital there. He was captured in the same battle and the same April 30 as I. When he, with five comrades hands up, came out the bunker the five of them were killed instantly.[13] He, the last one, got bullets from a revolver through his right arm and left hand. He showed me his wounds, which were beginning to heal.

[13] Once rarely discussed, the killing of soldiers who surrendered on the battlefield (the 'forgotten atrocities' in Niall Ferguson's evocative phrase) was less infrequent or isolated than many veterans cared to admit. Important recent works include Ferguson, *The Pity of War: Explaining World War I* (New York: Basic Books, 1999), 367–94; Tim Cook, "The Politics of Surrender: Canadian Soldiers and the Killing of Prisoners in the Great War," *Journal of Military History* 70 (2006): 637–65; Holger Afflerbach and Hew Strachan, eds., *How Fighting Ends: A History of Surrender* (Oxford: Oxford University Press, 2012), 265–311; Heather Jones, *Violence Against Prisoners of War during the First World War* (Cambridge: Cambridge University Press, 2011), 82–83. In the one instance cited by Kaufmann, French soldiers may have been angered by the fact that the German unit "fought to the last minute," only to then surrender, a situation in which the prisoners might be felt (by captors on either side) to have forfeited their right to surrender. It is important to recognize that there was no uniformity or consistency of behavior with regard to prisoner killing among the Allied or German armies. For an example of a French source indicating instances where soldiers simply disregarded orders to take no prisoners, see Louis Barthas, *Poilu: The World War I Notebooks of Corporal Louis Barthas, Barrelmaker, 1914–1918* (New Haven: Yale University Press, 2014), 108, 202.

In the evening I myself was witnessing a repulsive scene. The previously mentioned Alsatian ordered a captured non-commissioned officer to do a certain labor, contemptuously using the familiar form of address. The officer answered him that not even a simple soldier in Germany would be addressed this way. The Alsatian interpreter foaming with rage kicked the unfortunate soldier brutally with no let up. As if this was not enough punishment, at eight o'clock his overcoat was taken from him, his hands bound on his back and he had to stand upright and isolated against a tree the whole cold night.

We ourselves started to pass the night in the open as well as we could. When darkness came at nine we forty-eight prisoners, almost all without coat, lay down in a heap one after or upon another, like sardines in a can, in the middle of the enclosure, in order to protect ourselves, although poorly, against the cold. We were hardly fifteen minutes in this position when a motorized mortar battery drove up on the highway a few hundred yards away and started shooting with an infernal noise. Impossible to sleep anymore. On top of it a German battle-plane passed on his way to the French interior, pursued from French cannons all around our encampment. Luckily nobody was hit from the falling fragments, although we were in grave danger. One hour had passed when the German plane came back, but the mortars kept silent, so we finally could lie down and try to sleep. A half hour later the cold forced us to give up our try. In silent groups of two, three or four we walked around along the barbed wire till dawn came, welcomed with relief by all.

At six o'clock we began a fifteen-kilometer march on the old Roman highway in the direction of Châlons-sur-Marne past large encampments of soldiers on both sides of the road. Guarded by nine "Spahis"[14] on horseback, soldiers of a colonial regiment, we passed first through the village of Les Grandes Loges. Here we received a typical reception. We would later encounter [it] many times: women, children on their doorsteps and soldiers shouting: *Les Boches* [the Germans] ... *les vaches* [the cows] etc.[15] Behind the second village, ... we were separated in an enclosure near a tent camp. Around noon fifteen of us, one sergeant, six non-commissioned officers and eight privates with special technical skills in the army or machine gunners were ordered to fall in line. We received a half loaf of bread and some canned meat and were on our way to Châlons,[16] a distance of about eight kilometers. The hot sun shone mercilessly from a cloudless firmament, not the slightest wind was blowing. The swiftly passing cars whirled the highway dust in big clouds into the air. Soon we were covered with a fine white dust from head to toe, looking like a miller in his flourmill. When we arrived in Châlons pandemonium broke loose. Half grown boys pulled their knives, old men spit at us, women of all ages made typical French gestures, their flat hands pressed to their breasts or down on their genitals,

[14] Light cavalry regiments of the French army who were recruited largely from Algeria, Tunisia, and Morocco. The term derives from the Turkish word for soldier, *sipahi*.

[15] French civilians often "greeted" German prisoners with hostile words and occasionally threw items at them. Jones, *Violence against Prisoners of War*, 45–47.

[16] Châlons-en-Champagne, located in northeast France in the Marne prefecture, was one of the primary French garrison towns.

gesticulating as if to cut our throats and always shouting: *Sales Boches* [dirty Germans], *bande ... de vaches* [band of cows], *Kaisère kaput* [the Kaiser is useless or finished], *Kronprinz kaput* [Crown Prince is useless]. When the crowd came menacingly close our soldiers rode against them and pushed them back with their horses. I fully understood the feeling of the French population. The hatred of the German was the more intense the closer to the front they lived. The howling youth accompanied us to an old stone building with the inscription: "*Maison d'arrêt*" (prison).

Inside on a wide shady floor we were received by two sturdy jailers, who put eight of us in a cell on the main floor, where some straw was littered on the floor. After a while a jailer came and brought us to a common bath inside the prison to our great satisfaction. At the same time our belongings were deloused. Unfortunately this was done in the French way, i.e., two days later we had an equal amount of lice. We were delighted over the amount of soft soap at our disposal. We hadn't seen soap for well over a year. Back in our cell we received ½ gamelle (one liter) of soup, consisting of warm water with some grains of rice. Meager as it was, we appreciated it nevertheless more, since we hadn't had a warm meal for the last three days. In a separate room a brigadier of the field gendarmes, who were from then on our guards, wrote down our personal history once more. We were told we would stay here only a few days and then shipped to the interior. Glad over this prospect we slept well this first night in the prison. We didn't know how much suffering and privation we had to endure the coming weeks. Later we learned the reason for keeping us in prison was meant as a reprisal, because we belonged to the army of the hated "Kronprinz" and second the Germans supposedly did the same with some unfortunate French prisoners. We had of course no knowledge whether this last one was true or not. The next day, it was May 3. We were allowed to walk together on one of the small prison courts. The brigadier changed our German money into francs and the gendarmes interceded on our behalf and bought some food with this money. For the twelve Marks I had in my possession I got I exchanged 9.60 francs. With half of this amount I bought a loaf of white bread (at 15 centimes), a can of oil sardines and a chocolate bar.

On the afternoon of this third of May we prisoners were separated. Because Rüsche and I belonged to the same machine gun company we luckily were put in one cell. All the others became lonely occupants of their cells. Rüsche, in civil life a schoolteacher, was a very dull fellow, who didn't make my stay in the prison more bearable. For the next days the only contact we had with our co-prisoners was in the morning, when we furtively could exchange a few words while disposing of our excrements. After eight days this stopped completely. Thanks to my knowledge of French—even if a poor one—I was employed for ten minutes each day during the first ten days in the French office to make a list of the arriving prisoners, officers, non-commissioned officers and privates. During these same days we were allowed to walk daily for two hours and get some fresh air in one of the small with high walls enclosed prison yards. After ten days these daily walks were changed to two hours every fourth day.

Our cell was a bare square room. The entrance door, made of heavy iron, had a small peephole, which could be opened only from the outside. On the one side of the room was a water faucet. On the wall across from the entrance was a square board, which could be lowered to use as a table, also chained to the wall was a heavy oaken chair. Chained and upright against the wall was an iron bed without mattress or anything else; therefore, useless to us. Completing the "furniture" was a small cast iron vessel near the floor in a wall niche, which served as our toilet. We had to dispose of its content either daily or every second day. High up in the wall near the ceiling and towards the court was a small grated window, which didn't let in much light. All over the white washed walls were written the names of German prisoners since 1916. Sometimes they gave testimony in moving words about the plight and mental distress of the occupants. Some of the prisoners had been kept for five weeks. We of course added our names too. In order to keep track of the days, we marked down everyday with our pencil.

The next weeks were truly the saddest and most wretched of my whole captivity. Darkness came early to our cell. Around eight we lie down in a corner on our bed of musty straw. We had not mantle or blanket for covering, only the uniform we wore. Weak from the starvation diet and lack of exercise we slumbered for hours in the daytime. As a result, we were not able to sleep much during the night. A little mouse, which came regularly after darkness and ran around in the straw to our feet and which we tried without success to catch, didn't further our sleep either. Toward six in the morning we were awakened by the loud bark of dogs, which were let in after being in the courtyards during the night. At seven a gendarme brought us a cup of lukewarm coffee we had to drink immediately, because the cup—the only one in existence—went from mouth to mouth and cell to cell. At ten we got a small piece of bread and ½ liter of so-called rice soup, the same old lukewarm water with some grains of rice. The evening meal—at four o'clock—was exactly alike. No wonder that after ten days I was so weakened and had dizzy spells when I got up in the morning that I had to prop up myself against the wall. Although the sun shone warm at noon, the days when we could walk in the prison yard we all felt cold. Later I heard many prisoners sold everything they owned for bread. One comrade held out against his hunger till the day—not knowing it—before we left the prison and sold his watch to his greatest regret later for a few loaves of bread. Monotonously, one day went by after another. We suffered torments of hell not knowing when our imprisonment would come to an end.

During this time an incident made a deep impression on me. We heard for several days in the normally profound stillness of the prison a German lieutenant in a cell above us giving orders in a loud voice, marching in his cell up and down and knocking with his fists against the iron door. Whether he went crazy or faked, only I did not know. A very bad experience had comrade Münch from Münster from Res. Infantry Regiment 16, whom I met 1½ years later in Biscarosse. As he related to me, he and the captured sergeant-major of his company were a few times sent together to the courtyard for fresh air. They were joined by a non-commissioned officer in German uniform. Both didn't trust him and talked about trivial things in his presence. By accident Münch's cell door was once open and to his great surprise he saw this same officer in a French colonial uniform passing his way to the city. In no time Münch was taken out of his cell and put in one on the second floor. The solitude induced him one day to climb up to the not too high window of his cell.

From here he had a view of highway with passing cars and groups of soldiers coming from or going to the front. At the same time he could look into the apartment of one of the gendarmes. He was very careful not to be seen, but one day the wife of the gendarme detected him. A few minutes later two gendarmes appeared, one carrying a cudgel and pointing to the window they grabbed him and thrashed him mercilessly. For two days he didn't get anything to eat or to drink. Then they sent him to the country in the north of France. A beating got also co-prisoner Seligmann from Mühlheim, a mere eighteen-year-old boy. On his way back from the walking in the prison yard he tried to move the slide on a peephole of his door a little bit so he could see what was going on in the hall. A gendarme saw this and after beating he was put into a cell in the basement with double doors in the thick wall. As an additional punishment he had to stand up for twenty-four hours without food between these two doors. Then he was brought back to his cell.

On Sunday, May 20, in the early morning, my cellmate and I heard heartbreaking crying and weeping, which was followed by an unending moaning, accompanied by steady and heavy blows. We were terrified and resolved never to submit to such treatment. Listening with tension for further sounds, we were unable to penetrate the secret.

At 10 'clock two gendarmes came and sent us to the courtyard. I can't describe our astonishment and great joy when after the two hours walk, instead of going to our cell, we were reunited with our six year old comrades. They were assembled in a large cell on the top floor and had also been in solitude all the time. Still thinking of the meaning of all this, we were led to a large courtyard where we found the rest of the seven men of our original fifteen. Here we were finally told our prison days are over.

We received a two days ration of ½ loaf of bread and ½ can of oils and sardines and started our march on this radiant Sunday afternoon to the railroad station, emaciated to the bones as we were, covered with vermin all over our body, with beards and uncombed hair (we couldn't wash nor shave during these three weeks). As guards, we had three older soldiers in their forties. In order that the few Sunday strollers got a glimpse of us, we had to march on roundabout ways through the city. After several hours of waiting we finally boarded a cattle car with the inscription "*18 cheveaux ou Quarante hommes*" (18 horses or forty men) which was attached to a long freight train. Our guardians kept the car door wide open till darkness, so we were able to see the country through which the train passed. We went through St. Hilaire le Grand, St. Dizlier, Charunout (beautiful country), Langres etc. When our train stopped for a longer time in the early morning, we had to wake up our guardians from a deep sleep. They had put their rifles of an old vintage in one corner of the car. At 8 o'clock we arrived at the station "pont neuf" in Dijon, where we had to wait till noon in our car. Then finally we could start our two hours march past endless vineyards in a beautiful hilly country to our destination: camp de triage, Fort d'Arnières [*sic*], côte d'or.[17] Through a large old stone gate, cleverly concealed

[17] Fort Asnières, near Dijon

in the terrain, with the inscription: "Fort Brulé."[18] We entered a narrow courtyard, overflowing with prisoners.

We were told up to nine hundred were always in this camp. We were met with some excitement, because the night before two German sergeant-majors and one non-commissioned officer had escaped. In the following weeks several escaped prisoners were brought back, whose flight only ended at best in the French front-line. After our arrival co-prisoner barbers cut our beards and hair radically. After the evening roll-call, we received French suits (cotton) and wooden shoes, which were our equipment—besides our own uniform—for the whole time as prisoners. The old stone barracks of the fortress with about twenty-eight men in one room and always four iron beds together, two side by side and two on top, similar to our military barracks in Germany, became our "residence." The palliasses[19] of the beds were torn and of an unbelievable filth, full of lice and fleas. Our food consisted in the main of soup of grinded maize, sometimes with an additional "tripure" (tripe) which was often in a questionable condition. Naturally, we were always hungry. The food was barely the minimum to exist. Potable water was brought in daily in a big barrel from a distant spring and put into an enormous subterraneous reservoir of the fort. For the first time we had the opportunity to wash ourselves, something we had missed for such a long time. A small German library from the Red Cross gave us some precious hours to forget our misery. Our only duty was to assemble mornings and evenings in the courtyard for a roll call. The rest of the days we were idle. As on most of these days the weather was nice and a warm sun shining, we were sent down to the old moat of the fort. No sooner did we arrive and were sitting on the round when everybody took off his clothes and underwear and started hunting for our perpetual tormentors: lice and fleas.

During this time an agreement was signed between the two governments pertaining to the work of the "intellectual" prisoners.

The French text was [translated] as follows:

> An agreement was recently signed between the German and French governments which regulates the work of war prisoners who belong to the liberal professions. In the main they shouldn't be employed anymore as miners, diggers or long shoremen. The German government declares, however, that she never intended to free the intellectuals of all work in the mining industry, especially work in the open air, which she considers less wearisome.

In accordance with this agreement, my stay in the transit camp came after three weeks to an end. At 3 o'clock in the morning of June 10, 1917, we were aroused from sleep and after receiving a one and a half days ration of ¾ loaf of bread, a cooking vessel with rice and for every two men a can of oil sardines, we started at 4:45 our two hour march to Dijon. We were about two hundred prisoners. It was one of those radiant mornings presaging a very warm day. A deep breadth of relaxation went through our ranks, since we didn't get once out of our fort in the three weeks.

[18] Fort constructed to endure the shock front of the Prussian army during Franco-Prussian War of 1870–1871.

[19] thin mattresses stuffed with straw

Shortly before Dijon, close to the highway, we noticed a monument, erected in 1871. According to the inscription, it was a monument to the soldiers of the Garibaldi army, who conquered the first Prussian flag under heaps of dead soldiers of the Infantry Reg. 61. It made a big impression on me and reminded me of my beloved father, who fought with the Prussian army in France in this year 1871.

Arrived at the station, we didn't trust our eyes when told to board a waiting passenger train. Normally, only cattle cars were reserved for prisoners.[20] Leaving at 7:45, the tram carried us through the middle of France from the East to the extreme West. We passed the towns of Gevrey, Chambertin[21] with vineyard after vineyard, Le Creusot with the famous Schneider-Creusot works (the French Krupp)[22] till we arrived at Nevers, a city of 43,000 population, at 5:30 in the afternoon. At Le Creusot we saw thousands of Chinese at work at Schneider-Creusot. Here at Nevers our train was shunted to a side track till 5:30 the next morning. Soon swarms of civilians were all around us and the same spectacle was repeated: several of our men were so hungry they traded their watches for bread. Needless to say, the civilians got the best deal. After a two hours delay at Bourges, where we arrived at ten and received a two days ration of one loaf of bread for three men and two cans of meat, our next stop was Vierzon. Here we had a strange sight: Moroccans with venereal diseases, whose railroad car had been attached to our train on one of the stations we passed, were driven with whiplashes to the hospital in this city.

Rambling along the Loire, our train passed a hamlet named Bourré with the picturesque sight of its houses, hewed in the rock above the Loire, then further Tours, Saumur till we stopped about midnight at Angers, a big city, and stayed here till 6 o'clock the next morning, June 12. After passing the towns of La Passionère and Nantes, our train came to a last stop at Chanteney, a suburb of Nantes. It was 10:00 a.m. when we disembarked and marched to our final destination: base camp Roche-Maurice. Nantes, the big seaport with the hustling and bustling of a busy port, with its many sailing ships and cargo vessels, impressed us very much. We had a good view, because the railroad trains run in the old fashion at street level across the whole port region.

In Roche-Maurice we found the typical life of a well-organized and fairly clean prisoner of war camp. The old prisoners, for the most part captured in 1914 and 1915, several of whom had gone through hell in prison camps in Africa, welcomed us with great warmth and affection. In our honor a concert by the camp string band took place in the prison yard in the evening, while we had the opportunity to take a bath in the daytime. A large library, donated by the Red Cross, was at the disposal of the prisoners.

After only two days stay, the 200 of us assembled at 8:45 ... [on] June 14 and marched to the Loire, where barges were in readiness to transport us to our place of work. Towed by a tugboat we sailed slowly down the river till we stopped after two

[20] Both France and Germany used cattle trucks to transport prisoners (as well as wounded ones) because of shortages of hospital trains. Hence Kaufmann's surprise when he was transported in a normal train. Jones, *Violence against Prisoners of War*, 43.

[21] famous French wine villages

[22] Renowned French iron and steel works that became a major arms manufacturer

hours at an island named Isle de la basse Loire près Cordemais. Cordemais was the name of a village with a population of 2000 on the riverbank opposite our island. The Loire, spreading out here quite wide, had formed this island of a length of 13½ kilometers and up to 3½ kilometers in width, traversed by numerous ditches. While the island was completely inundated in winter, it served in summer as a pasture for the horses and herds of cattle of the many villages situated on both sides of the riverbank. After landing we were divided into four groups and placed in different parts of the island. Although the locations were not far apart, the Frenchmen saw to it, that no group met the other during our entire stay. . . .

June 15 started our real work. Using forks we had to pile up to haystacks the grass, which was cut with machines by old soldiers of the territorial (home) army. June 17 was our first Sunday and rest day. After the dense fog of the morning had lifted and the day had become very hot, we asked for and got permission in the afternoon, when high tide in the Loire appeared, to take a refreshing swim.

Many prisoners couldn't suppress their craving for a smoke and they employed every ingenuity to do just that. They made cigarettes from the discarded coffee grounds of our French guards, from sorrel and peppermint leaves, which both grew here. On of my saddest sights was when some of my co-prisoners, who called themselves "intellectuals," stooped so low to walk among Frenchmen eating outside on tables and picked up the bread rests [crumbs] thrown to the floor. Of course, I couldn't blame them. The meager food combined with the fresh invigorating air made everybody more hungry.

In the first weeks ourdaily schedule was as follows: reveille at 5, at 5:45 roll call and march to work, 11:15 return for lunch, departure again at 1:15 and work till 6:45. Monotonously, one day resembled the other.

June 28 and 29 were rainy days, so we couldn't go out for work. We were lying on our beds and felt cozy and comfortable, while listening to the steadily falling raindrops on the roof of our barrack. Not a small part of our wellbeing during the last eight days we did attribute to the almost complete absence of vermin. Our main conversation in these days turned always to food and work. My co-prisoners were a diversified lot in private life: teachers, businesspeople, students, bank employees, musicians (from regimental bands), one lawyer and one Ph.D.

July 1 was the first Sunday we had to work to make up for the rainy days. It was also the day one of my comrades, a corporal, was sentenced to jail, because while working he supposedly had used an invective vis-à-vis the French guard. I witnessed the occurrence and told the captain it was not true, the man didn't speak nor understand a word of French. Nevertheless, the punishment was ordered with the captain's remark to me, he believes a Frenchman more than a German. During my captivity I met this kind of justice more often, on the captain's order. The "prison" was built a few days earlier by some comrades from reeds in the form of a small doghouse and placed in front of our barrack. A prisoner in the "jail" had to lie flat on the floor or in the best case in a squatting position. In contrast to the hot days, the nights were cold, so a stay in the jail was no fun. The ten hours daily work all week (not including our march to and from the place of work) combined with the wearisome haymaking and our malnutrition (although we got used to our feeling of hunger as time went on) began to [take a] toll on us. No wonder we all looked forward to the free Sundays. It was always an enjoyment to watch the Loire with the high and low tide, the many seagulls, the passing sailing ships and cargo vessels, the light buoys in the river evenings and nights, and the magnificent sunrise and sunset.

July 10 the first mail and packages from home arrived. While there was great joy by the receivers, we others became very depressed, since we hadn't had any news from home in months, and our unrest increased more and more. July 14 (*fête nationale*, taking the Bastille by assault in 1789) all our "hommes de garde"[23] were drunk. At 10 o'clock in the evening they came noisily into our barrack, while around midnight the aide de camp appeared, accompanied by a sentry with fixed bayonet, in order to make once more a count of us, maybe fearing some prisoner might have escaped during the prevailing festive mood, which would have been sheer madness.

July 15. Three more comrades were sentenced to one day in jail and no lunch and supper, because they walked on the free Sunday without permission too far from the barrack to pick blackberries.

July 17. All Frenchmen were excited. A general was expected for inspection. Around nine he appeared in our barrack. He expressed his pleasure about the neatness of our barrack, asked the three prisoners next to the entrance about their grade in the army and their profession, was interested in a science book one was reading and—disappeared.

August 3. Finally, I and several of my comrades got their first and longingly expected mail from home. A load came off my mind.

One day in our prison life:

Early in the morning a French sentry, who is posted during the night in a round tent across the entrance of our barrack, awakes one of our three cooks. At six the cook wakes us. We receive a "gamelle" of "coffee," made from the coffee grounds the Frenchmen gave us "generously" after they had used it twice themselves. After that we wash ourselves in an old tin can. The wash water we get out of a pool, filled with creepers and all kinds of little animals, across our barrack. The pool with its smelling and stagnant water was filled only by high tide. After we drank our coffee a caricature in French uniform appears in our barrack at about 6:45, shouting: "Appell, rassemblement."[24] It is our French corporal, a man of the class '85 or '86, small and with an "embonpoint,"[25] round like a barrel, with little pig's eyes, which look at you good-natured, and with a drooping mustache. He makes the impression of always sleeping when standing, sometimes he staggers from too much wine. In general, he is a decent fellow. After his call one prisoner after the other comes out of the barrack. When some time has passed and everybody is assembled, the count starts. The corporal gives the order: "par quatre, en avant[26] or en route" and in a slow prisoner walk (about thirty steps in a minute) we

[23] French term for a watchman or guard
[24] "Name, fall in"
[25] plump or stout
[26] "Four forward"

German prisoners in France returning from work. *Library of Congress, LC-DIG-ggbain-24260.*

start moving, accompanied by the guards to a tent near the French barrack, where we pick up our tools: small forks and in bad weather pick axe and spade. Divided into several gangs, each group march with a sentry and several French soldiers who work with us—again in a snail's pace—to the different fields. According to the disposition of the sentry or the nearness of a superior, the ¼ hour break at 8 o'clock is prolonged to thirty or forty minutes and our return for lunch correspondingly at noon or 12:15. The same is repeated at 1:15 when we assemble again, and at our afternoon break at 5. At 7:50 in the evening we are normally back in our barrack. The work itself consists of gathering the hay and putting it later in huge stacks up to forty meters long and five meters high. The recreation, to which we were always looking forward, are on the Sundays. On these days we get up at 7, drink coffee and after the roll call everybody is on his own. Some read, stretched out on the bed or when the weather is fine, lying in the sun on a quilt in the grass, some are dreaming or talking, some doing their wash or fix their clothes, and almost all take the opportunity to bathe by high tide.

August 1, *1917.* The day when the war started three years ago was for us a day of quiet remembrance and a conversation subject all day long. My thoughts went back to August 1, 1914, when I was standing in the open place in front of the town hall in Elberfeld,[27] jammed with people, and the announcement came that war was declared. The enthusiasm and patriotism of the crowd had no limits.[28] For days the newspaper brought warnings that war might break out any day. The announcement was therefore

[27] city in North-Rhine Westphalia, Germany

[28] The degree of enthusiasm for war among even urban crowds, let alone those working on the land, has often been exaggerated, not least by government authorities at the

a relief from the uncertainty. I had mixed feelings, knowing that—according to orders I got six months before—I had to report for military service seven days after a war broke out. I remember also the happy time, August 1, 1915, when I was in Staumühle, . . . and beautiful summer days at recruiting depot in France near the frontier of Belgium on August 1, 1916.

On this August 1 our haymaking was finished. The delivery of the expected machines for pressing the hay into bales had been delayed. For us it was a godsend, we had a complete rest till August 8. These were happy days. One could read to one's hearts desire and dream and dream.

August 4. Twelve more men from the port city of Caen, for the most part longtime prisoners, joined us. Two lucky comrades among us, former medics in the German army, were exchanged after an agreement between the two governments for two French medics in German prisons.

On this date, the long awaited spring tide (full moon) arrived by which large parts of the island were inundated. On August 11 we had the opportunity for the first time while working to meet the old comrades of the other groups. Returning to our barrack we were told to pick up just arrived packages. Many like myself received their first packages in captivity and soon a joyful mood prevailed in the camp. I got four packages. One comrade received a package that was sent in November 1916, almost a year ago. As time went on we had formed ourselves according to our likes into small groups who stayed, worked and talked together. . . . I had several congenial comrades attracted to each other by common interests and more or less the same background, formed one group. We never lacked interesting conversation topics. I brought up my gloomy musing and brooding at times and was relieved when told they went through the same agony but found it a normal condition in a situation like ours.

August 15. Tonight I ate for the first time *des grenouilles* (frog-legs). A comrade, who was in private life a salesman in a fine food store, excellently prepared them. By now I have been through the scale of a prisoner's "delicacies." In Dijon the unbelievably stinking . . . tripe, also horse and mule meat, here quail eggs, which we found when haymaking and which we drank raw.

August 16. Came an order from our base camp that starting the same day all shoes of the P.G. (*prisoner de guerre*)[29] had to be put during the night into the kitchen for safekeeping, because lately prisoners had tried to escape. Three pair of wooden shoes were placed in the barrack entrance, if anybody had to use the toilet during the night. Every evening there was the funny spectacle of P.G.s walking in a procession to the kitchen with one or two pairs of boots or shoes in their hands. With the same

time and nationalist historians thereafter. Kaufmann's remark about the declaration of war bringing welcome closure to a period of nervous anticipation and mounting stress, however, is especially apt. See Jeffrey Verhey, *The Spirit of 1914: Militarism, Myth and Mobilization in Germany* (Cambridge: Cambridge University Press, 2000).

[29] prisoner of war

order came the prohibition of our innocent Sunday bathing in the Loire, supposedly to avert escapes. During these last times my main work was to ride one of the heavy workhorses mornings, noon and evenings to and from our working place. As I had no saddle my behind was soon brown and blue; nevertheless, I enjoyed this kind of work immensely.

August 23. The hay pressing for the time being finished, we had to carry now—each two men—the hay bales of forty to sixty kilos on long poles on a running board to large barges. Our daily fare since June consisted of potato soup and, in addition, alternating two days of rice and lentil soup. Today to our surprise we received instead of the last two soups bean soup.

Reading the French newspapers these last days was an ordeal and mental strain for us prisoners: Triumph for the allied forces on all fronts: victories at Verdun, victories of the Italians, victories of the English.

On August 26 (Sunday) and 27 we did not work. Lazily stretched out on our beds we listened to the melody of the falling rain on our roof and the howling storm around our barrack. We felt cozy and comfortable. Outside the landscape was gray in gray. What a contrast to the sunny days when we went to work with open collars, in cotton jackets and pants and naked feet, stuck in wooden shoes. I became acquainted with—and valued—a new dish, a vegetable from "nettles," which abound on the island and which we cooked ourselves.

The post exchange and mail conditions became more and more intolerable. Orders for the post exchange were delayed for two weeks due to the ill will of the French, and the incoming mail and packages were stored away for the same length before distributed. We were allowed to write home a postcard every Sunday and a letter every second Sunday, but this chicanery prevented us to answer mail promptly.

August 29. Our daily working hours were shortened from 6:30 in the morning till 11:30 (included ½ hour break) and from 1:30 till 6:30 in the afternoon, but today we worked only two hours, because the barges couldn't be loaded at the prevailing low tide. The rest of the day a comrade and I skinned caught young eels and prepared an excellent meal. When the tide receded, the eels stayed behind in the mud of the ditches. Easy to catch, it was tough to hold and skin them.

For the next eight days we always worked only half a day, because one of the heavy presses got stuck in the quagmire, over which we were not too much aggrieved.

On September 5 the prohibition to bathe in the Loire was lifted and we enjoyed it more as the river had overflowed its banks on account of the moon change.

September 7. Our *capitaine* died quite suddenly, mourned by no P.G. He was a rabid German hater.

September 8. We met comrades from our four groups of the island who told us they had gone on strike Sept. 1 and 2 on account of the untenable conditions of post exchange and mail delivery. The second day two German speaking sergeants from our group had come to persuade them to work, using alternatively the stick and carrot approach, but nobody budged, not even when they threatened to deprive them of their food. Only then the sergeants gave in and promised to deliver the exchange orders the next day and mail in time in the future. A punishment was dealt out anyhow. Ten prisoners were selected and sent back to the Camp Roche Maurice. The so-called "loader commando" group, to which I belonged, was idle for the next five days. There were not enough pressed bales to fill two barges, about 1600 bales. . . .

September 12. The French newspapers reported in big headlines "*guerre civile en Russie.*"[30] After the fall of Riga this was too much for the Frenchmen. We prisoners were overjoyed, although we expected some harsh reactions against us. We didn't have to wait long. At 8:30 in the evening a sergeant, girded with a revolver and accompanied by a sentry with fixed bayonet[,] appeared in our barrack and ordered in a rude tone to put out the light. While we were allowed to burn the one stable lantern "generously" given us by the French, for lighting with an unsteady and ghostly shine, the whole barrack till 10 pm. Lights had to be out from now on by 8:30. We ourselves had bought candles with the few *centimes de poche*[31] we received and which we could burn before as long as we wanted. Furthermore, we were strictly forbidden to be seen near the French barrack without a sentry, even to go alone, if we fell sick, to the short distant tent of the French medic. This paltry tactic of pin pricks I experienced later on more often, regardless of the camp I was in, whenever there was a German success in the war.

September 15. All of a sudden I became ill. A big carbuncle boil appeared on my left foot and I couldn't leave my bed anymore. The next day was the eve of Rosh Hashonah.[32]

Without consideration of my foot, I was sent September 18 with other comrades to the first group a distance of three to four kilometers, in order to board a ship back to camp Roche-Maurice. On my right foot a boot, on my left foot a wooden shoe, on my back a large sack with my belongings, across my shoulders my blanket. I hobbled under severe pain. . . . To our escorting sergeant, a very sympathetic young man from Amiens, who himself was severely wounded on a foot in the war, my sight was very painful. He told me he had been nine months in Budapest in 1911–1912 and spoke German very well. I noticed he made all efforts to get a carriage to transport me to the landing place, but to no avail. After we had gone half way—I always hobbled slowly behind the others—a cart from our own group came along and took me in whether [it was] sent intentionally or came by accident I did not know. The part of the island we passed was full of young horses and cattle guarded by civilians, who lived during the night in our built huts of reed. With twenty-seven comrades I waited on this second day of Rosh Hashonah on a boat in the middle of the Loire from half past two until five for the tug to take us in tow. We went upstream towards Roche-Maurice where we arrived at 6:45. There all our belongings were checked, above all they were looking for books. One comrade had to take off his

[30] "Civil war in Russia"—that is, the Russian Revolution
[31] pocket money or pay
[32] Celebration of the Jewish New Year began on the evening of September 16 and ended on September 18 at sunset.

boots where they found in his stockings letters and French money. He was immediately led away. It was the first night where I had to sleep again with my clothes on. I missed terribly the *Gemütlichkeit*[33] of the barrack on the island, the cleanliness of my bed, the pleasing conversation and the polite and considerate manner among all of us.

The next day an examination by a military doctor, an unusually nice man, took place. He ordered my removal to the *"Infirmerie"* (sick quarters). Here I got again a decent bed. Towards evening a lifeless comrade was brought in who had had an epileptic attack, a consequence of his captivity. The next morning he told me the story of his sufferings. When the war broke out he was already a year in the services with the regiment 25 in Aix La Chapelle (Aachen). His hometown was Frechen (near Cologne). Captured at the beginning of 1915, he was sent to North Africa where he worked in a quarry and road-making till June 1916. Returned to France, he contracted malaria and after that he suffered epileptic attacks. As a faker, they put him in a lunatic asylum. From here he escaped—barefooted and bareheaded—with two German fellow sufferers and two Frenchmen, and fought his way through for six days, then was caught and sent to a regular prisoner camp.

The stay in the infirmary was very monotonous. I missed painfully newspapers and books. In the nights we felt very cold. We had only one blanket for covering. The food was without variety, mornings, noon and evenings bean or potato soup and for drink cold tea, naturally without sugar. Every morning the doctor paid a visit. First was the round of the French soldier, then came the turn of the Austrian, almost all names to end in "titsch" or "anka," stupid Slavonic faces and the last ones were we Germans.

September 22. A Swiss committee, two men in civil dress, appeared. Accompanied by our limping *capitaine*, who was a German hater par excellence (I couldn't blame him, he lost his leg in the war), they took a look in the infirmary and disappeared again.

September 25 and 26. The Jewish prisoners were exempted from work. On request of the ten Jewish prisoners (eight Germans and two Austrians) a room in the camp was put at our disposal by the captain where a young teacher from Frankfurt (Rosenfelder) held services.

On the evening of October 2 I developed a fever of 39.8.[34] I already had 38.3[35] the night before and was transported to the infirmary for internal sickness. The food here was good; mornings and evenings we got hot milk but the trouble was I had no appetite.

Finally October 15 I could leave the infirmary. . . . The time started again to become acquainted with lice and fleas. Again I had to sleep with my clothes on—with only one blanket I felt terribly cold. In the meantime the old comrades from the island had returned to the camp. They told me they had gladly left, as in the last days the island was so inundated that the water at times was as high as the beds.

October 18: For the first time I worked at the port at the company "Cordon Bleu" to unload and pile up flour sacks. From now on my life as a prisoner became more

[33] German word that suggests an atmosphere of cordiality or conviviality
[34] about 104 degrees Fahrenheit
[35] roughly 101 degrees Fahrenheit

varied but certainly not more pleasant. I got a great admiration for the inventive faculty of my co-prisoners to steal food. The knowledge of going immediately to jail when caught didn't restrain them. Hunger was stronger than all punishments.

October 21, a Sunday. I worked at the shipping company "*Transatlantique*."[36] Our lunch, delivered from the camp, was prepared at the harbor and consumed in a wooden shed. This company contributed voluntarily meat and potatoes, besides eatables had often to be loaded or unloaded. No wonder to work for this company was in great demand by all prisoners. On this morning we had to unload barrels of oil, shreds of hemp, soap etc. In the afternoon we loaded cases of tinned goods, cognac and champagne and enormous quantities of chestnuts, which were sent to England. Altogether we were four prisoners and four Arabs and our task was to stow away these things into the deep ships hold. To allay our hunger we took advantage of the semi darkness of the hold and ate quantities of chestnuts. As a consequence, we became very thirsty. To quench this thirst the Arabs opened bottles of champagne, which went from mouth to mouth and were empty in no time. Not accustomed to this kind of fare, we returned to our camp quite staggering. Two of my co-workers couldn't suppress their hate of everything French, dropped quite a few cases of champagne in the hold, where nobody watched us. The next day I worked with this same Arab at another place and to my utter disgust I noticed in the daylight what a frightfully ugly man he was. A tall fellow, only skin and bones, with big unusually dirty yellow hands and yellow complexion, with big teeth sticking out of his mouth, wrapped in rags with a drooping, unkempt pitch black mustache. He gave me the creeps, thinking that I [had] drunk with him from the same bottle. The comrades who worked with me this day and saw the Arab, roared with laughter when I told them this was my bottle drinking pal, knowing how particular and sensitive in a physical way I was.

For the next days till October 31 I worked with this "commando" where much food (mainly chestnuts and figs) we had to load disappeared in our stomachs.

Generally, one day resembled the next in Roche-Maurice. A French bugler awakened us at 5 o'clock early in the morning. The whole camp stirred into action. One of us had to go the kitchen to get a dish with a watery soup for fifteen men, after delivering a token made of tin, at the kitchen entrance. We alternated for this job. The soup really consisted of warm water with some breadcrumbs in it. Then we washed ourselves in the open in wooden basins through which constant water was running. At 5:55 we had to assemble and at 6:10—still in darkness—we marched off to the different places of work. With each detachment was a French interpreter. Between 11:00 and 11:30 [we] return to the camp. As in the morning, we got a dish with soup, this time only for ten men. Scarcely finished with eating, the bugle sounded again and the same procedure was followed. In the darkness at 6:00 or 6:30 we returned to the camp and received the same soup for fifteen men. At 8:30 was roll call in the courtyard and at 9:00 the bugler sounded retreat. Every evening we could

[36] Compagnie Générale Transatlantique, or CGT, also known as the French Line, was a French shipping company founded in 1861. During WWI many of its ships were converted to warships or hospital ships.

wash ourselves in the wooden basin, while on Wednesdays and Saturday evenings we had the facility to take a shower.

Some comrades gave free evening courses in German, French, arithmetic, etc., few even delivered scientific lectures. The free Sundays we used to do our washing. A band of six prisoners also provided entertainment on Sundays.

November 6 (1917). ... [A] special newspaper edition was distributed: The Americans made the first prisoner. Starting today I worked with short interruptions at Nantes in the *Chambre de Commerce.*[37] Our work was to pile up sacks with sugar or cocoa beans, which arrived by ship from South America. While we were forbidden to bring sugar home to the camp, we were allowed to eat on the spot. ... For this reason every prisoner on this detachment carried his spoon with him. ... One day a ship arrived which had been torpedoed and had caught fire. The cargo of sugar, burnt and brown from the fire and baked together from the penetrating water, was a welcome change for us. On account of the prohibition to bring sugar to the camp, we had to undergo body inspections by customhouse inspectors before leaving the pier. Nevertheless, as hunger generates ingenuity, there always came the opportunity to smuggle sugar. With our German uniform we always wore a tie with strings around our neck. Some prisoners ... went so far [as] to tie the bag under their genitals. Little by little the custom officers found out these tricks. ...

Always fascinating was watching the teeming life of the big crowd at the harbor: the multitude of peoples of the different races: Arabs, Negroes, . . . Greeks, Serbs, Algerians, Spaniards, Americans and in between the elegant ladies and the demimondes from Nantes. America was trump all over in . . . the articles in the newspapers and—the fashion of women's hats. For the most part the ladies wore wide brimmed hats in gray, blue or black with two dents in the front, like the hats of the American soldiers. . . . Generally the elegant French women wore exquisite shoes. From the promenading of ladies, the sight fell on Negroes, dressed like perfect dandies, patent leather shoes with bows, silk stockings and pants with cuffs. Among the crowd the Greeks were a striking sight with their peculiar wraps around, similar to the one worn by monks, and their curious black nightcaps. Our civilians called them "sale people" (dirty people). . . . A typical daily street sight was the newspaper vender [and] at the same time a walking clock. He arrived on the dot at the same spot. A short blow on the horn and a flow of words started: "*Le phase*" (the lighthouse), "*le populaire*" (the popular one), "*l'ouest Éclair* (the enlightener of the West) latest edition. . . .

Even if we all believed in the final victory of Germany, the passing of the trains with American soldiers several times a day . . . gave us a lot of anxiety.

In the last days of my stay in camp Roche-Maurice, serious fistfights broke out in the camp of the Austrians, who were completely separated from us, had better lodgings and . . . always got extra food. The reason for the brawl was the soldiers of Czech nationality had gotten from the society of Czechs in Paris a button with the Czech lion on it to replace the gold button with the initials F.J. (Franz Joseph)

[37] Chamber of Commerce

on their Austrian caps. The German-Austrians and the Bosnians, who closed ranks with them, as well as the prisoners from Herzegovina and Dalmatia, were roused to anger, and the fistfights started. The French were of course on the side of the Czechs. The Austrians were threatened as punishment to be moved into part of our camp, with all its disadvantages, especially much worse food. Immediately after our capture, a selection was made among us Germans between Poles, soldiers from Alsace-Lorraine and so-called Danes. All those came in different camps, where they had, as I heard many times, a much more tolerable life. The same method was used against the Austrians. Nevertheless, it must be said to their lasting honor, they stood firmly together in spite of the difference in language of the various nations of the Habsburg monarchy. For the most part older men, captured in 1914 and 1915 in Serbia, were sent across Italy to France. Almost all of them had taken part in the terrible so-called Serbian retreat and endured unspeakable sufferings. Because their retreat lasted from one to two weeks and they had nothing to eat but grass, three quarters of them died on this march, completely exhausted.

November 23 was a special day: we received a second blanket. Only somebody, who was nightly robbed of his sleep, can imagine what this meant to us.

November, 1917. I was transferred with a group of comrades to the camp "Sainte Anne." As it turned out, I experienced in this camp the most wretched time of my prisoner life—already a gypsy existence—surpassed only by my stay at the prison in Chalons. After a one and a half mile march to the station Roche-Maurice and a short train ride, we arrived at 4 p.m. at the new camp, Sainte Anne, built as an island branching out of the Loire, [and] located close by the city of Nantes. Devoid of any vegetation and covered with beach sand, the island was the city's emporium for coal, wood, iron, etc. [In addition] there were several factories. After our arrival the usual search of our belongings took place. The next day—a Sunday—we were immediately sent to work unloading iron bars. At the pier in front of our workplace was the former proud German steamer "Bismarck," anchored, now the possession of America. . . . The camp itself was in a sad state. The barracks were so dark we could not even read when at noontime the sun shone brightly outside. The glass window-panes were replaced with unbleached muslin, drenched in oil, which became even more impenetrable with time. It seemed there was a shortage of window glass. . . .

The starvation diet—water soup in the morning, water soup at lunch, water soup in the evening—forced us to steal and steal. As soon as twilight arrived, the place outside of the barracks came to life with a peculiar aspect. Almost all prisoners had small stoves, made secretly by co-prisoners out of large tin cans, on which everybody cooked with stolen firewood. All over the little fires flared up, although it was strictly forbidden to cook. In order to avoid being caught, one man was posted in the first barrack near the entrance to the camp. As soon as he gave the danger signal, the fires were extinguished with the beach sand. After a while, the danger became too great and we decided to cook inside our barracks. As there was no ventilation at all, the smoke became so heavy that we almost suffocated, not talking about how much it hurt our eyes. But hunger surmounted all obstacles. The main coffee depot for the army was on the island, so we helped ourselves with coffee beans, which we roasted and made our own coffee. Three of us had joined together whenever two went for work, the third had to cook. While some had the opportunity to steal the precious firewood, others stole the beans and so a steady exchange took place.

On the evening of November 28[,] I was sent on night commando "Commerciale" to unload a large ship with phosphate. As a special inducement, we received at 9 p.m. coffee and a kind of liver sausage, and for every two men a bottle of beer. At midnight we were served a real meal and then we worked till five in the morning. After such night's work we were allowed to sleep the whole morning. While working on the ship's hold I found lots of American peanuts between the cross-beams, probably shipped for soap manufacturing on a previous cargo, which gave me a much appreciated variation in my diet for the next days

December 2. While unloading an American ship, I was lucky to pick up a box with canned meat from provisions piled upon the pier for the American army and protected by American sentries. It was not without danger because the sentries shot at anybody who tried to pilfer, without warning.

December 4. The camp supervisor, a German sergeant major, told us at roll call about the treason [committed by] a comrade with the name Dietrich from the guard regiment "Elisabeth." Born in Posen, he was captured on September 16 and since then he had been a cook in the prison kitchen. According to the custom in the camp, cards and letters, mailed by the prisoners but sometimes by mistake without address, had been given back to the supervisor. Because there was a new French interpreter in the camp, such a card with the following text was given back by error: "I hereby inform you that several prisoners are preparing for an escape in spring. For this purpose money is collected at places of work, Dietrich." We wondered how they had picked out and searched on several occasions certain P.G.s, who had more money and had them jailed immediately. The German camp elder had D [Dietrich] come to his office and told him to his face [that he had committed] a treasonable offense. D. [Dietrich] couldn't deny it, and the present clerks gave him a good thrashing. Scared, he ran out of the camp straight to the French guard. In order to protect him, the guard put him in prison as there was no other place available. When we prisoners heard all this, our anger rose to a fever pitch. He certainly would have been lynched, if they would have gotten hold of him. The same evening the comrades, who had thrashed the traitor, were thrown into jail. . . . D. was sent the next morning to the infirmary, supposedly on account of a fever, . . . was rigorously guarded, and we were forbidden even to come near it. The following day he was taken . . . [by] a corporal armed with a revolver to the cries of the prisoners—"traitor," "rascal," "Judas"—out of the camp. Our camp elder was sentenced a week later to fifteen days close confinement. The reason: he had allowed P.G.s to thrash D.

The terrible hunger in the camp forced everybody to steal. *Bon gré mal gré*[38] whenever the opportunity arrived and facilitated by working day or night on American freighters, packed to the hilt with all kinds of provisions. Because the control was very efficient, we had to devise all the time new tricks. From the night crew for

[38] whether willing or not

instance, four men had to take pails along to the camp to pick up the meal. Before entering the camp, the escorting guard had to report to the guard house. The prisoners took advantage of this short time and threw the stolen provisions (lard, canned beef, condense milk, chocolate, etc.) which they had packed into the pails over the camp gate, where they then would be picked up by other prisoners and brought into the barracks. ...

The treatment in the camp got worse from day to day. A newly arrived interpreter from Roche-Maurice, an Alsatian, was ordered to search every single prisoner of the returning work crews. . . . To bring along firewood was severely punished, sometimes with the use of a horse whip. . . .

January 23. Punishment for stealing was raised and intensified: sixty days jail now. Of these sixty days fifteen to thirty days were "close confinement" that meant four days bread and water and only the fifth day a warm meal. Mail, sent from home, was thoroughly censored. I often received letters by which a pair of scissors had been so much in use that it was impossible to make any sense out of the letter. . . .

From January 24 till the end of my stay in Sainte Anne I was attached as a handyman to a crew of P.G.s, who worked as bricklayers. I remembered this January 24 well, because it was unusually warm so we worked in our shirtsleeves. We had to build huge stone barracks, which were erected on a wide empty space near the stockpiles of coal, wood, etc., and meant as living quarters for the American civilian longshoremen. The ... [foundations] for the barracks were made of cinders and cement by Arabs from the French colonies. These Arabs in their turbans, the wide pants, their glaring red sashes wound several times around their waist, their blue military jacket and their bronze faces, partly covered with black beards, looked very picturesque and dirty. When they returned to their camp by sunset in the afternoon one started aloud in a peculiar singing cadence and the whole chorus fell in while walking. Finished, they all fell down, turned towards the sun, kissed the ground and performed their prayers. ...

I and fifty-one of my comrades were awakened at 5:30 on February 4, 1918, to get transferred to another camp. As it was my birthday, I considered it a good omen. After packing our few belongings, we assembled at 7:30, received a small food provision to last supposedly till afternoon, and marched at 8 o'clock to the station Orléans, not before being submitted to some searching at random of our baggage. Our German kitchen had saved some food for us, so everyone got an additional half loaf of bread and a small horsemeat sausage. At 8:45 we changed to train at the gare-état de Nantes for our going north to the city of Brest, a train ride of 340 kilometers. . . . It was a hilarious sight for us to watch the faces of the inhabitants whenever our train stopped at the several stations. First, they were standing, staring and gasping, then the bedlam started: *Des Boches* [the Germans], Fritz, kaput, etc. At almost all stations we saw lots of American soldiers. A new sight were the Bretton women and children, wearing their picturesque medieval dresses with the characteristic white bonnets. . . . I was thinking how odd it was to travel just on my day of birth as a prisoner on the extreme west coast of France. When darkness came, I fell into a deep sleep from which I only woke up when the train stopped at Brest, the capital of Brittany at 10 p.m. . . . we luckily arrived after a ten minute march at our destination: camp Brest Kéroriou.[39] After a superficial searching of our pockets and delivering of our baggage—with the exception of our blankets—we finally were led to a low wooden barrack with the customary oiled muslin as a window-pane. It was 11 p.m. The beds were double decker bunks, two together as in German troop barracks, which we found ideal in comparison to the other camps where we slept in two tiers in a long row of plankbeds. The only thing missing were tables and benches. As on the island, the palliasses were filled with seaweed and a pillow we received with the same, so we had an excellent sleep this first night.

The next morning we were awakened at 5:30 for the roll call at 6:30. . . . Half of my comrades from Sainte Anne were so-called "jail birds." One, from Hamburg, a very nice fellow, established a record. From his three years in captivity he was no less than 330 days in jail, hadn't received any pay since June and had to do another ninety days. For our work we got paid 10 to 20 centimes a day, but this was detained for the most trifling reasons. I admired my Hamburg comrade for his guts, but was at a loss to understand why he defied the French so often, knowing what it meant—to go to jail again and again. . . .

One of the disadvantages [of this camp] was to work eight days in a row before getting a day off. One other was our interpreter, who supposedly was born in Strassburg [Strasbourg] and had even served in the German army . . . , a violent German hater for whom the prisoners had quite some respect or fear, whatever one might call it. . . . The Frenchmen constantly insisted the reason for fighting this war is to stamp out once and for all Prussian militarism. The big advantages [of the camp] were: the daily bread was much better . . . , instead of water soup in the morning we got coffee made from malt, which we prisoners bought jointly, contributing twenty centimes from our weekly pay. For lunch we got bean soup with horsemeat or any other soup with horsemeat. The meals were nourishing and for the first time with enough salt, normally in insufficient supply. . . . Another advantage: the post exchange was managed by Germans by which the profit making of the French officers or sergeants was eliminated. . . .

In the camp confines were, besides Germans, Austrians and the French staff. Although our barrack was next to the one of the Austrians, we were strictly forbidden to enter theirs. We new arrivals received each a freshly washed white linen sleeping bag, which was changed every four or six weeks, a handkerchief and a fork, things we never had possessed before in captivity. The camp was on a small elevation so we could see a part of the city. . . . The city itself, surrounded by old fortifications, was located high above the sea. Two steep rocks with an old castle on top of each commanded the port entrance. One of the castles served as a navy cantonment, while on the other, according to the legend, the story of Tristan and Isolde took place. Every morning and evening at 6:30 a cannon shot was fired to announce the opening or

[39] a prisoner-of war camp and also a supply base for American troops located in northwestern France

closing of the harbor for navigation. When the weather was fine, two captive balloons were up in the air and an airship was flying back and forth to watch for Germans. . . .

February 9. Thirty men were discharged from the Brest military hospital and sent to our camp to be returned to Germany. Mostly young boys born 1896 from the Guard regiment or Regiment 57. They were taken prisoners October 17 in the battle on the "Chemin des Dames," seriously wounded. . . . An agreement existed between the two governments to repatriate seriously wounded prisoners.

As on other Sundays we had a savory menu today, February 10: potatoes, meat soaked in vinegar and cabbage.

February 11 saw me working at a coal barge, feared and detested by all prisoners; because this coal was of a fine and dusty kind, one became in no time black as a moor. Luckily we could take a bath evenings. In summer when exposed to this coal dust, the skin on one's face peeled off, while the eyes became severely inflamed. The French leader of the coal commando—a corporal—unfortunately originated in the north part of France, occupied by German troops. This circumstance, as well as a premium he got for fast unloading of the barge, . . . made life miserable for the P.G.s in this crew. A few weeks before P.G.s had complained to a Swiss emissary [about it], and as a result it became a bit more tolerable, but today, when we new prisoners from St. Anne formed the commando, it got worse again. One determined comrade from Düsseldorf, in captivity since 1915, couldn't control his feelings when the corporal touched him and threatened him with his shovel. . . . The final result for my pal was fifteen days in jail, eight of them in close confinement.

Working hours in this camp were from 6:30 in the morning till noon and from 1:30 till 6 p.m. . . .

Today we saw how successful our submarines have been when a 2,000–3,000 ton steamer, severely damaged . . . the day before, was berthed between two ships. Since the first days in the camp, I was able to subscribe to a French newspaper. It was interesting to read and detect the nervousness of the various papers . . . about an expected offensive.

February 15 . . . . An ever recurring amusement and laughter for us was tomfoolery and drollery of the numerous Chinese who were busily engaged, close to us, with wheelbarrow and shovel, doing the same work. To our great surprise our men had changed considerably in the last days. We received daily quantities of cauliflower in our soups. The farmers in Brittany on the advice of the government had planted great quantities of cauliflower and were forced now to sell them for one sou, due to the scarcity of railroad cars to transport them. . . .

February 16. While working deep down in the ship's hold, I couldn't help it that my thoughts were wandering back to the time of peace, when I was sitting on these evenings with good friends in a café, talking or listening to the pleasant music of a string band. (How many of these friends are still alive?). What a crass reversal. . . .

February 17. We got a new dish for supper: thick rice. The long-time prisoners didn't touch any, for them rice was distasteful. . . . They told us they had to spend the first months of their captivity in so-called "front work companies" where they had to eat rice three times a day for four to six weeks. . . .

It didn't take the French long to find out that for [an] additional wage of ten centimes a day, German prisoners would accomplish a record output. It was no wonder that they soon were demanding these record performances as a normal task. . . .

February 22. Six more prisoners, severely wounded in the October battles last year and discharged from the hospital here, were sent to our camp to be repatriated. Five of them were young boys on crutches with one leg and the sixth, a sergeant-major (Cohn from Charlottenburg) with one arm. Seeing these men, I felt a deep compassion for them and myself fortunate in spite of all the sufferings of a prisoner's life. . . .

February 23. Great excitement prevailed in the morning in the Austrian camp. While the German-Austrians, the Hungarians and Rumanians went to work, the Croatians assembled separately and were led by a German-Austrian sergeant-major to the reading room. Shortly after, a Serbian colonel . . . appeared, accompanied by the camp commander. Immediately, the Austrian sergeant-major, a giant of a man, was punished with ten days in jail and marched off, because he didn't give the order: "Habt acht!" (attention) when the Serbian colonel entered. We Germans were proud of this Austrian strength of character. Our delight was complete when we heard that none of the Croats, in spite of an hour long address and persuasion by the colonel, changed sides . . . to go [over] to the Serbian army. . . . [T]hese two hundred fifty Croats stayed together with the rest of the Austrians.

February 23 and 24 . . . . In the last days, the French showed great nervousness, probably a consequence of an offensive started by the German army. From experience, we P.G.s had to suffer for it. At all workplaces the prisoners were jailed right and left for the smallest infraction. I could write a book about the French morbid hatred of the Germans and their use of the word "Boche," an invective for Germans. Without exception, newspapers of all parties applied it copiously. The civilians, with whom we had to work together, were cautious enough to avoid this word. . . .

The last day of February, a day of terrible snow, hail and rainy weather, saw me at the unpleasant work of loading iron bars.

As a welcome change, I enjoyed the next day, March 1, a well-earned rest. . . . By good fortune, I had as a co-prisoner in my barrack a Dr. Adler from Württemberg, a fellow Jew and philologist, with whom I often had long conversation, so today we both couldn't be reconciled to the fact that anti-Semitism existed in the army among all classes, but particularly, the officer corps. In peacetime it was impossible for a Jew to become an officer in any but one of the German states (Bavaria). It had changed of course in this war. The perception of this fact led us again and again to ask the question: What do I fight for? On the other hand, as German prisoners, we were the hated "Boches" and had to endure privations and sufferings on account of our German being. An eternal dilemma.

March 2. I was sent again to my old commando to work with shovel and wheelbarrow at the fortifications. A Chinese sneaked by and furtively gave me a clipping from a newspaper with the headline: "La paix honteuse de la Russie."[40] During our whole captivity we were aware how deeply the Chinese sympathized with us and how they proved it by deeds whenever an opportunity arose. . . .

March 7. I decided to go to the infirmary for an examination of my beard infection. The doctor burnt out the infection spot, a very painful procedure. This was the reason for my exemption from work this and the following days. . . .

In the night of the 9th to the 10th the clocks were changed to daylight savings time.

The next day, Sunday March 10th, was a beautiful sunny day. Because the decree of no newspaper delivery to P.G.s was still in force, the most unbelievable rumors were going on in the camp. . . .

[With] my restful, pleasant days for almost a week over, I had to report to the doctor [on] March 13. . . . [H]e declared me able to work again. . . .

My work on March 14 was to unload wine barrels at the port. For several weeks American soldiers arrived daily. They stayed here in wooden barracks for a few days and were then transported by train to the East. Some acted disgraceful, calling us in German "Schweinehunde,"[41] "the Kaiser will be hanged," and used invectives in English. The majority, especially those of German extraction, were very nice. They gave us cigarette packs and asked, partly in pure South German dialect, whether we had to work hard. They told us they all were born in the U.S.A., that their parents or grandparents came from Germany, and they themselves would be drilled for three or four months behind the frontlines. Uneasily, they inquired whether the war would last long, who would win, etc. . . .

March 18. In the afternoon I went with a French interpreter to the hospital, a very large, old building, to get a prescription—at my own expense—for a pair of eye glasses (I was slightly shortsighted). Although we avoided crowded streets, we couldn't help it several times when I was spotted, people yelled at the "Boche."

The newspaper prohibition was finally lifted today to my great joy. . . .

In the evening of March 20 we heard outside of our camp a large crowd shouting, brawling, and whistling. We learned later that the mills hadn't received any grain, couldn't deliver flour to the city, and the bakers were therefore unable to bake bread.

March 21 was a beautiful day, worthy as the first day of spring. . . . A comrade told us about his two years experience as a prisoner in Morocco.

March 22 *(1918).* The eve or day of the German offensive.[42] Our French "tormentors" showed, on account of it, great irritability. In the morning the German camp leader told us an order had come from the French War Office to deal more strictly with the P.G. during the German offensive, [so] that they don't get too "insolent." At

[40] "The Shameful Peace of Russia"

[41] filthy dogs

[42] Reference to German attack known as "Operation Michael," or *Kaiserschlacht,* that launched the spring offensive from the Hindenburg Line (near Saint-Quentin) with the intention of breaking through Allied lines and ultimately seizing the Channel ports that supplied the British Expeditionary Force.

work, the French corporal marked down the names of P.G.s by the slightest infraction for deduction of wages, etc. At roll call in the evening punishment was dealt out right and left. Because clothing was hanging openly in the barracks (which had to be according to a strange order hidden under the palliasses), eight to fifteen days wage deductions were inflicted. On top of it, the group supervisor was made responsible and jailed.

One revealing incident occurred today when we marched through the city. A well-dressed elderly lady walked beside our column, insulting us with a face, distorted in a rage, and advised the accompanying sentry to ram his bayonet through our bodies. . . .

March 25. All over the streets at the port soldiers, marines and civilians were standing around with an intense air, studying the newspapers to find out about our offensive. Strangely enough, three quarters of the issue was devoted to a mysterious giant gun, which bombarded Paris from a distance of 122 kilometers.[43] Against this, our offensive in the English sector receded into the background.

In the last days the French newspapers brought sensational articles about the German infantry and methods. There were summaries from the notes of Count Lichnowsky, German ambassador in London, dealing with our diplomacy before the war, about the crown council at the beginning of 1914, from which one could gather that we wanted the war. . . . Revelations were made about intrigues of Count Luxburg, ambassador in Argentina,[44] about Count Bernstorff, about submarine hiding places in Spain, about bribery affairs here in France etc.

March 26. I was put to the torture once more; i.e., the doctor burnt out the infected spot on my face again. In the afternoon I was allowed to go to the city, accompanied, naturally, to pick up my eyeglasses at the optician. The city impressed me as quite clean almost like a German one. In the evening the newspapers informed the public, with some apprehension, that the war of mobility had started again.

March 27. Again treatment and burning of my infection. Back in my barrack I read "Tristan and Isolde" and "Parsival" (by Will Vesper). The mood of the poetry affected me strongly, evincing thoughts of one's unhappiness in captivity.

March 28. Lying in the morning on my bed when at 8 o'clock all church bells in the city started ringing. On my question I was told, it is "Maundy Thursday" (a Catholic semi-holiday). Captivity dulls a person so much that he doesn't think or care about Sun [day] or holiday. . . .

Easter Sunday—March 31[,] I spent in camp, having been exempted from work for the last eight days on account of my infection, which was burnt out again the previous

[43] Likely reference to the Paris Gun, or *Paris-Geschütz*, a German long-range gun used to bombard Paris between March and August 1918. It was capable of a range of about 130 kilometers, or about 80 miles. While not particularly accurate, the gun had value as a psychological tool.

[44] Karl von Luxburg was German chargé d'affaires in Buenos Aires, Argentina, not ambassador. He reportedly sent secret messages to Berlin via Sweden, urging that some Argentine ships be sunk.

day. Some comrades had to work on this holiday. Like everyone else exempted from work, we had after the roll call at 6:30 to peel potatoes. (In honor of Easter every P.G. got 1 ½ lb for his meal) After these chores I did my usual Sunday work: washing. The Easter weather was seasonable, sunshine alternated with hail and rain. In the afternoon our Bund [group] gave a concert and the chorus sang. For the last two days the newspapers are gleefully reporting the failure of the German offensive. On this Easter day they wrote about the victims of a projectile of the "Big Bertha," which landed on Good Friday among a band of worshippers in a church in Paris.[45] Seventy-five women and children had been killed, ninety wounded. As a human being I condemned and deplored deeply this act of barbarism, knowing well as a soldier that these acts of despair never would affect the outcome of the war one way or the other.

Easter Monday saw me pushing a wheel barrow with sand at Fort Fetteré. In the evening there was great excitement in the camp. One of the most feared commandos was the one called "Bastide." Under the commando of a redhead corporal, born in Lille, and known for his brutality and immoderate German hatred, PGs had to unload the fine, dusty coal. As the corporal was paid on the side from the company for quick unloading of the ships, he drove the PGs on all day long like a slaveholder. The fine coal dust clung to mouth and nose and made the work . . . intolerable. On the Easter day these comrades, blackened all over, arrived at the camp at 8:00, just after we . . . came out for roll call. Working since 7:00 in the morning fully twelve hours with one hour's break for lunch and contrary to the regulations that PGs shouldn't work more than ten hours a day, they were forced to unload after time for leaving work. They were so excited and yelled invectives at the French, and especially the young ones were in such a rage that they couldn't hold back their tears. We felt very deeply for them, while the French had only scornful laughter. . . .

On the morning of April 4 we were awakened at 5:30 from loud lamenting, sobbing and crying in the courtyard. During the day an Austrian told me what happened. While all Czechs changed sides and joined the Czech national army[46] weeks before, four of them chose to stay with the Austrians. In letters written to one of them, a sergeant major, by his mother in the Czech language, the French found out, although he had a German name (his father was German) that his mother was Czech, and therefore they tried by all means to make him a Czech. When the French [were] met [by] a resolute refusal [from] the four, they had put them in a cell the evening before. Early the next morning the guards gagged and tried to drag them to the railroad station after the French adjutant had slapped them in a brutal way in the face. The Austrians, informed [about] what was going on, armed themselves in the morning darkness with stones and came to the courtyard to liberate the four. In the meantime, the whole guard was mobilized and forced the Austrians back with their fixed bayonets. Feeling [weak] against [the French],

[45] English newspapers reported that the gun, which reportedly killed seventy-five worshipers and injured ninety, had a barrel eighty feet long and fired a shell eight or nine inches in diameter.

[46] Reference to the Czech Legion, a volunteer army that fought on the Allied side in the hope of establishing an independent Czech state upon the defeat of the Austro-Hungarian Empire.

they cursed and insulted the French and called to their gagged comrades to throw themselves on the ground. . . . When the French sergeant of the guard tried to push the Austrian sergeant major back, he let the French know through the interpreter, blood will flow if the sergeant would touch him again. After assembled for work, the Austrians decided with one voice as a protest to go on strike. In response to this threat, the [entire] camp administration, commander, manager, interpreters, etc., came out—afraid that something would leak out [about] the [incident]—to [cajole] the Austrians to go [back] to work [by] promising to agree to all their demands. They were told the colonel, to whom they could submit their requests, would come the same or the next day. The Austrian leader demanded, however, that a representative of a neutral legation should come to the camp so they could bring forward their grievances. . . . Only after these demands were granted, the crews went to work. As [it] became known later, the French didn't dare to force the four PGs to [convert to the Czech side]. Instead, they were sent to Tours where they were jailed for thirty days with the devilish argument "they had refused to be sent from one camp to another.". . .

Sunday, April 7, was real April weather—rain and sunshine. Several cases of homosexuality became known in the camp, but the affair was hushed up vis-à-vis the French. Today on the anniversary of the U.S.A. entering the war, all public buildings [flew flags]. What bitterness for us!

It was always comforting to see the show of sympathy for us [by] colored people, Chinese, Annamites [Vietnamese], Moroccans, pressed by the French to statute labor. A few days ago, while we were working on a street, a young Moroccan passed by and silently threw a cigarette to the ground, in the afternoon an elderly Moroccan, dirty, his face full of coal dust, came along and threw a coin—a franc to the ground, walked away without turning his head or [to] wait for a thank you. They all knew, if caught, they would [be] severely punished. . . .

April 17. Two comrades were jailed for two weeks, one week to spend in close confinement, because "they had bought bread from the Austrians."

April 19. "*Le Temps*" [published] an article that the first American Jewish regiment[47] had arrived in London in whose honor a banquet was given by Lord Rothschild. Letters we received from Germany in the last two weeks were in an unbelievable condition. In letters I got, the censor with his scissors had cut out so many words and sentences that it was impossible to understand the content. Whether it was for spite or for another reason, we didn't know. In any case, our ill temper grew. . . . As the war entered its fourth year more items of the daily necessities became unobtainable for the French population. One of these was meat. The scarcity of it forced them to eat horsemeat, while we got as a substitute three times a week fish.

[47] Reference to the British Army's independent Jewish fighting unit formed in 1917 to fight against the Ottoman Empire in what was then called Palestine. Attached to the Royal Fusiliers, the unit consisted of five battalions, one of which (the 39th) was composed largely of American and Canadian Jews.

April 27. Under the protection of an early morning dense fog, two comrades, one of whom was in his second year of captivity . . . (with intervals in between) in jail, escaped from the work crew at Fort Fetteré. . . . The German crew leader, a sergeant, was unjustly jailed immediately after entering the camp. We all got very excited and [for] the first time the word "strike" was heard.

April 30. The unhappy anniversary of my capture. The day was gray and rainy, typical for Brest, and exactly reflected my own mood. My thoughts went from the privations and sufferings to the uncertain future with the anxious question, how long our captivity would last.

May 1. Our daily bread ration was reduced from 600 grams to 400. As . . . compensation we got a little bit more potatoes and beans. As 5000 workers were on strike at the "arsenal," the longshoremen at the port, we PGs had to serve as strike breakers. The reduction of the bread ration, the many unjust punishments, the denial of undershirts (many PGs wore nothing but rags), the harassment and the many pinpricks we were exposed to [led] us . . . to the resolution this evening to strike the next morning. Soon the watchword strike went from mouth to mouth and barrack to barrack without a leak to the unsuspecting French. In every barrack we all vowed to stick together. . . .

May 2. In the morning the strike started. When the time . . . came for roll call, everybody stayed in bed. The German camp leader was heard negotiating outside with the excited French. Pro-forma, the German group leaders—sergeant majors—asked us to step out. As agreed upon, we refused, making known the reasons for our behavior: the small bread ration, the unjust jailing of the German sergeant, the inhuman treatment of the comrades [by] the coal commando . . . , the non delivery of underwear (undershirts and drawers). The withholding of the war offices decree relating to the treatment of PGs in accordance with the latest arrangement of Bern from April 15 etc., etc. [At] a quarter to seven our sergeant majors appeared in the barracks telling us that the camp commander had been informed. We should put on our uniforms in case we had to come out immediately to tell our grievances. Ten minutes later they appeared for the second time to tell us that the helpless French sergeant had read to them the war offices decree, according to which the bread ration for PGs should be 400 grams and the missing 200 grams should be made up with other food in the same price range. At 7:00 the sergeant majors appeared for the third time with an order of the French adjutant, [stating that] anybody who wants to work should step out. Unfortunately, our two hundred and fifty Austrian co-prisoners, who lived in separate barracks, were informed too late about our strike intentions and had gone to work; otherwise, the strike would have been complete. Lying on our palliasses and waiting for further developments, we heard at 7:30 a long and excited discussion outside. The lieutenant first class let us know through the interpreter that the shortening of our bread ration was a countervailing measure against Germany, that the decree of the war office didn't arrive yet (all of which we knew was a lie). The two other demands would be solved to our satisfaction. Then came a threat [that] if the men wouldn't immediately come out for work, twenty men of each group would be sent to the "chateau."[48] At 7:45 the bugle sounded: everybody to assemble outside for roll call. In groups we stepped out in our Sunday uniform. The whole guard was mobilized and standing with fixed bayonets in the middle of the courtyard with the commander, sergeants, interpreters, etc. After our count, the German camp leader had to repeat three times (on orders of the commander) the call for us to march to work. Nobody moved. Seeing this, the commander gave in and promised that all our demands would be arranged in a satisfying manner [if] we would go to work. Still we were not convinced. Then the order came [that] the group leaders should read aloud the name of each prisoner and have him come forward . . . but nobody stepped forward. When they saw nothing could be done, the order to the group leader came to bring the PGs back to their barracks. The two doors and windows with their oil-soaked muslin in place of glass (which kept the barracks even in daytime in semi-darkness) were tightly closed. In front of every door and window guards with fixed bayonets were posted. In order to economize our energies, we were lying on our plank beds. [Upon] our repeated complaints, we finally got at 9:30 a large bucket for every barrack as a substitute for the toilet. Because a great many men had to relieve nature after a night's rest, the air in the barrack got worse from hour to hour. At noon two men from each group—thirty in all—and two sergeant majors with the adjutant of the German camp leader were picked up and accompanied by guards with fixed bayonets (one guard to two prisoners) were marched through the city to the prison in the chateau. At one o'clock soldiers in marching order from the recruiting battalion arrived for reinforcements. At 1:30 the bugle sounded for roll call in work clothes. We, however, preferred to appear again in our Sunday uniform. While it was very hot outside, the stench inside was almost unbearable. We took advantage coming out and opened the windows wide. To our surprise, we found in the courtyard besides our guards a whole company of the garrison with their red cap and a commanding officer. Now the French used new tactics. The names of each man of the first working troop were called over and everyone had to stand at attention. The French interpreter read three times the following articles of war: anyone, who commits rebellion in a country at war, will be punished with five to ten years of hard labor, even with the death penalty. The German sergeant major gave the surprising order "*Im Gleichschrittmarch*" (to march). We all couldn't conceal our rage and shame. The same order came from the second troop, however, nobody budged. We breathed again with relief that the situation was saved. The first group had come back after refusing to work at their place. The second troop was meanwhile surrounded by the soldiers of the garrison. The same procedure was followed by the third group; all stayed put. Then the loud command, "attention," rang over the place. Again the articles of war were read three times. The camp leader called, "anyone who wants to work step forward," but all PGs [refused]. The order followed: "group leaders bring the men back to the barracks." Lying on our beds when at 5 p.m. the "coal commando" had to step out to go to the night shift. The French had hoped to persuade

[48] The chateau was a gloomy edifice from the time of Napoleon Bonaparte with a dark and dank subterranean prison.

this group [by] promising them plenty [of] food; however, they stood firm. As a consequence, the whole troop in groups of ten men were put in prison. At ten o'clock in the evening we were informed that the colonel had sent a telegram to give us neither bread nor water—what was anyhow done all day. Then the work schedule for the next day was made known with a promise that all questions would be solved satisfactorily once we started working.

May 3. In the morning we assembled again for the roll call, most of us in uniform. The thirty-five hour fast had unfortunately a bad effect on the younger among us and had made them waver. Knowing the state of mind and the psychology of PGs, the French had the clever idea of bringing large sacks filled with bread to the courtyard. The first group was marched in front of the sacks. The French held a loaf of bread under each PGs nose; the young ones couldn't resist the temptation. They grabbed the bread and the strike was over. It was as funny as it was sad. Everything was lost; we had to accept the commander's promises. Shamefully, we had to leave the thirty-three prisoners jailed in the chateau to their fate. Concerning our complaints, the commander explained to us that he had no more control over them; they were now under the jurisdiction of the admiral, the commander of the whole fortress. The strike with the resulting hunger had us all physically quite affected, due also to [us having been] locked inside the barracks with one hundred men in each one, their low ceilings, and the foul air from the provisional toilet and the heat. . . . If the strike didn't give us material success, it gave us an augmented self-conscience, teaching us that when we stick together, they can't cower us. . . .

Sunday, May 5. I had the pleasure to work at the port while the people—in the majority female—promenaded in their Sunday finery and watched us working. We were busy in our dirty work clothes, loading rusty iron from a burnt out ship on sloops. On such a sunny Sunday the captivity weighed very heavily on one's shoulder. Outside of the port our proud German boat *Vaterland* was anchored, filled with American soldiers. The sight gave us a sense of melancholy. For several weeks all PGs coming from or going to work were bodily searched. . . .

When I came back from nightshift on the morning of June 6, 1918, I was welcomed with shouts from all sides: "*Du kommst morgen früh auf Land Kommando*" (You are going tomorrow morning to a commando in the country). Nobody was happier than I. Weeks before I had applied for such a transfer to get out of the camp atmosphere. At the same time there must have been pressure put on the Red Cross from home to intervene. . . .

June 7, 1918. Accompanied by a guard, I boarded a train at 7:00 a.m. on a narrow gauge railway to Plabennec, a rather good size village, the fourth stop from Brest. I arrived at 8:00 a.m. and trotted with my guard to our quarters in the middle of the village opposite the church. Our sleeping place, the former ballroom of the village, built on top of stables, made a friendly and clean impression with its large windows. Naturally, all comrades were out at work. I counted twenty-eight beds made by the prisoners themselves from cudgels. The guards slept in the same room, separated by a partition of canvas used for the carriages. Hardly had I arranged my belongings and lay down on the plank bed when I fell into a deep sleep, at which not even the constant hammering of the forge below the ballroom disturbed my sleep. In the last forty-eight hours I had slept only six hours during the last night; sleeping in the daytime didn't replace the night sleep. At 12:30 the guard brought me my lunch, the inevitable French national dish "*pain soupe,*" a brown weak broth with "*pain blanc*" and a plate with an omelet, a long missed dish which I got thanks to the meatless Friday of the Catholic religion. In addition, I got a large piece of "*pain blanc,*" white bread. After lunch I continued my sleep till four o'clock. In the evening the new comrades with four guards came back from work.

June 8 was my first working day. We were awakened at 5:45 and departed at 6:45 without breakfast, which was supplied by the farmers. I went with a comrade, a farmer by occupation, to a "*ferme*"[49] at a distance of seven kilometers. The landscape of this part of France has a character all of its own. Each field was enclosed by an earthen mound as high as a man, grown over with broom shrub, blackberry and hazel bushes, which had a double purpose—to give the necessary firewood in summer and winter and to prevent cattle [and] horses, which were roaming on all the roads, from entering the fields. The landscape must also have formed the character of the inhabitants—very conservative, very religious and superstitious. It was if time for the last two centuries had stopped in Brittany (as we found out later). "*Les Bretons*" are of Celtic origin, related to the Irish and speak a sort of an ancient Gaelic language. They are very backward. . . .

When we arrived at the farm we got for breakfast coffee with milk in large bowls (the size of four normal cups), white bread in unlimited quantities and butter. After the breakfast we went, armed with a utensil for weeding, to the field . . . one plot planted with potatoes and one with turnips. While the younger daughter helped us in the morning in which she used very suggestive expressions in French as well as in Breton, the older came at times in the afternoon, but her talks were even far more suggestive. We got the impression we could have had anything for the asking, but the filth and ugliness didn't arouse any desire in us. . . .

At 11:30 we had lunch, the Breton national dish "*farz,*" a solid mass of buckwheat, which was cooked for several hours in hot water in a small linen bag and tasted very good. As an addition, we got roasted bacon. After lunch back to the field till seven. At four there was a break of coffee and bread. For supper we ate little cakes made from fowls and butter sauce. We met comrades from the various farms and arrived usually at 8:30 in our quarters. Striking was the wealth of horses the farms had. In our farm they had four horses, two fowls, two fillies, a dozen cows, but only two pigs.

June 9 was a Sunday, which resembled more or less all other ones. We woke up at 7:00, washed and drank coffee. . . . The washing, like on every weekday morning, was done with great difficulty. It took place in the courtyard or the horse stable with two or three pails and the same amount of tin dishes for the whole thirty prisoners. From an open draw well, we had to wind up mangle on which two pails hung on a chain. When there was little rain, the water was so scarce that we were forced to use the

[49] farmhouse

same dirty water for five or six people. At times we wound up in our pails with other rubbish and dead rats. It didn't deter us from our body washing. . . . On Sundays the village baker brought us the bread, four hundred grams for each prisoner for which the farmers had to pay. . . . If we wanted butter or other supplements to our bread we had to buy it ourselves. The first thing we did after breakfast was to take our blankets to the courtyard, put them on a clothesline and hunted for fleas. . . . After this we went to the brook pool of the village and did our washing. After a while I made a deal with a comrade, who did my washing for a few centimes, so I was exempted from this chore. The comrades, who made the morning coffee, took care of our dinner of potatoes, meat and gravy. As our Sunday dinner was always the same, the two became real experts in preparing it. We other PGs took turns in peeling the potatoes in the morning. In the evening everybody prepared his own food. The farmers were so greedy that we were forced to buy our own firewood, the bundle at forty centimes. My first try for my own supper was fried potatoes with roast pork. . . . The Sunday afternoons we passed with reading, writing or dreaming, lying on our beds. . . .

June 10. I was sent to a clean, better-kept farm. We worked in the field with several women, all barefoot. On this occasion I learned how deeply the church influenced the daily life of the farmers. One of the women, in her early thirties, for once clean and pretty, whose husband was at the front, mentioned how the curé[50] in a sermon a few weeks ago told his flock their patriotic duty dictated that they shouldn't have intercourse more than once in two weeks. It was unbelievable how primitive and backward these Breton farmers were. One comrade told us when he arrived at the farms two years ago, they didn't even have spoons. In the meantime we had spoons but not plates. For dinner the bowls served as plates, the tables naturally had no covers. For one dish we didn't even need bowl: buckwheat. This fare was placed in the blackened pot; it was cooked in the middle of the table and the whole family, including we PGs, helped ourselves by grabbing one spoonful after another. Our fare in the various farms was mostly either a bread soup or galettes (a kind of pancake), sometimes crêpe (think flour cake) or for a change (not too often) potatoes with meat or lard. For drink we got skimmed milk, from which I usually got diarrhea. Friday was a strictly meatless day. . . . Toilets were unknown. Any place in God's free earth was used to relieve nature.

Usually, we thirty prisoners left without any escort in the early morning for the forty-three farms, which were located a distance from four to eight kilometers, some at remote and lonely places. We arrived between 6:30 and 7:15. Our work was to weed the fields, to cut clover for feeding the cattle, to plough, etc. The most toilsome work was weeding, because we had to creep all day long on our knees. Before every dinner we had to water the horses, a job I was well acquainted with in my early youth. One of the most hilarious episodes happened to me one early morning. It could have ended in disaster. Before breakfast we were sent out to the field with horse and cart to mow clover for the cattle. For the other guys, experienced farmers from home, the mowing with the scythe was a normal chore, but I had no

[50] parish priest

idea. So I was assigned to watch the horse in the cart. When we were alone in the field, we always had long conversations. In order to join in these, I led the horse to the other side of the field in the middle of clover and grass to keep him content. All of a sudden my horse, a young gelding not three years old, started to urinate. His long genital organ must have touched one of the prickly stinging blades. He got frightened and before we noticed it, he disappeared in a gallop with his cart from the field. I ran after him but was unable to see him anymore, even less to catch him. Resigned that something unpleasant had happened, I arrived breathlessly at the farm and was relieved when I saw the steward had caught the horse and had quieted him down. For me it was always a wonder how the horse had found the right farm among the cluster of them in this hamlet. . . .

August 15 was a holiday. Because good drinking water was scarce, we suffered quite a bit from thirst. The time of threshing the corn, the heaviest and most tiring work of all, had come. Every farmer had postponed this work till he had us PGs for help. To give us more strength and as a compensation, they served us wine. . . . we all were happy when the season around August 25 came to an end. . . .

September 6. It is the first day of Rosh Hashonah.[51] My thoughts threaten to overwhelm me. What a contrast to my prewar life! I took out my secret notebook and started reading about the many occurrences since my capture, not a pleasant reading. To the physical pains and sufferings was lately added the terrible mental strain by reading the newspapers about our German reverses in the field. My comrades were almost exclusively workers or farmers by occupation, [and] therefore not susceptible to intellectual talks. . . .

September 7. [T]he second day of Rosh Hashonah. The hunger forced me to work again today (in the last twenty-four hours I hadn't eaten anything). It was one of those days when I was in a gloomy mood. . . .

Yom Kippur,[52] September 14, a Saturday saw me again doing heavy work. My head was heavy from all crazy and bizarre thinking on this day, accentuated even more by the fine rain coming down in the afternoon. . . .

September 15. For the last eight days one of our French guards was very sick with the "Spanish Grippe,"[53] high fever, headache and blood spitting. The day before two of my comrades also became sick.

September 16. I already felt a headache, nevertheless, I went, like the other comrades[,] to work which was cutting hedges with the sickle while a drizzling rain came down all day long. The more the day advanced, the more I felt miserable. When we arrived in the evening . . . , nine of my comrades came down with the grippe and four more the next day.

[51] the Jewish New Year

[52] Day of Atonement; day on which Jews fast and pray to atone for their sins during the previous year.

[53] The Spanish flu pandemic of 1918–19 killed more people than the campaigns of World War I. See Anne Rasmussen, "The Spanish Flu," in Winter, *First World War*, vol. III, 334–357.

September 17. It caught up with me; extremely high fever 39.8,[54] then 39.5 and last 40.2. I was in a mood where I didn't care anymore about living.

September 18. The fever went down to 38, but my bed was dripping wet from sweating, my bones were aching all over. Because we didn't get anything to eat before the doctor had arrived and examined us, we hungered already for the third day. The ones ... who felt stronger by now demanded that we get at least some milk. Thereupon everyone got:

1½ cups of hot milk ... as the only nourishment for the day. Finally in the evening the doctor came, prescribed two to three days rest. ...

For the last six weeks there was jubilation in all French newspapers over the coming victory. Our discouragement, which grew from day to day, was at its lowest ebb. For me it was an unbelievable mental torture. ...

September 19. [T]he day before a telegram had arrived from Brest that we had to supply—starting today—ten men for a transport of two hundred men to the South. In spite of our sickness we all reported voluntarily. I felt better but still had a bad cough, sore throat and headache. Luckily I was chosen with nine others, so we could say goodbye to Plabennec at 5:30 in the afternoon. My pains at this moment didn't count anymore. When we arrived in Brest, the first thing was the usual search of our belongings, which we had to hand over for this purpose. As soon as this was done the joyful greetings with the old comrades started. Through the common sufferings, a firm feeling of comradeship had naturally developed in the course of time. ...

September 20. [A]t 2:15 in the afternoon we left Brest. ... When we arrived in the afternoon at La Rochelle, our guards were replaced with another detachment. The station was crowded with American soldiers, nearby was a huge American machine shop. ... Passing through a few more cities, among them Rochefort, we finally arrived September 22 at four in the morning at the large main railroad station of Bordeaux. With our belongings on our back we marched past the port through the silent, sleepy city to the main cantonment of the P.G.s, St. Louis, a distance of seven kilometers. When they refused to take us in, we marched back to a small, old and very narrow barrack in the middle of the city, where we arrived at 7 a.m. These barracks, with a small courtyard and surrounded by high walls, served at the same time as a jail of the P.G.s of Bordeaux and transit camp for other P.G.s. Because we received by our departure 1½ bread for three days (that meant we had no other claims for those days), we didn't get any warm meal on this day.

The next day, September 23, the "wine commandos" were formed in troops from five to twenty men. In pouring rain our troop of twenty men marched at noon to the station, an hour's distance. Wet to the bones and surrounded immediately by curious citizens, we boarded a train in the direction of Charbon-Blanc St. Eulalie. Upon our arrival we were divided up to go to three estates. I went with six comrades to the chateau Malbec.[55] ... Here also Americans were seen all over. At the chateau, in the middle of a large park, we were welcomed by a gentleman in his fifties, one

[54] roughly 104 degrees Fahrenheit
[55] a chateau in the wine-growing Bordeaux region

of the owners. . . . After that we received palliasses, which were filled with dry rush (reed). A miserable hut in the vicinity of old houses in which the employees lived and about two minutes walk from the chateau was assigned to us as "residence." Our "room" in the old shed looked more like a hole than a room for human beings and served as a depository for fire and brushwood. Close by they piled up bundles of brushwood we put down our palliasses on the . . . loamy soil and set about improving our bed with a white linen sheet and two sleeping bags. . . . I explained to the people that we were very hungry since we didn't have a warm meal in three days. Thereupon they gave us bread and wine and . . . promised to compensate us in the evening. With our bread we could pick and eat as many grapes as we wanted. As far as the eye could see there was nothing but vineyards with juicy ripe grapes. In the evening we received a perfect meal of bouillion soup, cutlets, potatoes, wine, bread, etc.

Two days later, September 25, twenty civilians, men, women and children "*les vendangeurs*"[56] arrived from Bordeaux. Right away the real grape gathering started. Our work consisted of picking and putting one day the grapes into small baskets and the next day to fill the baskets into barrels. Then two P.G.s had to carry the barrel to a waiting wagon from where they could be transported to the chateau. This kind of work went on for days, from morning 8:30 till noon and from 1:30 till 6. The cooking was done by two female cooks, very tasty and clean, but the portions were not meant for P.G.s' hungry stomachs, so we always asked for more. For breakfast we got white bread and two oil sardines or some liver paste. As a substitute for coffee we received "pignette," a drink made of the rest of squeezed grapes with an addition of plenty of water. . . . Our meals at noon as well as in the evening were excellent: bouillon soup, meat (prepared in different ways), potatoes or vegetables and for every man and day a bottle of wine. While working, we ate all day long grapes, which I relished very much. It was a happy time, in fact the happiest in all my captivity (so far as it goes, speaking of happiness as a prisoner, everything is relative). Everyone was very nice to us. We had, of course, to work also on Sundays. As compensation, we had our washing done, normally Sunday work for us P.G.s. Here I was also officially designated by our commanding sergeant as the "*interprète*."[57] By now I spoke French quite well, understood the spoken and written words almost perfectly. Besides the peaches, there grew on trees delicious figs in the vineyard, which we were allowed to pick and eat as an addition to our diet, as much as we wanted. . . .

The second day one of our comrades came down with the grippe. We, who had experienced this sickness before, cared for him as much as we could, brought him every day bouillon soup. From the chateau they had sent for the civilian doctor, but on my urgent request the owner called up the camp at Bordeaux to have our comrade taken to the hospital. Soon afterwards an American officer with a medic appeared and told me he had heard that one of our comrades was sick and needed nursing care. They intended to take our friend to the nearby American military hospital. I explained the fact of the case and thanked him very much in the name

[56] grape pickers
[57] interpreter

of my comrades. This noble and selfless act of the Americans made an unforgettable impression on us, especially since they had nothing to do with us prisoners. . . .

When it became known, October 8, that we had to move the next day to another place, I was invited the evening before by the owner to come to the chateau to get our pay. We received for our work thirty centimes a day. The old chateau was furnished in an exquisite taste. The owner was a very fine, cultured man, a perfect gentleman of the older generation. I was offered mocha, fine white wine, cognac and cigarettes. I had a conversation with him for more than an hour, and he seemed to enjoy it. We talked about everything under the sun, among others, about my private life, but no word about politics. For me it was as if I was by magic transformed to prewar life and my own self again.

In the morning of October 9[,] the time had come to take leave. The whole female personnel was assembled. Some had tears in their eyes. With our behavior we had succeeded to gain popularity and their affection. The owner had placed horse and wagon at our disposal, and we were driven part of the way. The rest [of the way] to our destination we walked about five kilometers, accompanied by a guard. It was the estate of the brothers Dubosq at Yvrac, one of the biggest properties in the whole country, about 150 "Morgen."[58] One of the brothers spoke German fluently almost without a trace of an accent. To sell his wines he traveled before the war widely—six months of every year—in Germany, mostly in the East around Königsberg.

For the last two years six prisoners worked steadily on the estate. Immediately after our arrival we had to start working. We were twenty-one P.G.s with one hundred civilians, men, women and children, of whom about half were sick with the Spanish Grippe. These "*vendangeurs*" originated to a great part from the Spanish frontier. For the first eight days I worked with some comrades in the wine press room, while the others were sent to the vineyard to pick the grapes. Besides us[,] three Annamites worked on the estate and lived in the same building with us, separated only through a board partition. In the first days three or four comrades came down with the Grippe. A young girl from Alsace, who was on the estate, nursed them in an exemplary manner. When we were alone, she spoke to us in German, . . . deeply appreciated by us, to talk after such a long time with a female in our mother tongue. She told us about her "via dolorosa," her sufferings during the war. Surprised by the war, she had come to France shortly before the war broke out. She had no possibility anymore to go back to her family. Considered with suspicion as a German, she was under police supervision and had to report daily at the police station. She was an unusually pretty girl whose serious manners and cordial conduct with us, as a result of the same sufferings, made a deep impression on me. . . .

More and more gloom was spreading among us by the news of the French papers about the war. It seemed Germany was heading for defeat. Out of desperation we got drunk in the winepress room almost everyday. In this state we were able to forget all worries. The wine was black red like thickened blood, heavy and intoxicating. . . .

[58] about 90 acres

October 20. Most of the "*vendangeurs*" started to prepare for the next day's departure. A melancholic mood overcame us as the good times came to an end. . . .

We were supposed to go back to our cantonement the next day, October 27, so we had for the first time after five weeks a day off. For the last time I walked through the familiar vineyards to pick to my heart's desire figs, chestnuts and grapes. . . . The *regisseur*[59] had given us P.G.s as a farewell for tonight . . . a mug with . . . wine. Lying on our straw bed in the attic by candlelight, we seven got so drunk out of grief about our leaving and the long captivity, we couldn't get up anymore from our bed.

The next day we marched at 7:16 in the foggy morning to the railroad station Charbon-Blanc. . . . It was 9:30 when we arrived at our camp Bordeaux-Bastide. An intensive search of our belongings started immediately, so thoroughly as I never was subjected to before. The camp made a very dirty impression and the management seemed to be very strict with the P.G.s. We were assigned to the barracks of the Austrians. The palliasses we received were filthy and the straw in them was not replaced since the beginning of the war. My neighbor, a Hungarian, told me during the day of the many instances of bad treatment on the part of the French and their relentless pressure against Yugoslavs. For the last two months fifty of them languished in prison because they had refused to load ammunition. . . . A very interesting light about the treatment of the P.G.s was revealed on the notice board: P.G. X was sentenced to one year prison for ordinary theft, P.G. Y sentenced to five years confinement in a fortress for . . . escaping, P.G. Z to sixty days close confinement for joint escape.

October 28 is for us a day of rest, no work. With a heavy heart I thought back to the relative liberty and the exquisite wine of our command in the wine country. The past night was . . . very painful. The many fleas tormented me relentlessly. My nostalgia for the wine country became even more accented since it was the only flealess time of my captivity.

Arriving at the main railroad station in Bordeaux at 12:30 on October 29, after leaving our camp one hour earlier, we had long conversations with the many American soldiers around till our train departed at 2 p.m. in the direction of Bajonne (not far from the Spanish frontier). . . . Around four we arrived at a small station, Dehoux, where we stopped till 6:15 and changed to a narrow gauge railroad. During this time I had a stimulating conversation with our French sergeant, a young man from Angulême, gravely wounded in the war. In civilian life he was a salesman for a French company traveling extensively in Africa, Cameroon (A German colony), Duala etc., but didn't speak German.

People we met on this trip weren't as fanatic as the one in the North, naturally the word *des Boches* we heard here too. Soon the night descended. Everybody was brooding and melancholic, ... sitting in our compartment without any light. The familiar German trait came to the fore to sing our sad and nostalgic folksongs into the silent night. A quarter to nine we arrived at our destination. In the darkness we discerned some airplane hangars; the environ seemed to be desert, nothing but sand, sand, sand. In the distance a faint ray of light was visible, our future camp ... [which] consisted of

[59] director

low tents. We got very excited and angry and I was chosen as the interpreter to bring our complaints before the commander of the camp, an adjutant. He insisted that we had to sleep in the tents and refused to give us some meal, whereupon I had a sharp discussion with him. As we balked at his order, he alarmed the guard. With loaded rifles they drove us into the ... poorly lighted tents. ... We lay down on the naked cold floor. As a pillow we used our little belongings and for cover the tiny, thin blanket everybody owned. For a long time I lay down wide awake. The mighty roar of the nearby ocean, a distance of about one hundred fifty meters, robbed me of my sleep. Separated by a dune from the ocean, which was therefore not visible, our tents were erected at the base of the dune. After a brief sleep, the penetrating cold, besides the roar of the sea, prevented me from falling asleep again. At six the next morning we were awakened. In the daylight we saw some wooden barracks with prisoners nearby in the woods. After roll call we received a plank bed and a palliasse, some bread and rice soup. By chance I met Silberberg and Seligmann, with whom I was in the prison in Chalons and on the island. Silberberg worked in the kitchen and Seligmann was an interpreter. I was assigned to the office. We were in the middle of a large airfield. The fliers fascinated us with their going up in the airplanes and exercise in nose diving in the early morning. The name of the closest village was Biscarrosse. Its location was ninety kilometers from Bordeaux and one hundred twenty from the Spanish border. The ocean here is called the Gulf of Biscay, the stormiest sea of the whole French coast.

October 31. The cold prevented me again from sleeping. During the daytime the temperature is quite mild, but in the morning and evening it is very cold. At the "fall in" this morning, one group of P.G.s went on strike, because they worked already for ten days without a day off. To force them to yield, the French ordered them alternatively to stay at attention and stand at ease between 6:25 and 8:00 but the P.G.s didn't move. Finally, the French gave in and granted [them] the day off.

November 1, 1918. Besides the bitter cold we had to cope with the many fleas in the sand, which tormented us. Tonight I was chosen by the 125 new P.G.s as the speaker and trustee and delegated into the committee of five prisoners, which represented the interests of the P.G.s vis-à-vis the Frenchmen. . . . Immediately, I was urged to lay before the sergeant several demands, in this case as a spokesman for all prisoners.

On November 3, a Sunday, a pouring rain was falling all day. Completely cut off from the world in this desolate country, we all felt very lonesome.

November 5. Everybody is waiting for the news of the impending armistice and consequently peace. To improve one's diet the P.G.s here are toasting their bread in a pan. They buy the necessary fat from the guards at one franc a pound. The fat was for the most part "flotsam" and hurled ashore in barrels and cases by the raging sea. . . .

November 6 was my first workday; earth leveling, very monotonous and boring. They intend to build a huge airfield out of the existing one. For the first time I saw the ocean; it made a big impression on me.

November 10. Today—Sunday—is our day of rest. It has lately become my habit in the evening, on the request of my comrades who were all grouped around me and eagerly listening, to read and translate the French newspapers to them. Today's news about the collapse of Germany, of the harsh armistice terms depressed up as never before and overwhelmed us with grief. For such an end of the war we had fought and suffered so much for such a long time. . . .

November 11, 1918. Work again. In the afternoon the French captain arrived on horseback and informed us that the armistice has been signed by us. We all listen without any outward emotion. We were content that finally the day of our deliverance from captivity had come. *C'est tout!*[60] On the way back to the camp, the French airmen and mechanics shouted at us [that] the war is over. While they [were] . . . delirious with joy, we felt like crying, like running a gauntlet. Soon we heard singing the Marseillaise and noisy demonstrations outside our tents. In the night a couple of French officers, completely drunk, entered our tents. The angry comrades threw them. . . out.

November 12. Today there were no French fliers in the air, not any French soldiers or Annamites at work, the only ones working were we prisoners. The victorious air in the French faces was almost unbearable to us. In the afternoon the French sergeant picked up the newspaper and lent it to me. Reading to my anxiously listening comrades in a circle around me—the bad news. I hardly could speak in my excitement and barely hold the paper in my hands. In the evening nobody found sleep out of grief and sorrow. Till deep in the night we were discussing the events.

November 13. The Frenchmen are still celebrating. The papers in Paris and London are delirious with joy.

November 19. It was so cold last night that I couldn't sleep anymore after two o'clock. In the morning the ground was white with frost. In this temperature we were forced to sleep in a tent with only one blanket. On our complaint we were told a request for additional blankets was sent out. Now after the signing of the armistice, we felt we were completely at the mercy of the French. Immediately, they didn't recognize anymore the Treaty of Bern, regulating the treatment of P.G.s. The first thing they did was shortening the ration of rice by five kilos and beans by twelve kilos from the amount we were entitled according to the reciprocal treaty. To us, the committee, they advised maliciously [to] direct your complaints to the Swiss embassy with the threat: anybody who is in the possession of the list of calories, to which we are entitled, will be punished. This order came from Bordeaux. In the evening we swapped occurrences and stories during our captivity. One comrade told us [that] on his command "*pour le vendange*"[61] in the Gironde, one P.G. from Schleswig-Holstein, twenty-five years old, committed suicide with the rifle of the guard when called to account for his absence from camp the night before until five in the morning. The reason was a serious love affair he had with the daughter of the wealthy owner of the estate. . . .

November 21. Finally we moved into wooden barracks in the woods after the nightly cold was almost unbearable. We still had only one blanket and no stove.

[60] that's all
[61] for the harvest

A sack, which a comrade had lent to me and in which I put my feet and legs during my sleep, alleviated the terrible cold a bit.

November 26. Thanks to real beds everybody had built from the simple planks and little tables between two beds, our barrack is now more habitable. To have more light, we also had made little lamps from German vegetable cans. Gasoline was plentiful here. The cold had lessened but for the last six days it was raining, raining.

December 4. Although the mornings and nights are still cold, at noon it became comfortably warm like springtime. Grass seed, sowed weeks ago on the "plaine" is sprouting all over.

December 6. On the way to work at midday we were sweating. I noticed roses in full bloom. Two days ago we were supplied with stoves.

December 15. We are now 380 prisoners with fifty new ones who came today. Some of these were made prisoners November 15, four days after the armistice. All are full of lice. Some of the fifty were captured July 18. Theirs was to tell a sad story. For thirty-two days they had to live in the open behind barbed wires as a reprisal, because we had supposedly kept French prisoners for eight days in the open in St. Quentin. In reality, as I heard, it was only for four days and not in the open but in cellars. As food, our prisoners—7000 in all—received only water and four biscuits a day. Everyday a Frenchman asked: "How many are kaput?" Many, many died. Among a few prisoners, who came here three weeks ago, I met Münch fron Münster in Westphalia, also from my regiment 16, who was captured with me and was likewise in the prison in Châlons. He was the one who was severely clubbed in the prison. Twenty-five of the fifty new arrivals were sleeping for almost eight days without a blanket.

December 18. Since the first of the month I am officially the "*interprête*" with the "wood cutting commando." For the last eight days it is raining uninterruptedly. To get to our working place we had to march everyday four times five kilometers. Aggravated by the lack of a PX,[62] the specter of hunger appeared again as the French took off three hundred calories from every prisoners' daily food ration. Many comrades went in the evening to the Russian and Annamites' barracks to ask them for their leftover food. Some stole linseed oil, which the fliers used for gluing or painting the airplanes, and toasted bread in it.

December 23. My crew refused to work the afternoon in the pouring rain and I had, therefore, a heated argument with the captain, who threatened to put me in jail. With the argument [that] we had treated the French P.G.s in Germany the same way, they forced us to work. After the armistice, we unfortunately had no protection nor recourse to the Swiss embassy.

Back in the camp in the evening we got the news that a commando of one hundred P.G.s would be formed to leave the next day. On the top of the list the French selected the five members of the inconvenience committee. Three of our

[62] a commissary that sells food

committee swallowed their pride, bent their knees before the French and begged to stay. I would have rather suffered the worst misery before taking such a humiliating step. So the two of us with ninety-eight P.G.s were chosen.

December 24. Christmas Eve—we had the day off, as we are supposed to leave the next morning. We were in a wretched mood. The gray sky with heavy rains coming down intensified this feeling. Our anxious question, what will the near future bring us, stayed unanswered. Like gypsies, we have crisscrossed the country in all directions in the long years of our captivity, only they were free and we not. In honor of Christmas, the French had placed three tents at our disposal where our comrades gave a play and entertained in the evening. By 10 p.m. we went to bed.

December 25. We were awakened at 3:15, received warm water for coffee, our bread of 1000 grams for two days and a piece of liver cheese (kind of sausage). Assembled at 4:15, we departed at 6:15 in the pouring rain from the station Biscarrosse-Plage. After a stop at Ichoux from 8:15 till 11:00, we arrived in Bordeaux at 1 p.m. still in pouring rain. At 5:30 we re-boarded a train with compartments 3rd class for Chartres in the direction of Paris. Little by little darkness was descending, bringing with it a deep melancholy to all of us. While the train was traveling through the silent night, everybody was thinking of Christmas. A P.G. from Leipzig had in his possession a miniature Christmas tree with tiny candles, saved from last year. In such situations the typical German trait came to the fore—singing. Soon all were singing those melancholic folksongs and the ones expressing love to the native country. We kept singing till the candles burnt out. In the darkness—the train had no lights—extremely tired after the early morning wake up. The more aggravated by our grief and lulled by the monotonous rat-a-tat-tat of the turning wheels, we fell soon fast asleep. Awakened by daybreak the next morning—December 26—we saw the first winter landscape, fields white with frost but neatly tilled, trees bare of leafs, etc. . . . We crossed at 1:15 the Loire, which due to the ceaseless rain, had vastly overflowed its banks and arrived at Saumur, where I passed through for the second time in my captivity. It was the first time, more than 1½ years ago, on my way from Dijon to Nantes. . . . We frequently spoke to Frenchmen, freshly repatriated from German prisons and immediately discharged from the army. All were full of praise of the friendly attitude of the German civilians. We complained bitterly about just the opposite of the French population, what they already knew. Their complaint was the bad food and bad treatment on the part of the German officers and non-commissioned officers, besides the harsh discipline. It was 9 p.m. when we arrived at Chartres, shivering in the cold and longing for the warm south. We marched twenty minutes in ice and snow to the camp. At the campground we had to stand till 10:15 p.m. when the adjutant received us with the words "The rule here is stern discipline. We will teach you to run, when we give orders." As to confirm those threats, the same evening one of us was sent to prison because he kept his hands in his pocket. We were lodged in an icy cold new barrack with no stove, where we—about one hundred P.G.s—had to sleep on straw, thrown on the floor, most of us with only one blanket. Terribly freezing through the whole night, we were in addition tormented by the many fleas.

December 27. At 6 in the morning was roll call in the barrack. For breakfast we got ½ liter of coffee, but nothing to eat till noon. At 9 again roll call. An officer made the same speech about stern discipline here etc. Then everybody had to submit to a radical haircut. A demand for a second blanket or a shirt (our shirts were completely threadbare) was not even deemed worthy of any consideration. Our daily main meal at noon consisted of 200 grams wet black bread and half-liter soup of warm water in which a few little pieces of potatoes and turnips swam. After such a meal our hunger got worse. Twice or three times a week we got some horsemeat in our soup. Our mood in these days resembled the weather outside; the rain was steadily pouring from a gray sky. On the campground we sunk to our ankles in mud.

December 28. We received two stoves, but as firewood was very scarce, the heat was almost non-existent. . . .

December 29. Always fasting till noon, we got everyday the same menu. Today was inspection of our haircut, after which the adjutant looked at our hands for cleanliness. We couldn't suppress a smile that Frenchmen felt it necessary to look for cleanliness, to whom—according to our own experience—this notion was normally unknown. Yesterday I got a second—but only a half—blanket. Our camp was built only six weeks ago, so everyday new prisoners arrived. At the moment we are 1300. According to a notice at the board, the P.G. who was sent to prison the first day of our arrival (reason: "he didn't take his hands out of his pocket when speaking to a German sergeant") got six days close confinement and four days simple prison. Although I became fairly used to being hungry during my long captivity, I never felt as much hunger since Châlons. Since September I was not able to get out my money [that] they kept in deposit to buy some food at the existing PX here. Many a P.G. was sighing: "It is good our folks at home don't know under what terrible conditions we live here." I talked to some prisoners here who had been in prison. One of them got twenty-four days for stealing a few potatoes. Contrary to the reciprocal agreement, according to which every P.G. in jail is entitled to a warm meal every fourth day, this P.G. got nothing but bread and water in all those twenty-four days. No wonder P.G.s, who had been in prison, looked pitiful, nothing but skin and bones.

On New Year's Eve—*December 31, 1918*—there was some entertainment, music and comic songs, performed by our groups and one P.G. made a speech. Nothing could revive our spirit so we went to bed as usual every evening with an empty stomach.

On New Year—*January 1, 1919*—we got a half-liter substitute coffee before roll call at 7:15, then, in order to suppress our feeling of hunger, we lay in bed till 9, as this was a transient camp with no work done. In honor of New Year there was a theater performance in the evening but only for us "old prisoners." Every P.G. received today two spoonfuls of cocoa from the Red Cross. A few days ago distribution started of supposedly 4700 packages from the Red Cross.

January 2, 1919. From today our daily bread ration was reduced to 300 grams. While the food was getting less and less, the discipline was getting sterner, at which the French favored in a disagreeable way the German non-commissioned officers.

January 3. It's raining, raining. I feel very unhappy among the present new prisoners, a lot of riff-raff, mostly captured recently.

January 4. Everybody got a Christmas package from Barcelona at a value of ten to twelve francs. The content of my package was: one bar of chocolate, one can with cut green beans, one can with oil sardines, one bag each hazelnuts, figs and dried grapes. We were overjoyed to be able to eat a little bit better than usual.

On Sunday, January 5, at the roll call, we had to dress in our uniform and army coat to make sure everybody has imprinted P.G. on his cloth, and this after the armistice. It rains, rains, rains. According to the newspapers, all rivers in the country are overflowing their banks. By turns we had to peel potatoes and turnips. Every time a French sergeant was present and watched that nobody let disappear in his mouth perhaps a little piece of turnip. Nevertheless, watching every movement of the sergeant, we managed to shove furtively a bite in our mouths. . . .

The day of January 15 had an overcast sky. A week ago it came as a great shock to me to find again lice all over my body, a consequence of us old prisoners lying together on the straw with the lice infested freshly arrived ones. I am despairing of God and humanity. Hunger hurts severely. Many P.G.s were asking in vain for voluntary work. The most disgusting scenes took place at the distributing of the daily fare, endless quarreling and disputes, which never happened before. Everybody was watching that the other guy didn't get a spoonful more soup.

January 16. I observed that by the smallest exercise, bending down and going up, the old dizziness, dreaded and so often experienced in the prison at Châlons, came to the fore again. Due to the malnutrition, we all couldn't keep warm; we were always freezing. Underlying this situation was the lack of firewood to heat the two stoves in our barrack. Up to now we managed to steal some wooden planks but this source was stopped. The terrible hunger demoralized our men completely. The spread of vermin and to have to live among these depraved new P.G.s produced in me an increasing gloomy and desperate frame of mind.

January 17. After exactly four months I was happily able to take out of deposit some of my money. With it I bought margarine. Potatoes were also available but as we had no firewood for cooking, this . . . was useless.

January 21. Since I am in this camp I have almost every night terrible dreams, a consequence of the hard floor we are forced to sleep on, of the hunger and the cold. Many times I woke up and heard from all corners of the barrack frightful groaning and delirious loud cries of sleeping comrades, a sign that they were in the same state of mind as I was. One has to have a deep abiding faith and confidence in one's future to overcome these times.

January 23, 1919. Today we were divided into two "front companies" of 425 men each. My company is P.G. 193. What fate is waiting for us! As a belated Christmas present everybody got from the Red Cross Barcelona a fair-sized can with oil sardines.

January 24. Assembled at 8 a.m. we receive a palliasse and the usual morning coffee. Afterwards the rest of the morning was filled with distribution of our fare for three days: 1200 grams of bread, one and a half hard tack of biscuit, one piece of cooked horsemeat and a tint piece of cheese (the size of a lump of sugar). Furthermore, for every two men 300 grams corned beef and for every three men two cans of liver paste and one can of oil sardines.

At 12:15 we marched on the solid frozen road to the railroad station, glad to get out of this misery. Arrived at the station, we found out that our joy was premature. Instead of regular passenger we found those French cattle cars and instead of the normal forty men (or eight horses), we were squeezed into these icy cold cars—forty-five men to a car—which were then sealed from the outside. We departed at 2:45, destination Reims. . . .

From now on we were traveling along the Marne, where for four years the battles raged back and forth, bringing with them gruesome destruction. The villages, with their houses completely or partly destroyed . . . abandoned by their inhabitants, the surrounding field with numerous and large shell craters, uncultivated, all this made a desolate impression. . . . On this whole trip we were evenings and nights without light. To banish the brooding mood during these dark evenings, some started to sing, others fell in and usually succeeded in lifting the pessimistic general feeling. We were told we would arrive in Reims by 10 o'clock this same evening, which proved true, but were kept in the closed cars till 7:30 the next morning. This last night was endlessly long; nobody could sleep on account of the cold and the little space. (These nights in the cars we had to sleep in a sitting position; there was not enough room to lie down.) Dawn was, therefore, greeted with great joy. . . .

January 26, 1919. At 8:30 we left the railroad station and marched three kilometers to an old broken down barracks. The city streets were already cleared of rubble but the sight of so much destruction saddened me. Beautiful houses and churches, the work and genius of generations, lay in ruins. . . .

January 27, 1919. Outside the ground is covered with heavy snow, the city looks even more desolate under the wintry sky and the cold is almost unbearable. One of the sentries told me Reims had a population of 120,000 before the war, now 3 to 4000 had drifted back. From the 17,000 buildings only very, very few had been unscathed. Everyday old residents were coming back but seeing their ruined houses leave immediately again.

January 28. The leader of our company went to the French lieutenant complaining about the miserable quarters they had given "us old prisoners." The lieutenant, who himself had been in German captivity, got immediately in communication with the commanding general of Reims. As a result the lycée [school] for girls, in the middle of the city, was assigned as our lodging. At 9:30 we were on our way through the silent dead city and at 2 p.m. we were placed in a large hall located in the basement of the lycée. . . . As guards we had mostly very young recruits, who hadn't fought in the war yet, although they wore steel helmets. The guard of the city was entrusted to Arabs. . . .

January 29. We were still without work. In spite of ice and snow and without the necessary food provisions, two comrades escaped last night.

January 30. At 7 a.m. we marched across the dead city to a meeting place for the several groups of P.G.s, where work was assigned to each group. I was appointed as an interpreter. On our way we passed the cathedral, theater, palais de justice etc. It always made a deep impression on me to see this senseless destruction. My group had to fill up the trenches from the war and cut the barbed wires in the northeast of the city near Vitry les Reims. In the bunkers we found pianos and all sorts of furniture, which had been taken out of the city houses. The two escaped prisoners were unfortunately already caught in the morning and sentenced to thirty days in prison. From now on work started at 7 a.m. till 11 and from 1 p.m. to 4:30, leaving in the darkness and coming home in the darkness. Our fare is 600 grams good white bread and in the morning a half-liter coffee with sugar (ten grams to a person) and one liter rice or potato soup each for lunch and evening, but the hygienic conditions were still miserable.

February 1. As an interpreter I had many conversations with our guards. They told me the restoration of the cathedral would cost approximately twenty-two million francs, a staggering sum, also that 20,000 prisoners would be brought to Reims to work here and the surroundings. New P.G. companies are arriving already daily. Those comrades who work here for the civilians are full of praise and surprised about the decent treatment they experienced on the part of the civilians, something unusual in France. It was not so surprising when they heard [that] these people had known misery during the war as much as we P.G.s. They got from the civilians in the morning and also evenings bread, cheese, wine and cigarettes. A daily recurrence are these American soldiers (marine corps) moving around in the battle zone, looking for "German souvenirs." They even come to our quarters to buy things. A few days ago they gave a guard 250 francs for a German army revolver.

February 3. Since the first of the month the train connection between Châlons and Reims was restored and civilians are arriving in greater numbers. Today I went with a group as interpreter to the freight yard in the west of the city. This part was quite intact and the streets more crowded.

In a conversation with a sergeant I was reminded that today's date is February 4. I had completely forgotten that it was my birthday. In the afternoon we had the opportunity to steal flour. As the food on this day was very bad, the soup, we made from the flour, was very welcome. Since I was the interpreter, I couldn't avoid it to sometimes have very lively disagreements of a political nature with the civil population. It happened so today when I had a very sharp discussion with the employer of my group, owner of a firm for building material. He showed such a hatred of the Germans and tried to convince me that the German character, the German feeling and thinking is different from all the other people on this earth. As proof he mentioned the indiscriminate bombardment of open cities, the Kaiser, the iron discipline, the invasion of Belgium, after a solemn promise, laid down in a binding treaty, to observe for all times its neutrality. During my captivity in lonely hours when I was brooding about the war, its causes, sufferings, etc., I had ample time to draw my own conclusions. Besides as a lifelong and avid reader of newspapers, I was well informed about world politics. In this way I could refute most accusations, but on the one, the breach of Belgium's neutrality, I had no answer. I sympathized with the man and understood his feelings when he told me that he was wounded three times during the war, once gassed, that in Reims alone nine hundred civilians had been killed and fifteen hundred wounded.

February 5. I went with a group to civilians, who treated us royally. We got two cups of mulled wine, two glasses of regular wine, sweetened coffee, white bread and sausage in the afternoon. They also treated us with a good snack. While the group worked, they talked with me all morning. These were people who had stayed in Reims during the whole war up to our offensive 1918. Among other things, they told me that in September 1914 the Cathedral was full of German wounded soldiers, about two hundred of them. . . . The Germans had occupied Reims from September 4 to 13 and were forced after the defeat at the Battle of the Marne and a precipitated retreat to leave these wounded behind. On September 27 our artillery shelled the cathedral with incendiary bombs. The cries of the helpless German soldiers had been so terrifying that many French women wept. The French succeeded in saving a few of the wounded, all others perished. Even after four years the memory of this tragedy lingered in their mind. I remembered the outcry all over the world in September 1914 when our army bombarded the cathedral (churches were hitherto considered inviolable). The German High Command gave us reason for bombarding the cathedral visible for miles around the countryside—that the French were using the towers as an observation point to direct their artillery.

February 8. I had again long and sharp discussions with fanatical Frenchmen.

February 12. For the last eight days I went with a group as interpreter to the firm of Werlé, Veuve Cliquot, one of the largest champagne firms of France.

On the morning of February 13 our company moved to buildings of Veuve Cliquot in the south of the city—a march of about four kilometers. Half of the company was quartered in the horse stable, the other half—with myself—in the attic above the stable. We painfully missed the warm basement in the lycée. In the daytime we built our guard beds with wood we procured in dismantling the bunkers in the trenches. Unable to sleep on account of the severe cold, the nights were again becoming unbearable. In order to prevent an escape of P.G.s, the Frenchmen had ordered to hand over all boots in the evening. As a substitute we received wooden shoes (sabots). Our quarter was directly under the tile roof with no ceiling between. In this way wind and cold got through the fissures with the consequence that everybody had to go to the bathroom only after one or two hours sleep. As we had to go down a stairway, the continuous ratting of the sabots made a further sleep impossible. Since the armistice we had no rights anymore, a complaint was therefore useless. . . .

February 16. Our food situation was getting bad again. Starting today our bread is of an inferior quality, especially baked for us P.G.s. As I didn't have news from home in more than a month and couldn't take out money from my deposit in more than three weeks, to alleviate hunger my frame of mind became from day to day more pessimistic. Since we are here we received neither light nor soap nor writing paper. Our daily food is 180 grams of rice, 115 grams horsemeat and 23 grams of fat.

February 27. Since February 18 we received no bread at all. As a poor substitute, we got daily 1½ to 2 biscuits. Luckily civilians gave me some bread. I also received two packages from my mother. We awaken nightly from the stamping and neighing of the twenty company stallions—heavy workhorses—which were placed some time ago in the stable below our quarters.

March 2. Today the clocks were advanced one hour to summertime. As so often during the war, food packages, sent to us from home, were handed over in a ruthless way, everything broken into small pieces, partly even made unsafe for eating. In a cold rage we have to accept this. . . .

March 5. The first spring weather. At such time everybody is thinking of escaping. . . .

March 6. The hunger forced us to bring anything edible to our barracks. . . .

March 21. Two more comrades escaped. For the first time since we are here, we received our pay (20 centimes a day). At the same time the PX was opened but we still didn't get our deposit money. . . .

The radiant sunshine on this Sunday, March 23, gave three of our comrades the opportunity to escape in the night.

March 24. The top French civilian "profiteer," whose business it was to distribute the P.G.s to the different jobs, [made] a fortune. . . . Two more comrades escaped this afternoon direct from their jobs. . . .

March 28. Today five men escaped, while two, who escaped a week ago, were brought back. These two poor "deserters" had to stand upright in a piercing north-east wind in rain and sleet all night in a sentry box, on orders of the company leader, a Catholic minister. The sentry box was enclosed by "Spanish riders"[63]—an escape impossible. In addition to thirty days prison they didn't get any food.

March 31. Three more "deserters," among them a sergeant, were brought back. They were caught near Longevy.

April 1. Our working hours are now from 6:30 till 11:00 and from 12:45 till 5:30. Instead of the twenty centimes, our pay is now forty centimes plus a premium. To stop the many escapes, an order came that nobody is allowed to step out of the barracks between 8:30 in the evening and 5:30 in the morning. I was designated as the interpreter with the "city commando" in the main street of Reims, rue de Vesle. It turned out to be a very interesting place for me.

April 2. Some of my observations on the rue de Vesle, which I saw quite often and which distressed me very much: two field gendarmes on horseback with two "*Boches*"—escaped prisoners—with hands chained to each other marching in front of them. The hands of the poor guys were blue from the cold.

A second picture: "*Boches*" as "dog catchers" with a lasso on the streets looking for dogs without a leash or muzzle. In order to catch the many stray dogs, commandos of P.G.s were formed, whose activities developed many times into the funniest

[63] a barbed-wire obstacle

and most hilarious situations. I often had talks with Alsatians, who, although living here since 1870, were treated during the whole duration of the war as "*étrangers*."[64] They had to report every other day, their passports were thoroughly scrutinized and traveling under a strict observation.

April 9. A few days ago a commando of ten P.G.s was formed with the task to defuse or blow up unexploded shells around the city, a dangerous assignment at which several comrades were already wounded. . . .

April 11. We hold the record among the P.G. companies in Reims with thirty-eight escaped. Eight comrades escaped today. . . .

April 19. A French colonel appeared in our camp. He made a speech telling us we didn't work hard enough, so we would be retained till everything is built up again and the stolen industrial machines returned. Therefore, it would be in our interest to work hard. We were stunned and irritated about such an impertinent language. . . .

April 22. Four P.G.s escaped successfully today but two were apprehended. . . . I envy the comrades who escaped, the more since I am fully convinced [that I am] in a better position than anybody else to make a successful escape. I speak the language almost without a trace of an accent and have the whole country map up to Germany in my head. . . . How many P.Gs. made it to Germany is another story. I guess many were apprehended before reaching the German frontier. Usually an escaped P.G. hid in the daytime, walked during the night and used, as often as possible, freight trains. . . .

April 25. The French threatened to send us to the "Fort de la Pompelle"[65] to live in tents if the flight of the P.G.s didn't stop. Our company 193 has the worst reputation of all companies in Reims, which we are no little proud of; up to now forty-six from our company fled. . . .

April 30, 1919. Today I am a prisoner for two years. . . .

May 9. Since a few days we have beautiful spring weather. I had a nice encounter with a very pretty German girl or rather young women, "au palais de Justice," where I was busy as interpreter. It lifted my spirits to talk with a female in my mother tongue after so many years (the last time was June 1916).[66]. . .

May 13, 1919. The champagne corks were popping; my whole commando got drunk, For the first time we worked in the cellars of the champagne house Carl Heidsick[67] [*sic*]. . . .

May 19. We are still working at Heidsick [*sic*] and enjoy the champagne, red wine and cognac, the more so, as we know, it was strictly forbidden. . . .

[64] strangers

[65] a fort built around Reims in 1870 bombarded during WWI and left in ruins

[66] Either Kaufmann forgot about his encounter the previous October 9 with an Alsatian girl or he did not consider Alsace to be part of Germany. His reference to not having spoken German with a woman since mid-1916 suggests that he had not returned home on leave since that time, a period of ten months until his capture.

[67] Heidsieck

June 8. (Whitsunday): It is an unusually hot day. . . . My thoughts seem to overwhelm me: June 8, 1915—I came to the "Sennelager," to guard prisoners; June 8, 1916—it was the last time home with my mother and sister; June 9, 1917—I was sent to a farm commando in Brittany; June 8, 1920—where will I be???

June 10. A few days ago representatives of the "Suisse [Swiss] committee for prisoners" paid a visit and found everything in good condition. They were hardly gone when the French changed our working hours from eight to ten hours a day.

June 12. At the roll call a letter from the French general was read in which he praised P.G.s for their heroism in saving children from drowning. . . . It was already the third case in two weeks.

June 15. An order once more was given that we have our hair cut very close and the PG. Company number sewed on our uniforms.

June 21. Two more citations of P.G.s for saving the life of Frenchmen.

June 23. Tonight at 8 o'clock the official announcement was made that the peace treaty was signed and all prisoners, who were still in prison, would be discharged. Our early "retreat" is extended to 10 o'clock. At 9 o'clock the bells of all churches in the city started ringing to celebrate this event. . . .

June 25. One of the typical French chicanery against us P.G.s was today's order forbidding us to subscribe to French newspapers. There was no valid reason.

June 26, 1919. My closest friend, Berthold from Chemnitz, a comrade in the truest sense of the word and in captivity since the beginning of 1916 (our beds were side by side) died last night after he was admitted to a hospital a week ago. His disease was diagnosed as typhus. Self-educated and in private life a printer by occupation, he was one of those rare quiet human beings of a lofty, unselfish character. His tragic and untimely death affected me deeply. The only remembrance of him left to me was a picture of his grave in a cemetery with a wooden cross and his name. For a long time I couldn't overcome my shock, brooding what a tragic fate this was. He had survived several battles at the front and three years of captivity with the knowledge of a not-too-far off end liberation.

Saturday, June 28. The day of the final signing of the peace treaty. As a sign of general satisfaction, we were exempted from working at nine in the morning. It was gloomy weather outside, while a gloomy mood prevailed inside our camp, surrounded on all sides by barbed wire and barbed wire.

In honor of the American national holiday, we have today, July 4, our day off.

The next months passed monotonously. As the interpreter, I accompanied the various companies, whose work consisted mostly in clearing the rubbish from the innumerable houses and business places of the city, damaged from four years of war and bombardment.

November 12, 1919. In a blinding snowstorm and cold, we left Reims this morning. Our train passed Cernay, . . . familiar to me, near where our division occupied our defense lines. 1½ kilometers behind Époye on the highway to Pontfaverger was a former German restcamp called *Dessauerlage*. Only one barrack was still intact besides a few sheet metal bunkers. It was here where we lodged like sardines in a can; a space of twenty width was allotted to each of us for sleeping. The wind was howling through the fissures, the rain dripping from the cold metal sheets and in the night, the moon was shining through the cracks of the roof. To top it all there was terrible plague of lice and fleas. . . .

Our commandos worked at the old frontline to level trenches, eliminate barbed wires, etc. This work was not without danger.

November 15. Two P.G.s in my commando were wounded by picking up unexploded shells. While the snow outside was piling up high, we kept warm by using the wooden planks of the bunkers as firewood. During all this time I had ample time to read books and newspapers.

December 7, 1919. The previous day an order had come through that by the evening of December 8, all prisoners from the left bank of the Rhine should be assembled in Sillery, about fifteen kilometers from here. In the morning the French lieutenant made a speech, thanking us for our decent behavior and Godspeed. Unexpectedly, our replacement—one hundred men from Company 122 Versenay—arrived already at midday, so we "leftbankers"—about fifty in all—were forced to leave at 3 o'clock in the afternoon. Before we started our march, our German sergeant major delivered a speech, exhorting us, we should never forget what we had suffered and remain good Germans. Our "gleeclub" sang farewell songs and then we marched on. . . . My thoughts went out to our division cemetery near Époye, where comrades of mine were buried. In deep mud our march went on the high road to Beine, where I had walked so many times before my captivity. My baggage, made still heavier by the steady rain, was pressing me down. When we arrived in Beine, which was a heap of ruins, a mute evidence of the raged battles around here, dark night had come. . . . We crossed our old German trench positions between Beine and Sillery and finally arrived late in the night in Sillery. This whole march was like a nightmare, which I never will forget.

Here ends the diary of my captivity in the second half of January 1920. The day had finally arrived where we could board the train to our homeland, which I hadn't seen in almost four years. Instead of exuberant, we all were rather subdued, our sufferings lasted still heavily on us and we knew that our part of the country, the whole west bank of the Rhine, was occupied by French soldiers. . . . In a slow moving train we traveled all night, passing through the Eifel mountains. Still in the mountains when dawn broke, we saw a motionless, lovely figure of a woman in the door of a house up on the hill. Seeing us soldiers, tears rolled down her cheeks. Her sight intrigued me and kept my mind occupied for a long time. Was she crying because she lost her husband or son in the war, or seeing us coming home long after the war was over, or was she thinking of the four years of unheard of sacrifices of the German people to end with the prostrated Fatherland, occupied and at the mercy of French soldiers? For me, she was a symbol of the German fate.

SELECT BIBLIOGRAPHY

Afflerbach, Holger, and Hew Strachan, eds. *How Fighting Ends: A History of Surrender*. Oxford: Oxford University Press, 2012.

Aitken, Alexander. *Gallipoli to the Somme: Recollections of a New Zealand Infantryman*. London: Oxford University Press, 1963.

Angress, Werner. "The German Army's *Judenzählung* of 1916: Genesis, Consequences, Significance." *Leo Baeck Institute Yearbook* 23 (1978): 117–37.

Ashworth, Tony. *Trench Warfare, 1914-1918: The Live and Let Live System*. New York: Holmes & Meier, 1980.

Audoin-Rouzeau, Stéphane. *Men at War 1914-1918: National Sentiment and Trench Journalism in France during the First World War*. Translated by Helen McPhail. Oxford: Berg, 1992.

Audoin-Rouzeau, Stéphane, and Annette Becker. *14-18: Understanding the Great War*. New York: Hill and Wang, 2002.

Barrie, Alexander. *Underground War*. London: Muller, 1962.

Barthas, Louis. *Poilu: The World War I Notebooks of Corporal Louis Barthas, Barrelmaker, 1914-1918*. New Haven: Yale University Press, 2014.

Barton, Peter, Peter Doyle, and Johan Vandewalle. *Beneath Flanders Fields: The Tunnellers' War, 1914-1918*. Montreal: McGill-Queen's Press, 2005.

Becker, Jean-Jacques. *The Great War and the French People*. Oxford/Providence: Berg, 1985.

Boff, Jonathan. *Winning and Losing on the Western Front: The British Third Army and the Defeat of Germany in 1918*. Cambridge: Cambridge University Press, 2012.

Brown, Joshua, ed. *A Good Idea of Hell: Letters from a Chasseur à Pied*. College Station: Texas A & M Press, 2003.

Caplan, Gregory. *Wicked Sons, German Heroes: Jewish Soldiers, Veterans and Memories of World War I in Germany*. Saarbrucken: VDM Verlag, 2008.

Childers, Erskine. *The Riddle of the Sands*. London: Smith, Elder & Co., 1903.

Cohen-Portheim, Paul. *When Time Stood Still: My Internment in England, 1914-1918*. London: Duckworth, 1931.

Connes, Georges. *A POW's Memoir of the First World War: The Other Ordeal*. Oxford: Berg, 2004.

Cook, Tim. "The Politics of Surrender: Canadian Soldiers and the Killing of Prisoners in the Great War." *Journal of Military History* 70 (2006): 637–65.

Crawford, John, and Ian McGibbon, eds. *New Zealand's Great War*. Auckland: Exisle Publishing, 2007.

Cresswell, Yvonne M., ed. *Living with the Wire. Civilian Internment in the Isle of Man during the Two World Wars*. Douglas, Isle of Man: Manx National Heritage, 2010.

Cru, Jean Norton. *Témoins: Essai d'analyse et de critique des combattants édités en français de 1915 à 1928*. Paris: Les Étincelles, 1929.

Cru, Jean Norton. *War Books: A Study in Historical Criticism.* Translated by Stanley J. Pincetl Jr. San Diego: San Diego State University Press, 1988.

Doughty, Robert, *Pyrrhic Victory: French Strategy and Operations in the Great War.* Cambridge, MA: Harvard University Press, 2005.

Draskau, Jennifer Kewley. "Prisoners in Pettycoats: Drag Performance in Great War Internment Camps." *Proceedings of the Isle of Man Natural History and Antiquarian Society* 12, no. 2 (2007-2009): 187–204.

Englund, Peter. *The Beauty and the Sorrow: An Intimate History of the First World War.* New York: Knopf, 2011.

Falls, Cyril. *War Books, A Critical Guide.* London: Peter Davies, 1930.

Feldman, David. *Englishmen and Jews: Social Relations and Political Culture 1840-1914.* New Haven: Yale University Press, 1994.

Ferguson, Niall. *The Pity of War: Explaining World War I.* New York: Basic Books, 1999.

Fine, David J. *Jewish Integration in the German Army in the First World War.* Berlin: Walter de Gruyter, 2012.

Fletcher, Anthony. *Life, Death, and Growing Up on the Western Front.* New Haven: Yale University Press, 2014.

Foreign Office: Reports of Visits of Inspection by US Embassy Officials, 1916. London: H.M.S.O., 1916.

Friends of France: The Field Service of the American Ambulance Described by Its Members. Boston: Houghton Mifflin, 1916.

Fuller, J. G. *Troop Morale and Popular Culture in the British and Dominion Armies, 1914-1918.* Oxford: Oxford University Press, 1990.

Fussell, Paul. *The Great War and Modern Memory.* New York: Oxford University Press, 1975.

Gainer, Bernard. *The Alien Invasion: The Origins of the Aliens Act of 1905.* London: Heinemann, 1972.

Garrard, John A. *The English and Immigration: A Comparative Study of the Jewish Influx 1880-1910.* London: Oxford University Press for the Institute of Race Relations, 1971.

Grady, Tim. *German-Jewish Soldiers of the First World War.* Liverpool: Liverpool University Press, 2011.

Graves, Robert. *Goodbye to All That.* Providence: Berghahn Books, 1995 reprint.

Gregory, Adrian. *War of Peoples, 1914-1919.* Oxford: Oxford University Press, 2014.

Greenhalgh, Elizabeth. *The French Army and the First World War.* Cambridge: Cambridge University Press, 2014.

Grieve, W. Grant, and Bernard Newman. *Tunnellers: The Story of the Tunnelling Companies, Royal Engineers, during the World War.* London: Herbert Jenkins, 1936.

Grundy, C. R. *Local War Museums: A Suggestion.* London: W. Claude Johnson, 1917.

Habeck, Mary. "Technology in the First World War: The View from Below." In *The Great War and the Twentieth Century*, ed. Jay Winter, Geoffrey Parker, and Mary Habeck, 99–131. New Haven: Yale University Press, 2000.

Halpern, Paul. *A Naval History of World War I.* Annapolis: Naval Institute Press, 1994.

Hanna, Martha. *Your Death Would Be Mine: Paul and Marie Pireaud in the Great War.* Cambridge, MA: Harvard University Press, 2006.

Hart, Peter. *Gallipoli.* New York: Oxford University Press, 2011.

Horn, Daniel, ed. *War, Mutiny, and Revolution in the German Navy: The World War I Diary of Seaman Richard Stumpf.* New Brunswick: Rutgers University Press, 1967.

Horne, John, and Alan Kramer, "German 'Atrocities' and Franco-German Opinion, 1914: The Evidence of German Soldiers' Diaries." *Journal of Modern History* 66 (1994): 1–33.

Horne, John, and Alan Kramer. *German Atrocities, 1914: A History of Denial.* New Haven: Yale University Press, 2001.

Housman, Laurence, ed. *War Letters of Fallen Englishmen.* New York: E.P. Dutton, 1930.

Hull, Isabel V. *A Scrap of Paper: Breaking and Making International Law during the Great War.* Cornell, NY: Cornell University Press, 2014.

Hynes, Samuel. *The Soldiers' Tale: Bearing Witness to Modern War.* New York: Penguin, 1997.

Hynes, Samuel. *A War Imagined: The First World War and English Culture.* London: Bodley Head, 1990.

Johnson, K. B. "'It's Only the Ones Who Might Live Who Count': Allied Personnel in World War I." In *Personal Perspectives: World War I*, ed. Timothy C. Dowling, 161–203. Santa Barbara, CA: ABC-Clio, 2006.

Jones, Heather. *Violence Against Prisoners of War in the First World War.* Cambridge: Cambridge University Press, 2011.

Keegan, John. *The Face of Battle.* New York: Viking, 1976.

Kuhr, Elfriede. *There We'll Meet Again: A Young German Girl's Diary of the First World War.* Gloucester, UK: private printing, 1998.

Kukatzki, Bernhard. *Juden in Böchingen: Spuren ihrer Geschichte, 1548-1840.* Landau in der Pfalz: Gesellschaft für Christlich-Jüdische Zusammenarbeit, 1996.

Leed, Eric. *No Man's Land. Combat and Identity in World War I.* New York: Cambridge University Press, 1979.

Lyons, Martyn. "French Soldiers and Their Correspondence: Towards a History of Writing Practices in the First World War," *French History* 17 (2003): 79–95.

Lyons, Martyn. *The Writing Culture of Ordinary People in Europe, c. 1860-1920.* Cambridge: Cambridge University Press, 2012.

Mayhew, Emily. *Wounded: A New History of the Western Front in World War I.* New York: Oxford University Press, 2014.

Meyer, Jessica. *Men of War: Masculinity and the First World War in Britain.* Houndmills: Palgrave Macmillan, 2009.

Moore, A. W. *A History of the Isle of Man.* London: T. Fisher Unwin, 1900.

Morse, Edwin W. *America in the War. The Vanguard of American Volunteers in the Fighting Lines and in Humanitarian Service, August 1914–April 1917.* New York: Scribners, 1919.

O'Brien, Tim. *The Things They Carried.* Boston: Houghton Mifflin, 1990.

Omissi, David, ed. *Indian Voices of the Great War.* Houndmills: Macmillan, 1999.

Palmer, Svetlana, and Sarah Willis, *Intimate Voices from the First World War.* New York: HarperCollins, 2003.

Panayi, Panikos. *The Enemy in Our Midst: Germans in Britain during the First World War* Oxford: Berg, 1991.

Panayi, Panikos. *Prisoners of Britain. German Civilians and Combatant Internees During the First World War.* Manchester: Manchester University Press, 2012.

Pellew, Jill. "The Home Office and the Aliens Act, 1905." *Historical Journal* 32, no. 2 (1989): 369–85.

Pennell, Catriona. *A Kingdom United: Popular Responses to the Outbreak of the First World War.* Oxford: Oxford University Press, 2012.

Penzer, N. M. *The Tin Resources of the British Empire.* London: W. Rider, 1921.

Porch, Douglas. *The French Foreign Legion: A Complete History of the Legendary Fighting Force.* New York: HarperCollins, 1991.

Prior, Robin. *Gallipoli: The End of the Myth.* New Haven: Yale University Press, 2009.

Proctor, Tammy. *Civilians in a World at War, 1914-1918.* New York: New York University Press, 2010.

Pugsley, Christopher. *The ANZAC Experience: New Zealand, Australia and Empire in the First World War*. Auckland: Reed, 2004.

Rachamimov, Alon. "The Disruptive Comforts of Drag: (Trans)Gender Performances among Prisoners of War in Russia, 1914-1920." *American Historical Review* 111 (2006): 362–382.

Rachamimov, Alon. *POWs and the Great War: Captivity on the Eastern Front*. Oxford: Berg, 2002.

Rasmussen, Anne. "The Spanish Flu." In *The Cambridge History of the First World War*, vol. 3: *Civil Society*, ed. Jay Winter, 334–57. Cambridge: Cambridge University Press, 2014.

Retallack, James N. ed. *Saxony in German History: Culture, Society and Politics 1830-1933*. Ann Arbor: University of Michigan Press, 2000.

Reynolds, David. *The Long Shadow: The Great War and the Twentieth Century*. London: Simon & Schuster, 2013.

Roper, Michael. *The Secret Battle: Emotional Survival in the Great War*. Manchester: Manchester University Press, 2009.

Rosenthal, Jacob. *Die Ehre des jüdischen Soldaten: Die Judenzählung im Ersten Weltkrieg und ihre Folgen*. Frankfurt: Campus Verlag, 2007.

Scott, James Brown, ed. *Texts of the Peace Conferences at The Hague, 1899 and 1907*. Boston and London: Ginn & Co., 1908.

Shils, Edward, and Morris Janowitz, "Cohesion and Disintegration in the Wehrmacht in World War II." *Public Opinion Quarterly* 12 (1948): 280–315.

Smith, Leonard V. *Between Mutiny and Obedience: The Case of the French Fifth Infantry Division during World War I*. Princeton: Princeton University Press, 1994.

Smith, Leonard V. *The Embattled Self: French Solders' Testimony of the Great War*. Ithaca, NY: Cornell University Press, 2007.

Smith, Leonard V. "Jean Norton Cru and Combatants' Literature of the First World War." *Modern & Contemporary France* 9 (2001): 161–69.

Smith, Leonard V., Stéphane Audoin-Rouzeau, and Annette Becker, *France and the Great War, 1914-1918*. Cambridge: Cambridge University Press, 2003.

Speed, Richard V. *Prisoners, Diplomats, and the Great War: A Study in the Diplomacy of Captivity*. New York: Greenwood Press, 1990.

Stibbe, Matthew, ed. *Captivity, Forced Labour and Forced Migration in Europe during the First World War*. London: Routledge, 2009.

Strachan, Hew. *The First World War*. Vol. 1: *To Arms*. Oxford: Oxford University Press, 2001.

Strachan, Hew. "Training, Morale and Modern War." *Journal of Contemporary History* 41 (2006): 211–27.

Thomson, Alastair. *ANZAC Memories: Living with the Legend*. Melbourne: Oxford University Press, 1994.

Ulrich, Bernd. *Die Augenzeugen: deutsche Feldpostbriefe in Kriegs- und Nachkriegszeit 1914-1933*. Essen: Klartext, 1997.

Verhey, Jeffrey. *The Spirit of 1914: Militarism, Myth and Mobilization in Germany*. Cambridge: Cambridge University Press, 2000.

Vischer, A. L. *Barbed Wire Disease: A Psychological Study of the Prisoner of War*. London: Bale and Danielsson, 1919.

Watson, Alexander. *Enduring the Great War*. Cambridge: Cambridge University Press, 2008.

Watson, Alexander. "Morale." In *The Cambridge History of the First World War*, vol. 2: *The State*, ed. Jay Winter, 174–95. Cambridge: Cambridge University Press, 2014.

Watson, Janet S. K. *Fighting Different Wars: Experience, Memory, and the First World War in Britain*. Cambridge: Cambridge University Press, 2004.
Weber, Thomas. *Hitler's First War*. Oxford: Oxford University Press, 2010.
Williams, Bill. *The Making of Manchester Jewry, 1740-1875*. New York: Holmes and Meier, 1976.
Winter, Jay, ed. *The Cambridge History of the First World War*. 3 vols. Cambridge: Cambridge University Press, 2014.
Winter, Jay. *Sites of Memory, Sites of Mourning: The Great War in European Cultural History*. Cambridge: Cambridge University Press, 1995.
Winter, Jay, and Antoine Prost, *The Great War in History*. Cambridge: Cambridge University Press, 2005.
Witkop, Philipp, ed. *German Students' War Letters*. Translated by A. F. Wedd. London: Methuen, 1929.
Work of the Royal Engineers in the European War, 1914-19: Military Mining. Chatham: W. & J. Mackay, 1922.
Ziemann, Benjamin. *War Experiences in Rural Germany, 1914-1923*. Oxford: Berg, 2007.
Zombory-Moldovan, Béla. *The Burning of the World: A Memoir of 1914*. Translated by Peter Zombory-Moldovan. New York: New York Review Books, 2014.

INTERNET RESOURCES

BBC World War One Centenary
www.bbc.co.uk/ww1
A multifaceted website administered by the BBC, largely devoted to the experience of Britain and its Empire, including, for example, podcasts, interactive guides, photos, and articles about Indian and ANZAC troops and women on the home front.

Europeana 1914–1918—untold stories and official histories of WWI
www.europeana1914-1918.eu
A transnational collection of public and privately held materials, including films, letters, diaries, and photographs

First World War Centenary
www.1914.org
Created by the Imperial War Museum in conjunction with a network of local, regional, national, and international cultural and educational organizations, this website offers links to research databases and archives from around the globe.

National World War 1 Museum
http://theworldwar.org
The website for the U.S. National World War I Museum in Kansas City, Missouri, containing a variety of educational resources, including online exhibitions and a collections database, as well as lesson plans.

The United States World War One Centennial Commission
http://worldwar-1centennial.org
Site that provides classroom resources, information on American monuments and memorials, and links to historical resources.

Trench Journals and Unit Magazines of the First World War
http://media2.proquest.com/documents/trench.pdf
Available only through subscribing academic libraries, this site provides access to over 1,500 newspapers and journals, primarily British, produced on the front lines by soldiers for soldiers.

World War One
www.bl.uk/world-war-one
British Library site examining the war's key themes through primary and secondary sources, photos, and articles by experts.

World War I Centenary: Continuations and Beginnings
http://ww1centenary.oucs.ox.ac.uk
A teaching resource created by Oxford University that includes a variety of expert articles, audio and video lectures, downloadable images, interactive maps, and ebooks addressing the cultural, social, geographical, and historical aspects of the war.

ACKNOWLEDGMENTS

We would like to thank the following individuals for their help with this project: Ron Opie (Redruth Old Cornwall Society), Peter and Valerie Malindine, Diana Dowson, John Tonkin, Patricia Utuerhark, Wendy Dawe, John French, Penny Picton, Nicole Milano (Head Archivist, Archives of the American Field Service), Lisa Stiegel, Mark J. Grubbs, Anne Cate, Leon Miller (Head, Louisiana Research Collection, Tulane University Library), Sean Benjamin (Louisiana Research Collection, Tulane University), Sandy Levy (Executive Director, Jewish Endowment Foundation of Louisiana, New Orleans), Seymour Dreyfus, Elton and Doris White, Paul Weatherall (Library and Archive Services Office, Manx National Heritage), Sheila and Graham Dunbar, Jocelyn Chambers (Alexander Turnbull Library, Wellington, New Zealand), Vincent Villette (Archivist, Nogent-sur-Marne, France), Margherita Giubelli (Editions Denoël), Michael Simonson (Archivist, Leo Baeck Institute, New York), David Rosenberg (Librarian, Center for Jewish History, New York) and Deborah Naish (Executive Director, Congregation B'nai B'rith, Santa Barbara, California). It has been our pleasure to work again with our exemplary editor, Nancy Toff. Finally, thanks are due to our anonymous readers for their perceptive comments and to Kate Nunn for her expertise in shepherding our manuscript through the publication process.

INDEX